John Jay Chapman
May 7: 1924

M. A. DeWOLFE HOWE

John Jay Chapman
and His Letters

Illustrated

BOSTON

HOUGHTON MIFFLIN COMPANY

𝕿𝖍𝖊 𝕽𝖎𝖛𝖊𝖗𝖘𝖎𝖉𝖊 𝕻𝖗𝖊𝖘𝖘 𝕮𝖆𝖒𝖇𝖗𝖎𝖉𝖌𝖊

1937

The Riverside Press
CAMBRIDGE · MASSACHUSETTS
PRINTED IN THE U.S.A.

IN AFFECTIONATE AND ADMIRING
MEMORY OF
ELIZABETH CHANLER CHAPMAN
(*Died June 5, 1937*)

NOTE

NOT long after the death of John Jay Chapman, on November 4, 1933, his family placed at my disposal, for the purposes of this biography, a vast collection of his letters, unpublished manuscripts, and personal papers. From the same source and from many friends of Chapman's there has been besides a liberal bestowal of unwritten information. I assumed the responsibility this implied, with no obligations beyond those of gratitude for the opportunity to undertake so congenial a task, and of handling the abundant material to the best of my capacity and discretion. For any errors of omission, inclusion, or interpretation, I am therefore solely accountable. As for Chapman's opinions, whose were they but his own?

He was my friend for about the last third of his life. When he disagreed with his friends, as he did at times with me, there was no mincing of the disagreement. Thus one became aware of his challenging contradictions, and perhaps the better qualified to see, and present, him as he was. If his unique personality can emerge truly from the following pages, I am confident that it will be found a rich and significant product of American civilization. Under any civilization that personality would have stamped its individual mark upon its time and place.

M. A. DeW. H.

THE BOSTON ATHENÆUM
December, 1936

CONTENTS

ILLUSTRATIONS

John Jay Chapman

and His Letters

OF CHAPMAN: '*He is glowing and beautiful like fire, pure and purifying like fire, lambent, wayward, unshapeable, mischievous like fire, uncontrollable like fire, destructive like fire, seeking heaven like fire.*'

DICKINSON S. MILLER

Prelude

JOHN JAY CHAPMAN did his imagined biographer a good turn
when he wrote, long ago, as follows:

> I confess that I had rather stand out for posterity in a hideous
> silhouette, as having been wrong on every question of my time,
> than be erased into a cypher by my biographer. But biographers
> do not feel in this way toward their heroes. Each one feels
> that he has undertaken to do his best by his patron. Therefore
> they stand the man under a north light in a photographer's
> attic, suggest the attitude, and then take the picture; — where-
> as, in real life, the man was standing on the balcony of a
> burning building which the next moment collapsed, and in it
> he was crushed beyond the semblance of humanity.

Chapman knew himself quite well enough to realize that
the balcony of a burning building was much more his natural
habitat than any photographer's attic. The north light and
the pose would instantly misrepresent him, and the biographer
employing them would be doomed from the start to failure.
He would, moreover, need rare powers of devastation to
erase his subject into a cypher. Whatever Chapman may or
may not have been, he was not that. Merely to see him was
to be sure of it.

He wondered once why a man of sinister appearance, whom
he disliked, looked as he did, and exclaimed, as with the
joy of discovery, 'He looks like that because he is like that!'
Precisely this might have been said of Chapman himself.
One saw him approaching on a New York street, perhaps
Fifth Avenue, and felt at once the nearness of a notable

figure. Tall, with the commanding presence to which a prophet or poet might lay claim, bearded, in his later years, and then of a grizzled grayness, with small, piercing, friendly eyes, and clean-cut features, bending slightly forward as he walked with a shorter step than most men of his height, dressed with something of the sweet neglect that sits best upon the well dressed and well formed, wearing a woolen scarf about his neck and shoulders in nearly all weathers, and singular above all else through the lack of a left hand. There, you said (if you did not know him), passes somebody who is indeed somebody — I wonder who. If you did know him, you were thankful: it was Jack Chapman. He looked like that because he was like that.

Such apparitions do not merely happen. Inheritance and circumstance explain something but by no means all, especially when the man one is trying to account for possesses attributes of genius, in its very nature an unaccountable possession. The normal, average man is like a pendulum of small swing, with no excess of impetus to either side. A broader swing is, of course, not a sure token of genius, but without it and without some of the excesses, for better or worse, implied in such a swing, genius seldom finds expression. Chapman's nervous and emotional forces were never of that stability which affords insurance against excess. Indeed there were periods, in his teens, in his twenties, and as he was passing out of his thirties, when the instability went to formidable lengths. These were periods from which he emerged, tried as by fire, and sensitized to pity and other promptings of the heart as few can be who have not suffered deeply in spirit as well as in the body. Without these experiences, without his freedom from many of the responsibilities to which most men are subject, it is impossible to say what he would have done with his remarkable powers of thought and expression. For the biographer this freedom of Chapman's has the virtue of imparting a corresponding freedom: there is no need — as there might be in dealing with an active participant in politics, education, or what not — to justify his opinions or their expression. There was an impish quality in him, something of the joy he ascribed to an older critic suspected of liking to excite interest by his sallies: 'After one of them he would chuckle like a naughty gamin who has thrown a stone cleverly and knocked off an old gentleman's hat.' Chapman spoke truthfully of his more serious writings, however, when he wrote: 'I am saying things which will some day be thought of, rather than trying to get the attention of anyone.' Yet there were spirits, an alert minority, from whom he always got attention.

One thing seems certain — that for all the diversity, or, as it was sometimes thought, the perversity, of his manifestations, for all the contradictions between what was best and what was worst in them, a single unifying thread ran through the fabric of his life, the thread of deep, continuous concern for the spiritual realities of human existence, the ultimate truth underlying the relation between the temporal seen and the eternal unseen. The very subjects of his most characteristic writings in the field of literature — the Greek dramatists, the Bible, Dante, Shakespeare, Emerson — suggest this commerce with what is most important and best, the stuff that matters with your true aristophile, as I like to call one so catholic and yet so keenly eclectic. The trivial, minor figures and topics of his time were alien to him, except as figures and topics for the fun of which his great gift of humor made him capable. Centering his attention, then, upon the more enduring things, it was but natural that the most enduring of all, the concept of union between God and the soul of man, the unceasing search for it, should have run through all his thought. The term 'religious' for this habit of thinking, the term 'mystic' for this type of thinker, have as mere words so many connotations and such varieties of meaning in various minds that the definition of anybody as a religious mystic exposes itself to challenge. Yet no other single term can suggest so accurately the essential

3

quality that made a unit of this intense and vehement creature, or indicate more truly the midmost point to which his swinging pendulum would always return. The personal knowledge of him on which this belief is based finds confirmation from a study of his life and thought as recorded in published and voluminous unpublished writings.

Of what does the record consist? In the first place there are some twenty-five books, generally of slender proportions — critical essays (relating chiefly to literature and politics), biography, translations, plays, and poems. The most substantial single work was his 'William Lloyd Garrison,' not so much a biography as an extended essay on agitation and reform. Most of his writing appeared first in periodicals, with the result that the books in which the articles are assembled produce frequently a fragmentary effect, increased by the fact that the separate articles often lack the advantage of a definite element of structure. They prevailed in many instances through the brilliancy of single pages, through a rare rightness in imagery, humor, insight, and vehemence, working together for effectiveness of verbal expression. Again and again the books provide passages of autobiographic import, and, disheartening to their author as their restricted circulation must have been, they are bound, for this very reason, to serve a biographer well as sources of unfamiliar quotation.

Another abundant source exists in the form of an unpublished manuscript, 'Retrospections.' For several years before Chapman's death his latest publishers, through Mr. Ferris Greenslet, were asking him to produce an autobiography which might prove comparable with 'The Education of Henry Adams.' When I urged him to consider this suggestion seriously, he wrote to me: 'Perhaps I am to wind up with wheezing an accordion of memories. O Lord! By great good luck I cannot remember anything. I now realize why this gift was bestowed upon me. They say that dying men remember everything, and certainly aging and decaying men begin to do the same — and publishers feed on them and flatter and stroke them. Get thee behind me, Satan! I'd rather die in a pot-house.'

His misgivings were nevertheless overcome, and as he drew near to the age of seventy, one year before his death, he began to put his remembrances on paper. They fill 167 typewritten and several manuscript pages, but end, as a continuous narrative, with the year 1886, when he was a student at the Harvard Law School. In the course of them he wrote: 'I must tell the reader of a discovery that I have made since beginning to write these papers. Every autobiography speaks from the date of its composition, and there is nothing in which writers deceive themselves so readily as in evoking their own past. The more interested a man is in himself, the greater liar he becomes. Autobiographies are fairy-tales.' There is, of course, a measure of truth in this, yet the letters of Chapman to his mother, from which he quoted freely in describing his life at Harvard, have the value of contemporaneous record, and such a document as the uncompleted 'Retrospections' must indicate much of what a man has become, even if its dealings with the processes of becoming are inadequate or misleading. In any event Chapman's own attempt at autobiography will provide many illuminating pages in this book.

Then there are his letters. His talk was notoriously spontaneous, brilliant, and exciting. He believed strongly in speech, and that of the freest. In an unpublished piece of verse he wrote,

> 'How much of strength would overflood the weak
> If they but knew, I *am* what I can speak.'

Now the speech and the letters of Chapman were extraordinarily alike. His pen, at least in letter-writing, was as fluent as his tongue, and equally free from inhibitions. What crossed his mind at a given moment he wrote just as unrestrainedly as he would say it. This may well be why so many of his letters have been preserved: tearing up one was like destroying a piece of him. The letters that poured from him in rivulets confront me as a lake. Draw from it freely as I may, its level will hardly be affected; yet in every cupful a tang or savor distinctly his will declare itself. Thus in the books, in the unpublished 'Retrospections,' in the letters, countable by thousands, there is what an earlier generation would have called ' great store ' of material.

Out of it all emerges a figure as distinctive and arresting as the physical presence that has already been described. It is a figure of passion, ferocity, and tenderness, of extravagance in thought and deed, of violent contrasts, of an inward wildness needing to be tamed for almost every relationship of life, such a lover as only a poet could be, and beloved as few but poets may be. This figure would never serve to adorn an Arnold's tale of seeing life steadily and whole, for the unsteady and the piecemeal kept getting themselves into the foreground. Confident, often savage, pronouncements on persons, books, pictures, or all the works of God and man are poured forth in bewildering profusion. Nobody could be expected to agree with them all, any more than the Chapman of one period or mood could agree with the Chapman of another. The editor of his writings who should undertake to interpose 'At this point I agree with him — at this point I differ ' would have his folly for his pains.

It would be an equal folly to speculate in any detail upon what Chapman would have become had the circumstances of his life been different. His birth, breeding, and natural associations were all of the sort regarded as 'advantages.' Except for a few years of his younger manhood, he was unhampered by financial pressures, and was consequently free to choose the paths he liked best — paths that led him away from the market-place, into the realm of mind and spirit. Under other conditions, he might have been forced to winning a livelihood and support for dependents either from his profession of the law, or from writing, not so

6

largely as an amateur but wholly as a professional. Would he have served his generation more, or less, fruitfully under these compulsions? It is futile to try to say more than that conformity and compromise were alien to his very nature, and that he can hardly be imagined in another rôle than that of a 'minority man,' an individual in revolt. Standing in another place, he might have chosen other foemen for his steel. It would not have been permitted to rust.

The implications of Chapman's social and economic status will not be lost on every reader of this book. Indeed many in our day of special interpretations will be on the alert for them. Others will be scanning his psychologic chart, for whatever it may suggest of obscure or patent origins of tendencies and characteristics. This is a field in which the layman does well to leave the last word to the professional. But for fellow-laymen and professionals alike the materials for conjecture and theory are spread forth by a biographer who is by no means unaware of their possible value to the specialist.

The beauty of Chapman's letters, as of the best talk, is that much may be taken for what it is worth at the moment, and for no more. There are plenty of passages which can be related closely to the eternal verities, and plenty that cannot. The reader must be credited with the wit to discriminate. Particularly with personal allusions, sometimes quite outrageous, the discerning must be trusted to add the proper modicum of salt. If I cite here at the outset only two out of several expressions about myself, in letters to me and to others, I shall be the more free to uncover some of his devastating utterances to and about other friends. He avows his grief, on reading a book I had written, over my 'damaged intellect'; he remarks that my specialty, in biography, 'is cutting out the shadows and keeping the smiles — the grin without the cat ' — a stimulating word of warning in what now lies before me. To another friend he writes in violent denunciation, and adds a postscript pleading, indirectly, for an understanding of his own irony, humor, and subtlety.[1] Such an understanding must be brought to the reading of many letters in the pages that follow. William James, an amused target for Chapman's audacities in correspondence, is said to have found in the letters he received something too much of 'humorous denunciation,' though his responses seem never to have discouraged it. Wrathful letters to others than friends could not be expected always to call forth soft answers. But among Chapman's more regular correspondents it would have been hard to find a desire for different or fewer letters. There was no telling when any one of them might amount to the event of the day on which it came.

When he was away from home his letters of minute report upon everything he was doing and thinking were so full and frequent that it is hard to see how days were long enough both for his living them and for his accounting of them. Yet the sheaves of letters to his first and, through a far longer period, to his second wife survive to show that he could accomplish both. In these, and in many letters to others, he made an amplified supplement to the frequent traces of autobiography in his published writings.

It is naturally in his letters that he reveals himself most fully and truly — sometimes in much detail, often through a word or phrase. By the measurement of the world's coarse thumb, the tangible results of the activity of his mind seem small indeed. He knew this all too well himself. While his first wife was still living, he wrote to her, in his thirtieth year, 'God have mercy — to be my age and not only to be nothing but to see no chance of becoming anything!' Five years later he wrote to his second wife, not long before their marriage, 'It's an accident when I *do* right, but I *am* right.' And in these few words there was a large part of the whole truth about him.

Doing and being — the immemorial choice of values presents itself sharply in Chapman. If it was an accident

[1] See page 412.

when he did right, it was also an accident when, blundering and arrogant, he did wrong; for fundamentally he *was* right, in caring more for the truth as he saw it — in affairs, in letters, in art, in personal relations — than for all besides. 'Loyalty to truth,' he once wrote, 'is a fine thing; but loyalty to anything else is an attack upon truth.' There will always be a jesting Pilate to ask, 'What is truth?' and the answers will continue to be as various as humanity itself. But here is a man who had no doubt about his own answers, and made them with so extraordinary a vigor and pungency that he and his opinions are vital matters for inquiry. There is a challenge to serious scrutiny when a man of uncommon gifts invents for himself an aphorism of the Emersonian philosophy of individualism, and glories, as Chapman gloried, in declaring, 'After all it is just as well that there should be *one* person like *me* in the world.'

II

The Scene of Youth
1862–1885

CHAPMAN's 'Retrospections' tell so little about his ancestry that, if anything more is called for, it is only decent that there should not be too much of it. His father was the son of Boston anti-slavery parents, of good New England descent; one of them, Maria Weston Chapman, held a place among the abolitionist women of Boston quite comparable with that of Garrison and Wendell Phillips among the men. The Chapman family motto, *Crescit sub pondere virtus*, was engraved on a ring worn by Chapman's father. The arms were a mailed arm and fist holding a broken lance, with an olive sprig resting where the broken parts of the lance meet. Both the symbolism of this device and the motto meant much to Chapman. As the grandson, on his mother's side, of a John Jay who was himself the grandson and namesake of the first Chief Justice of the United States Supreme Court, he bore in his blood a Huguenot strain modified by the union of his Jay forbears with representatives of the early Dutch and other New York families of ample background. Both his grandfather John and his great-grandfather William Jay were active in the anti-slavery cause. On the score of inheritance Chapman could obviously lay good claim to Owen Wister's characterization of him as 'a belated abolitionist.' The backward look for ancestral traits meets with a severe check when it comes to that earlier progenitor, Chief Justice Jay, of whom another descendant,

George Pellew, has written, 'He was by his disposition so reticent and unimpulsive, so completely self-controlled, that there is scarcely any material for constructing a history of his inner, private life.' Chapman was so precisely the opposite of this that the name of John Jay seems in itself to have been his main inheritance from the Chief Justice.

Soon after the death of his grandfather John Jay in 1894, he wrote to his mother, 'The fact is that his name and the family tradition have been controlling ideas with me ever since I can remember — perhaps too much so, and while I do not speak of them very often they are in my mind about all the time.' A few months later there was an impressive meeting in New York to honor this grandfather's memory, with speeches by Choate, Depew, Seth Low, and Bishop Coxe. Chapman attended it with much reluctance, and wrote to his wife in Italy: 'I do a good deal dislike the sort of thing it was, and think these collections of sentimentalists are not very important.... To tell you the truth I don't think people are influenced by eulogies one bit. They go home and feel comfortable and someone else who didn't attend the eulogy meeting is the man who will do the work.' It was later in the same year of 1894 that he was justifying himself in a letter to his wife for a somewhat fantastic bit of misbehavior among friends. 'I myself am such a thundering swell,' he wrote, 'that what I do must be right.... Come down to it and you can find the paradox that only aristocrats are truly democratic in their social conduct and feeling. They only are simple — they only have nothing to gain and nothing to lose, and have the freedom and simplicity of human beings.'

So much for Chapman's place in the world and his way of looking at it. His 'Retrospections' may now be drawn upon for his later view of his formative years. Before he finished those personal chronicles he placed autobiographies in general, as we have already seen, in the category of fairy-tales. Yet in this instance there is no other such guide to a comprehension of Chapman's personality. Let us begin, then, at the beginning:

I was born on March 2, 1862, in New York City, in a house on Eighteenth Street near Fourth Avenue, being the second son of Henry Grafton Chapman and Eleanor Jay, his wife. My brother Henry was two years older than I, my sister Eleanor [1] two years younger, and a second sister, Beatrix,[2] about nine years younger. My father, Henry Grafton Chapman, son of Henry Grafton Chapman, was born in Boston on October 29, 1833, attended the Boston Latin School;[3] was for a time a student at Heidelberg, Germany; on his return to the United States was for some years a clerk in Goodhue and Company and made a voyage to China as supercargo in 1855. He came to New York in 1855 and became a member of the firm of Ward, Campbell and Company, stockbrokers. In 1873 he was president of the Stock Exchange. During the panic of that year he closed the Exchange and served on the governing committee of the Exchange for some years thereafter. He was a member of the Union and Knickerbocker Clubs of New York.

One of my earliest recollections is of New Brighton, Staten Island, on whose shores the newly married business men of the day used to reside in the summer, going up to their work in Wall Street by the ferryboat. There was a lady at New Brighton, Mrs. Leonowens, who kept a school for very small children to which I was sent. The idea struck me as such an outrage that I clung to the palings at the front of our cottage and howled dismally, with the result that I was not sent to school that year. I must have been about four years old, to judge from my recollection of the height of the palings. I remember a year or two later being taken to a small, private rowing club near the ferry, where the members, rather commonplace people — a hard-drinking set of young brokers and lawyers — were chatting and joking on the float. One of them, who was smoking a handsome cigar, announced with great gusto that he 'felt like a morning star.' It seemed to me a kind of sacrilege that a man of that type should make such a remark on that bright, glorious Sunday morning. I felt a really superfluous scorn for him, and have often thought since what a horrid child I must have been. I remember a few years later

[1] Later Mrs. Richard Mortimer.
[2] Now Mrs. Raymond de Candolle, formerly Lady Barclay.
[3] He entered this school in 1846, with Phillips Brooks and Henry Lee Higginson.

CHAPMAN'S PARENTS: HENRY GRAFTON CHAPMAN AND ELEANOR
JAY CHAPMAN

approaching a contemporary and saying — quite out of the blue — 'David, if you knew how I hated you, you'd cry.' I remember this because of my mother's laughter. She said, 'But why should you think he'd care so much about your opinion of him?' This fastidiousness made the Sunday fishing excursions on the bay in a deep-sea rowboat loaded with bait and fishing tackle and the horrible going up and down of the boat a purgatory to me. There were other outrages. I was obliged to eat a saucerful of oatmeal at breakfast before I could come to the chops. I remember several compliments, probably of a later date. My father, who as a rule took little notice of the children, once remarked quite pointedly after I had said something, 'Jack has a spark,' a statement with which I inwardly agreed; and I also remember my mother's saying, 'Jack is a very honorable child,' which pleased me very much.[1]

Some years later we moved to New York and lived at 130 Madison Avenue, northeast corner of 31st Street, in a house which my father owned; and later still, probably in the early seventies, we moved to Thirty Washington Square, which I think my father first rented and then bought.

The visits of my grandmother Chapman [2] were great features of our domestic life. She was a born children's friend and entertainer. She used to take Henry, Eleanor, and myself into her bedroom and amuse us, instruct us, and show us pictures by the hour — filling scrapbooks with cuttings from the magazines — using gum arabic which she bought at the apothecary's and melted down, and delighting us with her activity and her variety. One of her accomplishments was to make a bouncing ball by rough-hewing a cork for the center and winding twine very tightly about it till it was the size of a billiard ball. This she would cover with leather cut from old gloves and neatly sewn. She would then bounce the ball gleefully. On it she printed the adage, 'Perhaps you don't know I've a cork in my middle,' a phrase which I think comes out of Hans Andersen. At any rate, she applied the motto to herself, and we understood that she used it as a philosophy.

[1] A friend of Chapman's mother has been quoted as follows by his friend Richard Welling: 'She said that Mrs. Chapman had rather amazed her friends by her frank encouragement of the *enfant terrible* in Jack at an early age. On a formal occasion, if a caller arrived in a rather loud waistcoat, Jack would enter the drawing-room with him shouting, "Oh, look at the bright waistcoat," and was always rather encouraged by his mother. This aspect of his early training gave me much food for thought.'

[2] See 'Maria Weston Chapman,' in Chapman's 'Memories and Milestones.'

She was the least sentimental person and the most actively happy that I have known.

She was a great reader aloud, and had made a study of the art. If she were going to read something to us after dinner, she would eat little, in order that her voice and delivery might be clear. I was therefore much pleased when a page of Crabbe's poems was given me to read aloud, and I heard her say to my mother as I was proceeding, 'You see, he takes it in just the right tempo.'

The fact that my grandmother was a public character gave her a manner and charm that was novel to us. Some of our elders regarded her with the prejudice that commonplace people feel towards woman agitators. Of this we were well aware and it enhanced our regard for her. For about thirty years, say 1830-1860, she had in charge the Annual Antislavery Fair in Boston and was an important aide to William Lloyd Garrison. The close of the Civil War found her in middle life living in the Weston family house at Weymouth, Massachusetts, with two old maid sisters, Aunt Caroline and Aunt Deborah. As a child in my early years I was taken there once or twice and saw her mother, Ma Weston, a tiny bundle of an old lady in a close-fitting fringed cap, who used to send us hampers of pickles to New York she had made with her own hands. My father told me that the family tradition was that she had been chased by the negro servant of George Washington, and that when asked — 'But Ma, what did the man want with you?' she would purse up her lips and say, 'No good!' She was the sister of Joshua Bates, the banker, who founded the Boston Library.

The Weymouth house was full of portraits, souvenirs, presentation copies of books written by the French liberals of the mid-century; for the antislavery people were honored in Europe, whither my grandmother made repeated visits. One of her daughters married Auguste Laugel in Paris, and another Edward Dicey in England. But in Boston, antislavery continued to be taboo. Friendly relations were never re-established between the Garrisonians and the social life of Boston. The breach which began in 1829 lasted for a generation after the war.

Antislavery was from the beginning a religious movement led by revolting parsons, of whom the Unitarians were the most conspicuous. In the act of leaving their churches, with polite words, or sometimes with denunciation on each side, these men and women broke with ritual, with ceremony, with all the conventional pieties of religion, and they never thereafter had time to improvise substitutes of their own. Thus it was with my grandfather Chapman, who was in the ministry at the time of his marriage, but afterwards seceded from his church. My grandmother told me that she first saw him as a handsome young man behind the chancel rail where he was serving the communion table. He lost interest in his profession when he passed into the antislavery ranks, and died young. I have a story at second and third hand about his funeral. The mourners, being at a loss as to what ritual they should follow, gave expression to the only form of religion that they understood in antislavery speeches . . . .

There was indeed a strange contrast between the social position of the antislavery leaders in Boston, where they were thought to be superfluous, if not odious, characters, and their welcome in the capitals of Europe where they were accepted by the advanced thinkers of the times as prophetic voices.

The worst indictment I can draw against the American mind and temperament is that in our recognition of the value of the antislavery movement we have never caught up with the Europe of 1850. It is now one hundred years since our antislavery agitation began in earnest. We have had seventy years since the close of the Civil War to think over the whole matter, and yet the average American, the educated person, still thinks that our Antislavery was a misguided movement. It would have been better, he thinks, if the cure for slavery had been left to time. . . .

Antislavery was a Messianic movement. No argument could reach or express or arrest it. It was a flame that arose in the northeast and was destined to ravage the whole land until the soil was burned over. The Civil War was inevitable from the start, and any truce would have meant a mere postponement of war.

My grandfather Jay and his father William Jay were, like my Chapman grandparents, antislavery workers, and I believe that it was through this common interest (of their respective parents) that my father and mother first met.

People were harder at that time. There is a family story that when my grandmother Chapman's family went off to Europe, one of the children, who had at the last moment broken out with the measles, was left behind in charge of a boarding-house keeper. I suspect that my father was neglected in his youth. He certainly had no regular education in school or college. A very old Boston pal of his who had known him from the age of fifteen told me that he had never seen Henry Chapman when he had not had a drink in him by ten o'clock in the morning; and this, too, may be taken in the light of the customs of the period.[1]...

The wedding of my parents took place at the Bedford house,[2] at a time when my great-grandfather William Jay was still alive, and a very caustic old gentleman he was, with an exceeding sharp pen, as may be seen by his 'History of the Mexican War' and numerous other antislavery writings. (See 'William Jay and the Constitutional Struggle for the Abolition of Slavery,' by Bayard Tuckerman; Dodd, Mead & Co., 1893.) He was an unconventional person. The family tradition is that he wore a red tie at the funeral of his wife. At the time of my mother's wedding, an Englishman was staying in the house, and thinking to compliment the United States, he proposed as a toast at the wedding breakfast, 'The President of the United States,' who happened to be Buchanan. The old gentleman at the head of the table thereupon turned his glass upside down and said with great determination, 'I won't drink it!'

My grandfather, on the other hand, was a jolly person, and yet there were times and circumstances when he could show excitement. For instance, when my father, who was madly in love with her, had proposed to Mama — who was twenty-one at the time — my grandfather, who had three other unmarried daughters, said to her sternly, 'You must take him! it's your *last chance!*'

My father was a rough diamond, a witty man full of quaint humor and unexpected turns of thought. When I was a small boy he would come home after a hard day on the Stock Exchange, throw himself on the sofa and read Shakespeare, the only book I ever saw him read. He was extremely remiss in his attention to the care and education of his children, and my mother did all the work of finding tutors and schools. He was a man of granite chastity, and when I first went to

---

[1] Henry G. Chapman was a founder of the Knickerbocker Club. In its first days, before it was much frequented, he would visit it in the afternoon, wait for one other member to appear, and then take his departure, saying, 'I'll go now if you'll stay awhile.'

[2] See pages 17–20.

college he gave me a lecture on the subject, with the plain statement that he was preaching what he had practised.

He was a man of suppressed emotions, and was more or less inarticulate. At the time when I was at the point of death with pneumonia at the age of fourteen, he rescued a suffering dog from the street and kept him in his third-floor back bedroom, where there was no carpet, for he would never have a carpet, but only bare boards and a couple of old chairs and ancestral wardrobes. He tended the dog day and night, and had a superstitious belief that somehow my fate was wrapped up with that of the dog. That he was fundamentally unhappy goes without saying. His was an inward nature, whose emotions had never found a vehicle of expression. There were people who adored him, and could only speak of him with tears in their eyes. . . .

My mother and her sisters thought very highly of themselves as the flower of Revolutionary Society, and believed that the Revolutionary John Jay was one of the greatest statesmen of history. Their father, John Jay, was a handsome man of astonishing bonhommie and approachability, and had no pretentiousness whatever. In early life he had defended runaway slaves in court, hid them in the house, etc., and he had a thrilling collection of stories about that epoch. During the fifties he became one of the organizers of the Republican Party and was a prime mover in the group that called Lincoln to the Cooper Union Meeting in 1860.[1]

His wife, my grandmother, was a daughter of Hickson Field, a rich New York merchant, and she was a masterly character with a passion for all her descendants. She kept track of every one of them down to her rapidly multiplying great-grandchildren. At eighty-odd, she sat up in bed giving directions and writing notes with regard to each of them. She despised all public activities and regarded them as vanities — bubbles on the stream. She concurred with her husband in only one thing — a delight in surrounding themselves at Bedford with their daughters and their grandchildren, giving a month in each summer to each of the families. The dinner table there was a daily bout of festivity, the children, except the smallest ones, being at the great table. The sons-in-law[2] came up for week-ends from their work in town, and the ris-

[1] From 1869 to 1874 he was U.S. Minister to Austria.
[2] Henry G. Chapman, William H. Schieffelin, and Edmund Randolph Robinson.

ing generation was made to feel that it owned the place, indeed owned the countryside.

The farm was said to amount to a thousand acres, most of it woodland, and the title was held by Indian deeds to some old Dutch ancestor. The little old house was full of portraits, by Stuart and Trumbull, of Washington, Hamilton, Egbert Benson, and a remarkable Stuart of the Chief Justice himself and a fine bust of him by Ceracchi, which one could see bore but a faint resemblance to the man, but was a magnificent Romanization of an American patriot. There were two handsome portraits of William Jay and his wife, my grandfather's father and mother, by the American artist, Vanderlyn.

In addition to the good portraits, there were various old canvases of mythical ancestors in bad condition by unknown artists. One of them, known as 'The Patroon' — a Dutch title — had been repainted so many times that one could not tell whether it had originally represented a sitting or a standing figure. It was known to the grandchildren as 'The Sliding Poltroon.'

The Bedford house was well placed on the brow of a hill with a fine view to the west of the hills on the other side of the Hudson, thirty miles distant. Four great lindens stood in front of the piazza, and beyond them an open stretch of falling lawns, ha-has and cornfields toward the south. The flower garden, whose hedge proclaimed its age and sanctity, lay low along the eastern edge of the front lawn. 'What a nice little place you have here,' said some visiting Englishman. You see, to us it was Windsor Castle.

The 'Jay Farm' — to call it by its proper title — had other merits. There were Shetland ponies, sulkies, old hacks, dog-carts, haymows, arbors, an old cider mill, old stone cottages, a pond, a small rose garden surrounded by palings so old that nothing but their white moss was visible, moss like moonlight. The palings have vanished since my day, just vanished through the 'unimaginable touch of time.' . . .

My brother and I felt so much at home at the Jay homestead that when we went to college we brought our friends there for house parties, and the whole estate lives in my memory as an enchanted palace of youth.

More than ten years before writing these reminiscences, Chapman had put another memory of his grandfather's country-place into verse.

CHAPMAN IN EARLY BOYHOOD (RIGHT) WITH
HIS BROTHER HENRY

THE GRANDFATHER

There's a kind of morning prayer
    In the air,
That recalls the song and praise
    Of other days,
And the lilacs all in bloom,
And the sunny breakfast-room,—
Open windows to the ground
    All around.
Lawns a-glitter with the dew,
Scents from many a field and flower
In that early, quiet hour
    Greeted you;
For, in coming down the stairs
You could smell delicious airs, —
The whole country-place seemed theirs.
Were they creeping in to prayers
    Or passing through?
Or visiting the vases freshly set
On the mantel, in the corner cabinet?
Was it lilies, was it pinks or mignonette?
What they were I'll hardly say —
    Roses, roses anyway!
    I smell them yet.

Just a morn like this, and then
Came the maids (there were no men)
    One or two
Decent maids; then jolly children not a few.
And with shuffling of the chairs
They prepared the place for prayers,
    Romping through;
And scarcely grew more tame
When the silent moment came,
    For they knew
When Grandpapa appeared
He was little to be feared
    By the crew.
And their mothers were in bed.
(And surely for such notions
As family devotions
    There's little to be said.)

> So the ancient prayers were read
>   By that brilliant-eyed old man,
> Full of reverence, full of grace,
>   For the children of his clan
> In the quaint old country-place
> That had nursed the elder race
>   With its bloom.
> And he kneeled where they had kneeled,
> And the odors of the field
>   Filled the room.

October 12, 1920.

The 'Retrospections' proceed with the tale of other boyhood vacations at Narragansett Pier, 'a resort where, in the seventies, not too prosperous business men sent their families, and rejoined them at week-ends. We, at any rate, were not rich.' There was the perfect bathing, and 'the group of friends whose children grew up like first cousins.'

> They were active-minded youngsters, reading books of all kinds and discussing them furiously; acting charades and trooping across the country on picnics and crabbing parties, playing croquet and tennis and constantly undergoing discipline at the hands of their correct parents, of whom my mother was chief duenna. She was a *mondaine* and a woman of great will power who was determined that her daughters should marry well and that her sons should have a good education. Her own early education had been neglected, but she had a natural aptitude for the things of the mind. All her life she read constantly, German, French, and English books. Her outlook made her at home in Europe when in later life she was often there, and she came to resemble an old countess of the continental variety, experienced, worldly, formidable, classbound. Many is the battle I have had with her. Both her great qualities and her defects were steadily enhanced by the decline in our family fortunes during the seventies, when the boys were at school age, and the problems of life fell upon her alone. She made an inquest of boarding-schools and, deciding upon St. Paul's, Concord, N.H., sent my brother there, I following him next year at the age of fourteen.

Chapman's mother and St. Paul's School were each of great moment in his later life. The references to them in the

'Retrospections' must be read, however, with a special realization that they were written in a mellowing haze of later years. The records of early antagonism with his mother are of a violence which gave way by degrees to the more dutiful practices of a son. The 'queerness' which led to his leaving St. Paul's School seems, in the following passage from the 'Retrospections,' queer enough, but hardly so strange as it must have appeared to his schoolmates and teachers. Owen Wister[1] has told of his standing at cricket all oblivious of the ball bowled at the wickets he was supposed to be guarding, oblivious for the strange reason that he was lost in prayer. Travelling to and from the school on sleeping-cars, the presence of other boys did not keep him from kneeling openly beside his berth to say his prayers as if he were at home. There were legends at Concord of a woodland shrine of his own to which he would repair for religious rites. A schoolmate recalls a habit, when they sat next to each other in a schoolroom for Latin study, of passing his hands over the textbook as if warming them at a fire, on the theory that the language would enter his system through the pores. He was tortured, moreover, by a sense of physical inferiority, extending far beyond his ineptness at games. Yet the chief maladjustment between St. Paul's and himself lay in the heavily religious atmosphere of the School, which might leave the normally impervious all untouched by solemn thought, yet work destruction to so sensitive a spirit as Chapman's, merely through overemphasis on a tendency inherent in himself. Many years later, when his soul was harrowed to its depths by the adversity of grave illness, the spiritual significance and value of his schooling became quite clear to him.

Let us revert to St. Paul's as the 'Retrospections' disclose it, and to his further preparation for college:

> The place did not suit me. (This was, of course, earlier than the Narragansett period, but I must set down these things in

[1] See *Atlantic Monthly*, May, 1934.

the order in which they occur to me.) I was an inward creature, wandering about in worlds unrealized. I was not school-trained nor governess-trained, nor at home on the playground. I could not answer a question in class or catch a ball on the field, and I looked with wonder on my young contemporaries who could do such things. School life was to me a mysterious and gloomy whirl of things, a vast, complex factory-building of clock, bells, and automata. The meals were dreadful and the friendly attentions of the masters, mortifying; and besides, there was never enough to eat. On Saturday evening — or perhaps it was Sunday evening — the whole school was gathered in the large schoolroom; the masters and their wives ranged about the walls, and Dr. Coit on the platform. He made a holy talk, a hymn was sung — always the same hymn — and then everyone filed past the ghostly ranks of the Doctor and his underworld, shaking hands with each master, and then wandered toward his bed, with visions of the dreadful morrow — æons of dreadful morrows — rising in his heart.

At this period I got an impression as to institutions of all kinds which has never left me. A jail, a lunatic asylum, a summer school — community life of any sort, is a sanitarium. It says to me, 'Good morning; have you used Pear's soap? Now you may take ten minutes on the treadmill. It is such wholesome exercise.' I cannot bear to pass a town high school in an automobile.

On returning to St. Paul's School for the second year, my isolation was apparent to the naked eye. I was plainly in a dream. I wandered about and made mysterious gestures before imaginary shrines. I picked up torn papers and carried them to the dust-bin. If I were playing baby cricket on the small boys' green patch at the then Lower School, I would lay my bat on the ground and wait, then pick it up and face the occult ceremony of the 'service.' These things astonished and bewildered the not-too-watchful school authorities, and my father was sent for. I was at this period sleeping in the attic of the then Lower School, and the water froze in my jug at night. On the journey home with my father, I developed pneumonia by sleeping in a draught on the Sound boat and arrived in a fever that kept me out of my head for many days. At my bedside were Doctors Francis Kinnicutt and William H. Draper, whose kindness I never forgot.

On my recovery, my body was a shell, with a weak

left lung, and it was some years before my constitution was re-established. A return to school was out of the question, and the alternative was to prepare for college at home. For the next four or five years I spent the winters at Washington Square and prepared my daily task for a crack tutor, Horace E. Deming, then a young lawyer, who dropped in every afternoon for an hour or two, alternating with Camillus G. Kidder, an equally competent examiner, both of them Harvard men. The expense of this tutoring was a large item in my mother's budget. My work once done for the day, I was left to my own devices, which were to wander about the city, frequent bookshops and book auctions, go to an occasional matinee and to concerts. My mother was fond of music, and in her earlier married days had taken lessons of old Mr. Rackemann, whose family had, I think, been friends or pupils of Beethoven. She attended all such classical concerts as the time afforded. I was taken to hear Rubinstein, Thomas's Orchestra, and an occasional violinist. I wandered in to hear Kreisler in a concert hall on Sixth Avenue when he was almost a boy. He played some Bach solos. I remember Edwin Booth in 'Macbeth,' with a cast made up of scene-shifters, and a papier-maché leg of mutton to symbolise the Banquo scene. I heard Charles Coghlan play the 'Lady of Lyons,' and Fanny Davenport in I forget what, Montague, the gallery Adonis, Boucicault in 'The Shaughraun,' old Wallack in his own play, 'Rosedale,' Hackett as Falstaff, etc. I got my father to put up $9.00 for a Lucian in Greek text, 1503, because I wanted to own a folio Aldus. It is not the best edition, but served my turn. I have seen Milton's early poems, 1640, sold for $40.00, and Shakespeare quartos for $10.00 apiece. I bought a Brunet and a [blank in script], but I never had any system, resources, or ambition about book-collecting.

In my leisure hours I read Shakespeare, Spenser, and other English classics, Molière and 'Gil Blas,' etc. At this time I developed a great admiration for the writers of Queen Anne's time, especially Pope, of whom I had an early, much annotated edition.[1] I read the 'Dunciad' with gusto and was entirely

---

[1] After addressing a letter, in 1889, in the beautiful script of which he was capable, he wrote: 'Isn't it written like a copying clerk of the last century? There are old records down town in the County Clerk's office just like it. Why is it that clerks could write so? Nowadays nobody can but me, and I learnt it by imitating the writings in a Boswell's Johnson that contained facsimiles of Pope and Dryden and all those fellows.'

on the side of Pope in his excoriation of persons I knew nothing about who were his small-fry enemies. The later romantic poets, Byron, Keats, and Shelley, I regarded with contempt, and thought (as Byron himself pretended to think) that the heroic couplet was the proper vehicle for English verse. My discovery of the romantic poetry came very slowly. I remember closing the door for years on Byron with the single phrase, 'Byron was a blackguard' — words which incensed my most intimate friends, the young Lockwoods, almost to madness.

Our youthful group included Florence and Francis Lockwood (later Mrs. C. Grant LaFarge and Mrs. Henry Wharton), and their younger brother Benoni, who became sisters and brother to the three young Chapmans, Henry, Eleanor, and myself. At a slightly later date Owen Wister, a great pal of Henry's at St. Paul's, was added to the group.

The solitude of my Washington Square period fortified me against the opinion of the world and made me conceited. It was as if I had lived in a foreign country and had come to see my own as a stranger might see it. This made me too self-sufficient, not to say self-important; and when I went on to Cambridge to take my preliminary examinations, I was boxed-up, self-conscious, and quite determined not to change my opinions too easily for anything that Harvard might offer. I have a single recollection of a metaphysical sort that dates from the Washington Square period. Of course, my reading was apt to arouse ideas and questions in my mind that did not interest my family or my companions and were met with silent indifference. I said to myself, 'But unless I say these things, I shall lose them and lose the source and habit of them.' Therefore I continued to talk without the expectation of being understood, and I have done this ever since.

A long section of the 'Retrospections' is headed 'Harvard Letters, 1880-81,' ushered in and interrupted by reminiscent comments. It is unnecessary to present these pages in anything like their entirety. The letters, which extend but slightly beyond the first two years of college, yield bits of significance and spirit, but must not stand too long in the way of the maturer correspondence. They are addressed almost without exception to his mother, who, he says, 'must

have crossed out passages here and there and thrown away
the pages which she didn't like or thought unbecoming.
I seem,' he proceeds, 'never to have had an intimate relation
to her, but to have been conscientious in entertaining her
and nevertheless retaining a sort of incognito so far as my
inner self was concerned. My letters probably became the
chief interest of her life and I probably knew this.' He certainly knew it many years later when he found a note in his
mother's handwriting on a letter in which he had urged her
to remain abroad, 'Dear old Jack is so afraid I'll come home.
These scraps and letters are more than gold-dust to me.' In
the second year of his college course his father met with a
disastrous business failure, and it was for this reason that
his mother and sisters 'went to France, for economy's sake,
and lived in a pension. It was then taken for granted,' he
goes on to say, 'that Henry and I should be kept in college.
My grandmother Jay and even my grandmother Chapman out
of her modest income lent financial aid.' He had already
begun to fend for himself financially, by tutoring. This
piece of work came to him, as Chapman tells in his 'Memories and Milestones,' through the kindness and clairvoyance
of President Eliot: 'I had not known that it was within my
powers, but Dr. Eliot knew it.' A professor, who had found
himself while an undergraduate in straits like Chapman's,
offered, apparently without avail, to place a substantial sum
of money at his disposal for the completion of his course.
The college years had their full share of anxieties.

Some of the letters in this portion of the 'Retrospections'
may be prefaced by one of the interrupting comments:

> During two years of my college course I had an obsession,
> a sort of self-willed mania for learning to play the violin, for
> which I had no talent. The letters recur to this subject. I
> have not quoted many of such passages because they bore
> and shame me horribly. I have no intention of putting myself
> in an unamiable light in these memoirs. My musical craze
> came to a natural end at Harvard in the hurling of coal-scuttles
> at my room door, popular and effective demonstrations. This

outcome I count among the chief blessings I received from Harvard University.[1]

After his father's failure he wrote home, 'I shall sell the violin: it's no halfway business.'

CAMBRIDGE, *July* 2, 1880.

(After an examination)

... The young lady who is passing (handing out) papers here I should say was safe. Am inclined to agree with Milton that women were not meant to be learnéd. The cultivation which rubs off on them ought to suffice. The timidity that comes from conscious ignorance is by no means unattractive. Howsoever, this is great bosh. Subtract the time-consuming possibilities from N. England females and you'll throw a large mass of very questionable produce on the market. Take eyeglasses from a virgin about here, and what are you going to do with the remainder? Got through, I think, Greek prose, Grammar, Geometry.

J. J. C.

This outburst against the New England female was not so uncalled for as it seems. One of the humiliations of Freshman life at Harvard was the recurrent need of applying to a vulture who lived in a box in University Hall for information and for permits of various kinds. She was elderly, sharp-nosed, and sharp-tongued. Her face was flanked by long, black, curly ringlets, and she snapped out her information with exasperated contempt. I resented her; I resented the University for employing her. I took it for granted that she was a pet of President Eliot's and was employed because she was accurate and useful, and because Massachusetts didn't know that one must not treat ingenuous young men with unnecessary discourtesy. You will say that this was an error on the part of Massachusetts, but I say it was a crime. There! That's the first reminiscence that really bites me which I have gleaned from the package of letters thus far.

It so happened that before my college days my mother had taken the family to a summer boarding-house (Hood Cottage) at Nahant, and in this way we had come to know some Bos-

---

[1] His classmate, Philip H. Goepp, recalling this period, wrote after Chapman's death to Mrs. Chapman: 'It was in the hey-day of his study of the violin, when the sophomores hung clocks outside of his windows and burst his door, to stop his practising.'

tonians. The only incident that I remember of this Nahant
period is that Dr. Holmes came to call on Mama, and talked,
O grief! some pages out of the 'Autocrat,' which we had been
reading aloud the day before. Among Mama's Nahant friends
were the George Abbot Jameses. Mrs. James was a sister of
Cabot Lodge. Old Mrs. Lodge, Cabot's mother, was a live
miniature Puritan portrait, in a close black cap with white
tucks about her face, sitting bolt upright on a spindle chair
with a footstool, staccato in speech, experienced, a personality,
dry and kindly. While in college I used to call on her in Boston.
I always felt that she was a friend. Her daughter, Mrs. George
Abbot James, was a downright, plump, unimaginative, categorical, square-toed, friendly matron, whose apparel had the
definition of an old colored lithograph. Her hair was drawn
back tight and she wore pendant earrings and a brooch on
the breast of her tight bodice. The Jameses lived at Nahant in
a large, new stone palace of a house, with oak tables ten feet
long, rugs on the floor, and no small objects anywhere to be
seen. The kindness of the Jameses to Henry and to me began
during the friendless period of our first arrival in Cambridge
and endured as long as they lived. I still feel grateful to them.
We regarded their house as our own. James had come from the
Middle West — wherever that is — and was such a contrast
to the Puritans as did one's heart good. He was large, florid,
handsome; wore low-cut, standing collars, a scarab on his
tie, a ring on his finger, loud clothes. He had a passion for
the stage and for acting, knew actors, and he liked to make
friends of young men. Boston, of course, looked askance at
him....

November 14, 1880.

It will please you to hear that I had the satisfaction of
making a fool of myself before the whole college. There is a
debating society called the Harvard Union.... I was moved
to get on my legs... and when I got there I found that I had
nothing to say, so after a few incoherent sentences I sat down
again, remarking faintly to my neighbor that notoriety was
the next best thing to fame.... I supposed from frequent conversations that the words would come to me in addressing an
audience.

The letters hold many allusions to the books he was reading, often with mature perception, to the theatre, with special

27

rejoicing in Sarah Bernhardt and Salvini, and to music. The 'popular movement' which put an end to his own ambitions as a violinist is duly noted; so, more than once, is the pleasure he took in the best music he could hear. 'You don't know,' he wrote in one of his freshman letters, 'how playing the violin gives me an appreciation of music;' and, a little later, 'if I were ten years younger, I'd be a musician.'

The social life of Boston, habitual flings at his surroundings, a righteous disgust with a demi-mondaine ball into which he drifted with some friends, all found place in the letters. 'I make it a point to abuse Boston,' he wrote. 'They like it inside and it's good for 'em. Have yet to see a girl who is a human being, with a good mind well filled, yet no spectacles, no woman's rights. Don't believe there is such a commodity.' His grandmother Jay would not have relished such levity:

February 19, 1881.

Yesterday I got a telegram which made me laugh for a half hour by the dial. I had written to Grandmama Jay much such a letter as I write to you, saying how we flung the ham about at table, and mentioning the coming St. Paul's School's dinner at which I expected to see my friends overcome with wine, when behold! comes a telegram, 'Remember *Noblesse Oblige*! Monday dinner. Ham story wounds me. Love.' I had a good mind to write her back that though she must have been ignorant of the fact, it's quite the thing to be drunk at a dinner and that *noblesse* will *oblige*!

While a club election was in progress he wrote:

You must expect me to be awfully swell. I have shoes not two inches across and shaped like very sharp pencils, and long cut-aways with tails like walruses. My everyday suits are made by the Emperor of Russia's tailor; my hats are bishop's mitres, and my overcoats knock the unsuspecting beholder off his feet.

December 14, 1881.

The Boston world really treated the young freshman cubs better than they deserved to be treated. — I remember going improperly clad to a similar soirée at Mrs. Henry Russell's; and to cover my shame Colonel Russell lent me an entire outfit of dress clothes, shirt, pumps and diamond studs. The clothes were a bit too large, but the effect was stunning.

At about the time of his first marriage, in 1889, he reverted in a letter, to these college days in a reminiscence, certain details of which are repudiated by a surviving figure in it (Owen Wister). Yet, whatever its shortcomings in accuracy, it speaks for the young New Yorker in his Boston surroundings:

> I remember Wister once, being asked to a shindy in Milton, saying, 'Now I haven't got any dress coat, and I am going without a dress coat, and as I go in I shall apologize, etc. Mrs. Russell will say, "O, Mr. Wister, you must not think this is Philadelphia. We are always anxious to see our friends in whatever clothes,"' and by Jove she did! Just the little fling at Philadelphia — slightly conscious character of the Forbes simplicity. There is a certain very slight ostentation of simplicity at Naushon — which I intend some day to tell old Forbes and make him hopping.

> WEYMOUTH, *June* 18, 1882.
> I am passing Sunday with my grandmother and making great friends with her. I have always had the greatest admiration for her and can make allowance for all those things which neither a son nor a daughter-in-law can tolerate. She is the most remarkable woman I have ever known and I find her very instructive. Have lately been reading Henry James's 'Portrait of a Lady.' Haven't got through. It's too fine flavored for me. The characters are drawn with too fine a point and in too faint colors. As Grandma C. says, it's a picture of a peculiar phase of civilization rather than of life.... I believe James designs ultimately to write a play. I don't believe he can do it. In a play you want just what he lacks, plot, action. You may be exquisite, but you must be evident. Besides you must have a dash of poetry or splash or bombast — the Bulwer element.

AT PRESIDENT ELIOT'S
NORTH EAST HARBOR
Sept. 1, 1882.

I am happy to say that the elder brother (of my classmate, Sam) is gone on a cruise with the largest boat and it has been too cold or too still weather to sail in the smaller one. For if there is one form of idleness I dislike more than another, it is sailing, flipping along over the water with no end but to pass time, and every few minutes crawling across the boat from one uncomfortable position into another.

The President is sociable and set in his ways. He has the self-confidence (not to say egotism), the hard-headedness, and perhaps narrowness of the self-made man, which, with his real antecedents and education, make a very powerful combination, though not necessarily an attractive one. All the same he is very pleasant....

October 7, 1882.

Went to the X's funeral on Monday, where was all the world. The minister said we ought not to grumble when we think she's probably in good company, her old aunts and uncles — and they probably need her more than the (West Newton) Branch, that she was a sweet and lovely character who went to church regularly and we ought to profit by her example. Then some people in the gallery began to sing dismally and slowly a Unitarian hymn of comfort and the grave, all the church, which was packed, sitting still as milestones. Then everybody stood up and he gave a blessing like a blight. Then everybody sat still and wondered for five minutes, till the pallbearers, walking hither and thither on tiptoe and talking under their breaths, carried off the coffin with the flowers through the door, and when we had looked at each other for five minutes more, we got up and dispersed. I felt like crying out with Laertes in 'Hamlet,' 'Is there no ceremony else — no ceremony else?'...

Besides the letters from which these fractions have been taken — letters that do not extend into that later portion of his college course which is generally the most maturing — there is little to speak at first hand for him. A classmate will tell you of his demonstration of disgust with a dish of tripe served at a club table in Linden Street, by hurling it, platter and all, through the glass of a closed window. His clubs were those of the elect, and his contributions of audacity and rhyme to their gatherings enlarged their gaiety. A college friend, Frank R. Frost, of Charleston, remembers and describes the walks that he and Chapman used to take together into the country, when Chapman would gather flowers and branches and put them in his hat, and then round his neck and shoulders, until he was bedecked and garlanded like a sylvan spirit. Returning to the streets of Cambridge in this guise, he was so absorbed in the walk and the talk as to be quite unconscious of what the passers-by might think of him. It is recalled, moreover, that on one occasion he brought to a meeting of a literary club, the now extinct 'O.K.,' a paper of his own on a new Scandinavian poet, giving some account of the man and his work, and reading translations from his poems. The members of the club were much impressed, and Chapman himself agreed that he had produced an ideal O.K. paper, adding that he had invented the poet and all his verses only the night before. In print he bore his part as an editor of the daily paper so indolently that he was dropped from the board. His contributions to the more 'literary' *Advocate* strike one today as possessing no marked distinction. When his class came to graduate, in 1884, the authorities rebuked his repeated absence from compulsory chapel services — whether as the gesture of an individualist or because he was in temporary revolt against the beliefs on which his school had placed so heavy an emphasis — by withholding his degree until the Commencement of 1885. This, however, did not prevent his appearance on Class Day as Ivy Orator, a rôle ascribed to the wit of the class. His performance in this capacity was most favorably received, but, as read in print today, it cannot be counted definitely better or worse than the average of its kind.

One production of his college period should nevertheless

be rescued, in token of a spirit that was already stirring within him, and of a power to express it. In his volume of 'Songs and Poems' (1919) the verses, 'A Prayer,' bear no sign of their early origin. Yet among Chapman's papers I find a manuscript copy of it, endorsed in his mother's handwriting, 'August 1883,' and a second copy, endorsed, evidently by Minna Timmins, his future wife, 'October 2, 1885.' Before inclusion in his book it underwent a slight abridgment. In the earliest version, dated in the summer vacation before his final undergraduate year, it read, all prophetically, as follows:

A PRAYER

O God, when the heart is warmest,
And the head is clearest,
   Give me to act —
Turn the purposes Thou formest
    Into fact.
When I feel the love Thou sharest,
    Cast out fear.
O God, when what *is* dearest
    Seems most dear —
And the path of life lies straight
    With neither chance nor fate
    In my career —
When the spirit is up lifted
    For a moment and can see
    Through dark mists brightly rifted
    Its true felicity —
Then let me act — the wicker gate
In view — let me not wait — not wait.

We do not always fight —
    There is a lull
And nervous watching — after night
Follows dim dawn before the day is full —
    How can we see till there be light?
But there's a time to speak as to be dumb
    O God, when mine shall come
    And I put forth

My strength for blame or praise
Blow Thou the fire in my heart's hearth
    Into a blaze
(Who kindled it but Thou?)
And let me feel upon that day of days
    As I feel now — as I feel now.

Here also we should pause a moment to look at a letter, written in the same summer of 1883, to his boyhood and manhood friend, Florence Lockwood (Mrs. C. Grant LaFarge). Its frankly assumed sharing of his joy in the discovery of Browning foreshadowed many such instances throughout his life.

Lowland, Nahant, Mass.
July 20, 1883.

My dear Flos

Jenny Carlyle is not in the house after all, and I did not buy the pirated edition — from no deeper principle than economy, however, so I shall not be able to finish the letters till leaving. So far as I could guess — Francis, and her simple hard-headed view of the case, seemed near the truth. But even if Jane had been here herself and Carlyle and Brother John and Lady Harriet, all thinking and talking their best — I should hardly have listened — because — to put it very simply, I have had a revelation — Robert Browning. You will smile — fact all the same. I read him last night till daybreak — and cried. Can you believe it? It was as chastening to the spirit as a family quarrel. Really it is wicked to laugh at these things and immoral. . . .

I wonder if we shall all turn into steady-going inhabiters of 25-foot houses — with fixed ideas and a notion that all things are more or less the same now as ever — and there is no new thing under the sun. I trow not. Nothing is so evident as that this so easily quoted truism is one of the falsest things that a maker of half-truths ever got off. Not only would the reverse be truer — but would be absolutely the fact — i.e., that nothing was ever repeated. Each water drop falls to the earth — by its own particular virtue — so to speak an original idea. To say it obeys a law is a most misleading metaphor — the 'law' being only a chronicling of its action.

And so we too of this generation are new. There has been no one like us — there will be no one who will understand us,

33

as we now can scarcely comprehend the ruling generation. We can a little — thanks to that extraordinary simultaneousness with which modes of thinking pervade a country — discoveries — conceptions flash at once along the channels of all men's minds. We can hope to understand our contemporaries.

But the newest thing about us is that we expect to change every day — every hour. This should be an elixir to prevent us from growing old. Do you think when I'm sixty I'll advise a boy to read Herbert Spencer? Not if I understand that writer. I'd as soon send a boy now to Coleridge's Aids to Reflection — as my grandfather did me because forsooth it had meant something to him — and I could have sucked as much instruction from the Alcoran.

No, no, the boy shall have the textbooks of 1930 — and we shall regard Huxley (suppose we knew enough to do it) as we now regard the first steam-engine — or the first circumnavigation of the globe....

If you have ideas about Browning I wish you would hint them to me. It sort of came to me not to be critical — so I just read him — and stamp on the floor when I come to a good place....

Following the 'Harvard Letters' in the 'Retrospections' stand more than twenty type-written pages headed 'Harvard and Boston.' These are followed by a still longer section headed 'Europe,' early in the course of which Chapman wrote that he was obliged to rely upon his 'fragmentary and confused memories of the years that followed the Harvard letters preserved by his mother. He warns the reader again that 'an autobiography always speaks from the date at which it was written;' and so much of the 'Harvard and Boston' passage represents obviously the remembrances of later years that it is best to pass over them now and proceed at once to the year of European travel that followed his graduation. For all the desultoriness of his college studies, he passed this *Wanderjahr* as one anointed with the oil of cultivation — and cultivability — above his American fellows, indeed more as a young European fortunately placed in the world might have passed it. With many omissions and one in-

CHAPMAN, STUDENT AT HARVARD

terruption from a contemporaneous letter, suggesting how richly his soil was prepared to receive the seeds of travel, the 'Europe' section of the 'Retrospections' runs as follows:[1]

A young American should not go to college in his own state if he can avoid it. 'Home-keeping youth have ever homely wits,' and half the value of college life comes from transplantation. The Bostonians are at a disadvantage here; for with them there is nowhere to go but home — homes to which they welcome their friends of all ages from afar.

When I remember my earlier dinners and Sundays with the families of my Boston classmates, my visits to the North Shore and the Cape, I feel the tingle of travel and the tang of sea air. It is stimulating to find people who are not exactly like one's own people, and valuable to do this as early in life as possible. What any young man ultimately needs is *the world*. As Dante felt about the Southern Cross — when he speaks of the 'widowed' northern hemisphere, where that constellation never becomes visible — so I felt about Europe and Europe's constellations in the intellectual skies.

It was arranged that I should travel with William Amory Gardner, one of my very earliest acquaintances as a freshman — the youngest and the best educated man in the class of '84. Gardner was one of three orphans, Joseph '82, and Augustus, '86, being the others, and all three of them inherited a supernormal sensitiveness of nervous structure. They were essentially religious types. Jo, the wittiest man of his epoch, committed suicide in early life. Gus worked himself to death during the Great War, and Amory, who devoted his life to Groton School, among whose founders he must forever figure, died at the age of sixty-six, leaving such a host of impassioned friends that his funeral, which took place in the Gothic Chapel that he had given to the school, lives in my mind as the most impressive religious service that I ever attended....

The frailty of Amory's constitution was revealed on one of our first meetings. He and John G. Coolidge, his first cousin,

[1] There are no allusions here to previous visits to Europe, but in the essay 'La Vie Parisienne' in 'Greek Genius and Other Essays,' Chapman sets down a memory of St. Cloud when he was seven. 'I was struck dumb with delight,' he says, 'and I said to myself, "This is the sort of thing that I like! It is native to me; I have always been waiting for this. It must be that I am a king!"' Letters to his mother in 1881 show, besides, that he visited Europe in the summer vacation between his freshman and sophomore years in college.

and I decided to walk to Bunker Hill Monument. When we had ascended it, Amory had a taking, which he took calmly, simply bidding us hold him upside down by his ankles. This treatment seemed to restore him and we thought no more of the matter.

Amory was a prize scholar. Professor Goodwin said at the founding of Groton School, where Amory was to be the Greek Master, that Gardner was the best scholar that he had ever taught. Amory had a phenomenal memory and the conscience of an anchorite. He was the victim of his memory and of his conscience; and in his later years had to be humored when he talked; you could not detrack him; you had to let him unwind. It was due to my friendship with him that I became almost like one of the family to the group that founded Groton School; and I must say they are one of the dearest memories of my life. It was due largely to him that I became at home with his labyrinthine family connections, and feel today as if Boston was my native village. I dip into it and am happy....

I was to go abroad as a wandering student for fifteen months — live at the rate of $100.00 a month and return to enter the Harvard Law School. I began with a month in London, where, as I remember, I was alone, and after that two months on the Continent with Gardner. My grandfather Jay had supplied me with numerous letters to old friends and notabilities in England, and I had the necessary equipment of fine clothes and umbrellas for social emergencies.

It was the age when the doors of England stood wide open. The first thing anyone in England said on glancing at a letter of introduction was: 'Whom do you wish to see?' Now I will not swear as to just on which visit it was that I saw the persons I name — for one was always passing through London — but I remember the glamor of the personalities. I saw Tom Hughes at a sort of barn-place — the Cosmopolitan Club (?). I shook hands with Lord Salisbury at a reception in his palace, where he loomed like an Olympus in his great drawing-room; and on his daughter's asking me what I had seen that had most impressed me since I reached England, I answered with an aptness which somewhat surprised me, 'Your father' — which she immediately repeated to the god. It was true, all the same. He looked like the British Empire. I made one or two week-end visits to great houses. One of them recalled to me a remark made years before by my grandmother Jay —

that in all great establishments in England there was a crippled ancestor, a sacred being having every sign of extreme care in dress and attendance, who lay on a stretcher on the lawn or in a back library, and to whom one was introduced with dignity. This was a beautiful and extraordinary feature of English life.

I must not forget Tennyson, to whom Mrs. Ritchie, Thackeray's daughter, gave me a letter, which resulted in my lunching with the Tennyson family in the country. When I arrived, he was standing in the garden beside Lady Tennyson, who lay on an iron movable bed, collapsible, complicated, portentous. There was a strained pause, for I was speechless with reverence and oppression. Then Tennyson said, 'How much do you think a thing like that costs?' I hesitated; the question was so unexpected. 'Eighty pounds,' he said very ponderously. I endeavored to show proper surprise and sympathy; but I have never felt at home in drawing-rooms nor in the presence of distinguished persons. The family luncheon at the Tennysons' was colorless. We all seemed to be equally overshadowed by his greatness. It was the *mot d'ordre* to be speechless.

After lunch we sat in the shrubbery — and a minor poet dropped in. I think his name was Lewis Morris. Now, I thought, we shall have some poetic intimacies. And it really happened. Tennyson and Morris conversed about small water-creatures, newts and frogs, and little things that flit about on azure wings, and I felt I was seeing life. But I also felt oppressed. I had the desire to join in and didn't know how. Next the conversation shifted to larger animals. I began to nurse a hope that I perhaps might quote something; and on Tennyson's mention of the polecat — before I knew it I had quoted that magnificent line of Hamlet where he says, — 'He smote the sledded Polacks on the ice,' — only in my impromptu rush I quoted it in the form we used at home in the schoolroom, — which *égayés* the line a bit — 'He smote the sledded Polecats on the ice.' I admit that there was some malice in this, for the polecat is what the English call the skunk.

The effect was stirring. All three of us were knocked out. The poets couldn't laugh and I couldn't laugh. My own lack of small-talk and my crude excursion into natural history had ruined the day. There was no recovering the first mad, careless rapture of seeing Tennyson, whose fear of American visitors was notorious and whose anxiety to be visited earned all the agonies it caused him. I had a glimpse of the whole tragedy when I was saying good-bye to his daughter-in-law at the entry. She detached the last sheet of a weekly paper that was lying on the hall table and handed it to me as a memento of the visit. . . .

I heard afterward that Mrs. Ritchie had given Miss Georgina Schuyler a letter to Tennyson. Miss Schuyler was a very distinguished, experienced, public-spirited lady of New York. Throughout the visit Tennyson behaved toward her with his usual boorishness. In saying good-bye he endeavored to force out a polite word of some sort. Miss Schuyler coldly assured him that 'She was always glad to meet any friend of Mrs. Ritchie's.'. . .

People used to write essays on the uses of great men. The British had long understood the matter. Great men were to be shown off. 'Would you like to meet Lord Acton?' said a lady to me. 'I will get him to dine with us.' Now Lord Acton was the unique Monster of Erudition — almost a hieratic personality — as the most learned man in England; and I really wonder what would have happened if she and I and the sage — for such was the image in my mind — she and Acton and I — had dined together. Fortunately he was not in England. He was at his castle on the Danube, where he was writing so profoundly on the Roman Catholic question that his reputation plunged after him into the abyss. In later years, when every man of note was giving out the names of the hundred best books of the world, Acton suggested a list of works so erudite that James Russell Lowell said there were only four of them that he had ever heard of.

I saw Henry M. Stanley at a tea, and a tough customer he was, with rather terrible hands, and eyes as hard as quartz. I was taken to a family dinner at the Gladstones' — very informal and short — before a public meeting of some sort. I was taken to lunch, also informal yet vacuous, at Herbert Spencer's. He was an intimate friend of the Miss Cross, sister of John Cross who later married George Eliot, and of another brother who lived in New York and was a friend of my family.

I notice in reading memoirs that the authors attempt to conceal their vanity, — a most dangerous thing to do, — and I think of pursuing the opposite course as an experiment. There were some dear people with whom I spent some days in the country and whose name I cannot remember. One of them said to me, — 'You know we have a nickname for you, — we call you "the smiling tempest."' Now I always think of myself as a shy, oppressed person.

I remember a garden party or open-air spread of some sort where the abundance of the food — displayed upon long tables, and the delicacies of the season — especially the pyramids of nectarines and plovers' eggs — as well as the voracity with which the standing guests devoured them — talking at the same time in torrents — impressed me deeply. There was an abandonment about it which I envied. These people certainly knew how to enjoy themselves. It occurs to me to say here that from my early years I had a natal contempt for my own compatriots due to I hardly know what, perhaps to being a clever boy who was king of the nursery. At any rate, I despised Americans for their social timidity and colorlessness. In the meantime, I had drawn my impressions of the British from the old English works of fiction. The British appeared to me to be all expressiveness and ingenuous force. Thus when I reached England and saw them at play at a free lunch in a Jacobean garden, they seemed to correspond to my dream of them.

It required years of experience and hard thinking for me to throw off my impressions of the English as a race of supermen, and I couldn't have done it alone. But in later times I had one at my side who had been to school in England and had grown up with a whole generation of English intimates, had kept in touch with them in all her life and loved them. It was she who acted as a composite Hermes-Virgil-Mephistopheles in shepherding me through the underworld of ambition, selfishness, and savagery that lies, or used to lie, below the surface of social life in England. Strange to say, my reading of Thackeray had not sufficed to open my eyes. I was converted gradually, and came to suspect that I had been fooled by my bookish education, and that there were some things in life that books do not teach.

I do remember one experience in Piccadilly in 1884 which gave me a jar. I was walking past Apsley House, looking quite like anyone else, and certainly as well dressed, when a similarly outfitted pedestrian who was walking toward me, just as he passed me and when his face was within three feet of mine, looked straight at me and hissed, 'Cad!' I was puzzled. I said to myself, 'No, I am not a cad; I may be something equally ignominious, but the word is wrong. The cad is a British type.' The hostility of the man was unexplained, and by degrees I noticed that there was a certain *régime* as to gait and eye-work in all the well-dressed paraders. They kept their eyes focussed on a point forty feet ahead of them. Now Emerson had said in one of his books on England that 'The Englishman's eyes are fixed to his backbone.' But the eyes of the Englishman are no more fixed to his backbone than the eyes of the negro are fixed to his backbone. The Britisher's fixture is part of his costume and panoply — of his correct hat, tie, and umbrella. It is part of a self-protective pose. I have seen Americans assume the same sort of rôle on Fifth Avenue — perhaps not quite so convincingly. Such tricks are part of the *lingua Franca* of a period and are as easily picked up by a visitor as one picks up foreign idioms and intonations. I have seen Henry James employ half a dozen of them at a sitting. An American friend of mine once gave me a lecture quite seriously as to how to call a hansom. He gave me the correct words and intonation quite seriously.

But what was it that I felt the stroke of as I passed Apsley House? It was merely the too articulate expression of a sentiment that should have been conveyed more quietly — the idea being 'You be damned!' The Duke of Wellington had sanctified this gesture with his nod, which one of his contemporaries described as 'insufferable.' In the later Victorian age it was still in vogue in England.

As in England, so on the Continent; the lively young American, well equipped to get the best out of places and persons, to give and take of pleasure and profit wherever he went, roamed irresponsibly over Europe for several months. 'I seem,' he writes, 'to recall only the joy with which Amory Gardner and I gambolled up the Rhine like puppies at play.' They got to Homburg in the season and found his Aunt Anna Jay von Schweinitz and her many children established in a fashionable hotel while her husband was at his post in St. Petersburg as German Ambassador. At Dresden he fell in with a young Englishman, Henry C. Cust, later editor of the *Pall Mall Gazette*. His memory has recently been revived by a passage in H. G. Wells's 'Experiment in Autobiography' that is congruous with Chapman's early impressions of him.

> Cust [wrote Chapman in his 'Retrospections'] was first and last a great education to me. He invaded my crepuscular mind like a piece of fireworks. I never saw him for long at a time thereafter, but there was a strong bond between us — the bond of youth....
>
> Cust belonged to the generation that was later to become the Gay Nineties. These talented people had a quality of their own that was quite different from that of the elder Victorians. The Victorians were serious, weighty characters, who tilled their several fields of thought in comparative solitudes. The *mot d'ordre* in their day was *work*. The spirits of the nineties to be were gregarious. Their true gift lay in the discovery of how to enjoy life, and in this field they succeeded *à merveille*. The secret lay in pretending to be serious. Self-dedication to some ideal was distinctly in the air, but the choice of a sphere was left free to all. One great lady would make very gifted drawings; another would visit the slums; a third affect ceramics; a fourth revive the needlework of Elizabethan draperies. The spirit of the game was in the air. Of course, the intermingling of the professional artists added glamor to the atmosphere. Social life became thrilling.
>
> This view of social life, which came not as a view but as an inspiration, converted good society into a masked ball where everyone had a cue. With one it would be philosophy. Arthur Balfour I first heard of as a very serious thinker who had for the time being retired to Florence in order to set the higher metaphysical thought of the world in order. He was one of three brothers, all reputed to be mystics. Arthur opened the ball with a book called 'A Defence of Philosophic Doubt' — not *actual* doubt, you understand, which would be unseemly and subversive, but *philosophic* doubt. Now Balfour was the most astute, practical parliamentarian of the century, but to the social world he was an heroic figure.
>
> To show the depth to which this spirit of play had penetrated the talent of the times, one has but to observe that real artists like Whistler and Sargent and Henry James — instead of plodding away before their easels and at their desks, — as Watts and Trollope had done, — were constantly talking about their art. Indeed, the spirit of play entered their studios. Whistler wishes to paint a gray riding cloak that shall com-

pete with Velasquez. He sues Ruskin for libel, raises the wind by a newspaper-paragraph tea-chat about himself and his works and everybody joins in the paper-chase. Henry James is bent on writing a page that shall be as good as Flaubert or Stendhal; Sargent on painting a head *à la* Titian....

This passage, of course, bears all the marks of retrospect. From other passages the contemporaneous could be presented, in the form of an itinerary winding in and out of Germany, Austria, Italy, and Russia, where he visited his von Schweinitz relatives. The flavor of the 'Retrospections,' touching this early experience of Europe, has already been tasted. With all that remains beyond, it must suffice here to look at a few characteristic pages, prefaced by a letter.

To Owen Wister

(Date missing.)

... One ought to be as open to conviction at forty-four on any subject as one is at twenty-three. It is not the condition but the man that changes. He freezes up. He reaches his growth. He loses the power of readjusting his thoughts. Now this should be struggled against. We should live all the time like children to whom a fairy-tale is being read. Everything should be real and new and interesting — in a sense possible. If we do this perhaps the new poets will not die of starvation. Such a striving is the command and at the same time an antidote to the tendency of our age.

The conceptions of our time are greater than those of Elizabeth or the Medicis — since they include them. We have not their ability because our enlightenment comes from the top and is theoretical, theirs came from within — the development of a need — and was practical. They did what we but dream of. But their *Weltanschauung* — that of regarding everything as a great perhaps — which laid them open to so many new ideas and let them into so much no one had got into before in art and literature and history, and made them have so good a time — is what ours ought to be.

['Retrospections']

I went to Venice by night train, third class. I still remember the fatigue of it. I put up at the Hotel Danieli for a time, out of sentiment for the well-known people who had lived there — and later moved to a hired room. I walked the galleries and read the guidebooks, and seldom took a gondola. It was cheaper on foot. I bought the old Variorum Dante of 1821 in many volumes and have it still — minus a few volumes which disappeared in the course of time. I knew no Italian, but read it with a pocket dictionary. I lugged about Burckhardt's Cicerone, a thick volume in German, for I was originally anxious to be thorough; but this ambition soon evaporated, and turned into a philosophy of *laissez-faire*. For what is all criticism of art more than a Baedeker which leaves one standing before the picture or the building — criticism is a sort of hound who points the covey. I accept the expert's guidance but not his reasoning; for there is a mystery in the fine arts which analysis cannot fathom. No words can convey the taste of a strawberry, and all talk about art is merely a parlor game.

Many years later I was again in Venice, this time with four small boys whom we brought in order to educate their eyes a bit, and let them feel the inspirations of the Old World. We were floating one day in a gondola amid the palaces and domes, spires and vistas of the enchanting place, when we observed that the lads were showing interest. Their eyes were on the gleam of the waters and seemed to be drinking in the wonderful tints of the shadows and of the painted poles that pierced the depths. They chatted together as if in rivalry. At last my wife said to the eldest, aged about twelve, 'What is it, Victor?' 'That's the eighth dead cat that we have seen this morning.'

The mild climate and the enduring beauties of nature in Italy nourish the human race and are the origin of all the types that Italian art has recorded — types in which a kind of savagery is revealed, as in Titian's pictures. The two handsomest women I ever have seen were in Tuscany. One was opening the shutters of an upper window as my train passed slowly through the suburbs of a small town. She was a Juno. The other was the wife of a substantial farmer, was about twenty years old, and was standing in the market-place at Florence beside her husband, who was as magnificent as herself — both of them large, dominant, stupendous creatures — savage as the hounds of Thessaly. They were in holiday attire, but not gaudy — all solid, handsome, burnished. At Naples I caught a glimpse of a scene that suggested everything in the Mediterranean and reached as far back as Medea and Hecate. I was walking back to the ship after the opera across a large, desolate square near the water — after midnight. A great causeway ran along the flank of this desert and in the side of the causeway under a bridge I saw a sort of cavern. Twenty feet within the opening a fire of driftwood was burning in the middle of the cave, and above the fire a woman's figure was bending to warm herself. She was covered by a very large cloak. As she saw me pass the cave, she raised herself and threw off the cloak backwards to the ground — inviting me to the cave. She was absolutely naked, a hag about fifty years old. I certainly ought to have given her some money, but I was so overcome with the tragedy of it and the visual power of the scene that I moved away speechlessly. A French painter would have put me into the scene with my opera-hat and my impeccable black cape....

The Russian experience was disillusioning in the extreme, all external, while behind and beneath the externals, lay imaginable horrors. Midwinter, the Neva frozen and at night a soldier standing on guard beneath each bridge to guard against dynamite. Droschkies, generals, moujiks, adjutants, troikas, on the Nevsky Prospekt; enormous distances, palaces, police. Fairyland? No! Tolstoi had shattered that thought. Everyone knew what those costumed aristocrats were like. It could only have been done by a great genius who was also a noble, a plunger, a young man about town, a poet and dreamer — a misformed, amorphous saint and mystic. Turgenieff had helped — the man all sensibility and no will, the Russian poisoned by European cultivation, the lost man. Both of these men were nobles and incontrovertibly insiders. It was Tolstoi and Turgenieff rather than the nihilists who wiped out the Russian Empire. They prepared Europe for its fall; destroyed in advance all sympathy, sentiment or excuse that could be offered for its continued existence.

The Schweinitzes lived in a palace with nothing mysterious or uncanny about it — except one thing. If one came in late at night or wandered through the rooms, one met very docile and harmless dusk-animals, who prowled softly and disappeared behind the furniture. These were dusters, cleaners, and scrubbers. No one knew where they slept.

My aunt and uncle were in their glory; children handsome, affectionate, charming; Schweinitz the complete *grand seigneur* —

only not quite, because he was really the personal first servant of the old German Emperor, wore the chain of office, besides all the rest of his decorations; and he was all conscience. I heard him say to my aunt as the guests were departing after a grand dinner: '*Ich bitte zu bemerken dass ich noch nicht geraucht habe.*' He must have been the most agreeable gentleman in the German Empire.

I saw one of the annual state pageants at Petersburg, the 'Blessing of the Neva.' It took place on the ice — which was carpeted in red and crowned with a pavilion. The Grand Dukes were there, half a dozen of them, like Paladins in a group, magnificent in their pride and splendor. I had a good view of the show from a gallery, a sort of enclosure for secretaries and lesser foreign functionaries. I attended a ball at the Winter Palace, an ugly building about half a mile long. On the steps stood servants and gorgeous ministers holding glittering staves, tufted at the top with ostrich plumes, while imperial ambassadors and Russian princesses trailed up the great staircase, and diplomats greeted, soothed and heartened one another with their consoling duplicities. At supper, which was at an immensely long table raised at one side of an immensely long gallery, the Emperor and Empress were sitting under a canopy halfway down the table, the guests bowing low before the sovereign as they passed to their seats. I forget the rest, except that I danced with an American girl and was politely called to order by an aide to the Master of Ceremonies for reversing. This was a common occurrence and was, as it were, part of the etiquette of the occasion.[1]

I had naturally talked much about my friend Cust to my aunt and uncle. They asked me, with the conservatism common to conventional upper-class persons, 'What did I really know about Cust?' They seemed to think Plauen [where Chapman and Cust had met] hardly a town where we would find desirable acquaintances, and that a cramming house, to which

[1] Mrs. Philip Sawyer, of New York, a daughter of Moncure D. Conway, provides an anecdote of Chapman in St. Petersburg. The Conways were visiting the American Minister, Alphonso Taft. The young people of the diplomatic set used to gather each morning at a country club for tobogganing. Chapman, at the top of the chute, saw a pair of toboggans starting the descent side by side, but held together so loosely that a dangerous spill might well occur. Instantly seizing the two toboggans and holding them together, Chapman let himself be dragged on his stomach from the top to the bottom of the slide. The praise and thanks showered upon him for what he had done meant far less to him than the loss of all the buttons from his outer clothing.

British civil servants resorted for the sake of picking up the German tongue, was hardly a safe place in which to swear eternal friendships. I had no answer for such enquiries, but they remained in my mind. Some point was given to them by the news from Cust that he was coming to Russia very soon. He had a friend, Pashkoff, who himself remained in England, but was to lend Cust his apartment in Petersburg. One day in reading a Berlin newspaper, I came across a social item to the effect that one of the English royal family was staying with the Crown Princess in Berlin and that the group had been giving private theatricals. Among those mentioned as participating was Mr. Henry C. Cust. I showed the paper to my uncle saying, 'My friend Cust seems to be getting to know the right kind of people.' After this the air cleared considerably. A haunting doubt was banished from the mind of my hosts.

Cust soon turned up and directed all his batteries upon all the Schweinitzes. He and I had a silent competition as to who should win out in capturing the old gentleman. My aunt, who was a conservative to the backbone, was less sensitive to Cust's batteries than her husband. She never quite capitulated. Such are women. Yet she one day — perhaps in response to our curiosity — revealed what we both most wanted to know. Of course, I won. The General had said to her about Cust, '*Aller liebster junge Mensch!*' — and of me, '*Wie der junge Mann versteht Goethe!*'

Now Schweinitz was a conventional Teuton and accepted or thought he accepted Goethe as his guide to life. He had an edition of Goethe in many volumes in which he browsed, and marked the margins — *à la* Bismarck — with a large blue pencil — of those passages which he thought particularly wise. Considering that Goethe's conduct of his own life was in several worldly respects quite puerile, as e.g. in his early content to be the Grand Vizier of a toy dukedom, in his philandering and love affairs and in his marriage; in his nursing of his own personality and talents as if he were his own puppet; and finally in his choice of Eckermann as a man to whom he might confide the last whisperings of his vanity; considering all Goethe's failures in self-knowledge and practical wisdom, I then thought and still think it hard to explain how a clever man like Schweinitz could be so hoodwinked by the *mot d'ordre* of his own formal education. I must, however, have expressed these ideas differently in talking to my uncle....

46

My fifteen months of Europe affected me much as such wanderings affect other young Americans. I felt that Europe was the place for me. I had had a mere taste of it; I needed more. Europe was my natural habitat. By accident I had been born in a desert, a suburb, a penal colony. I felt that I was just beginning to get my eyes open and my feathers dried out after life in the shell. What I needed was more Europe — another dip in the elixir. If I had had any resources of my own, I should have applied them to more foreign residence, with a sense that I was fulfilling a Sacred Duty. But the conditions were inexorable.

The time had indeed come for the young man, so charged with promise but with his way in the world still to make, to set about it. This, it seemed, was to be achieved through the profession of the law. In the decade since his collapse as a schoolboy he had profited by many enlarging and stabilizing experiences — study, friends, music, travel, all the 'advantages' that provide the springboard from which a young man with talents such as his might plunge into a brilliant career. But a period of intense turmoil, charged with successive exaltations, sufferings, despairs, and reassertions of power, lay before him.

III

Fuel and Flame
1885–1897

WITHIN the dates above fall the years of Chapman's life between the ages of twenty-three and thirty-five. They held for him — as a lifetime seldom holds for others — a measure of personal drama inevitable in its tragic essence as that of the Greeks he came to love so well. The heights of happiness, the depths of desperation and sorrow, flights on the wings of the morning, periods in which he might well have cried with the Psalmist, 'The pains of hell gat hold upon me' — these extremes, with all the gradations between them, crowded the dozen years on which he entered when his professional studies began.

The external circumstances of his life could hardly have been more propitious. The time was one of relatively simple living, and it made no particular difference that most of his friends had deeper purses than his own. The comeliness and charm of his ruddy, vivacious presence, the daring brilliancy of his mind and talk insured him a welcome wherever he chose to challenge it. The transition from Europe was hard, but the 'Retrospections' show both how it was made and into what pleasant places it led:

> On landing in New York the ugliness of everything appalled me. I shall never forget my first look at Cambridgeport as I crossed the bridge from Boston — the signboards, the humble signboards, the packing-cases, wooden shanties on the streets; grocery stores; the glare and litter of everything. And this

unconscious sensitiveness of the eyes has remained with me as part of my experience in Europe. Many years later when first off the ship I walked into the Century Club in New York, there were some coins lying on a plate on the clerk's desk — quarters, dimes, and half-dollars. They looked monstrous, like undersea objects. I thought that they must be magnified, and felt the plate to see if there was water in it. On going home to a plain house which I had lived in for twenty years, the wainscoting, cornices and doors, looked misplaced, disproportioned, meaningless, horrible. But the horrors of the external world were as nothing compared to the gloomy forebodings awakened by prospective Law, the grim necessity of tackling its concepts, its wheels and cranks, presumptions, precedents, maxims — the interlocking images of a world that is neither science nor poetry, nor social life nor religion, though it impinges upon them all, and is pieced out of them all. This world is first presented to the ingenuous youth as part of the struggle for existence.

I think that the severity of my work in the Law School, to which I partly attribute my breakdown later on, would have been distinctly relieved if I had spent a preliminary year as a clerk in a busy office and had become familiar with the practical aspects and daylight realities of the law. When I did later on go into an office, I was moderately competent at making briefs, but I could do nothing else. My head was so filled with the higher metaphysics of legal theory and my ignorance of practice so complete, that when I saw a real mortgage or a real bond, I thought the thing would explode. The responsibility of drawing or filling a note of appearance affected my nerves. Thus in both fields, the theoretical and the applied, law was to me a phantasmagoria.

In spite of my gloomy forebodings as I returned to Cambridge, which appeared after Europe like an entrance to the underworld, with the Law, as Cerberus, on guard at the gate, I very soon, almost immediately, emerged into a life and landscape that distinctly resembled the Elysian Fields. The great thing about Elysium, after all, is that they let you alone there. If you really wish to improve yourself, you may consult Aristotle or take up the clavichord with Musaeus. You are allowed to be serious and hard-working, if that is your whim, and in the Harvard Law School it was every boy's whim.

A group of students, including Owen Wister, James J. Storrow,

49

Robert Simes, William Ropes Trask, Eliot Norton, and one or two others, hired a small wooden house on that sequestered village street that was known as Appian Way. I was not one of the residents, for I roomed elsewhere and took my meals with this fraternity. Hard work was the order of the day, and the law talk never ceased day or night.

The relation between professors and students was ideal. Occasionally some eminent elder man from Boston, Judge Holmes or John Ropes, would come out and take dinner with us, or ask some of us to his home; and our wider social relations and intimacies in Boston were kept alive by our perfect freedom of locomotion. We were a law unto ourselves and this held us in the harness. Regular exercise, tennis and long walks, lazy and paradoxical conversations, mingled with infinite humorous nonsense on serious legal speculations. In fact, the spirit of the Law School was what, with many allowances, the spirit of any university ought to be. Its chief and singular merit — the relation between the professors and the scholars — could easily be encouraged in any university. The teaching was oral. The old textbook method was abandoned and the Socratic method adopted. This was done deliberately at the time that Mr. Langdell was put at the head of the institution. The change not only spread rapidly to every Law School in America, but through the influence of his pupils in the next generation changed the very conception of law in the minds of our judges and practitioners. Thus Langdell, who had a genius of his own for infecting other minds with his methods of teaching, probably did more towards raising the standard of legal argument through the land than he could have done in any other capacity.

A law school implies, not only a library and classrooms; it implies a cockpit for debates and legal wrestling matches. In our day the students formed themselves into groups — small clubs that held moot courts, and this was one of the most serious and important features of the life. There was no element of private theatricals about these contests. They were gladiatorial struggles, prepared for by weeks of study and talked of for days afterward. My own share in these strenuous games was slight and by no means brilliant. I took part in only one moot court, and in my speech I broke down, or rather groped in a vacuum till the assembled Solons could not tell what I was talking [about,] till and at last I resumed my seat in a mist, a no-man's-land of legal verbiage. Owen Wister told me afterwards that it had been awful; no one else had ever made any approach to it as an exhibition of complete failure.

To judge by one or two expressions in my letters to my mother at this period — for she kept very few of them — I began toward the close of the first year to have trouble with my eyes. I attributed this to an experience in England. Henry James had given me a letter to Robert Louis Stevenson, who, with his wife, was then living at Bournemouth. I went down there for a week or so. I lived in a room in a neighboring cottage where I had only one candle — the kind that gives next to no light. I sat up all night for two or three nights and wrote a story — very tragic, about a man who murdered his wife out of quite mistaken jealousy. Will you believe it? I read this story aloud to Stevenson and his wife, and was so excited about it that they almost seemed to think there was something in it. Stevenson at that time was the whimsical, picturesque, enchanting invalid that he is in Sargent's sketch of him, and his wife was the blazing gypsy from New Mexico who contrasted with him like a big, tropical plant — and both were friendly and most dear. I found the story years afterward and destroyed it. It was feeble and extravagant trash. This was before the days of Stevenson's fame, but he afterward came to America and filled the whole sky with his success. It was a Stevenson shock. Why did I not look him up and thank him for his early kindness to me? Was this shyness or ingratitude? I don't know. I merely record the facts as they come back to me in connection with my eyes and the Law School.

I became hipped about my eyes, consulted an oculist in New York who pooh-pooh'd the matter and told me not to mind it, that it would pass of itself. The truth was that I was oppressed with the responsibilities of life, the dreaded hurdles, the fated race-course, imaginative pressures, perhaps the inheritances of a Puritan's conscience, or the drive of a submerged ambition. I hired poor students to read aloud to me for hours a day, and I became a kind of solitary. At the end of the first year of the Law School, I passed the examinations without difficulty and decided to work on a farm as a cure for my eye trouble. As a matter of fact, it did so; but it was one of the unpleasantest experiences of my life, and much shorter than I had planned. As I had never taken any interest in sport, athletics, or muscular development, couldn't throw a ball, drive a nail, lift a spade or lead a horse to water, I was not well fitted to make myself useful on a farm; yet I went across the border into Canada and did chores, digged holes for posts, picked cherries on a ladder. Such things to a novice are perilous and exhaustive work; for one's head swims, the landscape reels. I did odd jobs, and so badly that one burly farmer at first refused to pay me what he had promised. In this case I ran a real danger, for on his refusal I spoke to him with such heat that a fellow-laborer said to me afterward, 'I thought you were going to strike him.' Well, I *was*, but inasmuch as I knew nothing of 'le boxe,' it would have meant a week in a hospital for me. I quote a few lines from letters to my mother.

(Undated.) 'The worst of this day-laboring is one's sense of infringement of personal liberty — like a galley slave. My supper consists of a big bowl of boiling milk. After I've drunk a little of it, I pour a cup of tea into it, and, my God, how good it is. I wonder anyone ever drinks anything else. Then I get into bed and seem to fall millions of miles into sleep that deepens and deepens till I am a stone falling through an unfathomable abyss, — and in the morning I am rested. The work has been of a more various character for the last two days, but it bores me. Also the people bore me. I make no scruple to say that I have hated every instant. . . .

'Soft chairs to sit on, enough to eat and nothing to do. As you look up from a shovel, these things seem to be the only things worth having in life, — to sit in the shade on a piazza without effort — this is what I chiefly desire and is what the laboring classes envy the leisure classes for.' [1]

My experiment in roughing it soon ended off in a retreat into the Adirondacks, a region of small camps hired by city people and completely dominated by the so-called 'guides' — a region of sophistication, overcrowding and extortion. I closed my rustication by spending a few days there.

The summer and autumn that followed were taken up with more country-house visits and festivities than I had ever known before. Cust had turned up from England in the rôle of an interesting invalid, and a scion of the aristocracy. To me he represented social activities; for, of course, I wanted to do something for him in return for what his friends and family

---

[1] A member of his family recalls his return from this farm adventure: 'I can see him as he walked back on to the lawn up at Bedford dressed in ragged clothes, and with a shaggy beard. We none of us recognized him. He returned having made one dollar. He said that the greatest happiness in life was to lie in a hammock smoking a pipe after having dug holes all day to put in poles to grow beans on, or picking peas in the sun — thoughtless, brainless joy.'

had done for me in England; and I wanted to show him off. I became very busy over him. His health was shattered, and I confess I did feel some misgivings as to what he might do in the way of heart-breaking among the nymphs. Cust and I visited various country houses on the North Shore, shared the wonderful hospitalities of Mr. and Mrs. Forbes at Naushon, and went to the White Mountains where a group of intellectuals of an older day were making merry.

Letters to his mother describe these pleasures and others in the White Mountains, Cambridge, and Boston. 'The Brimmers' figure in them, and when these older friends, with two nieces of whom more is soon to be heard, visited New York in November, Chapman begged his mother to act as his agent in entertaining them: 'I am very fond of them, and, as you know, have done nothing but accept things from them for two or three years.'

Up to this point the 'Retrospections' have dealt almost wholly with the masculine side of Chapman's relationships. There was of course the other. When he wrote of his father's 'granite chastity,' and of his preaching to a son what he had practised himself, it was not as one merely endorsing the virtue of a previous generation. His own instinctive convictions were the same. With a certain naïveté he wrote in a letter soon after leaving college, 'I was walking out to Cambridge one night, and met a factory girl, and we began talking — about things, Longfellow's poetry and that sort of thing — and when I said good night to her she threw her arms round my neck and begged me sometime to think of her, not leave her, and I promised to send her Longfellow's poems, and swore I would see her again, but I never did. She was quite young — perfectly honest.'

With girls of his own walk in life he was much given to discussing books, more disturbing than Longfellow, and things of the mind and spirit. The young women of his circle, though withholding any such demonstrations as that of the factory girl, would have been unlike their kind, in earlier or later years, if they had not been flattered by Chapman's ways with them. Owen Wister's word about him at this time in this relation should be recalled: 'As far as could be discerned, it was a girl's intelligence that brought, not him to her feet, but her to his. At this stage of his life he could be heard to say quite frequently that Mary So-and-So or Lucy So-and-So was an exceptionally intelligent girl. But soon it seemed as if Mary and Lucy fell into the background, and it was Emily whose intellect was far out of the common.... The unusual brains of several young ladies did not protect their perfectly female hearts. An older woman who had observed some of these episodes remarked that Jack Chapman was inconstant.' Is something of the philanderer in his composition to be deduced from such a diagnosis? If it is, it must be reconciled with a high capacity for long-continued devotion to single objects of affection.

There was one girl in Chapman's early Boston circle so cognate with him in the passionate intensity of her nature that they seemed made either to have been kept entirely apart or to face all weal and woe together. The second alternative was their destiny. Through their Boston fathers they had a common ancestor in an eighteenth-century member of the Greene family. Their essential kinship may be ascribed much more plausibly, however, to his French and her Italian blood. Her name was Minna Timmins. Her father, George Henry Timmins, who had Mrs. Martin Brimmer and Mrs. Augustus Perkins for sisters in Boston, had married in Italy the Italian widow of an Italian count, and had left her again a widow in Milan with five Timmins children. A beautifully revealing picture of the eldest daughter, Minna, her background and inheritance, is to be found in the 'Memoir' which Chapman wrote to introduce 'Victor Chapman's Letters from France' (1917). From this and the sketch, 'Mr. Brimmer,' in 'Memories and Milestones' (1915), Chapman's vision of her, with her uncle and aunt and sister, might be reconstructed. In all of Chapman's writing there are no more vividly glowing pages than these.

54

Some attempt at such a reconstruction would be needed here but for the fact that a portion of Chapman's 'Retrospections' draws the picture afresh, and relates, as none other could, the loss of his hand to a tragic transmutation of friendship into love. He could bring to his 'Retrospections' even more than to the 'Memoir' and to 'Mr. Brimmer,' a calm and grateful remembrance of scenes and events which had once consumed him as in a fiery furnace.

Fuel and flame to each other were he and Minna Timmins. There was an outward and inward quality in this commanding half-Italian girl, powerful of body and spirit, which caused her older friend, Mrs. Henry Whitman, to bestow the name of 'Ombra' upon her. Keenly responsive to the mystical elements of religion, she was capable besides of all gaiety, and exulted in beauty in many forms. And there was in Chapman himself, though more gifted in humor, a ferocity of feeling — intensity is hardly a strong enough word — which rendered him in many respects her counterpart.

What could have nourished more surely the intimacy into which they fell than their reading of Dante together during Chapman's first summer vacation from the Law School? Each began, as he wrote to her at a later day, by wanting to help the other, and found 'that they could do it only with their lives. As we read that Dante, talking little, something was going on.'

In the autumn and early winter that followed this summer reading he saw more and more of her. The 'something' that was 'going on' — the beginning of their love for each other — went unrecognized. Then with a blinding stroke it was clear. In January Chapman, convinced that the happiness of Minna Timmins was in peril through another man, took it upon himself, quite without her knowledge, to give this man a savage thrashing. Then in a sudden revulsion from what he had done, and in a frenzy of expiation, he thrust his hand into a fire, and burned it so severely that it had to be amputated.

Such is the bare story. As Chapman himself related it, with something more of background and detail, it appears thus in his 'Retrospections':

> I now perceive that there is one truth to be learned from these old letters of mine [to his mother] which may be of philosophic value to posterity: — young people are not apt to reveal in their letters the important part of what is going on in them — especially when they are themselves unaware of it. I am quite shocked at the casual reference to the Brimmers as 'a family from whom I had been accepting hospitalities for two or three years.' This letter was absolutely misleading at the time it was written. I am amazed to find no earlier mention of the Brimmer household in my letters to my mother. There is a deep mystery at the bottom of the matter.
>
> Mr. Brimmer and his two nieces, Minna and Gemma, were the most vibrant people in Boston. They were like Europeans, he like some old continental noble — a feudal type. His physical frailty, his marked, serious features, his rare quietude were Castilian; but his laugh was spontaneous and his natural goodness inexhaustible. He was a leader in all matters of art, education, and every sort of civic interest — a self-effacing character whose ample fortune was always — and often secretly — at the service of the next forward movement in charity or reform. Mrs. Brimmer contrasted with her husband in a way that set them both off. She was very large, complacent, spoiled from youth upward, perfectly non-intellectual — a person on whom life had left no scars. Her maiden name had been Timmins, and Tom Appleton, the Boston wag, had said of her as a girl '*l'innocence de cette Timmins est immense.*' She was the daughter of an Englishman who became a merchant of some sort in Boston; and he must have been a good fellow, for my first wife told me that her grandfather Timmins used to visit the nursery in Milan and get down on all fours and pretend to be a bear till the numerous children screamed with rapturous horror.
>
> Mrs. Brimmer's taste was for the visible. She dressed visibly. Mrs. Bell, another Boston wit, said to a friend, 'I've just seen Marianne Brimmer going down the street looking like an escaped sofa.' [1]

---

[1] This saying, I am credibly informed, might more accurately have been ascribed to Mrs. Bell's sister, Mrs. Pratt.

56

It was the age when a dinner party meant a long table studded with silver monuments, candelabra and sheafs of roses; twenty guests, many sets of knives and forks; a colony of cut-glass wineglasses at each plate; innumerable courses and entrées followed by the final benediction of the majordomo as he decently proffered to each guest the sacred salver with six kinds of distracting, dizzy, romantic liqueurs. After that, at least at the Brimmers, came a short session in the crimson parlor where Story's marble statue of Medea was enthroned, and thereafter to the drawing-room for free circulation with guests dropping in.

The *finish* of it all outclassed anything that I had seen in New York. There was a colonial, ancestral touch about Boston that made New York seem shoddy. There were, for instance, always old servants about. And is there anything more truly dignified, poetic, and noble than an old servitor? A butler, a gardener, a housemaid of seventy recalls the Odyssey. He frames the picture and justifies the whole establishment. There were also certain old servitors who resembled solicitors and appeared at every large party in Boston — called in for the occasion — and whose glance of recognition meant more to me than the smile of the hostess. Whether it were the antique politeness of Mr. Brimmer or the conventionality of Mrs. Brimmer — who certainly did know how to do things — that made the charm of those functions at 47 Beacon Street — they certainly were impressive to the young.

Yet the chief attraction of the house was the presence of the two adoptive nieces whom the Brimmers had brought to America after the death of their father, Mrs. Brimmer's brother who had married in Italy. In their looks, tastes, and temperaments these young ladies were of the Mediterranean; but through their paternal inheritance and their residence in Boston and attendance at boarding-schools they had become domesticated into American life. By the time I knew them they had become — so far as such a thing is possible — actual daughters of Mr. and Mrs. Brimmer.

They were of contrasting natures and characters, and vaguely suggested the contrast between Rosalind and Celia in 'As You Like It.' The elder was tall, dark, athletic with a freedom of limb and motion that is not found north of the Alps — a spiritual vigor that seemed allied to Michael Angelo's Sibyls. The younger was of smaller stature, very gentle, feminine, affectionate. Both were pristine natures, approachable, fond of society, women's women with a large circle of friends, cousins and else. Each of them dressed according to her own taste and nature, the elder dramatically, the younger picturesquely; and I have always thought it a mark of superior wisdom in Mrs. Brimmer that she allowed them to dress as they pleased.

Mr. Brimmer's public interests brought the intellectuals of the day to the house and put his nieces in touch with current events. The girls had travelled in Europe and in the Near East with their aunt and uncle, who was president of the Museum of Fine Arts and they were interested in every kind of art and decoration. They collected needlework, bric-à-brac, bindings, fragments of manuscript; but always as personal souvenirs and private memoranda. The elder had a studio, painted a little and had a passion for manual work of any sort and for open-air exercise. She would stand for hours on a ladder hanging draperies, would repair a carpet, frame a picture, or walk for five miles in South Boston to visit an impoverished violinist of whom some friend had spoken to her.

I had come to know the Brimmer household very gradually. The merrymakings on the Beverly shore and in the White Mountains during the autumn of 1886 had advanced my intimacy with the whole family at 47 [Beacon Street], as far as my inner remoteness from everyone would permit. For I can see in retrospect that the solitude of my New York boyhood had never been really outgrown. I was always moving about in worlds unrealized and trying to shake hands with the present. As the autumn approached, Cust disappeared and Law School began once more. The Boston sociabilities, however, continued. There were boating excursions and garden parties, with now and then a trip to see some famous hill or headland. I saw the Brimmers often and easily.

I had never abandoned my reading of Dante and it somehow came about that I read Dante with Minna. There was a large airy room at the top of the old Athenæum Library in Boston whose windows looked out on the churchyard. It was a bare and quiet place: no one ever came there. And during the winter we read Dante there together, and in the course of this she told me of her early life in Milan. There were five children, three of them boys, and there were tempestuous quarrels between the parents. I saw that it was from her mother that

58

she had inherited her leonine temperament. The mother had been a fury. I could see this, though she did not say it.... The Dante readings moved gradually like a cloud between me and the law, between me and the rest of life. It was done with few words. I had come to see that she was in love with someone. It never occurred to me that she might be in love with me. An onlooker might have said, 'You loved her for the tragedies of her childhood and she loved you that you did pity them.'

The case was simple, but the tension was blind and terrible. I was completely unaware that I was in love.

The amenities of life went on as usual — calls, visits, a dinner here, a dance there — all of them commonplace. Yet my mind must have worked in a most unusual way and very rapidly, for I imagined the cause of her suffering and picked out an acquaintance of hers, a friend in whom she had little interest — how much I didn't know, for I knew nothing about him and she had never mentioned him. I do not remember having any intention to pursue or injure this man.

Now there happened to be the most innocent kind of party that you can imagine at a country house. A few pleasant people were there of whom I remember only one, who was a friend of my childhood that I had not seen for years and whose face comes back to me as I write. When the evening was half over, I invited the gentleman to whom I have referred to step on the lawn, and there I beat him with a stick — whence procured I don't know — about the head and shoulders. How I got away or what I did for the next day or two I cannot say.

The next thing I remember is returning late at night to my room. At that time I was rooming alone in a desolate side-street in Cambridge. It was a small, dark, horrid little room. I sat down. There was a hard-coal fire burning brightly. I took off my coat and waistcoat, wrapped a pair of suspenders tightly on my left forearm above the wrist, plunged the left hand deep in the blaze and held it down with my right hand for some minutes. When I took it out, the charred knuckles and finger bones were exposed. I said to myself, 'This will never do.' I took an old coat, wrapped it about my left hand and arm, slipped my right arm into an overcoat, held the coat about me and started for Boston in the horsecars. On arriving at the Massachusetts General Hospital I showed the trouble to a surgeon, was put under ether, and the next morning waked up without the hand and very calm in my spirits. Within a few days I was visited by the great alienist [*sic*], Dr. Reginald Heber Fitz, an extremely agreeable man. He asked me among other things whether I was insane. I said, 'That is for you to find out.' He reported me as sane. I took no interest in the scandal which my two atrocious acts must have occasioned. To this day I know nothing of what was thought or said on the matter. I know only of the extreme kindness of my friends in Boston and am grateful to my mother for having kept a few of my scanty notes from the hospital in which some of those friends are mentioned. My mother herself must have been the worst sufferer; yet there was somehow a hardy intellectual basis of understanding between us. I did not worry about her. As for Minna, I knew that she loved me and that all was well. A few intimates came to see me at the hospital. My arm healed up rapidly. My inner composure, so far as I can remember, was complete. When I left the hospital, Judge and Mrs. Holmes took me in till I was strong enough to be moved.

I do remember one shock. I received a note from Mr. Brimmer in a large envelope of very handsome note-paper, addressed in his beautiful handwriting. It began, 'Sir: — ' and summoned me to an interview. The note seemed to imply a doubt as to my 'intentions.' Yet I knew that Mr. Brimmer was a most sensible and humane person, and that he must have talked to his niece, and I felt that he would be governed by good feeling and common sense. The decision at my meeting with him was for an engagement with separation for at least a year.[1] I had one or two quiet meetings with Minna and soon left for New York.

The 'Retrospections' proceed with a few more letters from the hospital and the house of Judge Holmes to his mother, but do not include the telegram he sent to her on the day after his self-infliction of torture. It spared her the cold truth of the matter — a unique distortion of fact on his part — and this, no doubt, gave rise to the varying reports of the occurrence which gained credence:

January 27th, 1887, BOSTON, MASS.

To Mrs. Chapman, 191 Second Avenue, New York.

Please don't be scared by telegram from hospital. I had my left hand run over yesterday and taken off. I am perfectly well

[1] A period of five years was proposed later.

and happy. Don't mind it a bit — it shall not make the least difference in my life. If you can help it don't come on. I shall be here at the Massachusetts Hospital week or so with all science and comfort.

J. CHAPMAN

It needs no clairvoyance to see from what intensity of inward drama sprang the amazing deed here recorded. 'It shall not make the least difference in my life,' said Chapman, and he held himself unfalteringly from any outward dramatizing of it, and was soon to go his way as if it had not happened. Yet there was more than a year when his condition was hardly other than pathological. It is extraordinary that out of the tossings and surgings of an inward sea of violence he should have come even to such serenity as he attained. Nothing but a fundamental steadfastness of spirit could have saved him.

'If thy hand offend thee, cut it off.' Was none but Cranmer to burn away an offending hand? Joined with a Biblical austerity in Chapman's nature there must have been the exaltation of an Oriental capable of an incredible indifference to suffering. He might seek to comfort his mother by calling himself 'perfectly well and happy'; he might declare a fortnight later, 'I feel the loss of time a good deal, but that is after all a trifle'; yet his weeks in the hospital were weeks of the deepest agony of body and spirit. Too proud to summon Minna Timmins to his side, he did not know that when she came one day, unannounced, to the hospital, she was denied admission to his room.

> 'And to be wroth with one we love
> Doth work like madness in the brain.'

His brother Henry came to him and said, 'You know I don't understand you. I don't know what's the matter with you, but I love you.' Minna's gentler younger sister wrote to him as 'Yours in loving friendship, even if it is only poor little Gemma.' From Minna herself came a stream of written

61

messages of passionate devotion. If there had been a doubt
in either of their minds before the loss of his hand that each
belonged to the other, every shadow of it was dispelled.
From that time forth, they were irretrievably bound together.

So far, and a little farther, must the intimacies of a unique
situation be touched upon if Chapman is to appear in these
pages in anything like his entirety. Mr. and Mrs. Brimmer
could hardly have been expected to sympathize with a relationship in which the hottest blood of headlong youth was so
crucially involved. If the head of the house remarked, as
report has it, 'I hope we have seen the last of that unfortunate young man,' one cannot be greatly surprised. Willing to
postpone or to frustrate a possible marriage, the Brimmers
sent their niece, soon after Chapman's release from the
hospital, to visit a brother in Colorado; then took her to
England, the Continent, and Egypt. This period of separation was one of intense suffering for them both. How could
it have been otherwise when the struggle lay between her
lifelong sense of pious duty towards her uncle and aunt on
the one side and his dire need for her on the other?

When she went to Colorado, he returned to New York to
pursue, as best he might, his interrupted law studies. His
letters at the time flamed with the ardors and rages of a
tortured spirit. Then and thereafter there were wild and
whirling words from each to each. In June he went abroad
himself, in search of restoration to the health and calm of
which a diary he kept on the outward voyage showed him so
desperately in need. His friend Amory Gardner and others
from the newly established Groton School included him in
their holiday party. Mrs. Endicott Peabody recalls their
rowing down the Thames, 'taking turns at the oars, where
Jack, with his one arm, managed extraordinarily well,
bouncing the oar into its rowlock without help from anybody. It was just after the accident; he added enormously
to our fun and frolic.' This was not the only bright spot in
the summer, for Mrs. Peabody's remembrances continue:

When we crossed to the Continent, I was very anxious that we should all stop at a monastery well spoken of in a book I was reading. Jack parleyed with the Brother who came to the door, but when this one discovered that we were a party of seven men and one female, even Jack's emphatic argument, bringing forward that two were priests, did not gain us admittance. We then went on to Saint-Malo, where, as we were walking on the old walls, Jack caught sight of a bell with rope attached. His one hand was always busy, and with it he rang the bell feeling that something would happen; it did, and as this might get us all into trouble he turned and ran the other way, meeting the fire chief who told him he had committed a serious offense. However, it passed off.

With Minna Timmins in the same hemisphere it was inevitable that he and she should meet, as they did. The outpouring of letters continued. 'I hate my family,' wrote Chapman in one of them. 'I hate just about everybody, and shall till I have gained myself more or less and got back my heart.' And again: 'I'm going gradually to become well and kind and not miss those fields of glory I looked on like Moses. I see it coming, but I dread it and hesitate.' When he returned to New York in September, it was with every determination to fortify his spirit and mind with hard work, which bore its fruit, after study in the law office of Jay and Candler, in his admission to the bar in December, 1888. Not that he loved the process. 'As I worked in the office,' he wrote, 'I writhed in pain — the entire length and breadth of my physical system.... I got up and clutched the desk and prayed.... I had my head bound with a cap of iron, and when I used to stop working the suspended agony came down like a cataract, and I went uptown trembling, crying.' It was indeed a period of torture.

In the 'Heritage of Years: Kaleidoscopic Memories' of Frances M. Wolcott (Mrs. Edward O. Wolcott, previously Mrs. Lyman Bass) there are glimpses of Minna Timmins through the period of complete separation from Chapman which followed his return to New York. Mrs. Bass was one of the party that visited Greece and the Nile with the Brimmers and their nieces. She had made the acquaintance of Minna at Colorado Springs. 'Tall, dark, with the face of a benign lion or sibyl, her every movement free and untrammelled — she was a true child of the South.' So the older described the younger woman, of whom she wrote further that at Nauplia: 'Minna Timmins, homesick and longing for a sight of the man she loved and later married, talked till morning, saying that if she could only return to America, she would postpone her marriage as long as her uncle and aunt desired. In the fashion of Italian women who make an offering of their hair to the shrine at which they worship or the lover from whom they are separated, she had cropped off her splendid hair on the return Nile journey.' In London Mrs. Bass gave a dinner for her fellow-travellers and an Englishman she wanted Minna Timmins to like. The ladies were expected to wear Oriental dresses picked up in their wanderings. 'Imagine my horror,' wrote the hostess, 'when the door opened and Minna entered, wearing a shabby blue silk frock which had served full time in Africa, Greece, and the coast of Asia Minor, her cropped hair straggling from an insufficient number of hairpins. She paid no heed to handsome Renshaw, turned her shoulder and almost ignored him. It was the form of her loyalty to the man she loved in the United States, which demanded that she should in no wise either adorn her person or make herself fascinatingly agreeable. The evening was not a success.'

Of course it was not always like this with her — at dinnertables with James Bryce, Henry James, and Augustine Birrell, or sketching and reading voraciously at other times. Among the ardencies of her life, art and letters had always to be reckoned with. Her studio in Boston, her intimacy with Mrs. Whitman, the interests of her uncle, for many years president of the Boston Museum of Fine Arts, afforded outlets for a dominant interest of her own. When Martin Brimmer came, in 1892, to publish 'Egypt: Three Essays on

MINNA TIMMINS (DRESSED AS A SIBYL FOR A COSTUME
BALL)

the History, Religion, and Art of Ancient Egypt,' he wrote in the Preface, 'These essays were written during a recent journey in Egypt, with the constant assistance and able co-operation of my niece and fellow-traveller, Mrs. John Jay Chapman. They are indeed not less her work than mine.'

The five years' 'moratorium' desired by her uncle and aunt having been reduced to two, the engagement of Chapman and Minna Timmins, which could have been no surprise to their friends, became a matter of accepted knowledge early in March, 1889 — and then she was borne away to Mexico for a further separation of some weeks. She had no sooner gone than Chapman began following her in a stream of letters in one of the first of which he wrote: 'Coming up standing on the front platform of a car — suddenly occurred to me — suppose you should die. In an instant I have lived through my life. The first crash — the black clothes — the deadness — the indifference to the rise in salary that would come so easy then — so useless — the protecting and being near Gemma — I had married her and was thirty-five and prosperous enough and very respectable and so different. Why, in that instant I was transformed.... I had lived through a suicidal time. When I looked up I had gone two blocks, and you were alive, My Minna.' When she had returned from Mexico and the wedding drew near, there were communications in another vein. He insisted, naturally enough, on attending to the purchase of the ring himself. 'There is a correctness about these things you cannot disregard when you have been married as often as I have,' he wrote, and, 'Send me one of your rings, and be thankful if I bring you a brass one. Are we to lose one dewdrop that glistens on the leaves of human life because we have tastes and money — and elegance? You will remember as to those Turkey carpets, I feel in myself that if you get too many of them and silver lamps and incense, I shall spend my evenings in railroad bar-rooms. Luxury gives me indigestion — like peach trees that must be manured occasionally with ashes.' Yet again: 'Sup-

pose we had none of it — damn all the beautiful things —
they'll get here all right. I wonder if you'll be dusting them
and wanting me to keep my feet off them. I wish we were
going to live in two rooms with horsehair furniture.' This
wish was not fulfilled: he wrote instead, 'I think I've got a
gash in the wind-swept Apennines for you' — which was
a house numbered 327 West Eighty-Second Street. They were
married July 2, 1889, at the Brimmers' summer place, Wood-
rock, Pride's Crossing, Massachusetts. In a nervous moment
before the ceremony, when the best man, Amory Gardner,
was quitting the room in which the bridegroom and two
surpliced clergymen stood waiting, there was a cry from
Chapman, 'Oh, Amory, do not leave me with these two
men!' For all that had gone before, Chapman was even as
the rest of mankind at this point.

When Chapman and his wife began their married life in
New York, he was already deeply committed to an interest
which was to engross him for more than another decade —
the interest of political reform. In the spring of 1888 he had
written to Minna Timmins: 'I think there are no more books
that need to be written in the world just now. The world
has got all the books it wants.... The time is for action and
political organization. Better cast a vote than write a book.
I am inclined to think that these people organizing charities
and setting germs of self-betterment to sprout on a large
or small scale are the important people.'

Though his zest for reading suffered no abatement, it was
not long after his applying himself to the law in New York
that political activity began to claim his energies, far more
than the distractions of letters. 'I have never been connected
with a cause,' he wrote in 1895, 'for which the time was ripe,
and never expect to be. Such activities as this ripen the
times and bring them to fruition.' In the eighties and nineties
of the nineteenth century there was, in fact, plenty of ripe-
ness for action in New York against the rule of both Tammany

and Republican bosses, and into this conflict Chapman threw himself with the zeal of a crusader.

A surviving colleague of Chapman's in all this work, Richard Welling, recalls its general tenor in a letter from which the following passage is taken:

> My classmate T.R. and I, among others, in 1882 started the City Reform Club one of whose major tenets was that no member of the club should hold public office. T.R. very soon had to resign in order to go to our State Legislature and when Chapman came to New York he immediately joined the club and laid down the principle that all temporizing was fatal and that if our compass pointed north it must always be *true north*.
>
> As a watcher at the polls Chapman was very soon with his one arm arresting and taking to the police station a law-breaker, and his spirit and activity were grand in this decade 1883–93. We were hammering the District Attorney for laxity in enforcing the election law. We were indicting excise commissioners who allowed saloons to be open near polling places. We were very much on the front page, though not actually very effective, and when Edmond Kelly retired from a great, lucrative practice in Paris (having lost his wife) and came to New York to stir up his lazy classmates and friends who were submitting to Tammany, he immediately joined the City Reform Club and induced us to expand into the City Club, clubhouse, prominent citizens, etc. The directorate was made up of solid citizens of the town linked with half a dozen or more young firebrands like me and Chapman. Kelly was my most intimate friend and always complained to me that Chapman had no element of compromise in his nature and while fully appreciating Jack's idealism, he used to marvel that a man with such brains could not see that the practical way to get things done often required compromise.
>
> Kelly invented the Good Government Club idea and, after one long winter vainly trying to get artisans and laborers to join his club, resigned in despair and became a socialist. Jack and I, each president of the large 'G. G.' Club, held on, and in 1895, after vain efforts to agree upon an anti-Tammany city-wide ticket with the Republicans, ran our own campaign to defeat. Just before this Carl Schurz had several long talks with me urging me to compromise and agree with the Republicans, but I could not see it, although I might feel otherwise today.

While I was out of town Jack summoned the Republican leaders to a dinner with the Good Government Club leaders, and Choate was the leading Republican while Bishop Potter stood with us. I have never ceased to regret my absence from that dinner, for I always heard that Jack was at his very best, made sport of those who would allow an ideal to be tarnished, while Choate in his best humorous vein ridiculed the 'G. G.' ticket. Bishop Potter retaliated on Choate back and forth, and those present were embarrassed at the tilting, and Bishop Potter had the last word.

To follow the details of this battle for reform in New York politics and of Chapman's part in it all would be to enter upon a long chapter of local history. Here we must be content to indicate a few of Chapman's most important points of contact with it, and to illustrate these, on later pages, with passages from his letters of this period. His confidence in his own motives and methods was supreme. His consecration to the truth as it appeared to the 'belated abolitionist' in him, his antagonism to compromise of any kind, his ambition to apply to public service the gifts and powers of which he honestly felt himself possessed, made him a firebrand of energy, a constant disturber of the peace for those who preferred to leave things alone and ascribed 'queerness' to young men whose mission it was to stir things up. In tangible accomplishment the results of his labors were not impressive. One cannot 'have it both ways.' The consistent idealist must make his choice between conflicting satisfactions — and Chapman made his. He could no other, nor could he have been expected to achieve satisfactory results in a pursuit calling, as politics does, and often legitimately, for the very qualities of compromise and co-operation which he so signally lacked.

For his methods of dealing with people — we have his own word for that. 'There is nothing one may not do. I almost throw some men out of the window — I get so violent, and I suddenly turn as heavy and icy as cold lemon-pie. Some men are to be taken by the throat, some jollied, some taken aside into an alcove — and, by Jove, all men are nothing but dough so far as I can see.' Sometimes he prided himself on his extreme self-control in addressing an audience. Again he could open the speech-making after a dinner at which he presided by declaring, 'No doubt many of us will say things that we regret. My own endeavor shall be not to say anything that I shall not regret. The opportunity is too good to be lost.' In November of 1895 he wrote to his mother: 'My line of politics is war — war — war — with an ideal of absolute good humor and self-control. The latter become doubly surprising and doubly powerful when they come from such a source, and they are in order and shall be forthcoming now in all dealings and reorganizations.' He believed in laughter, ridicule, and plain speech. 'Denunciation is well enough,' he wrote, 'but laughter is the true ratsbane for hypocrites.' On occasion he could act as vigorously as he spoke. A 'Tammany Ruffian,' looking like a ward politician, but 'with the instincts of a gentleman,' brought to remembrance an episode in a city campaign when Chapman was making a cart-tail speech on behalf of a Good Government ('Goo Goo') candidate. 'He never got over my once jumping from a cart,' wrote Chapman, 'and collaring a ruffian in the crowd who was interrupting me, then finishing the speech, and then having drinks with the ruffian — all of which was purely the result of excitement — but which had a romantic and courageous appearance, greatly enhanced by the fact of my having only one hand.'

In the *New York Times* for Sunday, February 10, 1895 — to cite a single source — there was a full-page article 'The Clubs in Politics,' telling in detail how the City Club sprang from the City Reform Club, and the Good Government Clubs, then twenty-five in number and active in all parts of New York, sprang in turn from the City Club. It was in constant co-operation with the leading spirits in these enterprises — chiefly young men of independent thought and unselfish aim — that Chapman labored in one good cause after another, writing, speaking, appearing before legislative committees in Albany, spending himself, often to the detriment of his law practice, in endeavors for the general good. Dishonest excise commissioners had to be attacked; a bill passed at Albany, and signed by the Governor, to provide a speedway along the west side of Central Park for the fast horses of Tammany politicians and their friends, had to be repealed — as it was; an Independent ticket of Good Government candidates for city offices in 1895 had to be supported — though without success; every occasion to waken and excite the public conscience, at the very time when Theodore Roosevelt and the earlier 'muck-rakers' were beginning their labors to this end, had to be seized. Of the many books Chapman was yet to publish, the second and third — 'Causes and Consequences' (1898) and 'Practical Agitation' (1900), which he described long afterwards as 'a tract' that 'never was read by one man' — sprang direct from these efforts at political reform. So did an effort in political journalism, to be described in the following chapter. It came to be called *The Political Nursery*.

The Chapman nursery of this period was domestic as well as political. His oldest son Victor Emmanuel was born April 17, 1890; the second, John Jay, November 23, 1893; the third, Conrad, December 24, 1896, a month and a day before his mother's death. Of Minna Timmins after she became Mrs. Chapman her husband wrote in the 'Memoir' introducing Victor's Letters:[1]

> ... When I think of her it is as a tall young matron full of life, entering a room with gaiety, bearing an armful of flowers for the pots and vases — crowned with inner dignity, ready to meet the thoughts of all, domestic and full of common sense. It was life that glowed in her and flowed out in her correspondence, her friendships, her pursuits, her passions. Her vitality seemed like extravagance because of its fullness, but in her it was nature and the modesty of nature. I think that the rarity of her came from a sort of double endowment. She had

[1] From 'Victor Chapman's Letters from France,' By permission of The Macmillan Company, publishers.

the man-minded seriousness of women in classic myths, the regular brown, heavy dark hair, free gait of the temperament that lives in heroic thought and finds the world full of chimeras, of religious mysteries, sacrifice, purgation. This part of her nature was her home and true refuge. Here dwelt the impersonal power that was never far from her. There have been few women like her; and most of them have existed only in the imagination of Aeschylus and the poets.

But Minna's seriousness was not the whole of her; and perhaps the part that is played on the stage is not the whole of Antigone and Medea. Within the priestess there lived a joyous nymph — a kind of Euphrosyne; and this is what makes her doings indescribable, because, when she ran riot, it was the riot of the grapevine. There was divinity in it.

She and her sister were exceedingly religious, with a touch of old world Catholicism which they had from an old padre whose name, if I could remember it, ought to be recorded here; for he lived in the memories of the sisters as one of those quiet Saints which the Roman Church still gives to the world. The piety of this padre passed over into the Protestantism which awaited both of the girls. They lived in a sanctuary of prayer, religious books, observances, meditations. . . .

She acted upon her impulses which were loving and headlong, tender or fierce, personal or impersonal as occasion gave rise to them, but always large, and done with a sweep. Some people she terrified by her force, others she melted by her warmth. She once met on a doorstep a very beautiful young girl of her acquaintance, and who was wearing a new hat trimmed by herself with imitation sweet peas. Minna was enraptured by the vision, but the colors were wrong. Some of the tints in the sweet peas were inharmonious. She took the hat from the head of the vision and picked off the offending colors one by one and threw them to the winds. Yet she did this in such a way as to endear herself and explain the action. . . .

I must admit — what the reader will have surmised — that her unconventionality and habit of spontaneous expression did not please all people. There are those who cannot enjoy nature in this geyser form. A friend reminds me of the following story, which is probably true. Minna and I were walking on Fifth Avenue, apparently engaged in moral discussion, when someone met us. It seems that she had taken the tortoise-shell pins out of her hair, and her braids fell to her waist. Her plea was that she had a headache. My sense of propriety was shocked, and I was vainly supplying her with sound reasons for a more seemly behavior. At length I gave way to her point of view, took off my coat and carried it on my arm. This policy of non-resistance worked like a charm, and she put up her hair. I resumed my coat. Now it is impossible to make *all* persons understand a being of this sort. But on the whole, Minna was well understood and rightly all but worshipped by many....

Her sister was in a lingering and fatal illness at the time Victor was born. I think it was for this reason that his christening was hurried. About nine days after his birth, his mother wrapped him in the pelt of a mountain cat and went to Boston for the christening. Phillips Brooks was his godfather. Soon after this, Minna became possessed with the idea that if Gemma could be fed with milk from her own breast, she would be saved. I remember only the tragic passions of this crisis, and I do not know whether the plan was carried out or not; but I seem to remember another journey to Boston with this end in view....

She was a great housewife and loved accounts, kept her bills and beat down the tradesmen like a peasant. I used to find my old friend and neighbor, Thomas Ward, the coal merchant, holding long sessions with her in the parlor. I used to say to him — 'Mr. Ward, how can you make money on this system?' — But I suppose he did it somehow; for I had an affectionate letter from him at the time of Victor's death. Minna was also a believer, or half-believer, in astrology; and I have somewhere in a trunk a large engrossed horoscope of Victor, predicting for him almost incredible glory and greatness.

It is needless to say that the sharing of life with such a force of nature was a perpetually exciting adventure, especially for one so responsive to emotional stimulus of every sort as Chapman. She threw herself intensely into the new life with which she found herself surrounded — social, artistic, literary. Fortunately for this book they were separated often enough for Chapman to put his letter-writing propensity to extensive use — when summer drove her from New York, when Chapman more than once visited Colorado to look after real estate they had bought for investment, and when, from motives of economy, he left her with two children for some months of 1894 and 1895 in Italy. Now 'on his own' as a lawyer, he was reaping the small financial rewards of the young attorney quite imperfectly subdued to his profession. Her income was hardly adequate to all the demands they would have liked to make upon it, and irksome small economies were constantly required of them both. His wife, like a true Italian — or New England — housekeeper, made no scruple of sallying forth with a market-basket, and getting her provisions on the best possible terms. They were surrounded at home, however, with objects of beauty, and their house soon became a focus of friendship and hospitality. It was also, in spite of Chapman's preoccupations with politics and law, the scene of constant activity on his part as a writer.

His confidence in his own powers through these ardent days was unbounded. In society, in public speaking, in writing for the stage, in agitation for reform, his reach and his grasp seemed to him co-equal. '*The people like to be agitated*,' he wrote to his wife. 'That's the great secret. The people like a cause, and all it takes is a sort of instinct as to how far they will go before they need a rest, and when to strike afresh.' While the 1895 campaign was in progress, he wrote to Martin Brimmer, 'I swear by all the Egyptian gods at once that I will reform anything and everything that comes in my way between now and November 5 so long as it doesn't hinder the campaign.'

Obviously this state of mind imposed many tensions. Nor was it only in politics and reform that he felt them. Music, drama, and letters each added its stimulus to an exciting existence. '"Lohengrin" magnificently given,' he could write in 1895, 'kept me in tears for two hours with worse effect this morning than if I had drunk quarts of champagne. The truth is I get excited too easily, and swear off now and record it.' Only a few weeks earlier he had written about a friend: 'He was exceedingly nice and looked well, but I found him spiritually light. I had to put paper-weights on

73

him to examine him. I was afraid a wind would come and
blow him away. I myself am, as you know, spiritually very
heavy — like a wet sponge or some densely hard mahogany
wood. You pick it up thinking it's a cork and it turns out
to be a piece of railroad track. That's the way I impress
myself anyway.' In another letter of 1895 he wrote: 'I've
known Shakespeare so much in infancy, that he's given me
a stage feeling about Life generally, and I'm only at home
on an imaginary stage — that's the fact. I'm always on a
stage, and the whole world is a stage.' And a little later,
about a farce he was writing: 'If I find this a good thing —
however unpublishable — my amusement in life will become
the writing of plays — which will be worse for me than
drink, opium, and gambling all at once.'

In reality the writing of plays, especially for children,
did become a frequent amusement for him. Furthermore,
his first separate publication was in dramatic form — an
anonymous pamphlet, 'The Two Philosophers: a Quaint Sad
Comedy' (Boston, 1892). It was a broadly humorous
treatment of a conflict between Professor Josiah Royce of
Harvard and the Reverend Doctor Francis Ellingwood Abbot,
who served as an Instructor in Philosophy at Harvard in
1887–88, while Royce was abroad. This quarrel disgusted
Chapman. 'It's enough,' he wrote to his wife, 'to discredit
the name of professor, and a great justification for the popular
prejudice against professional philosophers. There is really
no seat reserved in the universe for the professional thinker,
as I've often told Royce.'

When the 'Sad Comedy' appeared, William James told
Chapman that the best thing about the drama was that it
bore no relation to the facts. At this later day its interest
lies in its revelation of an unterrified spirit in dealing im-
pudently with dignified figures. In this respect it was prophetic of later effusions from Chapman. The fact that his
own college had to share in the obloquy and ridicule aimed
at individuals acted in no wise as a deterrent.

Desultory, and 'occasional' as Chapman's writing was through the first half of the nineties, it included even in 1890, the year after his marriage, an important contribution to the *Atlantic Monthly*, 'The Fourth Canto of the Inferno,' a translation in terza rima with preliminary comment. This translation, commended, I am told, by Charles Eliot Norton as 'the best ever written,' reappeared, much later, in Chapman's 'Dante.' Before 1897 he was, moreover, producing other non-political studies. His wife's friend, and his own, Mrs. Henry Whitman of Boston, believing deeply in his powers, was enlisting the interest of Walter H. Page, then editor of the *Atlantic*, in Chapman and his essays. In November, 1896, the magazine printed his article, 'The Young Shakespeare: a Study of Romeo.' This lively paper, recognizing the danger in any attempt to 'size up' Shakespeare, and declaring that 'we cannot help setting down as a coxcomb any man who has done it to his own satisfaction,' was included in Chapman's first acknowledged book, 'Emerson and Other Essays' (1898).[1] It was, however, the long essay from which the volume took its title that gave general notice of the arrival of a vital critic of letters in America.

When a 'new and revised edition' of this book appeared in 1909, it contained a preface containing bits of spiritual autobiography not to be spared at this point:

> As I look back over the past, the figure of Emerson looms up in my mind as the first modern man, and the City of Boston as the first living civilization which I knew.
>
> New York is not a civilization; it is a railway station. There are epochs of revolution and convulsion — times of the migration or expulsion of races, when too much happens in a moment to permit of anything being either understood or recorded. Such times have no history. They are mysteries and remain mysterious. Such an epoch has been passing over New York

---

[1] Only the year before he had written to his wife about a lady in New York: 'She actually told me once that I was like Romeo, which made me so annoyed (for he was a perfect fool) that I told what I thought of Romeo and read the play over again in order to demonstrate what an inane character Romeo was. It may be true I am like him, but I resent it throughout.' Here may well have been the origin of his Romeo paper.

The essay, now nearly forty years after, still stands not only as one of the most admirable examples of Chapman's original thinking and effective writing, but also as a penetrating, stimulating study of Emerson, secure in its place as a classic of interpretation. In its autobiographic aspect it is notable especially for the passage relating to Emerson's mysticism, for here is revealed the apprehension of spiritual values in which Chapman a few years later was to include the specific values of religion and to show forth that quality of the religious mystic in himself which was so vital a part of his nature.

There was one early reader of the essay to whom its success gave a triumphant pleasure. This was Chapman's wife, all cognizant and confident of his powers, and certain that their general recognition had been too long deferred. At the very time her third son, Conrad, was born, on the day before Christmas, 1896, the inspiriting response from the first installment of the essay doubled their occasion to rejoice together. But the recovery from her confinement did not proceed as her rare physical strength and her previous experience gave every reason to hope. For a month her condition, though causing no special alarm, remained unsatisfying. Then, on the evening of January 25, as Chapman was reading aloud to her, lying flat on her bed, she suddenly sat upright, and then fell back dead. Chapman rushed to a maid downstairs and sent her running for a physician near-by — all too late.

After what has been told of Minna Chapman in previous pages of this chapter, it would be superfluous to enlarge upon what her sudden, wholly unexpected, death meant to Chapman and to a multitude of friends. Out of the flood of letters of intense sympathy that poured in upon him, a single expression from Mrs. Josephine Shaw Lowell struck a note to which a vibration in Chapman's heart must have made a special response; 'Do not for a moment allow yourself to think that anything could have kept her here. The passage of that great soul from this life to a larger one was too tremendous a change to be caused by anything but her own spiritual readiness, and you must never let yourself think of it as in any sense an accident or anything dependent upon physical causes.'

In the desolated household Victor 'would stand silently by the window for hours' — as we learn from the 'Memoir' of many years later — 'with unshed tears in his eyes, watching the sky and the street. A loving Irish maidservant, still with us, said to him, "Victor what are you thinking about when you stand like that?" He replied, quietly, "I am thinking of someone, and you know who."' Chapman turned his own thoughts, for solace and hope, much to his children. 'The small baby, whose name is Conrad,' he could soon write in a letter, to Miss Elizabeth Chanler, in Europe, 'is very much the handsomest, strongest, largest, and most intelligent child I have ever seen.' In the same letter he wrote besides, as to one whose sympathetic, affectionate friendship had been a common possession of his wife and himself: 'The Emerson was such a success I am only happy that Minna saw the beginning of it, and a few letters, so that she knew it. There have been a great many since and they keep coming. Scribner writes and wants to publish a volume of anything I have.... If Minna could only have lived a year or a month longer these things would have made her so happy — but she was happy and had not even a moment's knowledge that she was to leave us. This is infinite blessing forever.' It is needless to speak in detail of his grief: the bottom had dropped out of his universe.

The twelve years to which this chapter is devoted came thus to a blasting end. The chapter itself remains to be completed by extracts from Chapman's letters written through this period. The spirit of gaiety which so largely pervades them bore out his resolution, on losing his hand, that 'it shall not make the least difference in my life.' Another spirit, revealed alike in the extremes of scorn for pettiness in persons and ·ideas and of exultation for the highest beauty in letters and art, was the spirit of every true aristophile. In that revelation the letters are Chapman himself.

Letters

To Minna Timmins

[*Fragments from letters of the summer and autumn of 1887.*]

Do you know, Minna, the one time in my life during which I lived was that twenty days of pain. I read 'Henry Esmond,' Dickens' 'Christmas Stories,' one morning — I never shall forget them — 'Mr. Barnes of New York.' Every word of it is glowing with life and love. There was fire in everything I touched — the fire of the activity of that part of me which was meant to be used, which got suppressed all my life till it broke. The depth of the intentions and remote unkempt wells of life and feeling. Browning I used to read anywhere.... Somehow I have known the meaning of things, if not for long, and all the while I thought I need rest. I need sleep. You see life is an experiment. I had not the least idea but what [if] I met you all this would run the other way and the pain turn into pleasure. I thought I had opened life forever — what matter if the entrance was through pain.

You know people who are made strongest smash once, and badly. I did not believe that any ill could come to me myself. I did not believe that I was like other people. I thought I could weather anything and wait any length of time and suffer anything and that it didn't make the least matter. I had no instinct of self-preservation, and I knew, I have always known, that I could do any one thing I wanted to, and I set out not to be hurt in my feelings and to be magnanimous, and it happened to come when there was no material left in my body.

I cannot see why there was not charity enough about Boston last January to forgive and deprecate. Yes, I think there was charity — only to shock people, feeling oneself a monster and man of blood and iron, and unapproachable, made the strain. Dear me, if another fellow should do such a thing now, I should go to him and say, 'My dear fellow, you've been a damned fool, but it don't make any difference, there's nothing diabolical or insane or inhuman' — and I would give him what he wanted then and there, tho' it cost me the respect of everyone in the world. This world is a terrible place if one makes it so, and people take you for what you think you are.

It was all foolish, beloved, and wicked — all I did, and yet in moving away from it — it was my youth after all. I do think there was something promethean in it, in the capacity to yield.

To Minna Timmins

48, WALL STREET, NEW YORK
April 22, 1889

... Of all the volumes of letters how few are interesting *per se*. They are simply so from a human point of view — and because of our eternal interest in the personal knowledge of conspicuous people, but they never strike me as remarkable in thought. I think Byron's letters the best I have ever read. I hate all the Carlyle correspondence. It is as stuffy as an ill-kept suburban cottage — all clothes-lines and dustpans and bed-bugs and not enough to eat — hairpins-in-the-soup sort of people.

Mentioning C. to my grandfather last night, rather surprised at his acrimony. That Carlyle was a thoroughly bad fellow. The explanation is that Carlyle was rude to him — the only time he saw him in '48.

My Grandmother Chapman's reason for disliking him was a better one. She and the rest of the antislavery agitators in 1835 and '40 — Carlyle being one of the prophets of the times and writing all sorts of pamphlets about free thinking and being and high things generally — went to him for support, but they got only sneers. He was a man of words, whose profession was snarling. They ought to have known better.

To Helen Dunham [1]

48, WALL STREET, *February* 28th, 1890

... Last night I went to a studio uptown to see a Spanish dancing girl — the most wonderful dancing I shall ever see. She was like the daughter of Herodias — quite young, and very agreeable, and got so excited that she wanted to dance all night. The twenty people who were there, John Sargent, Frank Millet, the painter, etc., got so excited they would have liked to have let her, but humaner counsels prevailed. Sargent says nothing so fine is to be seen in Spain.

It was a study to see the people. My taste for such things is rather uncultivated, but most of them had been to Spain and got a notion. Enough to cry out Spanish exclamations of approval. Besides, they thought it was very much the thing to admire, and they *were* all artists, to whom grace of line, etc., appeals, and they really were wild. The girl herself was most charming; hoped she had not done anything to shock the sensibilities of the audience (someone had evidently told her Americans were prudish), and prefaced one dance by saying she did not do it very well, but wished to, to express her gratitude for the pleasure she had received. She sang at the same time that she danced. She is about twenty and like a young panther. Her name is Carmencita.

To Minna Timmins Chapman

COLORADO SPRINGS, *July*, '90

... O these law books — how I used to hate 'em. They used to be like the gate to Dante's Inferno. I saw the inscription written in invisible ink on every title page — all hope abandon ye who enter here. They contained nightmares of insoluble problems that must be solved, labyrinths that led nowhere and must be threaded, sphinxes on all sides — unseen and threatening hierarchies of power that must be overcome and checkmated. Pshaw — they are nothing. They are counters. They are mere pawns and useful formulas that will demonstrate anything. Set 'em up one way you have a sword. Set 'em up another way you have a shield. This is the whole law — and the prophets are in a different department.

---

[1] Later Mrs. Thomas Holmes Spicer.

To Mrs. Martin Brimmer

327 W. 82ND ST. *Sept.* 22, 1891

... At the '85 class dinner all the men were making speeches about the progress made by the different members of the class (a class dinner you know is a market day for folly. Everyone brings all he has collected during the intervening year). One man J. Simpkins was State Senator — another had had babies — Grafton Cushing made a speech on education in which he climbed up a high moral pole — and then forgot why he'd come up and slid down again. One man talked about the influence of Harvard and Harvard men in general and the conquering class of '85 — and they were all very dull speeches.

Trask came in very late — but when he'd heard about ten of these speeches — he was moved to arise and make a résumé of what he had heard. He said he was rejoiced at the spread of the class. That most of the men seemed to have had babies and some of them boys. That the class seemed to have produced every species of greatness and kind of man — statesmen, lawyers, navigators, inventors, historians, contractors, philosophers. In fact the only two kinds of men it had not produced were a Yale man — and an orator.

I think this is exceedingly witty, because you know on these occasions the Harvard man becomes glorified into a magnificent being and Harvard becomes [a] mysterious and sacred fountain of these men — as if she could produce any other kind of men if she tried — but held her own glorious course in producing only Harvard men....

To Mrs. James T. Fields [1]

[*Chapman had recently sent his translations of Michael Angelo to Mrs. Fields.*]

327 WEST 82ND STREET
NEW YORK CITY
September 27, 1891

MY DEAR MRS. FIELDS

I am almost ashamed at the great study you have given the sonnets. They ought to have been kept for ten years and

[1] Original in Huntington Library, San Marino, California.

84

worked over once in two — to give them the right to such careful consideration, but as I did so hastily despatch them I am going to reap the benefit of all you say and thank you ever so much for your notes. I have put your letter with them for future struggles.

I have been reading M. Angelo all the morning and he really is one of the few poets whom it pays to read because he only writes when he has something to say. When he can't end a line he just don't end it, and when he thinks of a rhyme but doesn't quite see how it can be worked in, he just jots it down at the end of an imaginary line — and occupies himself with some other thing. This is a great deal better — than trying to fool the reader — as almost everyone else does.

I hate sonnets because they are the most literary of all the forms of verse — even our best English poets are on their best literary behavior in the sonnet — their best foreign manner gloved and scented.

Shakespeare's sonnets stand by themselves. They have the charm of his poetry, his songs and madrigals — and it is his own. They don't pretend to be sonnets. They don't follow the traditions of sonnets and they don't smell like sonnets. Michael Angelo being an Italian was at home, so to speak, in the sonnet and wasn't obliged to imitate anyone in particular — (for an Englishman to write a sonnet is as if he should try to say his prayers in French) and Michael Angelo was constantly taken up only with the endeavor to say the thing — he was not giving sops to literary tradition. He was like a powerful man packing a carpet bag — when he has too many things to go in. You can see the veins swell on his forehead as he grips the edges and tries to make it close. Half the time he takes everything out again on the floor and makes a new arrangement — with the shaving brush at the bottom — and then he is so uncertain which is best that he allows both readings to stand.

But they have thought in 'em. There is not a fraud nor a paper stuffing nor a filigree ornament in the volume — and O, how can we ever be grateful enough for this! Here is a man that writes poetry which is as good as prose.

Their language is colloquial and simple — anything but

literary. They are so purely intellectual in their aim — their
effort to express an idea — that they would be dry and
frigid, if it were not for the man's violent nature. Do you
know I really believe that there's a great deal of humbug
talked about workmanship and form in poetry. These things
are results — the shimmer and gleam that come from saying
things well. They are not entities. They are no more things
in themselves than the relation between two lights is a thing
in itself, and anyone who sets to work to put good form on
his poetry is like the man in the story who wanted good
architecture put on to his house.

These Aldriches who think style is the *means* of saying
things well! How false is a philosophy of composition which
admits that there is such a thing as beauty — as an end to
be reached — and yet this simple proposition seems like a
paradox — what better proof could we have of how thoroughly the plagiarists have overcrawled the world? 'Use
beauty-wash!' they cry — patent Italian sonnet-varnish —
the only thing that has stood the test of time. Use the celebrated 'Milton finish' for odes, epics and epitaphs — cures
lame feet and rhymatism. Use the Petrarch burnisher —
porcelain-lined, it secures fame. Use Shakespolio, Words-
worthene, and Racine — they never vary and are *Reliable'* —
Is it a wonder a man will not arrive anywhere if he spends all
his life in getting forward and backward over his style?

But you will not think I really bear a personal ill will
against the refined poets — except the sonnetteers. You
will — I am sure you will — allow me to except the sonnetteers, those mouthing profaners — may not one have a
preference — a strong prejudice against a particular class of
mortals — and yet be full of the treacle of human con-
descension towards the rest?

I hardly know whether I ought to send this letter — it
having become — really against my will — so extravagant,
but I perfectly trust to your understanding it in as good a
sense for my reason as it will bear. With many more thanks,

I remain very sincerely yours
JOHN JAY CHAPMAN

To Minna Timmins Chapman

[*In preserving this letter, written on one of Chapman's business visits to the West, his wife endorsed the envelope, ' La miraculosa littera d'amore.'*]

[Postmarked LITTLETON, COLO. *Sept.* 21, '92]

I have sealed up each one of these letters thinking I had done — and then a wave of happiness has come over me — remembering you — only you, my Minna — and the joy of life. Where were you, since the beginning of the world? But now you are here, about me in every space, room, sunlight, with your heart and arms and the light of your soul — and the strong vigor your presence. It was not a waste desert in Colorado. It is not a waste time, for you are here and many lives packed into one life, and the green shoot out of the heart of the plant, springing up blossoms in the night, and many old things have put on immortality and lost things have come back knocking within, from before the time I was conceived in the womb, there were you also. And what shall we say of the pain! it was false — and the rending, it was unnecessary. It was the breaking down of the dams that ought not to have been put up — but being up it was the sweeping away of them that the waters might flow together.

This is a love letter, is it not? How long is it since I have written you a love letter, my love, my Minna? Was the spring hidden that now comes bubbling up overflowing curb and coping-stone, washing my feet and my knees and my whole self? How are the waters of the world sweet — if we should die, we have drunk them. If we should sin — or separate — if we should fail or secede — we have tasted of happiness — we must be written in the book of the blessed. We have had what life could give, we have eaten of the tree of knowledge, we have known — we have been the mystery of the universe.

Is love a hand or a foot — is it a picture or a poem or a fireside — is it a compact or a permission or eagles that meet in the clouds — No, no, no, no. It is light and heat and hand and foot and ego. If I take the wings of the morn-

ing and remain in the uttermost parts of the sea, there art
thou also — He descended into Hell and on the third day
rose again — and there art thou also — in the lust or business — in the stumblings and dry places, in sickness and
health — every sort of sickness there also — what matter
is it what else the world contains — if you only are in it in
every part of it? I can find no corner of it without you —
my eyes would not see it. It is empty — I have seen all
that is there and it is nothing, and over creation are your
wings. Have we not lived three years now together —
and daily nearer — grafted till the very sap of existence flows
and circulates between us — till I know as I write this —
your thoughts — till I know as a feeling, a hope, a thought,
passes through me — it is yours? Why the agony of those
old expressions and attempts to come by diligent, nervous,
steady, fixing of the eye on the graver's tool, as if the prize
depended on drawing it straight, those pounds of paper and
nights of passionate composition — did they indeed so well
do their work that the goal was carried — or was it the silent
communion — of the night — even after days of littleness
or quarrel that knitted us together? It does not matter, love,
which it was. It put your soul so into my body that I don't
speak to you to convey meaning. I write only for joy and
happiness. How diligently have we set fact to fact and
consideration against consideration during the past years —
as if we were playing dominoes for our life. How cloudy
I have been — dragging you down, often nailing useless
nails, cutting up and dissecting, labeling, crucifying small
things — and there was our great love over us, growing,
spreading — I wonder we do not shine — or speak with
every gesture and accent giving messages from the infinite —
like a Sibyl of Michael Angelo. I wonder people do not look
after us in the street as if they had seen an angel.

TUO GIOVANNI

*Che non è bimbo nè vecchio non ha età — nè maturità nè gioventù
— ma nel nascimento è tuo e nella morte è tuo e in tanto che spira.
spira la tua anima — e vive solamente in tuo corpo e tuo cuore.*

To Mrs. Martin Brimmer

Dec. 28: 1892

... The house in 82nd Street is proving cold. Whether it comes in through the said roof, or, as I think more probable, straight through the walls — being in it is like sleighing in a duster. Maggie had put all the blankets in the house on the bed and added — the lap rug, the red Italian blanket, the yellow counterpane, the eiderdown thing, besides leaving on the regulation embossed coverlet. I anchored these things down on the side opposite the window with a very heavy bolster. The cold, however, being frustrated on this side went round and came up through the mattress — so tonight I shall probably begin by reinforcing the mattress with the dining-room carpet. I had a fire made at dawn in the parlor — at which I dressed and had breakfast. This state of things has two consequences — 1. That Minna ought not to come back to such a cold house. 2. That I remain at the Club most of the time....

From Minna Timmins Chapman to J. J. Chapman

[*This letter on the death of Phillips Brooks reveals so much of the first Mrs. Chapman and her deepest interests that the whole scene now spread before the reader gains illumination from it. Her strong sense of individuality colored a letter written to her husband in the following year, when it was planned to give her name to a niece: ' Somehow it did not smite to my soul. It is rather a funny feeling. I would spare that name even from a daughter of ours, not of its special sacredness, but to have it given to another child it seems as if every time I should hear it I should be scalped. Another Minna Timmins rushing with the west wind in her through the streets of Boston! Could it be!! I wish indeed this little girl would suffer as much and love as much and be so wondrously blessed with love as the first Minna Timmins!! Still, people have a right to call their children by whatever name they choose.' Her individuality expressed itself in many memorable terms, none more characteristic than those of spiritual perception.*]

47, Beacon Street
Monday, Jan. 22, 1893

Mr. Phillips Brooks gave up the ghost this morning. Two days' sickness, pneumonia. I can only think of his splendor now, the great privilege of his entering into the fuller life, so much does my spirit glow with this thought of his joy that nothing else — our little loss — is to be compared to it — the mystic, the soaring, fighting soul in the greater life.

I never saw him more resplendent and serene than this winter. I saw him three times — real joy. The last time, only a week ago last Friday, he was here, he had invited himself to luncheon when I went to see him the day before — and such a delightful visit — because he wanted to see Victor — and so he came — and *you*, even you, would have acknowledged his humanity and splendor of himself — only to see him play with Victor. He had a great feeling for Victor because of Gemma — I still have Gemma's letter where she wrote down the things that he had spoken when she told him that Victor was born — his desire to be a youth again to run the race of life with the new generation. You know how Victor used to be frightened at Mr. Brooks. This time instead he ran right up to him at table, perched himself on his knee and laughed and gabbled to him all during luncheon time. And after, up in the library, Victor would not leave him but caressed his face, his big eyes, of which he was no longer afraid, and all manner of endearing things he did, to my surprise and delight, and then his warm-hearted glowing good-bye — Mr. Brooks — when he went I shall never forget it. I remember so well talking to him about the one hundred sonnets (Mitchell protégé) and how he scorned the spirit and soul of the man.

If there was anything that made him wild it was 'agnosticism.' True *he* could not say just what he believed in, but he believed in the hot glowing fire of faith — whether mystic or theological — he did not care, but it must be faith red hot — his nature always for life. I have always loved Mr. Brooks — somehow Gemma and I were favorites of his, and we could get to the truth and splendor of him always and right away, whether like five years ago — great, giant-hearted in despair and broodings of the worthlessness of his life's mission — or when in the joyousness of travelling in Spain together — all his soul out — a perfect companion — a glowing friend — a rich soul.

Quite a piece of oneself — memories' riches of one's past all entangled with him — suddenly scooped out of one's heart and thrust like a stone on the very forehead of night and there to glow like a star.

Gemma and he — how dear and beautiful together from the very first when we met him in Europe and we counted on going to India all together — and he had told Gemma that he would look out for her till the very last moment in Venice on the P. and O. steamer, and when the doctors told Uncle he would not be strong enough to go (being after his fever) and so the plan was given up much to our distress, Gemma taking it seriously that Mr. Brooks would expect her indeed, and so she must write to him that she was not allowed to come to him — all half-earnest, half-playful — to our great amusement — and his little presents to us when he came from India — and then Spain together — what didn't we do! In Sevilla to run up the Giralda — that beautiful high tower — go up four times a day — and then our antiquarian hunting and all the serious beautiful hours of talks together, especially the long evenings on the train when we went West to California together — all the others would go to bed early — and Gemma and I — Uncle and Mr. Brooks up talking till one o'clock always. Many times reciting poem after poem — his favorites — he knew so many — and then all his visits to great men in Europe. I told you about Browning.

I long to see you again — *averti amicino amor mio* — *I tuoi sogni sono le leggende della vita e debbono esistere sempre.*

TUO AMORE

To Mrs. Martin Brimmer

120 BROADWAY, *Feb.* 15, 1893

MY DEAR MRS. BRIMMER

I am delighted to hear both from you and Mrs. Whitman that Mr. Brimmer is doing well and that the long delay is the normal course. We have been doing lots of society, more than any winter before. Minna is devoted to it — though she thinks she has no taste for it. But she would go ten miles in the rain to a church sociable. My more serious turn of mind makes these things a distress to me, but I have always been quick to recognize the claims of married life and so give way graciously and go to dinners and musicals and pretend to enjoy them when my heart is in my office and intent on the preparation of motions and schedules. I have sorrowfully consented to go to a dinner party tonight. Last night we had a funny time, at my cousins' the Eglestons'. The guests were an ancient maiden aunt-cousin, a young singer, very vigorous and from New Orleans, a reciter young lady, Fitch the writer of plays, a nondescript nitrogenarian, a bearded Cyprian sculpture, and one or two unclassified floaters. But the host and hostess are such agreeable people that they cast a charm about the motley crew and we enjoyed ourselves immensely. I think all depends on the hostess and really it don't make much difference who the people are provided they have individuality. Then we went to a still queerer reception at the Korbays', where they played on pianos with the tops taken off, with hammers, and made so much noise that you felt as if you were drowning and the whole ocean was atop of you, and the room was so packed that you became intimately acquainted with strangers by apologizing for being squeezed against them, and the supper was arranged in [a] passageway so that no one could get any without preventing three others, and a young English bull of Bashan sang Hungarian songs in English — all of them to the effect that he was about to murder his lady love, and was on horseback and was warning the next county that he was about to ride into it, and yet we had a splendid time and saw lots of agreeable people and came away thinking it was a splendid thing to go to evening receptions.

Yours very affectionately

JOHN JAY CHAPMAN

To Helen Dunham

June 27, 1893

MY OWN LITTLE HELEN

... I must warn you as usual of English influences — adopt a strong tone in seeing the English, read and collect disgraceful episodes in English history — as the forcing of the opium trade on China (the greatest crime in history), the bombarding of Honduras, their conduct during our Civil War. Have these things handy — to use as required in repartee. Never forget to resent an insult — but anyone can do this. But never forget to give an insult. *Resent* the English generally. If you do like any English people, be careful always to say you like them because they are not like English people — and in fact you would take them for Americans. Quarrel also with their accent and ask them to repeat words. Correct their grammar without fail and make memoranda of their ridiculous usages. This sort of treatment they understand and enjoy.

I half doubt your loyalty. You have lived so much abroad — you are getting tolerant of abroad. You see good in abroad. You are a border state likely to secede. You desire to be just — you wish to be intelligent — you are an optimist — you wish peace — you wish brotherly love. Confess you desire to be friends.

You are in for Walt Whitman and the sentimentalists — the poseurs. Can you answer me now this question: The Chicago Fair — is it of heaven or of earth? When Kelly was at school in England there was a discussion on our war, and he remonstrated with Knox Little who was a master then upon England's giving aid to the South, and Little said, 'Ah, but the Southerners were gentlemen.' Can you give the true retort to this? The answer is half the history of England and the whole of its philosophy. I once charged Cust with the same charge and he said, 'Well, after all why should we have cared?' Do you know the true retort to this? You are not fitted to be abroad unless you have some of these sharp knives in your pocket.

Remember that every American abroad is an ambassador. He represents the cause of the American people in the history of the world. Now ambassadors must be not only good but clever. At home they may be stupid ad lib. You will say my instructions [are] a bore, don't square with the general notion of how an ambassador should behave — but that is trifling. It is a mere question of sheaths and passes — Marquis of Queensberry or Hoyle. I speak of the substance and sinews.

And write occasionally to

Your loving JACK

To Minna Timmins Chapman

Friday night Aug. 11, 1 A.M. [1893]

I am too tired to write. Went to the Century, where I happened to sit down next to Charles Peirce, and stayed talking to him ever since, or rather he talking. He is a most genial man — got down books and read aloud. He began by saying Lincoln had the Rabelais quality. It appears he worships Rabelais. He read passages from Carlyle in a voice that made the building reverberate. He also read from an Elizabethan Thomas Nash — a great genius whom he said Carlyle got his style from, but he is wrong. Nash is better. I almost died over the language of this Elizabethan — he is a gargantuan humorist of the most splendid kind, as good as Falstaff, and Peirce read with oriflamme appreciation. He then talked about — plasms — force, heat, light — Boston, Emerson, Margaret Fuller, God, Mammon, America, Goethe, Homer, Silver, but principally science and philosophy — a wonderful evening. It was ask and have, and, but that he talked himself positively to sleep with exertion, he would be talking yet, and I have many more things I want to ask him, chiefly Helmholz. He is a physical mathematician mechanician, that sort of a man of a failed life so far as professional recognition goes, but of acknowledged extraordinary ability, and is positively the most agreeable person in the city. He is a son of old Professor Peirce, is about 55 and is like Socrates in his willingness to discuss anything and his delight in posing things and expressing things. In fact I got to answering him in the style of Plato's dialogues. 'But do you not see, O Socrates, that you seem here to be confusing two very different matters, for when you speak of

the future as different from the past — you do not seem to
be aware that the future as we know it is only a portion of
the past in our own consciousness, and if it is a portion
of the past, how can it be different from the past?' Only
I was a great deal more astute than the sophists and other
answerers in the dialogues and only came in on the last moves
with, 'I perceive that it must be as you say, O Socrates,
and that I do not know what I am talking about,' or words
to that effect. He told me Emerson took no interest in anybody but practical men.

When you remember that I do not know anything whatever about the scientific things he was talking of and talking
most earnestly and most patiently most of the evening, you
will see he is a very remarkable person.

What started him off was at dinner I said the difference
between Walt Whitman and the American people was that
Walt Whitman didn't know what he was about and the
American people did know what they were about. At this
he burst into a flame and said he was inclined to think the
American people did know what they were about and the
man who should tell it would make a stir. He suddenly
seemed to believe that I was about to divulge it, and I felt
a momentary responsibility, but got out of it by recurring to
W. W. who I said as usual was only the notion of the English
Universities of what the A. P. *might be*, and I said I only read
him because the English U.s had talked about him and I
wanted to be in the swim of polite small talk, but as for the
man himself, etc., etc. I told him I doubted a real resemblance
between Lincoln and Rabelais, though I was glad to believe
in it, but rather thought his discovery of a likeness was
due to the natural tendency to assimilate the things we like.

It appears he had a controversy in which he chewed up
Edmund Gurney and Myers' book on Phantasms of the Living.
It appears he explained most of the tales on the theory of
inaccuracies and mendacities of the unimpeachable witnesses,
and he made one or two good guesses at mistakes afterwards
verified. He had never met Myers before, but seemed to get
on with him very well the other night. Tonight I took the
ground that Myers & Co., in taking up a study tainted with

charlatanism and every kind of reprobation, were really doing a heroic thing, etc. He reluctantly assented to this, but said there were other more important scientific things, and I rolled up this and boiled it down into a mere question of opinion and pointed out that Myers *would not* do any of his other suggested pursuits, but if he didn't, psychic research would be writing poetry and that Myers was doing more good than harm in the economy of the universe, to which he reluctantly assented. He has a theory that the laws of mind and matter are the same and he don't believe in the conservation of energy. He explained this at length — and he frightened two or three other gentlemen who came near while he was doing it so that they won't come to the Club for a month. They looked at him in wonder, crossed themselves, and went away.

It all comes down to the motions in germ-plasm — the law of internal friction in fluids which Fourier discovered and the formula for high numbers, which it appears are all fundamentally the same thing. Ergo mind is matter; matter is mind and energy is *not* conserved. I am sure I have expressed it accurately and if you don't understand it — it's your own stupidity. It's very likely to be the coming doctrine of science, so I advise you to try, that's all. I am pretty well grounded in it.

To Mrs. Henry Whitman

120 BROADWAY, NEW YORK
August 12, 1893

... What is there that a man can do in authority that doth not debase him? Teach? — no. Teaching dethrones the intellect. Edit? By no means. Keep a gate at the Elevated Railway — or distribute soup tickets to beggars? One and all give the wheezes to humanity. (The wheezes is a disease I have just thought of. When a man is able to draw in his breath but not to breathe it forth again. Consequently he turns into a force pump, gets by every breath more inflated — and the only reason he does not die in agony is the incredible capacity for inflation of the human system.) Charles Peirce wrote the definition of University in the Century Dictionary.

He called it an institution for purposes of study. They wrote to him that their notion had been that a university was an institution for instruction. He wrote back that if they had any such notion they were grievously mistaken, that a university had not and never had had anything to do with instruction and that until we got over this idea we should not have any university in this country. He commended Johns Hopkins and Gilman. It is a singular coincidence that Gilman is about the only college president a-going who impresses you as primarily a man and secondarily a professional man. I told Peirce I never could see why anyone teaching anything or conducting a study of anything with pupils could help being overwhelmed with the idea — that very possibly *some one* of the young persons before them were of such capacity that the instructor might later be dignified by having known them. It is an idea which does not, however, in general oppress our instructors much. Peirce told me that the man of his elders whom he had got most encouragement from was Elliot Cabot (I was abusing Cabot for eating buns at lunch. He admitted the damnability of buns). I harried Cambridge generally, which I think he sympathized with. It has sloughed off its intelligent men — (like Fiske and himself and Maximo Intervallo Perry) — because they can't keep dormitory. On the other hand there are better times coming. Eliot was put in as dictator and it was easier to let him have his own way and on the whole he has done wonders. These things were to be. There is about as much love of learning in Charles Eliot as there was in Jay Gould. Yet if we had the flowering humanities on top at Cambridge — very likely we'd be saying — (the college would have remained its old size and shape) we'd be crying out — 'O, if we could only have some business ability to run this machine and keep it abreast of the times. There ought to be examinations for Harvard held in every state of the Union!' — as there are.

Very sincerely yours

JOHN JAY CHAPMAN

To Minna Timmins Chapman

[*The serial letter begun by Chapman on his return voyage from
Italy to America had filled* 55 *pages of manuscript before he left
the ship. After several months in New York he lost track of the
paging at about* 250. *In one of the shipboard passages he wrote,
'Everyone thinks I am engaged in some literary work, seeing these
myriad pages.' They touch on many topics — from his fellow-
passengers to Dante, Zola, and other writers whose books he was
reading. Here it must suffice to preserve a few of his observations
on Dickens.*]

S.S. Werra, Sept. 2, 1894

Read all day yesterday Dickens. It happened to come in a
sympathetic hour and I enjoyed him immensely. Let us
acknowledge that he is sentimental with a cheap and often
vulgar and theatrical sentiment. Let us acknowledge that
his characters are not real for the most part, that the Sam
Wellers and Boffins and dolls' dressmakers and Mr. Micawbers
and Mantalinis never existed or could exist, that they are
fantastic creations of wit and humor, not meant to be real,
belonging almost to a realm of farce, or to marionettes rather
than to the theatre, yet there remains the genius of the man.
I am positively appalled at the prodigal brain that could
throw out this civilization of grotesques — at his will come
more and more of these creatures, goblins, elfs, Mr. Squeers,
Mr. Dombey, the fat boy, little Nell. I don't say I like 'em
or many of them — the goblins have lost their terror and
there is a certain amount of pasteboard in the angels, but
there is enough of human nature in human characters about
them to make them dance to the eyes, to make them surprise
us with their smartness, their magic-lantern definiteness —
saucy angels that they are — and the stream of them, the
hustling and crowding and trooping of them, the hatching
of new eggs with the little creatures jumping out of them and
jauntily proclaiming themselves as fast as the hatching of
fish eggs, hastening and bustling into the scene — I say I
read Dickens yesterday and I was impressed with the wonderful originality and stupendous readiness of the magician.
And then, after these French books, Dickens was a high

and pure soul and wrote with his heart — the bad taste is a trifle — the infinitely fine human spirit of the man, an immense love of the common people, a love of all that is good and holy lifts not only Dickens but shows as the light at which the whole of English literature is written, after we have wallowed for a day or two with the French.

To Owen Wister

56 WALL STREET, *Oct.* 4, 1894

DEAR DAN

I will now withdraw the curtain and rend the veil and you shall have the inward wisdom hidden under a boorish and humorous appearance.

There was a man on the steamer talking religion — and he said that President Eliot had had a grand discussion with President McCosh on the sanctions of religion and President Eliot had summed up his religious beliefs in the phrase which he said meant everything to him — 'Underneath us are the everlasting arms.' I replied flippantly — 'O yes, all free thinkers have some phrase they chew on — mine is "Male and female created he them"' — and the dolt thought I had debased the conversation. But had I chosen I could have filled the air with mystical wings and showed that this — the most famous line of Goethe — was, unconsciously to himself, the central idea of Dante's Comedy — and was what gave both these poets their modern hold — and so on deeper than ever plummet sounded. And so it has occurred to me with regard to stories and writing generally, that the best things, the good things, have been drawn from the life among which the writer spent his early years, and if you are to become a good and great writer of fiction, you will sooner or later gravitate back east of the Mississippi and all this western debauch will have been a magnificent training and, more than that, a fulcrum to move the world with and a mound to be seen from. Now go your way into his gates with gladness and into his courts with praise.

Affectionately yours

JOHN JAY CHAPMAN

To Minna Timmins Chapman

... Went to a concert — to which Eleanor Robinson sent me a ticket — a young man of thirty called Schenck, who has been studying in Germany, an American, his début. He is a leader. My own belief is he is a wonderful leader — one of the best ones I ever heard in the world — just a master. His own music is imitation of Wagner — beautiful orchestration but nothing in it.... It is wonderful how well Damrosch's orchestra can play. It must surprise the men themselves — and he *leads* — such time, such delicacy, such understanding. He played Schubert's Unfinished Symphony. Now I will tell [you] I always have had a dream that someday I should lead that and that I could lead it. But I crawl and apologize. It is, you must know, the most beautiful thing in the world or in human life. It stands alone in a curious way. It has not got the moral or conventional character of Beethoven nor the strength — but it has a genius as great as Beethoven. It is as beautiful as the Pheidian marbles — but modern or ancient and modern at the same time. If you want to know what I am — not now but in the infinite in the next world, in the revelations — that symphony is what it is. It makes me so moved I feel as if my head was lifting and my sides were bursting. It is like a deification to hear it — and he played it as it should be played. You know only two movements of it exist. They were found among his papers. He never heard it played. It has in it all the things that Keats was yearning for, but which poetry says about as adequately as a block of wood can sing. It is more like Keats' feeling than anyone's I can think of, but Keats was a sick boy yearning and this is a sane wholesome man realizing. It is a glimpse into fairyland which brings the feelings of early childhood and early dawn, and mature manhood, and sweep of pleasure so unalterably pure, so new, so forgotten, it gives almost a pang to reawaken the forgotten infinity of it. My Jove, what a being Schubert was! It is almost like being God. Beethoven impresses me as if he had been God — and in another way so does this Schubert.

To the same

[*On a talk with a daughter of Charles A. Dana, of the Sun.*]

Dec. 9, 1894

Sunday aft. called on various people and found them out. Then it occurred to me that Mrs. Draper had sent me a card to a musical and as I was just passing the street I went in. Stayed two hours and a half. Saw some of the children. Had a long political talk in which I had the chance to explain the City Club movement and its importance from a national point of view — with regard to the government of American cities — an impersonal view of the movement and its aims. This was a complete novelty to her and impressed her a good deal. She is a perfectly frank and very clever person and her face went through forty expressions. I described the tyranny over the poor — and the practical incidents of what corruption meant. We have had enough of them lately and to spare — touching very lightly and then moving to the effect, the immediate and practical effect, which the mere existence of the City Club or such a body had — and some account of its rise, aims, and weaknesses.

She has not much outfit for a defense of it, and said only one or two commonplaces about party government and reformers, and there I took the time to analyze and expose and show — or at least say just how and where she was wrong. Perhaps I ought to say she is more frank than she is clever. At the end she said she would so like me to meet her father and say the same things — but I had to get out of this. She was exceedingly nice and exceedingly intelligent and let me explain how I could not take the things he did on an intellectual basis and meet him just as a man with differing views and so on. She said he often took views and did things she couldn't follow or understand, but that she several times had found out a year late that he had been in the right and thought that he had broad, wide, deep principles governing his conduct, etc. I said, with that mixture of humor and truth that alone can carry such a remark, that I had studied his career beginning with Brook Farm and that I thought he was the devil — that I couldn't down or help the indignation against him, or vivid antagonism, nor help taking seriously and as facts and realities the matters and things advocated in the *Sun.* It sounds like an extraordinary conversation to have with a man's daughter about the man — but you must remember she brought it on, she wanted to have it, she was perfectly competent for it, and it was friendly and natural to the last degree.

As a matter of fact I do not want to meet old Dana, and to meet him willingly or dine with him — or in anyone else's house, to do more than the civilities of the occasion required, would seem to me a sort of injury to justice and insult to all good things.

To the same

Jan. 4, 1895

... Mrs. —— is a woman with a round high forehead, very ugly the forehead, and wore a low dress very tight so as to create the impression of a wealth of being which did not exist — with the effect of exhausting the subconscious attention of beholders as to just what was wrong, just why she was wrong. N.B. One ought not to wear anything that meets and occupies the subconscious attention of other people with problems. That's why I hate a false arm. People find it out by degrees and are worried all the time until they do — and then by that time — they can think of nothing else. A glass eye I should wear — for the alternative is too bad.

To Owen Wister

Jan. 7, 1895

MY DEAR DAN

The essential lack in Wagner is after all a want of sanitary plumbing. No amount of sentiment or passion can wholly make up for this. One feels all the time that the connection with the main is fraudulent. I should be grateful to you or anyone else who will tell me what is the matter with Wagner, and why I am against him, body and soul, sleeping and waking, and think him a bad man and a bad influence.

Once out of five times I find a person who both appreciates his greatness and acknowledges his wickedness, but what

I want is a formula, a simile — something, to explain his sinister character to those who don't see it by nature. I see many excellent and beautiful young ladies whom I passionately love who think Wagner is a good and beautiful soul. There must be some way of reaching their minds, and drawing a line between Wagner and Beethoven, or Wagner and all the rest of the great artists.

The Schopenhauer element is so plain, the philosophical intention of Wagner so obvious, I'm so sure I understand the man as a man — and disagree with him so utterly. His works are pamphlets, special pleading, the appeal he makes is to the insane, piercing, sweet, sad, unattainable mysticism of despair. It is the strongest plea for Evil that ever has been made on the Earth — I think, perhaps. If I were a musician I could illustrate it — by playing some Tristan or Parsifal — and following it by an old Scotch song.

But I want some touchstone and catchwords to express it to drawing-room idiots. The fact itself I am not in doubt about. I will die for it at the stake. If all extant humanity contemned me I should still know I was right. If Bach and Beethoven should rise from the dead and place their crowns at the feet of Wagner I should call them liars. But I want a mode of expressing this. If you think of any send me word.

Yours

J. J. C.

To Minna Timmins Chapman

Jan. 12, 1895

... I cannot help thinking you and I are a good deal alike in being passionate sort of people — though I am more self-controlled and less penitent....

How is it you dare to go off to Europe and leave every woman in New York ready to fall on my neck? How is it that, knowing my weakness of highly organized and contemptible flirtations, you don't think I'll indulge in them? Well, the real old intrinsic burning passions of life are enough alive in me to keep me out of them — and unless moral decay sets in with advancing years (as it does sometimes) I don't think I shall. I think on the whole I am as near to you — you as a presence, a being — a past, present, and future fused, as if you were in New York — perhaps nearer — and the clarification of setting all things down in black and white in writing to you, making the present into history every day, is a steadying thing. I am not far from the compass.

Polly was going to give a dinner the other night, but Eleanor was in bed and only Elizabeth Chanler, Polly, uncles, and I dined together. Elizabeth C. was in the dumps — way down in Hades and could scarcely make conversation, and though I went determined to be cheerful and succeeded — for if one has not got absolute self-control in such a matter one is a boor — it was all I could do. Then I went to the Century shindy, where I had a good time. Then I wrote Elizabeth Chanler a note:

> *My dear Miss Chanler*
> I have a desire to write you and it is no more than speaking — and it's not about anything in particular — and you needn't answer because there is no question.
> There is a certain cut fate has for us — against which there is no defence — namely the misfortunes and unhappiness of other people. I had a sort of feeling that you had had some form of this dealt to you recently.
> It is the only real suffering in the world. One may cry out — Lord, let me not know of the things I cannot remedy — but there is some cowardice in the idea — for the knowledge itself is a kind of remedy — and may lead it — who can tell at what time.
> Yours sincerely
JOHN JAY CHAPMAN

Now the electric flash in this was that she in casual conversation had mentioned going to see Amélie Rives and her brother who were passing through town, and though I don't know either of them — this whole bogey flapped its wings all over the drawing-room — I mean a cat-and-dog life in the Amélie Rives family. Now do you see the dangerous sort of creature I am? I don't do these things, I don't think or care about them, but the air is full of voices, demons — and angels speak and struggle in people's hearts, and trumpets

blow that drown the dinner table small talk, and I need all
my wits and all my prophets all the time — *Qui si convien
lasciare ogni sospetto, Ogni viltà convien che qui sia morta* — the
Dark Tower of Childe Roland — looms across the mere
through someone else's voice — and I cannot see the candles —
for a second.

I'm exaggerating these things so as to express them in a
clear way and blow the mists away with a fine literary wind.

In my college room I had written up on the ceiling with a
burnstick — 'Be fearfully afraid' — which meant to me be
afraid of getting into unwise complications through your
quick sympathies. So I am in training for some years. Sup-
pression is dangerous on the other hand, and dangerous to
the normal temperature, but I think it will be as well if I
keep suppressed to everybody except in these letters, and my
note to Chanler seems to me at this moment unwise and
unnecessary — though nothing will come of it more than
of a compliment.

Now I must set to work all day — and carry out my vow to
refuse these distracting invitations which seem so harmless
and are so vicious. It will be apparent to you that being
separated from you has a little raised my key out of a nervous
lack, the lack of that constant discharge of social force, and
made me like a man during the first six months of the opium
habit, just floated above his natural self. The scientific
phrases may offend you. We must grasp such handles as we
may, as the times throw towards us. No doubt the same
things could have been said in Greek or in the Persian language of old fountains, rose leaves, and broken pottery....

To Elizabeth Chanler

Feb. 5, '95

MY DEAR MISS CHANLER

Much talk about the complexity of modern life and little
upon the unity of human nature makes us warped and queers
us. Strikes, and the refinements of drawing-room conversation, charity organization, the tariff and cleverness, the newspapers, the cheapness of ink — have taxed our brains a little,
and because the horizon of each is expanded to some compre-

hension, some claim to be heard of a thousand subjects. It is the development of the *means of communication that we have* to thank for this.

We are staggered by a cataract of ideas. I admit it — I feel it as much as you could wish, and yet the code we live by, the feelings we rely on, are religious in their nature, they come from within. They are not born of the intelligence. I state this as a fact. I do not doubt it has some explanation — that perhaps the ultimate resultant influence of all these educative forces has its share in the feeling and that we are different in some sense from former generations. But the extent to which we are different will take care of itself. It is sane not to worry over it but to deal with the world unconsciously — to trust to our own nature — to fight for the right as we feel it, no matter how mistakenly. Until our experiences and beliefs have been through this alembic and come from within, they are crude, they are undigested, they are fictitious. That's why this *fin de siècle* talk makes me irritated. I don't happen to feel *fin de siècle* in the smallest degree, and other people seem to me to have a large share of primeval naturalness about them. I say don't worry about the generation — ginger is hot in the mouth still, and men are full of vanity, selfishness, courage, and heroism, and women of tears and laughter. It makes me mad to have you squinting at the earth and pulling out two-cent botanical instruments of dissection. Your analyses are nothing. They are old maids' gossip, and beware of them. Your Monday Clubs and your Tuesday Clubs are full of chlorine gas and take the tint out of wallpapers. It is utter nonsense, this great passion and little passion — this upper clef and lower clef. All life is nothing but passion. From the great passion of love to the regard for a passing stranger is all one diapason, and is the same chord. The whole of it vibrates no matter where you touch it — tho' in different degrees. Will you draw out Leviathan with a hook or stop the sweet influences of the Pleiades? You will measure the deeps with your plummet and prove everything by your slate and slate pencil.

Now there's no use in your writing a long pleading to justify your right to have opinions — I understand it, and

I know just what degree of exaggeration and injustice is contained in all the foregoing — and I want you to see just what degree of truth is contained in it, and not bother your brains to find it out either, for it is either utterly apparent or else inscrutable, and also I want you to believe I am Sincerely yours — and don't resort to poetry or compliment, beautiful and good as you are — this is part of the beauty of goodness of the world, and the joy of life. I am so glad to know you and do so much delight in seeing you, and have broken and battered down the doors of silence once and for-ever years ago, and go about the world escaped from that prison, I thank the powers of Life — and so write openly and that is all there is. Everyone feels so in his heart.

JOHN JAY CHAPMAN

To Mrs. Brimmer

56 WALL STREET
April 23, 1895

MY DEAR MRS. BRIMMER

I just have a letter from Minna in which she speaks of the money you and Mr. Brimmer sent her. It was very kind of you and I am ever so much obliged to you. The fine of all is money. It blesseth him that gives and him that takes, the rich man's peace, the poor man's comforter, tired nature's sweet restorer, the balm of life, the content that passeth all understanding — to be able to pay your bills. Why doesn't someone write a poem on money? Nobody does anything but abuse it. There's hardly a good word for money to be found in literature. The poets and writers have been needy devils and thought to brave out their beggary by pretending to despise it. This shows what liars poets and literary men are. The chief cry of their hearts has never found its way into their books during the last three thousand years....

To Minna Timmins Chapman

Sept. 19, 1895

... At Century Club. My humble fare of beefsteak better than the viands of Arabia.

I am full of poetry and blood. I may write some poetry.

I read before dinner a half hour in the 'Golden Treasury....'
Read some Shelley. Shelley is a great artist but hasn't got anything to say. He is a mood painter. He gives the mood —
there is not much in the mood — and it's not a very good or
valuable sort of mood. It's a weak, vegetarian, sinking-of-the-
stomach mood, but he does give it — that's his wonder. I now
know what I think of Shelley and of those that worship him.
They are either weak creatures who like him because he
depicts *their kind* of mood — or else people who like him for
the artistic pleasure of seeing him depict a mood, any mood,
so completely as he does. He is a great genius but he has no
stomach, no guts, no heartiness, and he was anemic. He was
in the state you or I should get into if we ate nothing but
vegetables for a week and read Schopenhauer and the Greek
Dramatists — a very decentralized state, by the way. That's
enough of Shelley. I could have cured him of being Shelley
if I had got hold of him early and fed him up. Your true
Shelleyite won't believe this, but it's gospel.

To the same

[*This long narrative letter, most of which survives in a copy in
the handwriting of the first Mrs. Chapman, describes a 'Good
Government' dinner on November 7, 1895, immediately after the
New York election of that year. The 'Goo Goos' had been bitterly
assailed for their opposition to the 'Committee of Fifty,' which
counted itself the strongest opponent of Tammany. The 'Evening
Post,' in the editorial vein of Godkin, was on the point of denouncing
Chapman and the Goo Goos as the blundering obstacles to reform.
The air was electric with charges and counter-charges. The dinner
here described gave Chapman, who presided at it, the occasion,
already cited, to strive towards saying nothing which he would not
regret. The passage of arms between Joseph H. Choate and Bishop
Potter was the chief event of the evening, and must take precedence
here over portions of the letter which are omitted.*]

November 1895

You must remember that this dinner was one riot of merri-
ment from beginning to end. Everybody was laughing all
the time — and this license of raillery was carried off by the

good humor of the occasion. I can only remember my own part because I was so occupied with making the wheels go round — stop and start the speakers and get off my little jokes — that I didn't listen to anyone else, but there was an infinite lot more of chaff which I have forgotten....

You may not know that New York is oppressed with deadly respect for wealth. The William E. Dodges and Morris K. Jesups are on top. It did my heart good to think there were fifty men in the city that could laugh so heartily, and it shocked and frightened Choate.

N.B. I hate and despise respectability.

The dinner was about fifty Goo-Goos including eight guests — of whom were Choate, Bishop Potter, and Adler's two candidates. We had it very early and it began on time; at quarter of nine. I pounded a plate and got up and when silence was completely restored, I said:

'We are the people — and there are 1066 of us — 1066 rock-ribbed, crow-footed Goo-Goos — that cling to their principles. That is an enormous number of such fellows as we are for a town of 2,000,000 to produce. Moreover, there are 39,000 people in the city who even when they have registered *won't go to the polls* until we tell them to.

'This is a peculiar dinner. The doors are locked for two reasons. First to prevent the reporters from coming in and second to prevent the guests from getting out. I told Mr. Choate when I invited him that the Goo-Goos were really a school of political philosophy, and if he would come and dine with us I would get them to recite. That we should have a set of five-minute speeches representing the different points of view — and that he would get a composite photograph of the Goo-Goo mind. Gentlemen, I trust that you will do your best. While Mr. Choate is a member of the Fifty — I still think him worth saving. He is very intelligent, he is anxious to learn, and he has to a very large extent kept himself unspotted by the Fifty!!!! You will all kindly respond when called upon and not quarrel with the titles of your speeches. The titles have been assigned to you. You are responsible only for the substance. One of the great points in the art of public speaking is the art of stopping, and this will be supplied to you, for each of you will not be allowed to speak more than five minutes.' ...

[*Then follow brief summaries of his introductory remarks and of the speeches by Messrs. Pine, Tucker, Mason, Davison, Klein, Page, Pryor, Leavitt, Nevius, Rothschild. Chapman then records what his summary defines as a 'perfectly unjust and outrageous' introduction of C. C. Beaman, in* absentia, *ending with the introduction of Joseph H. Choate as 'the partner of this man ... responsible for him, identified with him,' and, hailing the speaker, 'you fine mixture of Ariel and Mephistopheles whose wit has illuminated the city for thirty years, yet never carried a heart-stain away on its blade.' The narrative proceeds.*]

Mr. Choate made a speech in which he said two very clever things. First he described how he had been left alone in a country house which was being cleaned and could only find one book — Nordau, 'Degeneration' — so he had been obliged to read it. The summary of Nordau's creed seemed to him to be a summary of the Goo-Goos. Especially there was one chapter whose title summarized them and which he had not completely understood until he had come here tonight. The chapter was headed 'Mysticism and Egomania.' He had listened to Mr. Chapman both this evening and in private conversation in his office and on the stump and he had *never been able to understand a single word that Chapman said.* (The second good thing he said was this:) One of your speakers, Mr. Klein, has dwelt on the fact that the Good Government Clubs have been too exclusively composed of the educated and that you had *neglected* the masses. It occurred to me while he was speaking that the masses had *reciprocated* this neglect! Mr. Choate then became serious — and said he had been growing seriouser and seriouser through the evening and went on to deprecate our making fun of the Chamber of Commerce and the wise and well-meaning leaders of Fifty, so that I had to call everybody's attention to the conversion of Choate into solemnity and his attempt to bind the Pleiades and prevent a lot of young men at a dinner from making fun of their elders. I said the only reason that we did not pat the Fifty on the back for their *motives* was that we had tried it and that had insulted them more than anything else. We had in reality an idyllic attachment towards the Fifty. The Fifty were virtuous — 'but thinkest thou because they are virtuous there shall be no cakes and ale?'

Professor Felix Adler the first human voice that reached us.

Adler made a very thoughtful speech comparing a city to a church — the organization of each must be conducted on business principles in its government, but the end and purpose of each was something above and beyond mere business management. He was followed by a prolonged and renewed applause — in fact I had to stand waiting for some time to get attention — and when everybody was quiet I waited for fifteen seconds and then said in a loud voice with a sort of challenging and savage emphasis —

HENRY C. POTTER — There was a perfect stampede of applause — then I added solemnly — no more was needed at the moment — no more need be said now.

Bishop Potter made a few excellent remarks and presented a loving cup to Klein (Campaign Manager) given by the rest of us — and that ended the proceedings proper.

Then happened a funny incident. Choate, quite white, rose to his feet and said he had one word to say and that was to challenge anyone *inside* or *outside* the room to say that the Fifty had done anything that could be described as 'a deal.' In fact Choate had lost his temper. The effect upon me was regrettable. I leaped from my scabbard and said I took up his challenge in the name of the 39,000 stay-at-home votes. My friends instantly thrust me back into my scabbard, and I instantly apologized in public — for the form of my remarks. (It was a momentary flare on both sides — then Potter arose and said with the greatest courtesy and politeness that he was 'sorry to have to tell Mr. Choate that from knowledge he had obtained *from one of the Committee of Five* — (i.e., part of the Fifty who made the Fusion) — Mr. Choate was mistaken.'

All the boys then surrounded Choate and made friends with him, as I did also — and explained to him that he was not accurately acquainted with the facts — and we broke up in great good humor.

Nobody ever saw Choate seriously moved or rattled before. In fact he was in a hard position — one man against forty-nine — and I directed the whole proceedings against him all through the dinner. It wouldn't have been fair against anybody but Choate, but he has never spared anyone in forty years and is able I guess to take care of himself in a chaffing match.

To Mrs. Brimmer

January 16, 1896

MY DEAR MRS. BRIMMER:

Mr. Brimmer's death will be a shock and personal loss to all classes of people. I don't believe there was a man in Boston so much beloved. To have known him was one of the best chances of my life. I always had an affection for him even before I met him. He used to come out to the Porcellian lunches on Class Day. I remember coming in to such a lunch one day where everybody was sitting down at a long table with great festivity going on. Now I hardly knew Mr. Brimmer at the time save by sight, but I must have felt some lack in the assembly, and after looking up and down the room, I sang out in a stentorian voice, 'Where's Martin?' He turned out to be sitting immediately next to me and greeted me with such infinite courtesy and kindliness that I couldn't tell what I was doing for some moments. It is impossible to think of Boston without him. It seems as if half the place were lost. . . .

To Mrs. Henry Whitman

July 16, 1896, DUBLIN, N.H.

MY DEAR MRS. WHITMAN

The relation of Shakespeare to his art is a thing no feller has ever known much about — and only a coxcomb, or a theorist, will pretend to have much light on. I admit it is a splendid subject for a holiday speculation, and if anything could stir my slothful blood your tingling letter playing upon every impulse — vanity, pugnacity, omniscience — I almost think I will solve the problem just for your amusement of a leisure hour. Not that the present would be too valuable, but I should hate to have it so finished — so cleared up and smelted out. I read Shakespeare a good deal from year's end to year's end and always with the instinct that if I should draw all points together and put him in an essay I should dry up my own understanding — my own essay would be all that I ever could see in Shakespeare thereafter. Within the last six months I've taken to writing sibylline leaves, notes, and memoranda on the plays as I read them — on scraps of paper with no consecutive idea.

Walt Whitman disliked Shakespeare because he said Shakespeare was rank feudalism. Howells dislikes him. George Pellew was bored by him — and thought him a bombastic writer (though Pellew was fond of Webster — Beaumont and Fletcher). Jo Lee has got a bee in his bonnet about the masses. Minna dislikes him because of his lack of religious quality. I like him because he is a wit — and is so thoroughly indeterminate. I should say at a guess that people who are fundamentally theoretical — and require to understand and pigeonhole the world — would be apt to boggle over Shakespeare. They want him to stand and deliver — and he is dead and they can't get at him and corner him — and so they make up bad names for him. I doubt very much whether even if they had him in Lipsbury pinfold they could get a straight answer out of him. After all, life and the world — hunger, thirst, and the instant stream of experience in which we live are vivid, rapid, mysterious, and unfathomable, and Shakespeare has the same effect on us — you cannot size him up and pocket him — you instantly pocket yourself if you try. Look at Barrett Wendell — click, and he pops in the pocket. The only safe way is to say O, O, O, like a child looking at fireworks. I have no opinion whatever about Shakespeare except that he is a wit and a humorist and has a passion for metaphysical questions. He also had more intellect at his disposal for purposes of illustration than any other man ever had. He thought so fast that, as Taine said, it's like following Bellerophon to read him — he's by you and then he plunges and ploughs the clouds — and before you know it he's on the horizon. He's always three deductions ahead of you.

He gives me the impression that all the thoughts of all the characters are going on in his head all the time — and each one of these characters is apt to have as full a head as any one of us. In fact some of the characters who had broad-gauge natures like Othello are totally beyond our understanding even of themselves. We cannot more understand them than we can assume the expression of Michael Angelo's sibyls. The relation which the mind and nature that created these exhalations of humanity bore to them, is tolerably beyond our understanding. I could much easier explain Jo Lee, for I know some of the terms and elements of which he is made. I can make a guess at the reason he thinks Shakespeare heartless, but as to whether Shakespeare was heartless or not it seems that the question is like a djinn coming out of a bottle and me with my tin cup to decant him into....

To the same

DUBLIN, *Aug.* 7, 1896

... Minna took some of her daubs to Thayer — Thayer, by the way, is a hipped egoist who paints three hours, has a headache, walks four hours — holds his own pulse, wants to save his sacred light for the world, cares for nobody, and has fits of dejection during which forty women hold his hand and tell him not to despair — for humanity's sake. So Minna attacked him in his studio, daubs in hand. He looked at them with lack-lustre eye — looked at the skylight — for she stood between him and the door — staggered, drank a bottle of salts — and faltered out — 'That he had — never — painted — in — that light.' The next day Mrs. Thayer — (second wife, aged fifty, light and fleet, a benevolent witch, looks like a field-mouse in spectacles) writes to Minna that Mr. Thayer says she has talent — but that a 'lesser painter' can probably do her more good — still that Thayer will give her lessons at $7 for five minutes. The veiled prophet comes high. Thayer is sick and sickly and covered with hot-house glass and very selfish and spoiled — and of course he can't paint. He is very poor — teaches classes to help him out and grudges his instruction — overtires himself — gets up and paints by candle-light — destroys his good work — swears he's the greatest painter that ever lived and his friends had need be worried about him. . . .

To Mrs. C. Grant LaFarge (Florence Lockwood)

DUBLIN, N.H., *Aug.* 11, 1896

MY DEAR FLOS

. . . It has been so frightfully hot even here — which is in the Alps — that any whole family that survives the summer ought to be grateful. We are well so far and living in a house in a clearing, very rural indeed — almost camp life — the best place for summer life you can imagine. Narragansett is Newport and Threadneedle Street compared to it. . . .

. . . Our friends seem to have been bursting into literature. I liked Grant's thing very much. Harry Sedgwick is too affected and dilettante. He says he puts on this style to please the *Atlantic* — but how ignoble, besides being false. He ought to train himself for six years writing — 'The cow has four legs — I see a man,' to get back to some healthy directness. Twiddlededee — what has he said about Montaigne that we all didn't know? It's unmanly to go simpering through fourteen mortal pages — Stevenson banality — Virginibus Puerisque — I should say so — Senilibus Canibusque.

Stevenson's manner of writing is the last form of whipped up literary froth, very well done. It's the last charge of *ces messieurs*. The content is, can be expressed only, with four decimals of chemical formulas. It can't be seen, only surmised. Stevenson is a bad influence because he's so highly artificial. He struts and grimaces and moralizes and palavers and throws in tid bits of local color, fine feeling, graceful ornament, O my, ain't he clever — the rogue — hits you in the mid-riff — don't he — so beautiful — did you catch that — how smartly he led up to that anecdote — how well he lays in his Scotch pathos — his British patriotism — his nautical knowledge — and such light diet! I swear I am hungry for something to read every time I lay down Stevenson — give me rye bread, give me notes to Dante, give me a book about the world. I say I can read Wordsworth's poems and find them full of exciting reality and honesty of talent, after an hour or two of this fictitious fellow Stevenson. It's sham literature. It's all of it sham. The romances all sham romances, the essays are sham essays, the poems are sham poems. I have read 'Treasure Island' many times and the first time or two enjoyed it. 'Kidnapped' which always seemed to me the best of them — those I had read — (for some I stuck on) is a remarkable work of art. What talent — what talent, but sham!

Now the 'Vicar of Wakefield' is a work of art. It seems to me greater every time I read it, but it succeeds. The means of art are concealed. It is a real thing. It imitates nothing. It is a work of genius and a wonder of literature. But 'Kidnapped' is an attempt. I feel Stevenson sweating in every line. I feel an echo in every syllable. I labor with him — to perfect the work. It is the tradition and sentiment of literature, the secondary traits, catchwords, and paraphernalia of writing.

His popularity is a good sign perhaps as showing a certain knowledge and approbation of the literary forms of the past — very widely spread, but it's a bad influence on a man with as much native talent as Harry Sedgwick. It leads him astray — not into a bog, but into a dancing school.

After Harry's first Haggis in the *Atlantic* I told him that he would do better after he had used up the collection of clippings, tag phrases, and polyglot stuff that had collected in his table drawer and which he unloaded so swaggeringly — and I think he is doing better. The scum of quotation and heel-taps of foreign adage is getting cleared off. It reminds me of Miss What's her name — with the thin face — maiden lady — Repplier — Agnes Repplier. The Spectator and Joseph Addison are responsible for all the twaddling superfluity of writing for writing's sake that has been done since....

Affectionately yours

John Jay Chapman

To Minna Timmins Chapman

THE CENTURY ASSOCIATION
Sept. 6: 1896

... Reading Rabelais really struck some ideas that exploded me. I could wake up in Nirvana and laugh. I can't tell whether I have a gross and grovelling spirit, but there is a broadness of design about Rabelais, a gigantic quality, Cyclopean, it makes out Shakespeare to be little and fanciful. This Rabelais will burst me open. I shall be left like a broken vessel behind him and not care — it was only to meet this that I was born. He seems physically to fill the room, to stretch his arms out through the windows. I go wading in Rabelais bored to death, wondering why his volume comes down to posterity, disgusted, and then suddenly there grins from some farrago of learned nonsense and obscenity a humor so profound, a mockery so wholesome, so far reaching, so vital, so beyond books, the human thing that never gets into books, that I seem to be in the clutches of the greater myself. I wrote the thing myself. Nobody else could have written it....

To the same

[Undated: postmarked NEW YORK, *Sept.* 8, 1896]

... I think of writing an essay on James Russell Lowell, which, after the entering wedge of a few purely literary articles, I might get into the *Atlantic*, under the new régime, and which would make a stir in the tea pot. Just think over this notion and see whether you can't take essays as letters for twenty days or the rest of the time you stay. You have a notion that it's easy for me to write. It's really very hard. I sit down and grind things out, correct, throw away, rewrite, murder myself over it, but I have a notion that possibly there is a point of view both scientific, poetical, and literary which had *no* representative in current literature. I seem to myself to have things to say. I may be wrong — I never before thought so, and I feel like sitting down in these few days and trying it to the uttermost. You can judge better than I, for the Browning essay is the best thing I ever wrote — or else it is a poor thing. I don't know which....

To the same

... Henry has some very intelligent writing in the *Bachelor*. I agree with you about the Roman Catholic Church. Its attitude towards science is not of the smallest importance in the present age of the world, and is not worth writing about. I wrote as much to Henry. I hope he will write a book about some real question, Democracy or Socialism, or some kindred thing. He gets to be quite a competent writer and his things are very well put together. Ever so much better than they used to be. The habit of writing is an essential. Otherwise you can't say what you want. I have so little the habit that my things are apt to be too condensed, too much like algebra equations, or Emersonian mysticism, but I hope in time to break through it to current speech.

Nothing but practice will give it to you. Burke or Gibbon or Tacitus are all fair styles. You've got to invent and develope a vehicle out of constant experiment, and then you've got to write so much — so much that you have a public which is accustomed to it. If you only write a little you won't be read unless you adopt some current style, something *connu*.

Here I have sat reading two or three volumes of Lowell and let the mail time go by. I always take the letters to the Grand Central, but it is too late. I will telegraph tomorrow and write you a good letter. I am getting some pretty clear ideas on Lowell and had a most entertaining evening with him.

I don't dislike the man. I think him a fine man, a little dandified and genteel perhaps, but still a good story character. His poetry is nothing but a fine talent, a fine ear, a fine facility — too much morality and an incredible deftness at imitating everybody from Milton down. I cannot read his poems with any comfort — but his early essays I still think the best things he ever did, witty, snappy, 'smart' to a degree, and quite natural — they are the only things he ever did that were quite natural. In later life he got all barnacled with quotations and leisure. He pulls out pocket-books and gold snuff boxes and carbuncled cigarette-cases, and emerald eye-glasses, and curls and pomatums himself and looks in pocket looking glasses, and smooths his Van-dyke beard and is a literary fop — f-o-p, fop. Too much culture — overnourished as Waddy Longfellow says — too many truffled essays and champagne odes and lobster sonnets, too much Spanish olives, potted proverbs — a gouty old cuss in his later essays. But in '54–'65 he wrote rapidly and most clearly. Belles Lettres is the devil after all. It spoils a man. His prefaces — sometimes very nice, in spirit — but his later prefaces are so expressive — O my! so expressive of hems and haws and creased literary trousers. I feel like running him in the belly and singing out Hulloo! old cockalorum.

To the same

MY DEAR CHILD

I have got to the key note of what I was seeking in Emerson's deficiency — the Essay is a mere piece of work and rhetoric to put together now. The false note in Emerson that jars — everywhere — is 'The last revelation of intellect and sentiment is that in a manner it severs a man from all other men, makes known to him that *the spiritual powers are sufficient to him if no other being existed.*'

This is false. It is a false statement about human nature and is at the bottom of New England culture. It is the destructive principle that makes their literature barren, their life thin, their morality falsetto.

Every time I send Page an article or a proof I write him a little familiar and jocular note so that he won't be keeled over by the things I say about Emerson and New England generally.

I have not written a line, and I am only about half through review of Emerson's 11 volumes, for I go off into excursions — but I think I have so much to say that I shall have to write a volume of other reviews. It is laborious and tiring, this fumbling over the universe to find your own in it.

The lawyer's training makes me trust only authority and documents and citations. I am always making a brief — even in my dreams, even in my poems.

Emerson himself must be called as a witness and speak his falsehoods. We will have no hearsay. Suppose I say Emerson has been telling me a lie all his life. Somewhere in him I resent a lie on every page — a denial, a blindness, a weakness. Who will believe me? — no one. But if I bring the sacred old man and let him kiss the book and deliver his cracked oracle right before the effulgent seat of Truth, I need not say a word. Emerson said to Judge Holmes when as a boy he brought him a paper on Plato, said as he handed back the paper, 'If you strike at a King — you must kill him.'

I will not kill Emerson, but I will deal with him honestly.

To Mrs. Henry Whitman

56 WALL STREET
NEW YORK, *Oct.* 9: 1896

... Why get excited over such a thing as a window? The window is of no importance and will go backwards instead of forwards unless you are in good training. You can't get health into the window unless it is in your sinews. I'll tell you my philosophy — that there's only one real joy in life — but fortunately there's likely to be lots of it — the joy of casting at the world the stone of an unknown world.

If you don't do something so good that everybody abuses it — you are lost. I'll tell you what you ought to do. You ought to stop work and go to Japan. O my, how quick you would destroy your old stuff and begin over again when you came back. Get some Japanese and teach them how to cut lead and glass.

Do you know what I'm wondering — in a subconscious way? I'm just wondering how Boston will look after my Emerson comes out — All the steeples down. Now don't tell anybody, not even your most intimate friends, because I've just written to Mrs. Dorr that I'm not going to do any such thing but am going to be as mild as mild — which is also true. I say I wonder whether James or Royce or any of those fellows will understand a psychological critique on Emerson. I'll bet they won't. I lay odds they won't.

I have hopes of James — I will not give up James. James is the son of Henry James — who by the way was the only decent human man that ever lived in Massachusetts — and I must remember that James is his son. I will be patient with James.

JACK

To Elizabeth Chanler

56 WALL STREET, *Dec.* 29, 1896

[*First announcing the birth of his third son, and touching on Choate's candidacy for the Senate:* — '*I will worship virtue nascent, virtue inchoate and virtue in Choate'* — *and proceeding:*]

... Mrs. Wister and Dan Wister sat in solemn conclave, I hear, all night over my first Emerson article and then decided it was original, brilliant, literature, new, noble, a fine piece of criticism. This scares me a good deal. I'm afraid it's the small pattern and retrograde stuff after all. But I have hopes the second part will upset them. The first is all adulation. The second has some circular saws, files, gimlets, and gunpowder. Mrs. Whitman who saw it in proof spent 1½ hours trying to get me to leave out some remarks about Lowell as unnecessary, interfering with the general high tone — hurtful to Lowell's old friends, revealing a tartness on my part, etc., etc. Mrs. Dorr begged me not to say some things about Margaret Fuller for like reasons. This is more encouraging. Our people are as thin-skinned as babies and the Massachusetts crowd has never been criticised. I have hopes from this second part.

Beware of the approbation of your elders. I never knew a boy at school who got the approval of his elders who amounted to anything.

Yours

JACK

To C. Grant LaFarge
[*Apropos of forming a dining club*]

Dec. 30, 1896

... The Round Table Club, the Saturday Club in Boston, Dr. Johnson's Club, the Mermaid Tavern — they were well enough in their day. I don't think I'd have any special initiative idea — as to any crowd of men in this town or country during the last 50 years — I think we're a better set of fellows than any of them. They were small pattern. We may find we like heavy drinking, throwing plates on the chandelier, which used to help Coleridge to his illumination. We may find ourselves turn into a ladies' lunch club. These things are in the hands of Providence, but we can make a beginning. We ought to have done it ten years ago, but then we didn't know the town.

There has been since the death of the revolutionary fathers no generation of men here who were not caked in pomposity. John Marshall would leave the bench, and ten minutes after was to be seen crawling in the grass with a straw in his mouth measuring disputed throws at quoits.

Apropos to the Boston Immortals — Clarence King told me he had dined with them in the seventies and Longfellow, inquiring after Bret Harte, asked if he were a ' gen i us.' — 'Why, Mr. Longfellow,' said King, 'I didn't know there was a three-syllabled genius in the country outside of Massachusetts.' Upon which the gloom of offended Saturn fell upon the company, and even Dr. Holmes didn't dare to laugh, but came privately afterwards and pressed his hand....[1]

To Elizabeth Chanler

December 16, 1896

... I say I want you to write how the Emerson strikes you — abuse is as welcome as commendation — just how it strikes you. For myself I am unable to tell what it is like in the least — and would like to forget it and pick it up and see how it sounds. It seems to me chiefly rapid, the rapidest thing I ever read, like somebody playing too fast on the piano, and like catching glimpses out of a train window — too quick. It is so strange to find this outcome. It seems like a thing written rapidly, yet I sweated and trudged over it. It seemed as if I were making the solidest, dullest, most accurate brief-like statement, very ponderous, very reasoned out, rather heavy. These illusions about what one does are strange. You try to make brandy and you make currant

---

[1] This is one of the few bits in Chapman's letters which he turned to account for print. See the essay, 'Julia Ward Howe,' in *Memories and Milestones*, page 242.

wine — light volatile eau de Cologne, instead of vitriol. The second part which comes out next month, February, has not been cut down nor expunged. This whole world is so much a world of compromise — of being persuaded to qualify, to modify, to mitigate — just not to say the thing you want to say that I simply can't believe that I shall actually be permitted by Providence to print these things just as they stand — though I have the proof which the editor has gone over and on which he painstakingly made some admirable corrections. It is a little longer than the first half. The only two people who have seen it except Mrs. Whitman, i.e., Mrs. Dorr and Agnes Irwin, have deprecated its publication — thought it 'unnecessary' — for 'my own sake.' That last suggestion the time-honored plea — merely because I don't worship at the New England shrine. You see all the writing of this country has been done by New Englanders and they are unconsciously accustomed to incense burning, fumes of self-appreciation, throughout any book touching on New England. It seems sacrilege to omit these fumes. I have just read over the proof and some of it seems incoherent. It will require more work.

To Thomas W. Ward

56 WALL ST., *Jan.* 2, 1897

MY DEAR MR. WARD

I send you the enclosed scrap which has just been sent to me to show you what I expected. I want you to send it back to me because I begin to see that I am going to have some fun and I shall collect the scraps. If this first part 'draws' the old Concord fellows, the second part will throw them into convulsions. I didn't mean to imply in my last note that Mrs. Dorr disapproved the whole of the second half but only certain passages.

Now I may say I am certain that the second part will in many ways be unsympathetic to you, but if you will try to take it on a purely intellectual basis (which is asking a good deal considering it's about your personal friends) — why, I'll try to do the same at the age 80 when I read the essay of some young smart fellow. It distresses me extremely not to find a single person of the older generation who isn't horrified by the younger generation's conduct in attacking tradition — irreverently destroying old sentiments. The very radicals of the last age seem to think they are to be the last radicals — the last chartered iconoclasts — and that what they leave is to last forever. Now I expect you to disagree with what I say and not to like me for it — but don't destroy my illusions. I want to find someone on the earth so intelligent that he welcomes opinions which he condemns — I want to be this kind of a man and I want to have known this kind of a man. It is strange that local prejudices, or rather time and era-prejudices, are stronger to divide people than identity of spirit is to unite them. Thus the kicking spirits and protesters of each age are at odds with each other about trifles — when they ought to be in sympathy. I know you didn't bargain for all this when you wrote your note but it is too late to apologize.

Sincerely yours

JOHN JAY CHAPMAN

To Elizabeth Chanler

56 WALL STREET
NEW YORK, Jan. 19, 1897

I hope you are not in the plague district — I don't like your going to the Continent at all. I suppose you think your letters of introduction will protect you from the plagues of God. Don't trust to such things. Put not thy faith in Indian Princes. Minna has had a horrid siege — a week of high fever, a week of low fever, now recovery, and all absolute immobility — enough in itself to give her fever. She is doing well, eats and sleeps well, but still can't be moved till the clot of blood has been thoroughly absorbed....

My general impression is that the Emerson paper is a ten strike. The second part comes out in a day or two. I have had some letters from Emerson's old friends who say it is the Emerson of their youth, and several from Mr. Cabot, his biographer and lifelong friend, mostly flattering, and one man, Thom. Ward, really spoke of the literary value of it in a way to turn my head. Said no such historical sketch — so few words, so true — had ever been done here. *No* one could write so — that it was Montaigne and Montesquieu rolled into one — that it would be read forever — for the light it throws on the times. How had I written it? When — in what way? He thought I had been visited by the muse of History, etc. Some of it he thought grossly inferior — the part (of course) which I thought important, and wanted me to leave it out — destroy the *Atlantic* or defer for six months but not mar the essay with such passages. It was too late, and I'm glad it was, for I wanted those passages just as they were. I give you the best account I can to cheer you. You will find me Plutarch, Thucydides, John Fiske, and Macaulay all in one. The best fun has been to see the way people took it — and that is beginning, for you'll see by the text I send you of the concluding part it will not be sympathetic to a large number of people. It will raise a protest.

Naturally we haven't seen many people for the last month. I wish we could, for Minna needs to see people. If I had time I could give you a funny account of petty politics — of Henry, Dan W., and LaFarge trying to sit on my dinner club and doubting whether they could come — poor waifs, they have not enterprise nor acquaintance enough to start one of their own and will be blown into my dining room next Saturday for all their protests. . . .

To his Mother
[*When Chapman's wife died in January,* 1897, *his mother was in Europe. The following sentences were taken from a letter addressed to her there*]

325 W. 82, *January* 27, 1897

Minna's death came quite suddenly when she was supposed almost to have turned the corner of recovery. . . . The children are all extremely well. The small baby . . . is by far the strongest baby I have ever seen. . . . I do not want you to come home. My whole idea is to have as little change as possible made in everything. I have not got farther than that at present. The family and all Minna's and my friends have done what mortals could do, and are taking care of me. . . .

IV

Noontide to Darkness
1897–1905

THE plight of Chapman, the widower with three children, of ages ranging from six years down to one month, suddenly bereft as both he and they found themselves, wrung the hearts of his friends. What he meant to them, which was much, they also meant to him, and it was they, joining their forces with a force within himself, who sent him undefeated on his way. Among these the young women of his circle played an important part.

The names of Lockwood, Dunham, and Chanler over a number of letters in the preceding pages speak for three households in New York to which, in the loneliness preceding his marriage and through the months of 1894 and 1895 while his wife and two children were in Italy, he was a frequent visitor. The two Lockwood sisters, with their mother, and the three Dunham sisters, were of a circle in which Chapman could count on the sympathy and understanding of lifelong intimates. With the Chanler family his closest friendship did not begin until the winter of 1894–95. Here too there were three sisters, Elizabeth, Margaret (later Mrs. Richard Aldrich), and Alida (later Mrs. C. Temple Emmet). There were also five brothers,[1] young men of extraordinary spirit and gifts, whose exploits at home and abroad in art and exploration, in politics, society, and affairs, would furnish forth

---

[1] Their names were John Armstrong (who changed his surname to Chaloner), Winthrop Astor, William Astor, Lewis Stuyvesant and Robert Winthrop.

an exciting narration. Their father was John Winthrop Chanler, a Democratic Member of Congress from New York in the sixties, and their mother, Margaret Astor Ward, whose mother, Mrs. Samuel Ward, was a granddaughter of the first John Jacob Astor. Mrs. Chanler died in 1875, and her husband only two years later. The oldest daughter (and third child), Elizabeth, had grown, by the nineties, into the feminine head of the household. Her physical strength had been slender since childhood, and the older cousin, Miss Marshall, chosen by the father of this large family to care for the children after their mother's death, had brought her up to believe that she must never marry. There were, however, many lessons taught by Miss Marshall which she never unlearned — the basic lessons of character and its development through a strong religious faith. To these were added the demands of a four-square accuracy of mind, and of a controlling preoccupation with fundamental sincerity.

The experience of schooling in England, and of society in London, New York, and Newport bestowed an outward grace of the sophisticated world. Her delicate beauty bore a close relation to the distinction of mind and spirit within. The family life was of the gayest, whether in the houses successively occupied in New York or at the country place of 'Rokeby' at Barrytown on the Hudson, where the Chanlers and their forbears had long been established among the 'River families.' The free play of intelligence, mirth, candor, and seriousness, made the household peculiarly attractive to one of Chapman's temperament and gifts, and all that he had to offer in return rendered him a welcome family friend.

When his wife returned from Italy in May of 1895, the sisters that Chapman had come to know so well became, more than ever before, her friends also. He was bound that there should be no misapprehension of relationships in any direction and, with the knockdown frankness of which he was capable, had said to Elizabeth Chanler, 'Remember, you are nothing but a sick kitten I am bringing to Minna in a basket.'

But the two women instantly began to fill a large place each in the life of the other, and after visiting the Chanlers at Rokeby in the first month of reunion Minna Chapman wrote to Elizabeth Chanler of 'the blessed reception in your hearts' with which she had met: 'Blessed, lovely sisters, I love you well.' The intimacy with Elizabeth Chanler ripened most of all, and became, for her and the Chapmans, a relation of uniting affection. The fruit of it was that when, at Minna Chapman's sudden death, there fell upon the desolate father and his three children the deepest of human needs, the rare sympathy of heart and mind into which Chapman and Elizabeth Chanler had already entered soon proved the very blessing of his existence. She was in India with her sister Margaret when they received the appalling news of Mrs. Chapman's death. They returned to New York in April, 1897, when Elizabeth Chanler and Chapman were soon to face the fact that she was to enter the vacant place in his life, and his children's. What they could not have foreseen at the time was that she would fortify and fulfil him, in mind and spirit for all his remaining days. The sentiment of pity — for her limitations of physical strength and for what he called her 'motherlessness' — had colored his first feeling for her, and now her pity for him came forth to meet it. But there was so much more, in spiritual and intellectual sympathies, in a grateful masculine dependence on a rare feminine balance and clarity of vision, that their friends would have been glad to know sooner than they did what lay in store for them both.

They were not married until April 23, 1898. Their intention to become man and wife had seemed to them so strictly their own affair that they avoided much appearance together, and would meet in such places immune from observation as a Paulist church on Tenth Avenue in New York. The humor of these precautions sometimes overcame Chapman, as when he accused Miss Chanler of indulging herself in the romanticism of youth 'that loves mystery and clandestine meetings,' and declared, 'You shall have all the fun of it. I'll wear a

Photograph by H. L. Mendelssohn

ELIZABETH CHANLER

cloak and give the countersign, evade the eyes of hotel clerks, pass you in public, and leap through your casement to the sound of twangling instruments.' Through all this period the thought of the beloved Minna was never far from their minds, and in a letter of May, 1897, Chapman wrote: 'Joy, Elizabeth, nothing but joy and happiness shall there be for those who come within reach. I resolved that when Minna died. It is the only thought to meet life with. There is no one shall take death as back setting and despair, not one moment of it. If I have any grief it is that I should not before her death and always have seen this light and given it to her instead of my worry and cloudiness over the world. She should have had this. That is the only grief. I say we must bring a full measure to every man we meet pressed down and flowing over.' Only a fortnight earlier he had written, apropos of an address he was about to deliver: 'I am lost without Minna in these things and have only the memory of her criticisms to go by, but I have it with a certainty, like a conviction. I envy all success for myself and am jealous of it. It should have belonged to her. I don't want it except for her. It's within my reach — what I wanted — and it belongs to her.'

During the summer of 1897 Chapman established his children in a small hotel at Saunderstown, Rhode Island, near his friends the Lockwoods, and under the same roof with Mrs. Adolph Borie, of Philadelphia, and her two daughters. These ladies showered his little family with kindnesses. The Chanlers were in Newport, and there were frequent meetings with the oldest daughter. It was a summer, besides, in which Chapman expressed himself abundantly in verse. There was gratitude for what had gone before, and there was the mood of solitude, finding expression in such lines as these:

> Bear your sorrows into the fields —
> Sympathy their silence yields
> Deeper than mankind can give thee

> For they know not and they care not,
> And they pry not and they stare not,
> But with green religion growing,
> Their unconsciousness bestowing,
> Carelessly accept, receive thee.

A series of 'Sonnets to Elizabeth,' addressed to the woman he was yet to marry, transcended their immediate occasion, and must take their place in any complete view of him who made them. It mattered not that only a few years had passed since he likened the writing of any sonnets in English to an Englishman trying to say his prayers in French. It was consistent with his inconsistency that in practice he should discard his theory. Let two of the sequence speak for the beauty of the entire nine:

> The universe is newly recreated
> Whenever Love gives us new eyes for seeing;
> And all of life must then again be stated
> In the fresh language of the newer being;
>
> And all of books must be re-read with passion
> And all of thought must be re-thought with feeling;
> For the New Spirit doth the outworn fashion
> Touch and transform in his transcendent dealing.
>
> And old, sad closets closed up long ago
> Are opened, and behold our newest care,
> Garments that with immaculate freshness glow
> Because the power of love has kept them there.
>
> Rehearse then, loved one, all of life with me
> And don these garments kept so sacredly.
>
> If all the love I send thee were made known
> And all the world were called upon to note;
> If every word I spoke were written down
> And every line were printed that I wrote;
>
> Nay, further, — if unholy curious eyes
> Should ravin every corner of the scroll,
> Probe undecypherable mysteries
> And catalogue the contents of my soul;

> And if each indiscriminate pillager
> Were let to rummage to his heart's content,
> The loving one to find his forage there,
> The cynic to piece out his argument;
>
> So but thy name untouchable remained,
> That sack would leave the shrine all unprofaned.

The marriage of Chapman and Elizabeth Chanler would have been deferred even beyond its actual date but for the Spanish War, in which her sister Margaret took immediate part as a nurse, and her brothers Winthrop and William in active service in Cuba. Each of these had known what was impending, and each proceeded to the front the better satisfied that their sister was entering at the same time upon a honeymoon at Rokeby.

More than a year before this marriage, Chapman had begun the foray into political journalism mentioned in the preceding chapter. The first issue of his small periodical, the *Nursery*, later *The Political Nursery*, was dated March, 1897. It continued, at intervals of a month or more, until January, 1901. There were thirty-six issues in all, besides two supplements. Chapman was the chief, though not the sole, contributor to its pages, usually four to a number. Not until its title became *The Political Nursery*, in October, 1898, did Chapman's name appear as editor, as it did thenceforth, with the names of his friends Isaac H. Klein as manager and Boudinot Keith as publisher. The contributions almost invariably were unsigned, except in the first few issues, when such nursery pseudonyms as 'Georgie,' 'Willie,' 'Aunt Serena,' and 'Silly Sally' were used. No disguises, however, suppressed the internal evidence that its publication was primarily a vehicle for Chapman's personal views. In sending the earliest issues to his mother, abroad, he called it 'an irregular periodical for which I get the credit,' and proceeded: 'It's anonymous and I deny all knowledge of it in any shape or form, at all times, now and hereafter. So I only send it to you to show the sort of thing people think I do. — This

131

town is so sunk in ignorance and apathy that my friends *don't think the Nursery clever*. I mean my little social friends and first cousins. It seems to me just most terribly clever, and if it can be kept up to anything like this standard it'll become famous. Don't say anything about this to anyone, or that I sent it to you, for the anonymity is useful.'

The motto of the *Nursery* from beginning to end was, 'Let break what must break, we shall soon see the way.' The purpose of the journal was frankly announced in its first issue. 'The object of the *Nursery* is to tell the truth. There is no publication at present which seems to cover this exact field. Truth is best seen by the light of example, hence the *Nursery* does not shun personalities, when they are in point. Written contributions will be considered if sincere and short. Cash contributions will not be returned. *Nursery* will be published so long as the demand for truth exceeds the supply.' (This would surely have been more than four years but for the impending break in Chapman's health.) It was announced a little later that 'Future issues are not promised, but may be expected,' and that 'Persons who desire to risk a dollar on a year's subscription may address "The Nursery, P.O. Box 1750, New York City."'

These were not the terms on which most periodicals are conducted, but they departed from the normal less than the reading matter they heralded. When Chapman came to write his 'Practical Agitation,' and to rationalize some of his pamphleteering methods he declared, 'there is no such thing as an abstract truth. You must talk facts, you must name names, you must impute motives. You must say what is in your mind. It is the only means you have of cutting yourself free from the body of this death. Innuendo will not do. Nobody minds innuendo.' Elsewhere in the same book, he wrote, 'We shall not note the increase of virtue so much by seeing more crooks in Sing Sing, as by seeing fewer of them in the drawing-rooms.' These were the principles and objects that controlled his writing for the *Nursery*.

Only eight of its issues appeared before the end of 1897. From the very first it was obviously no respecter of persons. In its second issue Seth Low, with whom Chapman had once worked in harmony, was held up to scorn for a desertion of principle, and the antagonism between the two leading editors in New York at the time, was explained on the ground that 'Each is the *sort of hypocrite* the other most despises. The narrow and good Godkin hates the smiling devil — the frank hypocrite. The cultivated and cynical Dana hates the white choker — the canting hypocrite. In hating Dana so insanely Godkin shows a certain lack of humor, and it is this very lack of humor which exasperates Dana and unhinges his mind.' (Who does not remember that in these years the *Sun* was reputed to make vice attractive in the morning only for the *Post* to render virtue unattractive at night?) When a daily paper reported that the *Nursery* had been removed from the files of the Chamber of Commerce, the fact was celebrated in lines of impudent pleasure, introducing such respectable names as Godkin, Low, Beaman, and Hewitt, and ending with none too reverent gratitude to the *Nursery*'s defender, Bishop Potter.

> Then sleek as an otter rose Henry C. Potter,
> And smiled with the smile of his race.
> 'My friends,' he said calmly, 'I reckon you've gotter
> Accept with your usual grace
> The *altered conditions*, for signs of the times
> May sometimes be read in the ribaldest rhymes,
> And seen in the silliest face.'

When Theodore Roosevelt gave up his work as Police Commissioner, the *Nursery* commended the result of his service in the past, and proceeded: 'He was false to his character as a fighter only in this, that he threw up the sponge eight months before time was called, and left the field to the knave who betrayed him and the fool who opposed him. We will not accept from Theodore Roosevelt the excuse for not staying of "cui bono." His departure was the cowardly act of a brave man.' Two years earlier Roosevelt and Chapman had differed sharply on the Good Government Campaign and other matters. Roosevelt had written to him, 'O heavens on earth! You are the most delightful but the most puzzling piece of humanity with which I have ever come into contact'; and Chapman had written to his wife in Italy, on a special grievance against T.R., 'If it had been any other man than Roosevelt I should have let it slide as a trifle, but I remembered that I was going to live thirty years in this town with Roosevelt, and the only way with such a man is to be right behind him with a club.... He is muddle-headed.' In the second year of the *Nursery's* existence (1898) the two men, as we shall soon see, came into more serious conflict.

By the spring of 1898 the *Nursery* was in full swing. Through 1898 nine numbers were issued, chiefly at intervals of two months. The tone of the little journal was obviously pitched to provoke irritation and dissent in the circle to which Chapman himself belonged. In the March (1898) issue, for example, there was an article, headed 'Mr. Morgan,' exquisitely suited to this purpose. In the next issue (June, 1898), apropos of Charles Eliot Norton's disapproval of the Spanish War, came an irreverent blast against that former teacher of his — 'a phenomenon of great interest: a man born blind with the religion of pictures, a deaf man worshipping music, a man devoid of sensuous experience erecting altars to the Aesthetic.' The article was attributed to the *Worcester Evening Gazette*, but the hand that wrote it was manifestly the hand of Chapman — a younger, more abusive hand than that which produced some years later, in quite another vein, the 'Charles Eliot Norton' chapter in 'Memories and Milestones.' He could then write of Norton that 'at the age of eighty he was plainly nothing else than a darling old saint, with a few sophistical hobbies which, if you went to see him, he drew from his cabinet and showed you with glee — old philosophical gimcracks. These things you perceived at once to be of no importance; while the man himself was everything.'

A similar contrast might be drawn between his earlier and later expressions touching President Eliot of Harvard. In 'Memories and Milestones' he appears in a mellow light as 'one of the great figureheads of the age.' In the *Political Nursery* of February, 1900, the reader was invited to 'bend down and look through the peep-hole into this man's mind, and the whole world looks like a toy village, lighted by Arctic moonlight.' Such instances might be multiplied indefinitely — besides many that represented opinions which did not change. Of these there was none more striking than the poem, 'Bismarck' in the 'Midsummer Supplement' to the *Nursery*, 1898, beginning

> At midnight, Death dismissed the chancellor,
> But left the soul of Bismarck on his face.
> Titanic, in the peace and power of bronze,
> With three red roses loosely in his grasp,
> Lies the Constructor,

and proceeding into such lines, prophetic of Chapman's feeling twenty years later, as these:

> The age is just beginning, yet we see
> The fruits of hatred ripen hourly
> And Germany's in bondage — muzzled press —
> The private mind suppressed, while shade on shade
> Is darkening o'er the intellectual sky.
> And world-forgotten, outworn crimes and cries
> With dungeon tongue accost the citizen
> And send him trembling to his family.
>
> Organized hatred. Educated men
> Live in habitual scorn of intellect,
> Hate France, hate England, hate America.
> Talk corporals, talk until Napoleon
> (— Who never could subdue the mind of France)
> Seems like some harmless passing episode,
> Unable to reveal to modern man
> What tyranny could compass. Years of this
> Will leave a Germany devoid of fire,
> Unlettered, unrebellious, impotent,
> Nursing the name of German unity

And doing pilgrimage to Bismarck's shrine,
Bismarck the god, who having but one thought,
Wrote it out largely over Germany
But could not stay to read it. Those who can,
Who reap the crop he sowed may count the grains
And every seed a scourge. For on the heart
One or a million, each envenomed throb
Relentlessly records an injury,
While the encrusted nation loses health,
And like a chemical experiment
The crucible gives back its qualities.

The Spanish War, the Philippine question, the Boer War afforded frequent opportunities from 1898 onward for Chapman to express himself with vehemence against the governments of both America and England. Some of the heresies he uttered seem now the truths it would have been wisdom to follow. Before the *Political Nursery* came to its end, its scope was extended beyond local and national politics to include papers on new books by William James and Münsterberg, or philosophic questions which they raised, besides an admirable address of Chapman's own on 'The Doctrine of Non-Resistance,' which found its way later into his 'Learning and Other Essays' (1910). Chapman's article on 'The Will to Believe' was neither more nor less impudent than the letters we shall find him writing to William James. He had small patience with philosophers as such, and less with those who were beginning to be called psychologists. Some years later he wrote, apropos of Josiah Royce: 'There is no such thing as philosophy. But there are such things as philosophers. A philosopher is a man who believes there is such a thing as philosophy, and who devotes himself to proving it. He believes that behind the multifarious, contradictory, and often very unpleasant appearances of the world there is a unity which he can put into typewriting. Probably there is, but certainly he can't.' [1] In the *Political Nursery* for November, 1899, he wrote: 'If Mr. Münsterberg or anyone else will sit

[1] See 'Portrait of Josiah Royce, the Philosopher,' *The Outlook*, July 2, 1919.

down and write an account of the universe without using any words that begin with phy- and psy-, or end with -ology and -istic, it will be the best bit of mental training that ever befell him. Münsterberg is just the man to try it.'

Of the *Nursery* in general it may be said that in its pages the essential Chapman first revealed himself to a larger circle than that of his friends as a vehicle of vigorous thought and expression in the field of current affairs. Owen Wister has classified him with the zealots, who are 'at once impracticable and invaluable.' Here, indeed, is the very antinomy suggested by Chapman himself when he wrote, 'It's an accident when I *do* right, but I *am* right.' He was not only right, but among the pioneers of clear vision, in ascribing the low estate of party government in the United States to the dominance of business and money. It would be impossible to modernize many passages in his writings of forty years ago.

The paper on Non-Resistance had set forth Chapman's disillusion with respect to political reform. The phrase 'Resist not evil' seemed to illustrate his predicament, and he came to the conclusion that 'it was a mistake to try to induce others to act. The thing to do was to act myself, alone and directly, and without waiting for help.' He was in fact soon to fight shy of organized movements until the end of his days. The second half of the paper is concerned, in searching simplicity, with the teachings of Christ, and strikes a note to which Chapman's thought and writing were so often to revert that it became definitely a characteristic note.

The disillusion to which reference has just been made was related closely to an episode in the career of Theodore Roosevelt. In Roosevelt's 'Autobiography' and in the books about him the complications attending his candidacy for the governorship of New York in 1898, while the laurels of the Spanish War were still fresh on his brow, are represented as rising chiefly from a question of eligibility, on the score of non-residence. Elihu Root dealt with this matter to the requisite satisfaction of the Republican State Convention at its meeting to nominate a governor. Another complication was cleared away to Roosevelt's satisfaction, and Chapman's intense disgust, only a few days earlier. It is very much a part of Chapman's record, and should hardly be omitted from Roosevelt's.

The story, in bare outline, is this. A group of Independents, among whom Chapman bore a leading part, wished to nominate Roosevelt for the governorship of New York. In the September (1898) issue of the *Nursery* there were two articles 'The Governorship' and 'The Rough Riders,' the first of which began thus: 'Now for a State ticket with Roosevelt at the head, and decent men from both parties behind him, men known to the whole state if possible, unknown men if necessary, honest men in any case.... He is to be the instrument of the citizen destroying the Boss.'

To accomplish this purpose Chapman and Isaac H. Klein visited Roosevelt at Montauk Point on August 24, and laid the matter before him. There was a second conference on September 1. Roosevelt agreed to run on the Independent ticket. Then the regular Republican nomination was also offered to him. He would have been willing to run on both tickets, and to this the Independents did not object. But Senator Platt, the Republican Boss, did, and at his insistence Roosevelt withdrew his acceptance of the Independent nomination. There was much anguish of spirit on both sides. When Roosevelt's decision was made, the *Political Nursery* — expanding its title for the first time from the *Nursery* — contained an article, in its issue of October 17, 1898, entitled 'The Catastrophe,' and beginning thus: 'No matter how long Roosevelt lives or what he does, he can never again furnish such a terrible example of the powers of the boss as he did when he refused to allow his fellow-citizens to vote for him except on the Platt ticket.' After Roosevelt had been more than a year in office Chapman was still unappeased, for the June, 1900, *Political Nursery* published an article in which nobody but the editor could have written these words:

'Perhaps some old friend of his, by rummaging with a strong arm in him, could find the original Theodore Roosevelt, or put together the broken pieces that once gave the thought and made the world believe that there was such a man. But the chances are that you might, with as much hope, grope in a tree for the sapling.'

Such were Chapman's immediate feelings, and such in brief is the story. Further details would so impede the progress of this narrative that, for the benefit of those who would explore a by-path of political history, some of them may be found in an Appendix.[1] Here, however, are two contemporaneous letters written by Chapman to his wife on the very eve of the final rupture between Roosevelt and his would-be supporters:

42 E. 23. *Sept.* 24, 1898

... Roosevelt met us last night at City Club and two hours talk. Fuller and I met him this morning and had an hour's talk with him. The situation is severe, but there is nothing that has not been said — no point not covered. My own mind has become very clear. I want to save Roosevelt, and I believe it can be done. He hadn't an idea of the forces he was to encounter. ...

The resource remains to get Roosevelt to let us lay the matter before friends of his — politicians or otherwise in whom he has confidence. They would see his ruin clearer than he can himself. At any rate, the more desperate the situation, the heavier and stronger we will lay on. You will say why do it. The reason is that Roosevelt is a boy — a child — he is honest — spite of all he is honest. He thinks he didn't understand — he really thinks so.

A mere collocation of the correspondence without a word of comment would damn him. And yet if you talk to him you see he didn't listen when I talked. Remind him of my words and he agrees I said them — 'but Jack will say anything — Why, Jack said — "My dear fellow, can't you see that if you let us go on now as a practical matter you can never stop us hereafter."' He quoted that last night. Show him his letter to Tucker indorsing an address — he says he glanced at it —

[1] See Appendix A, p. 465.

but didn't understand. And yet he is good — by Jove, you can't help saying he is good. Of course half of our men say he deceives himself, he *did* understand — he did commit us, and let us go ahead. Each man judges him with a different shade of meaning. I see in him only a very muddleheaded and at the same time pigheaded young man, who needs to be shoved right at this crucial point....

Sept. 25, 1898

Last night I went down to Oyster Bay at 4 P.M. and by some cross purpose Roosevelt stayed here and had his final interview. He came out to O.B. by a late train and I saw him this morning. Our personal relations I won't say are unchanged — but are friendly. I had a long quiet talk with him. Yesterday in N.Y. at his house Klein talked to him for an hour. He cried like a baby — I don't mean in a babyish way. They say that last night — he could hardly walk when he left, and that Fulton Cutting (if you know Fulton Cutting, you'll see how remarkable this is) dismissed him like a French noble dismissing a lacquey. A great big Jew called Seligsberg, whom [*sic*] I didn't think had much dramatic taste, told me it was the most terrible thing he ever saw. 'Mr. Roosevelt, I don't think we need discuss the matter further.' The poor fellow is broken up, I am afraid. Our address of explanation has been divested of every possible sentiment, and made as nice as we could make it. The documents in support of it are really very strong, and the more interviews we had with R. the more our men began to think ill of him — for he backed and filled. He was rattled — thinking of himself — last night they say he was threatening, etc.

He is a baby and, with eight of the best heads in town against him, no wonder he broke. A man like Roosevelt is competent for a million if he has been *quite* straight. But if he hasn't been *quite* straight and begins to use his wits and make a case, he's lost. That's the fact, I'm afraid. He cannot be such a fool as he makes out, and then one reflects what sort of politics he has lived his life in, and his belief in compromise and expediency and the impossibility in actual life of distinguishing expediency and compromise from ways that are a shadow of a shade off straight. I begin to think ill of him myself. In all the politics I have ever known compromise means change of faith. At any rate he's off all our minds and we go *en masse* to

Albany at 8 tomorrow, Monday, and I'll come to Rokeby as soon as I can get away from there.

JACK

That this should come out of the war record, and San Juan Hill, and right on top of it — that I should be the instrument of it — that I couldn't have done it if I hadn't misjudged him, thought more of him than he is, tried to make *somebody else*, out of him, is very strange.

Nearly twenty years later, when Quentin Roosevelt died the aviator's death in France which Victor Chapman had died two years before, their fathers came together in the sympathy of a common loss. When Roosevelt himself died, early in 1919, Chapman celebrated him in verse as the savior of Paris, through his trumpet-calls for preparedness. Before the end of that year he committed to writing his remembrances of the Independent campaign of 1898. Time had tempered the bitterness of his feeling. Roosevelt had passed into history, and the following pages shed upon the story that has just been told a fresh light of retrospect.

(Memorandum by J. J. Chapman)

December 21, 1919

I confess that in handing to the future historian a key to some of these shadows in Roosevelt, I am somewhat actuated by malice and the rancors of a personal experience, long since survived and yet of which embers still burn in me. It gives me pleasure — I say it without shame, though perhaps I ought to be ashamed — I find that it gives me pleasure in reading Roosevelt's letters to find on him here and there the marks of my claws.

Roosevelt on Mugwumps
  'Lecky was thinking of the people analogous to our mugwumps; the people who actually pride themselves on a fantastic and visionary morality, utterly unbalanced by common sense; the people who attracted the scorn of Macaulay's eminently sane and healthy mind.' (T. R. to [Sir G. O.] Trevelyan, Sept. 1905. Scribner's Mag. for Oct. 1919, p. 393.)
  'It is of course easy for the mugwump or goo-goo who has no knowledge whatever of public affairs to say that the proper

thing is to refuse to deal with such men or pay any heed to such considerations.' I.e. meeting demands of party heeler, etc. (T.R. to Trevelyan, May 13, 1905; ditto p. 392.)

This testy condemnation of the idealist as an enemy to society was never far from Roosevelt's thought, and cropped out in his conversation. A philosopher might wonder why the man whose whole life was one long fight for righteousness should feel harshly towards men of any sort for being inexpediently, rashly, and ignorantly righteous — fools of idealism and mere prophetic agitators. One would think that such persons might be commiserated but must certainly be approved by the standard-bearer of righteousness. In this world, however, things work out differently, and the Prophet is always the enemy of the King.

The attitude of Roosevelt towards the idealists grew out of an episode which was extremely simple in its setting, yet the elements of it went to the essence of democratic politics. When Roosevelt came back from Cuba, he came back as a hero. I shall never forget the lustre that shone about him; for I went to see him at Montauk Point, and my companion accused me of being in love with him, and indeed I was. I never before nor since have felt that glorious touch of hero-worship which solves life's problems by showing you a man. Lo, there, it says, Behold the way! You have only to worship, trust, and support him. He was of course the obvious Republican candidate for the Governorship of New York, and the election was imminent, but he had not yet been named by his party.

The Republican party in the State was in bad hands. It was ruled by a cabal of politicians and had lost the confidence of the public. In the meanwhile there had grown up in New York City a group of very theoretical reformers (popularly called Goo-Goos, because of their Good Government Clubs) who in studying Tammany Hall had come to see that Tammany in the city and the Republican cabal at Albany were parts of a single machine, and that the only way to point this out and educate the public was to run independent candidates, sacrifice-candidates if necessary.

These theoretic persons now decided to widen their scope, enter state politics and strike a blow at the Republican cabal. Their method was as follows: — Roosevelt was to be nominated for governor by petition, and as an Independent. His nomination by the Republicans was a foregone conclusion.

Thus he would appear on two tickets. But — here was the venom of the idea — he would poll such a large vote on the Independent ticket that the Republican party could not claim his glory. The whole plan was a blow aimed at the Republican cabal.

I explained this to Roosevelt, as it were with diagrams. I told him that the reform group was not nominating him because they loved him, but because they desired to make use of him. I said that all we asked of him was that if he rejected the proposition he should reject it at that moment, — i.e. not take our nomination and then later throw us down by withdrawing from the ticket. Well, he allowed us to make the nomination, and then, very shortly before election day — he resigned from the ticket. In this way he had got the benefit of a non-partisan send off. Our ticket staggered, but was kept in the field. It was saved through the almost algebraic idealism, and certainly very mistaken, impolitic, ignorant, vicious, unwise, political heroism of Theodore Bacon of Rochester, a lawyer of note, and an upstate Goo-Goo, who allowed his name to be used that at least the shadow of a non-partisan movement might be seen in our state politics.

The Goo-Goos' relations with Roosevelt did not come to a break in a moment. Two weeks of interviews, explanations, and recriminations preceded the rupture. I spent the night at Oyster Bay on the day the axe fell; for it fell after I left the city, and there was no train back that evening. The reader will imagine that it was not a pleasant evening; for I was not going home leaving any mist or misunderstandings in the air as to how the Good Government Club group viewed the situation. But I went further. I unloaded the philosophy of agitation upon Roosevelt and pictured him as the broken backed half-good man, the successor of the doughface and Northern man with Southern principles of Civil War times, the trimmer who wouldn't break with his party and so, morally speaking, it ended by breaking him. He received all this with a courtesy, deference, and self-control that were absolutely marvellous. I never expect to see such an exhibition of good breeding as Roosevelt gave that night. We shook hands the next morning at parting, and avoided each other for twenty years.

But Roosevelt never afterwards told the truth about the episode. He persuaded himself that he hadn't understood my original proposition — whereas he had understood it; only events had caused him to change his mind as to the expediency of it.

Of course the memory of all great politicians is their weak point. There is a story about Nicholas Murray Butler which illustrates this. 'They tell me,' said he, 'that all college presidents lie. Why, they said this about me, — and they *proved* it too!'

Our little campaign for Theodore Bacon as Governor was amusing but fatiguing and was colored, I regret to say, with acrimonious literature. Both the great parties of course desired to suppress the news that there was any such candidate as ours in the field and they succeeded.

The best advertising we got was through Roosevelt's denunciation of our conduct as idiotic and subversive. There was really nothing either foolish or even novel in the Goo-Goo undertaking: to run independent candidates is the proper mode of injecting new ideas into politics: witness the Prohibitionists. Roosevelt was at this time so benighted a partisan that he would not allow his name to be voted for by independent men. He withdrew his name under circumstances where it was to my mind dishonorable to do so, because he had taken the benefit of the nomination.

The Club world, however, of New York soon got news of the misunderstanding between Roosevelt and the Goo-Goos v. Roosevelt. It was at that time that I joined the Ananias Club. The Goo-Goos' ticket suffered yet another calamity. George E. Waring, Jr., a popular and noble figure was our candidate for, I think, State Engineer. He wrote to Roosevelt at the inception of our movement, an enthusiastic letter expressing the hero-worship which every one of us felt. After Roosevelt's withdrawal I went into the City Club one evening and found Waring, — in a rage, of course. He shewed me a copy of a denunciatory letter which he said he had sent to Roosevelt, a copy afterwards found among Waring's papers, for Waring died before election day, leaving a halo above his name. On the Saturday before election day Roosevelt's campaign committee republished Waring's original letter in praise of Roosevelt.

Such things as this happen in all politics. They are the woof and web of which political life is made, and no one is to blame for them. In reality no one knows just how they are done or who is responsible, and the inner animosities, death-blows, and knifings, the interplay of action good and bad, passes so rapidly that there's no tribunal that can ever discover or weigh them. They exist in a fog and a welter. It was out of this fog that Roosevelt beamed.

His was a mind that consumed its own smoke. He could do the most desperate things in the way of putting a friend down a well and shine on the world like Phoebus the morning afterwards. His genius, his personal power, was so very great that it polarized the minds of all who saw much of him. He was surrounded by adulators. I doubt whether he had a true friend, for his friends were dazed by him. One had to avoid the subject with them, and thus they became a glamorous circle of myth-worshippers, a sort of body-guard of non-conductors. Criticism couldn't get through them to the man. Roosevelt lived on earth in an apotheosis, flaming swords surrounded him always. One reason for this was the extreme ignorance about political matters in which his social friends were born and brought up. Whatever he said became their political gospel. If he said, 'I must obey the Bosses in regard to the sewage question,' they shouted, 'Of course! You must. The idealists who wish you to defy Tom Platt in the sewer question are meddling idiots.' If he said, 'I shall break with the Bosses in regard to the Hospitals,' they exclaimed, 'Galahad, Jack the Giant Killer, George and the Dragon!' As Roosevelt's social circle widened and melted into the grand public as a sort of metaphysical cult, the alternate anathemas and hallelujas remained the same.

Roosevelt didn't really know that there was any principle at the bottom of the matter; but he did know just exactly how far he could go in each case and remain a party candidate.

I have always believed that if he had defied his party in the governorship campaign (1898) he would have become a dominant figure much earlier, though he might have suffered a defeat or two in between. But Roosevelt couldn't bear the thought of a temporary eclipse; so he kept on conciliating his party till events and his own qualities, both the best and the worst of them, threw him out of the party, and he took the position we had urged him to take in 1898. Of course it now became illogical of him to abuse the idealists, Goo-Goos, etc., but he continued the practice out of habit to the end of his life.

I have called up in this paper a few shadows out of the past in order to show the sort of limbo that engulfs political life in America, perhaps everywhere. Roosevelt passed his entire life in this welter and yet became the most vital, most interesting, most important figure of his generation. Whether it be that the makers of the picture books don't know about all this gloomy background, or are shy of depicting it I cannot say; but unless somebody paints it in, the figure of Roosevelt will lose half its permanence and all of its educational value.

This adventure in practical politics was but one out of many tests of Chapman's endurance during these exciting years. The care of his children, the approach and arrival of his second marriage, the preparation of the two books, 'Causes and Consequences' (1898) and 'Practical Agitation' (1900) which followed rapidly upon his 'Emerson and Other Essays' — all these held his emotions and his mind at a high tension. The buoyancy that marked the letters at which we have already looked continued, perhaps even increased, in those of the years immediately following 1897. His ardor for exerting a direct influence in political affairs was not yet quenched, and the two books that have just been mentioned were studies in the philosophy of American politics which, after nearly forty years, possess an astonishing vitality and appositeness to the present. Chapman never sought, or desired, political office for himself, and therefore could say with the better grace: [1] 'As soon as the reformers give up trying to be statesmen, and perceive that their function is purely educational, and that they are mere anti-slavery agitators and persons of no account whatever, they will succeed better.' In 'Practical Agitation' [2] he wrote of the anti-slavery people: 'The reason of some of them canted a little from the strain and stress; but they were so much nearer being right-minded than their contemporaries that we may claim them as respectable human beings.' It was the essential rightness in Chapman, and the vigor of it, that made him the human being he was and his writings what they were. They had their share of wrongness in unessentials,

[1] See *Causes and Consequences*, page 33.
[2] Page 53.

146

they were sometimes ill-ordered, to the manifest loss of effectiveness. But in these earliest books, as in their successors, there was a sort of lasting contemporaneousness which caused so representative a spokesman of a later day as Mr. Edmund Wilson to declare that 'perhaps no writer of his generation had dealt at once so realistically and with so much clairvoyance with the modern American world, and has in consequence so much to say to the younger generation.' Mr. Wilson has found, moreover, that these books of 1898 and 1900 'mark the turning of the tide in the open discussion of the relations between American public life and business.'[1] In one of his later books[2] Chapman wrote, 'I am saying things which will some day be thought of, rather than trying to get the attention of anyone.' Of course he would have liked immensely, early and late, to get more attention than he did, but the saying of things that would some day be thought of was after all, and constantly, his chief concern.

The distinctive quality of Chapman's writing can always be suggested much more clearly by illustration than by definition, and a passage from his 'Practical Agitation' may well be read at this point. It bears upon what Mr. Wilson has said, and, perhaps as well as any single passage may, shows forth the directness of Chapman's thinking and writing at this time. Many other passages would speak with equal force for other phases of his general subject.

> Almost every man who enters our society joins it as a young man in need of money. His instincts are unsullied, his intellect is fresh and strong, but he must live. How comes it that the country is full of maimed human beings, of cynics and feeble good men, and outside of this no form of life except the diabolical intelligence of pure business?
>
> How to make yourself needed — it is the sycophant's problem; and why should we expect a young American to act differ-

[1] See *New Republic*, May 22, 1929.
[2] *Letters and Religion*, page 90.

ently from a young Spaniard at the Court of Philip the Second?
He must get on. He goes into a law office, and if he is offended
at its dishonest practices he cannot speak. He soon accepts
them. Thereafter he cannot see them. He goes into a newspaper office, the same; a banker's, a merchant's, a dry-goods
shop. What has happened to these fellows at the end of three
years, that their minds seem to be drying up? I have seen many
men I knew in college grow more and more uninteresting from
year to year. Is there something in trade that desiccates and
flattens out, that turns men into dried leaves at the age of
forty? Certainly there is. It is not due to trade, but to intensity
of self-seeking, combined with narrowness of occupation. If
I had to make my way at the court of Queen Elizabeth, I should
need more kinds of wits and more knowledge of human nature
than in the New York button trade. No doubt I should be a
preoccupied, cringing, and odious sort of person at a feudal
festivity; but I should be a fascinating man of genius compared
to John H. Painter, who at the age of thirty is making $15,000
a year by keeping his mouth shut and attending to business.
Put a pressure gauge into Painter, and measure the business
tension at New York in 1900. He is passing his youth in a
trance over a game of skill, and thereby earning the respect
and admiration of all men. Do not blame him. The great
current of business force that passes through the port of New
York has touched him, and he is rigid. There are hundreds of
these fellows, and they make us think of the well-meaning
young man who has to support his family, and who must com-
pete against them for the confidence of his business patrons.
Our standard of commercial honesty is set by that current.
It is entirely the result of the competition that comes from
everybody's wanting to do the same thing.

The distractions of politics and authorship were of course
unfavorable to Chapman's progress at the law. He was
clearly equipped with certain gifts for that profession. But
when he wrote to his mother, in Europe, on January 5,
1898, about his professional prospects, it was evidently
without illusions or regrets: 'I am not making any money
at the law, and never shall, but I'm glad of it because the
power to see business relations and the money in them blinds
the eyes to everything else, and I doubt whether any mortal

intellect can be put to both uses at once.' His mother had different views of worldly success, and within a few weeks Chapman was writing to her again: 'I got your two delightful contradictory letters, the one telling me to go ahead and be great, and the other telling me to look out that I didn't lose money. Of course, you can't do both, and I intend to be great and lose money. But you needn't worry about it, because in the first place I have all the money I need, and in the second place I can make as much more at any moment I choose by taking the lecture platform.' In the same month he was writing to Miss Chanler: 'You ought to have heard those fellows laugh last night when I was expounding [?] that it was because of my great abilities, and *not merely* because of my honesty, that I couldn't make any money. The age makes this seem a paradox, for in the thought of the age ability = power to earn money.'

It has been seen already how he dramatized himself — 'I'm only at home on an imaginary stage.' Of the kind of part he wanted to play, an intimation appears in a letter of the summer of 1897: 'What is it about Jowett that bores me? Is it that he's always inside certain bounds, never extreme, never slops over, never tragic, never keyed beyond G natural? Is it that he *is* what you want me to be, but the Lord forbid my becoming!' At this very time he was writing again: 'I tell you the kind of man I am thrives only in romance. In real life he does murders, loves, revenges, heroisms, and crimes. He gets into places where no human agency can reach him. How much *good* is he? For business, for politics, for anything but poetry and possibly war?' As for poetry, he declares on another day that 'one needs to be a blackguard in order to write verses,' and, again, he calls himself a 'sentimental blackguard.' He realizes his own need of self-restraint, and exclaims, apropos of the *Nursery*, 'I have to keep copper hoops on myself to be merely humorous.' Restraint was difficult. About to encounter a bore he writes: 'I intend to present the surface which a circular saw presents to a pound of cheese'; and, having achieved reticence on another occasion: 'No man ought to keep his temper if it makes him feel so virtuous as I do now.' The self-scrutiny goes on, in another letter: 'I tell you what — I give you a confession. It's always been an amazement to me how I could have the horrid, ruthless, intellectual, inhuman, logical, outrageous [1] fanaticism to do the things I do.... Lord, it is act first and think afterwards. It is Emerson madness. Imagine a man taking Emerson *au pied de la lettre*. I say all wretchedness, Elizabeth, comes from thinking of ourselves. The machinery begins to destroy itself right off.'

The 'Emerson madness' was much upon him in this time before his marriage to Miss Chanler. On February 1, having completed an essay on 'Social Results of Commercialism,' which was printed in the *New York Times* [2] he wrote to her: 'The thing seems to me about this — Emerson made coherent. It's all Emerson. I should have had neither the ideas reduced so clearly nor the public to understand them if it hadn't been for Emerson. I can't imagine what I should have been if it hadn't been for Emerson. As it is, I don't think — at any rate I don't recollect any man who has had so coördinate a view of life as this essay represents. It's all one thing. It ought to create a school or way of thinking. It ought to answer the questions of a generation. But it's silly to lay down one's manuscript with tears in your eyes and praise God — for a prophet at last.'

The high spirits that fill these passages picked almost at random from Chapman's letters of the time pervaded the vast bulk of his correspondence. Sometimes the vein was that of pure foolery — as when, refurbishing the larger house next door to his first 'gash in the wind-swept Apennines,' he took

---

[1] When a profitable law case and the writing of an essay were engrossing him at the same time, early in 1898, he wrote: 'I would give the whole thing for a good adjective in the essay.'

[2] February 20 and 27, 1898. Slightly changed it appeared under the title 'Society' as a section of *Causes and Consequences*. This book was 'Dedicated to the Members of Club C' — a unit in the 'Good Government' organization — and, according to its Preface, 'arose out of an attempt to explain an election.'

a sample bit of Japanese wall-covering and wrote on it, by way of suggestion for its possible uses as note-paper:

> Mr. John Jay Chapman regrets that it is policy not to dine with anyone who has not $3,000,000. per year.
> Three twenty-five West
> Eighty-second Street
> Thursday.

(This, incidentally, was of a piece with his use of all manner of odds and ends of paper for the purposes of his incessant correspondence — telegraph blanks, concert programmes, restaurant menus, 'scratch blocks,' anything within reach). Sometimes the vein was combative: 'Politics takes physique, and being odious takes physique. I feel like Atlas, lifting the entire universe. I hate this community and despise 'em — and fighting, fighting, fighting, fighting an atmospheric pressure gets tiresome.' Often it was in happy revolt against his natural surroundings, as when he wrote (in October, 1897) to Mrs. Whitman: 'My own family and connections, being a lot of well-meaning bourgeois, are horrified at me. But I enjoy it.'

These bits from Chapman's letters serve a double purpose — to illustrate his characteristic spirit and at the same time to indicate the many-sided pressure under which he was living. When friends began to fear that it might all prove too much for him and were urging a moderated tempo, 'As for insanity' — he exclaimed in a letter — 'why, I was once examined for insanity by the two most distinguished physicians in Boston. It has no terrors. I talked to them like Plato. I was sitting in bed, and they left laughing and good friends.' He therefore felt secure against that danger; yet there were other dangers. The agitating activities not merely of the three years following his second marriage but of the preceding decade had wrought an insidious work. Even before that marriage he was writing to his future wife, 'I need to ask you to direct and command me at every moment. Please call me down, correct, and chastise me'; and she was bespeaking a quieter spirit in him. 'When you are excited,' she wrote, 'it puts a double burden of balance and steadiness on me. . . . I want [not Typhoons and Monsoons but] a strong westerly wind, steady, steady.' In the winter of 1899, during the first year of their marriage, they fled the turmoil of New York and sailed for England, to visit London — the place of many friends, to whom Chapman's pro-Boer sympathies were generally repugnant — to settle with the three children in Wells, and to return home in October, 1899, after a visit to the continent. Then began again the exacting round of law, politics, authorship, and social obligations, devised for pleasure, but leading to exhaustion. In the summer of 1900 Gerrish Island, on the coast of Maine, was the family base, but Chapman had to be much in New York. Here, after attending the Indianapolis convention which nominated the 'Gold Democrats,' Palmer and Buckner, to contest the presidential election with both McKinley and Bryan, he spent himself — in vain — on a 'Third Ticket Movement' to nominate Donelson Caffery of Louisiana and Archibald M. Howe of Massachusetts as candidates of a 'National Party' — an honor which they both declined. It was in the following winter, when pulled down by an attack of grippe, that he suffered a physical and nervous collapse of an alarming character.

The first manifestations seemed of such little moment that his wife felt free to leave him for a visit to Washington. On her return, shortly before the birth of her only son, Chapman became so weak that he could not walk. There were, besides, grave fears for his sanity — but not with Mrs. Chapman. At her insistence he went at once, with a nurse, to Rokeby, and a darkened room.

Some months after the long illness began, and while still his few letters were dictated and scrawlingly signed, he wrote to his mother that 'too much will and self-will' had caused his breakdown. In an uncompleted portion of his 'Retrospections,' written 'for consultation' in August and September, 1931, he ascribed his collapse to his attempt at combining the philosophy of political reform with its arduous practice: 'Now philosophic concentration,' he wrote, 'is one of the severest forms of work, and ought to be done in the closet by a man who is not running the practical side of the factory.' More specifically he went on: 'The crisis came with a crash. I was making an address to a small, highly intelligent audience in a small town somewhere near Philadelphia. I broke down. I wallowed on. I heard questions from the audience. I heard someone say, "He doesn't understand." I somehow got to the Princeton Inn, and I was frightened. The next day I went to New York and thought I probably needed exercise. I took quite a long walk. At one point I felt something break in the inner part of my left leg near the thigh. I knew that this was serious, but the leg still worked. I went home to bed.'

In less than a month after Chapman's removal to Rokeby, his son Chanler was born in New York, and just as soon as the journey could be made his wife and the infant followed him to Barrytown. If he liked darkness and a bed, she decided, let him have them — they were good things. If imaginings disturbed him, let him see that they were imaginings, not realities — and so he did. His brother-in-law, Temple Emmet, came to be near him. 'My psychological analysis of my own symptoms,' he wrote in 1931, 'was diagrammatic and alarmed the listeners. But Temple announced that I was perfectly sane though imaginative, and thus kept me out of a private asylum, for which I am still daily grateful.' It was of such as Chapman, especially at such a time as this, that Emily Dickinson wrote:

> 'Much madness is divinest sense
> To a discerning eye;
> Much sense the starkest madness.'

From his own narrative of the experience other bits should be rescued: 'At night I often felt like Poe's man in "The Pit and the Pendulum." I must lie perfectly still while the circular

saw or swinging scythe filed the core of me. If I resisted
I destroyed myself. Some of those midnights were unforgettable. In the early morning the dim light that came in a slit
from above the roller shade smote me like a mace and waked
me to pain. At this time began the normal awakening and
development of my nature which had been interrupted by
the St. Paul's School experience. I was no longer merely intellectual. I was religious, as I had been cut out by nature
to be. I was a unity. The rest was patience.... So far as the
consciousness of being the creature of divine power goes, it
has never left me. It is as strong at the present moment as
it was in the first midnight visitation. On the other hand I
have no impulse to express or impart it directly. It must
impart itself, — at any rate so far as I am concerned. I can
deal only with the old symbols of the intellect and let them
tell what they can.'

But the ground lost as by an avalanche had to be recovered
by inches. There was a year in bed. Then a basket phaeton,
into which he could be helped, and a mule named 'Clara
Barton,' played their part in the process. For many months
he could not walk without crutches. Daily drives became
longer, until at length there was a drive of two days to a
house high in the Catskills, when he seemed strong enough
to be called from his room one evening to see a superb sunset.
The beauty of it proved more than his shaken nerves could
bear. When he had gone with his family, to Europe, in the
autumn of 1902, seeking a full restoration of his strength, he
was similarly overcome on entering an Italian church into
which his wife had summoned him to see the whole beauty
of Europe embodied. Though his recovery was then considered well under way, there was still a long road to travel —
and at one of its turnings a cup of the deepest sorrow was
pressed to his lips.

After a sojourn in Venice, and a visit to the castle of friends
near Udine, the family cavalcade of eleven — parents, children, tutor, and maids — proceeded to Ober Tarvis in Austria.

Thence Chapman, with his two older boys, Victor and Jay, and their tutor, made an excursion which took them to Römerbad, a watering-place on the river Sann, some ninety miles from Ober Tarvis.[1] There was a bathing pool, fed from the river. Here, on August 13, 1903, the tutor took the two boys, and left them in charge of the bath-keeper while he went to check their bicycles. On his return within a few minutes Jay was missing. He had slipped through the outlet into the rushing river, and was drowned. Mrs. Chapman, at Ober Tarvis, immediately received a telegram: 'Jay drowned this afternoon. Body not found. The Lord gave and the Lord hath taken away. Blessed be the name of the Lord.' Two days later the body was recovered on the river-bank, far below the baths.

Meanwhile, Mrs. Chapman, setting forth on a complicated journey by night, had come to Römerbad. His first words to her, 'I would rather it had been you,' gave, in terms that met her perfect comprehension, the instant measure of his grief and of his feeling for the boy he had lost. As he wrote of his children before his second marriage, so he continued to feel: 'I never saw children like them — they are King's children in disguise, and I am a stepfather to them.' Jay, with his tenth birthday only three months ahead, was peculiarly the apple of his father's eye. His beauty, the sweetness of his nature, the high promise of his artistic gifts, gave him a place of special sacredness in Chapman's affections and hopes. Far from the top of his own strength, how was Chapman to face and bear such a nightfall on his firmament?

> Diseases desperate grown
> By desperate appliance are relieved,
> Or not at all.

So, truly, it appears to have been with him. The call for instant action in circumstances doubly difficult in a foreign land had to be answered. Future movements had to be

[1] On an Italian Touring Club map (1933) of Jugoslavia, Römerbad may be identified as Rimske Toplie on the river Savina.

planned. This necessity seems to have hastened the ascent from the depths into which Chapman had sunk more than two years before. 'Now we can go home,' he declared, and in September of 1903 they returned to the United States. His crutches meanwhile had been discarded.

Not yet capable of taking up his old existence he passed the ensuing winter at Edgewater, a country house close to the Hudson River at Barrytown, adjoining the Chanler lands of Rokeby. Here he remained, often in solitude, broken by visits from his wife, and sojourns of Victor and his tutor. The serious study of harmony under a professional master (Percy Goetschius), while his wife was studying the violin, became an important matter both of interest and of therapy. 'The only difference between me and Beethoven,' he could write to Mrs. Chapman in a moment of gaiety, 'is that when I think of a tune it takes me *longer* to write it down. (It is his tune).' For all such diversions, the shadow of his loss was still over him. Once, when a visit from his mother was impending, he wrote to her, 'Don't talk of Jay.' Talk might be prohibited, but thought could not. To its poignancy, and its long continuance, a sonnet dated October 20, 1920, found among Chapman's papers, with its first heading 'Jay in a Dream' changed to 'Bereavement,' bears memorable witness:

> When sleep has piled his mountain on my breast,
> Then through the portal of a silent room
> Which many rock-hewn years of life entomb,
> As from a jail, my child, thou issuest,
> Like some sad infant of a home unblest.
> What would you have me do? — and wherefore come
> In such a guise, so woe-begone and dumb,
> Thou poor, neglected, famished little guest?
>
> Did we not break our hearts above thy grave,
> Giving thee that which never comes again
> Save in a twilight and a spasm of pain?
> Tho' joy to life her after-blossoms gave,
> Thou cravest something, What is it, my son?
> Thine eyes make answer: 'Not oblivion!'

156

When Chapman, after a second winter at Edgewater, emerged from his long retirement, the beard that gave him thenceforth so marked an aspect might have stood as a symbol for a change that could not be seen. He spoke of Edgewater afterwards as 'the coldest place I was ever in. I was there alone one winter and lived in furs like an Esquimaux.' His loneliness was mitigated by his friendly dealings with his village neighbors — one of them a sick old 'Mr. Plass,' confined to a house-boat moored by the shore of the place. Chapman paid him frequent visits. 'What do you talk about?' asked his wife on one of her visits to Edgewater. 'I don't talk to him,' said Chapman, 'I just sit there.' 'Well, what do you think about while you are sitting?' 'Oh, I keep wondering whether the black things in his beard are melon-seeds or cockroaches.' His whimsical sallies endeared him to his obscurer neighbors and friends, and they in turn helped to rebuild his strength.

Through all this slow process he had learned not merely the lesson, never wholly to be forgotten, that he must refrain from extreme demands upon his strength, but also that an intensely personal inward life of religion, through its more mystical, less patterned influences, was to become more and more his refuge and invigoration. In his young manhood, as we have seen,[1] there was a period of reaction against the overemphasis on formal religion from which his boyhood had suffered. Before his second marriage he had written to Miss Chanler, 'Do you know, my dear one, I sort of hate the idea of having a regular pew and going and sitting in it — (and sermons I hate and will not listen to) — but I like to enter and sit back by the door during the service.' When they were married, and Mrs. Chapman, always a devout Episcopalian, continued her church-going habits, to which Chapman, reared in the same tradition, willingly conformed, she found good reason for sitting as far back in the church as possible. There it became her office to twitch at

[1] See *ante*, p. 31.

his coat-tails as he remained standing after the rest of the congregation sat down, even as he would remain on his knees, absorbed in prayer, while others were sitting or standing. In religious observance as in politics his resolution to 'go it alone' stood firm.

What concerns us here, however, is the reënforcement of Chapman's reliance upon religion which came to him in the period of sorrow and illness at which we have been looking. His *Nursery* article on 'Non-Resistance' already mentioned [1] gives clear proof that before his illness the essentials of Christian feeling were close to his heart and mind. In so far as their new importance to him can be described with any accuracy, his own word for it — beyond what has already been quoted — is to be found in two of his essays, 'The Influence of Schools,' in his 'Learning and Other Essays' (1910), and 'The Function of the Church School,' in 'Memories and Milestones' (1915).

In the first of these papers he tells of his breakdown at St. Paul's: 'In consequence of this experience my views about the school were thereafter quite gloomy. I regarded the place as a religious forcing-house, a very dangerous sort of place for any boy to go, especially if he were inclined by nature toward religion. I habitually abused the school, and I even took the trouble to go back there and have a quarrel with Dr. Coit about something he had said or done which seemed to me to deserve the reprobation of all just men. I poured over him a few vitriolic letters; and I still believe that the right was on my side in the matter, though perhaps I was wrong to assume the rôle of the Angel of Retribution.'

'It was at a date,' he proceeds, 'about twenty years after my leaving the school, and at the age of forty-odd, and through the medium of another and very severe illness, that my nature began to take up again the threads of the St. Paul's School influence, and to receive the ideas which Dr. Coit had been striving to convey, though in forms that

---

[1] See *ante*, p. 137.

would have been incomprehensible to himself. The school
had somehow been carrying on its work within me through
all these years.'

This essay, beginning with the workings of a mind in
illness, has to do largely with the austere figure of Chapman's
headmaster, 'a tall man in a long black coat,' to whose final
influence and power he makes full acknowledgment. In the
later essay, addressed to the boys of the school, he told them
they 'must not expect to understand very much about school
just yet.... It is a very rare matter when any of us at any
time in life sees things as they are at the moment.' Then
comes a passage in which the religious philosophy to which
his life had brought him finds this expression:

> I am speaking all this time in terms of education; but I am
> really thinking about religion. Now religion is not so much
> a thing by itself as a way of feeling, an inward experience as
> to the nature of life, which colors and changes the world.
> It is a personal experience. No one can describe it or convey
> it to another. There has always been this incalculable element
> about religious experience. The wind bloweth where it list-
> eth — even so is everyone that is born of the spirit. Religion
> is the consciousness of the presence of God. It often descends
> upon people in trouble, in moments of crisis. When all else
> is taken, it rushes in — I should say, *seems* to rush in; for
> it is really always present in all men, — only disguised and
> concealed by the clouds of other interests and occupations.
>
> You boys must often wonder, as I used to wonder in this
> room, what it is all about? — What is this religion that seems
> to be of so much importance? It is evidently at the bottom of
> St. Paul's School. The founders are founding it, the rectors are
> preaching it, the choirs are singing it. We walk in and out
> of the chapel, and rustle it in hymn books and undergo it in
> reproachful lectures for our misconduct. Some people seem to
> believe that it is pocketed in scriptural texts, and surely fitted
> into the catechism. All this language of religious feeling that
> surrounds you at St. Paul's School is the language of the
> mystery of life. That mystery will endure forever. It will
> outlast contemporary science, and over-shadow future science.
> It comes to you in the voice of many generations speaking

about the profoundest truths of life. You are here living in
the sound of that voice. You hardly understand it; you hear
it unconsciously; at times you catch a few syllables that seem
intelligible, seem meant for you — they are somehow communications from the great power in the midst of which our life
goes on, the power which drives and is our life. If there were
any sure way by which the child could be put into conscious
relation with God, — if he could be shown these mysteries,
as he may be led out and shown a waterfall — then all this
machinery would not be needed: — all this literature, this
music, discipline, prayer, praise and worship of God might
be dispensed with or replaced. But, as the old Jews used to
say 'No man hath seen God at any time.' This whole matter is
not a thing by itself which can be grasped. It is a part of
everything else. It underlies all thought: it is something which
grasps us. When it comes, it comes. It is not a universal
experience. Some people, great people, men of power and
sanctity, who fill the world with good deeds, and fill us who
gaze upon them with a sense of religion — have lived without
that sense themselves. The power that works in them is
veiled from them.

In his illness, moreover, as before it and afterwards, with
the sympathy of both his first and his second wife, he had
relied not solely upon doctors but upon those healers of the
spirit of whom he wrote: [1] 'I am constantly meeting people
who heal the sick through prayer and live in a whole-hearted
simplicity of feeling which brings to mind New Testament
times. I am thinking of individuals, men and women, not
of any church; for they frequently belong to no church, but
are mere children of the New Testament.'

Whatever these helpers may have done for Chapman's body,
there can be little question that his spiritual life was quick-
ened by their ministrations. In considering what he became,
it is well to consider what a mystic is. This elusive character has been brought to book in a dictionary definition:
'one who, whether Christian or non-Christian, seeks by
contemplation and self-surrender to obtain union with

[1] See *Memories and Milestones*, p. 81.

or absorption into the Deity, or who believes in the possibility of the spiritual apprehension of truths that are inaccessible to the understanding.' To this end there is no more travelled road than that of docility and prayer. For all of Chapman's confidence in his own opinions and the show of arrogance with which he would assert them, the habit of prayer — certainly through all the later years of his life — was constant with him. If there was one petition more than any other into which his yearning for a power not his own would pour itself, it was 'Teach me, O Lord, the way of thy statutes; and I shall keep it unto the end.' This, or the abbreviated 'Teach me, O Lord,' was on his lips, I am told, with extraordinary frequency. It came from the heart of one who, seeming often to have learned his lesson ill, could write, in the soul's sincere desire:

> There is a sort of docility of mind, a knowledge of our own impotence, that is very near to the threshold of intellectual vision and to the threshold of religious feeling. Whenever a man has this sentiment very strongly, people almost always give him credit for being somehow a religious person — even if the man protests he is not interested in religion. It seems to be true that great intellects are almost always filled with this sense of not quite understanding what truth is, of being powerless and ignorant. Emerson said that it has always been the mark of an intellect of the first order that a man should feel about the world as if the explanation of it could not be given here; but that the whole matter must draw its meaning from something else, something we do not know. The people who feel like this are not always conscious of God. I would not cite them as examples of religious feeling. I cite them as examples of that docility which is very near to religion.

Such books of mysticism as 'The Cloud of Unknowing,' one of many supplements to the perpetual reading of the Bible, held his spirit in a state from which the steady practice of prayer was inseparable. Having found it such a power in his own life, how could he have failed to employ it — for himself, for other persons, for the world at large? If the

Kingdom of God is found to be within us, it cannot be held in solitary confinement. When he travelled from home he was wont to pack among what he called his 'toys' a small wooden cross which for many years he liked to clasp firmly in his hand while he bent his thoughts, either in meditation or in prayer, on the intangible forces in his life. It remained with him to the end, broken, to be sure, a few days before his death by the pressure of his elbow as he turned himself in bed, but placed at the last in the coffin with his body.

In relating Chapman's fundamental concern for religion to the discipline of loss and illness, the sequence of external events has been outrun. In returning to their course it should now be said that the two sad winters at Edgewater were the last of their kind. The large tract of land on which this house stood had been acquired by the Chapmans and named Sylvania. Their friend Charles A. Platt had designed them a house, high above the Hudson, with a noble view of the Catskills across the river, and this habitation was ready for occupancy in the spring of 1905. Many of its furnishings had been assembled during their visit to Europe two years before. On Easter Day there was a happy family lunch party, though the house was still in considerable disorder. By that time, however, Chapman had regained much of his strength. His wife had worn herself to exhaustion in the processes of settling. Immediately after lunch, ignoring the unpacked furniture that cluttered the rooms, he ordered her to bed for three weeks. Their life in the new surroundings was not to begin with weariness, and was to continue under a standard of all possible detachment from haste and worry. A desperate chapter had ended. A new long period of unbroken health and relative serenity was about to begin.

Some of the letters that preceded it are, however, still to be read.

Letters

To William James

56 WALL STREET, NEW YORK
March 17, 1897

MY DEAR PROFESSOR JAMES

I am driven to write to you because I so narrowly missed
seeing you and regretted it so much — also because I am
concerned about Royce. I never heard a man talk so much
nonsense in one evening — and a man too who is such a
splendid fellow, a unique nature, and a very wonderful mind.
The inroads of Harvard University upon his intelligence
however, have been terrible. He said he was writing a paper
on originality and his conversation betrayed some of the
things he is going to say in it — this was that everything
was imitative — in art you 'imitate the ideal.' This ought
to be stopped. He is misleading the youth. I see why they
killed Socrates. I say it is pernicious emptiness he is teaching
your boys out there.

I know you would say that it's mere philosophy and not
to be taken seriously; but these things do have some influence sometimes. That man — mind you I love and revere
him — but he's not as interesting a man as he was ten years
ago. His mind has less of life in it. His constant strain and
endeavor to evacuate his mind and have nothing in it but
destruction is beginning to tell. I hear he is going abroad —
I am awfully glad. Let him have no money. Let him come
in grinding contact with life. Let him go to Greece and get
into a revolution — somewhere where he can't think — I
mean do this thing he does, which is not thinking. Let his
mind get full of images and impressions, pains, hungers,
contrasts — life, life, life — he's drawing on an empty well.

I am just awfully glad you are going to speak at the Shaw
Monument. Down with the literary people. It might have

been Norton or Eliot — very good — no offence in them — but Lord God, we have had literature done enough — hawked and styled to deadness. Let us express ourselves with brick-bats or pictures of ganglia — it's what we're coming to — but no more traditional English grace. Get up and say Shaw did well and sit down.

And do remember this — if your speech pleases that audience, it's bad. If you get adopted into that hypocrisy — the war reverence — the war cant — the eulogy business — any enthusiasm which doesn't concern the present instant! These very fellows you're talking to are brought up on this tradition. I think Judge Holmes' speeches are the veriest rot — the veriest unmanly sentimentalism and arid stuff — I know you couldn't do this, and he can't help it, but I don't want to lose you as figure of a live creature. Every year I hear more about you and I know you have put life into your whole science all over this country. I see the younger generation — run across them in one way or another — and trace back their vitality to you —

Please remember me to Mrs James.

Very sincerely yours
JOHN JAY CHAPMAN

To Mrs. Henry Whitman

March 25, 1897
677 FIFTH AVENUE

... I must send you copies of a recent periodical called *The Nursery*. I get the credit of being at the bottom of it — till I am tired of denying it. At any rate I believe in it and think it's the only page with a ring of Truth in it ever published in this miserable town.

Yours

JACK

This is a note I was writing to James but I dassent send it.
MY DEAR MR. JAMES —

Mine enemy has written a book. I saw it on Miss Dunham's table — and I have borrowed it. I have not yet read it — but I may read it — and I may write to you about it. What I want you to understand is that I have no malice and that whatever I may be called upon to say about the book will not be the result of my reading the book — nor be influenced by the book in any manner. I trust I have enough judgment and mental training to keep the matters apart in my mind. In the first place the mere writing of essays is very much against any man — and *philosophical* essays — and *literary-philosophical* essays — with gamboge and style in them — with 'howevers' and 'moreovers' and semicolons — this is terrible.

The pretenselessness and sort of damned and wretched charm which I know will hang about these essays — I am steeled against. They are a weak device of a personal nature — and I will stop my ears to both of them. The grand fact remains that you did write the Essays and you cannot get away from it.

[*The letter which Chapman did write on March 30, after reading the essay on 'The Will to Believe,' is printed in Ralph Barton Perry's 'Thought and Character of William James.' There Chapman repudiated, with humorous extravagance, James's conception of faith. More than two years later, in the* Political Nursery *for July,* 1899, *an article on 'Prof. James' Will to Believe,' shows Chapman returning to the attack, happily conscious that James would not take too seriously even the opening sentence of the final paragraph in the article: 'Mr. James's paper is cousin-german to every lie in the world.'*]

To Elizabeth Chanler

[*Enclosing a clipping from a Memphis, Tennessee, newspaper about the loss of his hand.*]

April 6: 1897

ELIZABETH — I had just thrown this away, but I keep it. It is too interesting and unexpected — and on the whole very accurate. Like catching sight of oneself in the glass. First I was shocked — then I laughed, then I threw it away, then kept it. What eternal blazon unfit for ears of flesh and blood have I lived in till I don't even hear it — and let's not hear it. . . .

To the same

May 1897

... I have had to spank Victor. He got out on the extension roof. Fortunately he was in his nightgown, as he is very active, and I never could have got him undressed to begin with. He fought like a tiger — but I spanked him, and I hurt him. I smacked him well. You know I don't believe in spanking. In fact I'm principled against it. *Never strike a child.* For any mere moral offence I shouldn't dream of spanking a child — but when it comes to a question of his continued existence, why, I'm ready to do him the moral injury — at any rate as a matter of fact I did, in violation of theory, spank him — very thoroughly. He was extremely outraged by it — really very indignant. I left him alone for half an hour, and then talked to him affectionately. Jay was very philosophical about the matter, but I couldn't get Jay to admit that he, Jay, would be *glad* to be spanked even if he had been naughty....

To the same

NEW YORK
CENTURY ASSOCIATION
May 16, 1897

[*Here is one paragraph from a letter of elaborate fooling (and genuine solicitude) about 'agony over other people's affairs' — especially Miss Chanler's concern for members of her own family.*]

... Or else you'd say, 'Jack, I want to tell you something. Winty has determined to join the Jewish church — and Daisy has found it out and has had him baptized in his sleep to save his soul, and Margaret don't know it — and it appears that by the marriage contract and under the Romish ritual this new child will (if Winty turns Jew) being the child of a Jew have to be devoted to the flames. I sat up eighteen hours laying the case before Stanford White who says the way to do is to wait and do nothing — but I know that if Margaret found it out she'd endow a dissenting chapel and *then* — *then* she'd die of a broken heart.' And I'd say 'My dear child, I think the fibre and grain of the family is tough enough to live through these religious wars. I was a Jew myself for eight years.'

Keep your health and keep your head — but I know you will do both. I understand it and take your word for it....

JACK

To William James

NEW YORK, June 3, 1897

MY DEAR MR. JAMES

I hear nothing but good of your address.[1] This is damning enough. They say 'a fine bit of English' — 'such fine feeling' — etc. I put the worst first, for I concede that it went well with the occasion — and 'Forward the 54th' belonged in the ceremonies as a keystone belongs in an arch. I don't see how you had the face to do it all the same.

But seriously I delighted in the part about any country having lots of boys like Shaw, and the praise of the mugwumps and civic virtue. I wish the whole occasion could have been devoted to the idea. It was a good little celebration — aunts, uncles, and cousins. Do you know it made the Mass. community seem so small — of course just the '61 crowd were there and about all of them were there. It lacked the present.

Booker Washington was the only man who took the matter seriously — for even you made your moralities rather reflections. I say damn the war. I believe these celebrations send every body home comfortable and happy and prevent 'em from subscribing to the lost causes on which the future depends.

Booker Washington was grinding his axe. The rest were celebrating and waiting for the strawberries and cream....

We went to see Mrs. Shaw on getting to New York and found her waiting for news. She said, 'How Rob would have laughed if he could have known they were going to make so much fuss over him. For you know he was very modest and simple and took the command because he thought Governor Andrew would find it hard to get another man.'

I told her I went on reluctantly because war celebration,

---

[1] At the unveiling of the Shaw Monument in Boston.

pension frauds, fine sentiments, and scoundrelism, and Republicanism were so mixed up in my mind. She said, 'Yes, I know, I had the same feeling somewhat.' But the girls gave her a glowing account of it and she went to bed in good spirits.

Mrs. Shaw takes a more vivid interest in the present and gets more excited about it than anyone in New York.

I understood you to say that something I had said about 'truth' was rot. Do you know that in your big two volumes of psychology there's an advertisement stating that your psychology is based on *American facts?*

Sincerely yours

JOHN JAY CHAPMAN

To Elizabeth Chanler

[*Written from Beverly Farms, where Chapman was visiting Mrs. Whitman, with William James as a fellow-guest.*]

July 11, 1897

... 11 P.M. James very dear. Came in to my bedroom when we went to bed, put his hands on my shoulders, and told me, 'Jack Chapman, you talk like an angel.' (This was not in the least true because I had been holding forth in a most dogmatic way about how the Shaw monument celebration looked towards the past, and the important work of the present was to be done more by sack-cloth and ashes.) He went in to see Victor asleep and said he wished Victor could know his boy. He's a most human creature and clever and comprehending.

To the same

[BEVERLY FARMS], *July* 12, 1897

... There is one subject about which I hardly like to speak — but I think you may help me. Mrs. Whitman insists upon kissing me. She always had an inclination this way because she has a kissing inclination. I hate it. I dread it. It horrifies me. It gives me the blind staggers. Now she has always had this. I used to take precautions against it — stiff elbows — running good-byes — public good nights.

Minna never gave me the least aid or sympathy, but used to laugh at me, not without resentment against Mrs. W. for being a foolish person and idiot — but Minna thought it so ludicrous and contemptible of me to get shattered in my nervous system, and yet not to know how to protect myself, that she didn't help me, but only laughed.

Now I am victimized and horrified and insulted — and please tell me the natural way. Shall I just tell her I can't stand being kissed or shall I continue my elusion, avoidances, and escapes? I tell you it is horrible to me.... I don't mind somebody like Mrs. Shaw as an act of grace and greeting and sort of blessing unexpectedly once in eight years — but to kiss good-night to Mrs. Whitman. It ain't a thing I can stand. I've been very gentle to Mrs. Whitman because of her troubles and because I've been softened — but she's kissed me twice — too quick for me — since I've been here. I think I shall have to tell her.

[*A few days later Chapman reverted, all humorously, to this subject, still bewildered, still self-defensive — ('I keep it off with the crooked elbow') — yet philosophical: 'Go your ways. You must leave me now to fight this out alone. It's one of those problems no one can help another in. I grieve over it, but I must with solicitude and prayer face it, and you can stand by and wait.'*]

To the same

NEW YORK, *July* 28, '97

I gave Grandmama the Walt Whitman to read. She said she had never seen so many different kinds of words in her life. That the reason people wouldn't publish my writings was they didn't like my arrogant tone. That I seemed to be one who took the tone of having read everything and knew everything from the beginning of the world and for whom everyone had been waiting from the beginning of time. That I never said 'by your leave' or 'don't you think so' or 'it seems to me' — but just laid down the law. That I was an egotist as bad as Walt Whitman. That I must 'bow down my spirit within.' On my asking whether I wasn't humble in private life she said 'Yes — you *pretend*, but that's not enough.' I tell you my grandmother is hard to deceive. She scouted the idea of American poets, said we'd never had a poet, that not more than one or two of them could write as good verses as mine, and she thought I was a poet and was glad I was going to publish, as she heard, everything I had ever written. She also said I needed some one by me every instant to tell me how to behave. That she wouldn't give two cents for my opinion on any subject.

If that's not a wonderful woman. . . .

To the same

[*In 'Letters and Religion' (1924) Chapman wrote: 'The Bible is a luminous congregation of vapors, a cloud by day and a pillar of fire by night; and the darker the skies grow, whether above an epoch or an individual, the more light it emits. Of all the media of communication between man and man, the Bible is the greatest mindtouching influence that swallows us into union with God, and with all men, dispelling the crass illusion of the moment, leading us to rely on the unseen.*]

OFFICE, 10 A.M.
Sept. 14, '97

. . . I read the Bible all the time and carry it about when I don't read it, I don't know why. It is the only power and opening of one's self.

There is a depth of human feeling in the Jew that no other race ever possessed. We do no more than imitate it — and follow it. David, for instance, and his conduct about Uriah's wife and the child that died — and Absalom — and Jonathan. Compare the Greek — the Chinese, the Roman. These Jews are more human than any other men. It is the cause of the spread of their religion — for we are all adopted into Judah. The heart of the world is Jewish. There is the same spirit in the Old Testament as in the New. What monstrous perversion — that we should worship their God and despise themselves! We admire the Pyramids and the Egyptians, but the history of the Jews is the most remarkable, the most notable thing, on the globe. Their sacred books and chronicles and traditions and history make the annals of every other nation mere rubbish — and I feel this same power in the Jews I know. They are the most humane and the strongest people morally mentally and physically. They persist. I'm glad I'm a Jew. I believe that's the reason why this paper-faced civilization impresses me so little...

Take Habakkuk:

'For the vision is yet for an appointed time — but at the end it shall speak and not lie. Though it tarry, wait for it. Because it will surely come, it will not tarry.

'Behold, his soul which is lifted up is not upright in him, but the just shall live by faith. For the stone shall cry out of the wall, and the beam out of the timber shall answer it. Woe to him that buildeth a town with blood and stablisheth a city by iniquity.'

Greek literature would have lived if it had any such human touch and bang in it. It is a washed-out rag — a *jeu d'esprit* for cultivated intellects.

Why was it Homer got preserved but because of the human touches in him? The Greek tragedians — we probably have about all that was best in them — and how little it is — how little, how mannered, how artificial, how local, how conventional. Take the 'Prometheus' of Aeschylus — and compare it to the two pages of Habakkuk — (and please read them today).

The New Testament has not the literary magnificence of the Old. It is hard to tell much about it — because we are born between its pages and have never read them. It is inconceivable that anything should be closer to life than the Old Testament — but the New Testament is much closer. The ignorance and dethronement of the times — the Roman captivity — there is no temple in the New Testament — whereas you feel the temple and the ark and the tables on every page of the Old. It is hard to understand how Christ broke down all these things.

I mean in his own mind. It would have been impossible but for the long destruction and desecration of all the outward symbols of mystery. Don't think I'm profane. Examine it in your own way. But I say with the Temple in full blast, Christianity would have been impossible.

I hate St. Paul. He is clever. He has the wit of Greece and the interest of doctrine and its application at heart — whether women shall wear long hair and speak in church — divorce — meats offered to idols, etc., etc. I don't say he was not a good man and did a useful work and that his letters aren't full of wonderful things — but I feel the vestry-room. He is responsible for the clerical manners of today and there are in him the beginnings of that asceticism that the Christian Church fell into and which is the danger of — I suppose it's one of the inherent dangers of — any religion.

I will try to like St. Paul if you have any very strong feelings about him, but he is not sympathetic. If I had gone into the Roman Church and become a preacher I'd have been that kind of a man — a Gentile with the enthusiasm of a Jew, and the intellectual training and ways of looking at things of an educated man.

To Mrs. Charles Howland Russell

City Club of New York
Oct. 27: 1897

... We've all been trucking and orating in halls like mad — three more nights of it. It's carnival. It's the only season worth living in. It's the one excitement this iron grey commercial civilization affords. I only hope good government won't come during my life time. If we had *that* it would be the crowning jewel of ennui. If on top of our goodness of heart, our prosperity, our smug contentment, our uniform, and moderate, unambitious, comfortable thrift — we had decent honest quaker government with men like Seth Low filling all the offices — everyman's mouth with a bun in it, and *no possible cause for excitement* — my Jove — I'd go — I'd leave the place. I pray these great reforms may not come in my time. I'm sort of frightened when I see how rapidly our ideas are being adopted. In 1899 I came to N.Y. — or '89 — and these things were silly heresies — and *they're all I know* — they're my stock in trade. Am I to be cast on the world at 35 — with no cause? ...

Affectionately
JACK

To Elizabeth Chanler

[*Written from Hotel Adirondack, North Creek, N.Y., before reaching a camp where some fellow-workers in the New York mayoralty campaign were resorting for rest. Arrived at the camp, Chapman wrote, 'Billy* [*Schieffelin*] *has lent me a rifle, and we go out at dawn, each with a guide, for deer. I can't shoot, of course, but what matter? If I only don't kill my guide, and I'm going to try not to.'*]

November, 1897

This is the end of the R.R. — a shanty at a river head. Rains — mud. The fun of these expeditions is the togs you bring. Every man has two guns — patent shoes — peculiar gaiters — tarpaulins — caps — of arctic types — overcoats — undercoats — cartridge belts.

Schieffelin has a pair of *snow shoes*. Immense fun they get out of these things. It's not so cold as New York City so far — and the country not unlike Westchester Co., only milder. LaFarge — who is by way of being a big game hunter and belongs to a self-advertising clique of champagne drinkers including Owen Wister, Teddy R., Willy Chanler, etc., who call themselves the Boone and Crockett Club and write memorials to the Secretary of the Interior on the preservation of the buffalo — and publish little club books giving their names — Grant LaFarge regarded this crowd as duffers and beneath him in sport. But I rather guess these fellows get as much fun out of their gimcracks as the others. The fun of sport is the outfit. The reels — the snells — the hooded caps — the favorite flies and snaffles, and charges and paraphernalia. It's luxury — sportsmen just have everything they want. I almost spent $50 yesterday — out of mere sporting instinct. If a man with $2,500 a year and a wife and three children needs a rod-holder that costs $8 — he orders three sent home and writes to the Rod and Gun to say which is the best. In short you're a swell, you're a lord — you have what's needed. It's your holiday. I never saw such a collection for the Smithsonian as these fellows have among them and what fun they get out of it.

Ludlow is loaded like a caravan to cross the Desert. He has eight waistcoats and sweaters and straps all over him.

My only solace is my boots — only one place in America they're made *right* — and very heavenly they are. Why not found a Strap and Buckle Club? Have a club house with lockers and go and put on these things.

To Mrs. John Jay

56 WALL STREET, *Dec.* 21, 1897

... The Jews have in my experience more faith than the Christians. They have clever heads, better hearts, and more belief in the power of good every way. They gave to the world all the religion it has got and are themselves the most religious people in it. I work with them day and night and most of the time is spent in prying up some Christian to do a half day's work.

Your affectionate Grandson

JOHN JAY CHAPMAN

To Elizabeth Chanler

Dec. 31, '97

The last chapter of George's book ['Progress and Poverty'] where he gets to describing the New Jerusalem of Single Tax, with fruit trees growing in the streets — no courts — no crime — no poverty — are really so much like Don Quixote that I was startled. He is rapt. He is beyond reach of the human voice. He has a harp and is singing — and *this* is the power of the book. It is preposterous. It is impossible. It is a romance — a rhapsody — a vision — at the end of a long seeming scientific discussion of rent, interest, and wages — (in which discussion his *destructive* criticism of other people must be admitted to be very strong — conclusive — but which leaves his own work subject to his own criticism). This burst of song, being the only lyric poetry of this commercial period, is popular.

To the same

Tuesday 11:40 A.M. *March* 18 (1898)

... Read the essays of (Pres.) Eliot. There's no offence in them. Two by six. Everything in Massachusetts is deal

boards. You can put every man in a box — Smug, Smug.
He has a good word for poetry too. It's the Dodgedom of
Culture. My God, how I hate it. He's the very highest type
of a most limited and inspiring pork-chopism. My God, he
is hopeful — calls his book 'American Contributions to
Civilization' — thinks we don't understand small parks and
drainage — but will learn and are doing nicely. Has a chapter
on 'the pleasures of life.' It's all one size. Every word in
this work is the same size. The Puritans — the war — the
problems of labor and capital — education — all excite the
same emotion — i.e. that of a woodchuck eating a carrot....

To the same

[*Enclosing a notice from the Society of Ethical Culture of William
M. Salter's lecture, 'What is the Permanent Value of the Bible?'
See Chapman's essay, 'Ethical Culture,' in 'Memories and Mile-
stones,' a lecture of his own.*]

56 WALL STREET, 12 M, *March* 26, 1898

I send you some selections from the mail to amuse your
leisure — Ethics and Extensions — and Permanent Value of
the Bible — this is the region of education nowadays. When
I get this stuff typewritten I want you to read it through
slowly with a microscope and cavil at every word and make
me work it over till every bit of its terminology and this
spirit is sweated out of it. I don't deny that the Bible has a
permanent value, but no man who has the faintest suspicion
of what the Bible is about could use that phrase about it.
Really I can't think of anything analogous or more picturesque, for this is the apogee of a fool. I am going to mention it in lecturing before those cusses. It's so ignorant, —
ethically, spiritually unenlightened. Everything this fellow
knows or values not only comes out of the Bible but is better
expressed there.

This is Ethical Culture, is it? Well, give us religion. Give
me idol worship. There's more truth in it. It's more respectable. There's more hope and seed of life in it than in
this chatter. Why, the whole advance of any man through
life is a mere excursion into the Bible. He dies on the edge

175

and understands some fragment of it — according to his capacity. He can no more outgrow it than he can outgrow his skull and frame work.

The New Testament, and to a very large extent the Old, *is* the soul of man. You cannot criticize it. It criticizes you. See what it has said about this man.

He has little knowledge of human nature. He has read a great many books — from Comte down. He has formal manners. He is self-conscious. He does not laugh easily — nor crack jokes — and he doesn't think he understands anything until he has connected it with somebody else's formula. He does not make his own formulas, but his greatest flight is a suggested variation on some detail or someone else's philosophy, — as for instance that: 'Mill does not allow for the law of diminishing returns in framing his altruism.' 'Instinct according to Laferrière is self-regarding,' but he forgets to qualify this, for the instinct of sex certainly regards the race.

Now what do you think of this sort of a cuss? I think I have seen him — a Jew — but no more like a Jew than I to Hercules.

Your loving

J<small>ACK</small>

To his Mother

[*The Chapmans had landed at Liverpool two days earlier, and were paying a visit on the way to London where they took a house at* 18, *Cowley Street, Westminster, before proceeding to Wells for most of the summer.*]

O<small>SSINGTON</small>, N<small>EWARK</small>, N<small>OTTS</small>
Monday, April — about the 8th or 9th [1899]

D<small>EAR</small> M<small>AMA</small> —

... I certainly want to see you in London, especially as we may see the interesting people and, having a house and living under the shadow of the House of Commons and next door to Alfred Lyttelton whose wife is a school friend of Elizabeth's, we can ask people to supper. I don't care about doing the season especially, but I should like to know a dozen of the people like Trevelyan and Morley and who not — whoever

Photograph by Dawkes and Partridge

THE CHAPMAN FAMILY AT WELLS, 1899

they are, the intelligent people in England —and get to know them well — and find things out. I rather believe both England and America are in the same lines of going to the devil so far as that side of it goes, and I feel in a vague way as if all the other forces pulled together and it will be apt to be useful to America in the future if I for instance know personally and am known by the English. My own impressions are that both countries are mad just now over bloodshed, commercial interests, and jingoism. But there must be large masses of people in both countries who hate all these things and hate cant and see that the moral interests of both nations are one. The prestige of the Anglo-Saxon race is today in America — the imaginative thing — and, by Jove, the English for all their talk are in danger of being too much influenced by America. I noticed this fourteen years ago when I was here as a boy — America is the future with a big F. Well enough — but we need their virtue and we need *nothing else*. Their hypocrisy (as now half of this sudden love of us is fear and trembling), their humbug won't do us any good, nor them either. In so far as they love us because they have seen we can shoot straight — there will come out of it nothing but antagonism.

To William James

18 COMMONWEALTH AVE
BOSTON. *March* 1, 1900

MY DEAR JAMES

My wife and I are spending three days with Mrs. Dorr and saw a handsome boy of yours last night at Mrs. Whitman's, but didn't get a chance to more than shake hands with him — most distinguished looking fellow. We have seen the whole astronomy here — and a joy to find how little everyone has changed — all the people old and young I ever knew — and each one more so than ever — Royce especially in good form. If he could only get rid of the notion that there is such a thing as philosophy what a fellow he would be. Poor babe — he claims the privilege of not worrying over politics on the ground that he has more important things to attend to, and must perforce rely on the opinions of his nearest lawyer friend as to how to vote — little dreaming that he is giving the same reason that the average American gives — and furnishing a key to all our political life. O learning, and devotion to learning, how little dost thou differ from any other pursuit!

This surrender of Cronje makes me sick. The Lord will provide, but it blackens the whole sky. My, but the process of kneading decency into the human race is slow. The dawn and then clouds again. By the way, the people of Massachusetts are the most unselfish people as a community, the most self-respecting and honest and agreeable, in the world — I notice it in the streets and in social life. The old puritan religion has got into them and qualifies them. Have had a splendid time here — seeing so many people I know — and not having to be hostile to them — for life in New York is a steady fight, steady discomfort. I can't go out to dine without armor on, and no doubt it would be so here, if I lived here and made myself so unpleasant as I do in New York. It is a great and wonderful change coming on here — and I'm going to try to remember how it feels to really give way to liking people and try to apply it to those sons of Belial in New York when I go back.

Look here, the *Manchester Guardian* is the ablest paper in the world; and the sort of Anglo-Saxon alliance that is needed is an international monthly or weekly on those lines. Just bear it in mind — I don't know how I could benefit America more than to send a copy of the *Manchester Guardian* for a year to every editor in America. The degree of gross ignorance that exists in the U. S. as to the principles of liberal government — the ignorance of what the Boer war means — an ignorance accentuated by the fact that our sympathies are with the Boers — and yet you don't know why — gives me the shivers. By the way, you don't know anything about England — you see enlightened people when you go there — awfully educated and nice people, people of ideas — now listen — *Those that you know* are about all there are in England. You've got to see London drawing-rooms — the average M. P., the average banker and merchant and swell and nobody — to see 'em for four months as we did to get any notion of the state of civilization on the island. I like the Americans much better. They are religious beings compared to the English — I mean the English from May to August 1900, for this war will qualify the whole temper of every one — make an — epoch — and I hope an epoch for the better before it is finished. . . .

Affectionately yours

JOHN JAY CHAPMAN

To the same

NEW YORK, *March* 4, 1900

MY DEAR JAMES

But this gives me a horrid fear you may have missed other numbers of the P. N. [*Political Nursery*] besides the one on 'Will to Believe' which I am now mailing you — and as I write them — I won't say chiefly for you — but for three or four persons, most of whom you are, I have to swallow the chance and see that you do get them in the future anyway. Dickinson Miller maintained stoutly at the time that I hadn't any idea of what the 'Will to Believe' was about at all — that the whole subject was something different — I don't know what — somehow some other subject. This is very likely so.

I am going on to Harvard at the end of this week for a séance of some sort with the Civil Service Reform association. I do hope we can make it discussion and not lecture. Of course if an audience is cold piety and comes to learn — you must give your talk, bow, and move. But the things I'm interested in, anybody knows about — and I'm going to make a hard try to just have a conversational evening and let the thing take what direction it may. There are many signs of life over here. If only the Boers can beat back the barbarians till our fibre gets a little stronger, we may develope a civilization — I am horribly afraid this militarism which arose in North Germany, swept over Europe and is now threatening England, may conquer us. It's a terrible reality. England has lost her head. The state of mind of the average Englishman is *bête* and pitiable. The thing is like an infection — I'm afraid I'll get it myself and these ignorant well-mean-

179

ing fellows, the American citizens, will catch it — and then — why, we'll have to wait for a new era and five hundred years later a rediscovery of free government.

J. J. C.

To Elizabeth Chanler Chapman
[On receiving the honorary degree of L.H.D. at Hobart College.]

[GENEVA, N.Y.] *June* 20: 1900

I forgot to say that I was given a degree of Doctor of Letters, $25 for travelling expenses, made a member of the P.B.K., and taken round in hacks. The degree is a danger. I'd have stopped it if they had told me they were going to do it, but I had no notion of it till it was announced with the others. There is something about an academic degree that is like I don't know what. It's like knighthood. It's disgusting and I shall avoid them if I can. It went through my head to write a *Nursery* article on College degrees and protect myself. But this is petty cash. The whole occasion — including an alumni dinner in the gymnasium — where I made another very short speech (on a presidential third ticket), an afternoon tea here with little tables on the large veranda — on a high country-place cliff overlooking the lake — and everybody and everything has been charming in the extreme — quaint, intelligent — *kleinstädtlisch*.

Tonight there is a President's Reception. The size of the whole thing may be given in the fact that the graduating class consisted of about nine. But don't think the speech-making in the town opera house wasn't a fine thing — for the place was full of women and families and friends and a band of four pieces — and a procession through the town led by the President with everybody in gowns, ribbands, and I marching with the faculty with a mortar board on my head, very proud.

JACK

To the same

[*After a talk with Grover Cleveland about a third-party candidate for the presidency in* 1900.]

[Boston], *August* 7, 1900

Two hours' talk alone with Cleveland. He is about the best man I ever met. But won't play our game. It's unreasonable to expect him to. He don't know how. He's of another generation. But when you consider that the ideas were new to him — the notion that you could do anything useful in this kind of way, the whole scheme of it was new to him — naturally enough. But he is perfectly unselfish and a very religious sort of person who knows human nature and thinks hard all the time — and he took in the notions and saw the points in a way that was very remarkable. Never was more glad of any visit I paid. He has one weakness. He is sensitive to newspaper criticisms and to the injustice and meanness of former associates — especially reformers. He has a touch of sentiment. In fact he's full of sentiment — dreads being thought ungrateful — perhaps of *being* ungrateful to the Democratic party — and hopes — still hopes — in which he is less astute than Benedict — that that sacred old fraud can be rescued from the barbarian hands.

I laid out our view of the need of the American people on the broadest basis — fifty-year basis — and talked without stopping for an hour — gave him local history and illustrations, etc., etc., showing that it wasn't politics but something deeper than politics that was needed. He kept nodding and following and assenting — and do you know he really did understand. But for a man who has always had a big party behind him to be turned into a John the Baptist by a conversation showing that it would be a useful thing if he did is hardly to be expected. Then he talked for half an hour and then we both chattered about everything for another. Like Benedict he expects a movement to regenerate something later — a resurgence of the good in the land — perhaps a recapture of the Democratic symbols — but all this vaguely. It's quite true he would get a terrible hammering if he joined us. He suggested that he would cause us to be ridiculed to have him. 'Ridicule!' I said, 'we *want notice.* That's one reason why we want you.' It's true it would be a magnificent spectacle to see the old fellow leading the boys — and having even his college professors and mugwumps doubt his wisdom. But he is not a great enough man to do it. That's the fact. Though he is a great man, the greatest among us — the simplest — with a very quick mind too, which I didn't expect — a most analytical powerful thoughtful direct weighty mind; and he wants nothing — except activity which he is going to miss if he doesn't look out — for he half thinks his activity ought to be over. He is very well in his health — next year his partisans, Edward M. Shepard & Co, will be pulling his leg to get him into a movement to get them some offices — and I shall be coming down to see him to tell him to keep clear of the gang — and make his life unhappy by dividing his conscience. He was so quick in seizing the meaning of phrases descriptive of our function — e.g. that all a reformer could do was to raise the moral issue — and raise it again — and again — and the good he did was the discomfort he gave to the club men who had to settle it — that we were now at the maximum of purity and minimum of power — that nothing was the matter with politics except personal selfishness and the only cure was personal unselfishness — the rest was illusion — the more metaphysical I was the closer he followed. The connection between these ideas and having *no organization* — he even seemed to understand. But for him to plunge and *do* it — lead it, create it! But I think he will know what we are after next year and that there is method in our madness and not take his understanding from Shepard & Co.

Well, that's all and it was very much worth while.

Yours

JACK

To William James

January 8: 1901
325 W 82 St., New York

My dear James

I don't seem to hear very good reports of you. They say you are in Rome — why Rome? a place of no stimulating power, full of catacombs inhabited by dead Americans.... I believe I could cure you of whatever it is you've got, if you would definitely give up ambition and come immediately back to this country. Ambition ruins any man — poets and philosophers above all others, for it contradicts — as a man who shuts his mouth can't sing, and the wheels and mael-stroms going round over here — why, the centre of force is over here — and — everything has changed during the last six months — does every six months — every man I know is different from what he was a year ago. You'll be an old flintlock discharging antiquated shrapnel when you get back. As for instance — everybody — every schoolboy, legis-lator, stockbroker, M. D., and clergyman is better up in spiritual science than you were, the time they used to throw bricks at you in Boston. Mrs. Whitman I have hardly seen — but I hear Mrs. Dorr has turned Christian. Henry Higginson rules peaceably over Boston and corrupts the youth by weep-ing in public on Decoration Day and voting for sound money in November. A bad man — a bad influence. I saw him last summer. He is so soft-voiced and soft with old women's caresses that, as Caliban says, I'd like to 'paunch him with a stake.' Every word he utters is low-browed concession — every example, the example of good business. Jim Storrow has been apotheosized into partnership with this holy smugness — L. H. & Co., Jim, who might have been a strong, steady, and straight force....

I believe I shall get Dickinson Miller to invite me on again to talk to the boys. It would be a good idea to keep in touch with the College and go once a year if it could be managed. So long as one preserved a perfectly indifferent or hostile attitude towards the university, it might be good to meet the undergraduates — so to forestall the doctrine that all decency is damn fool which they will get as they issue out of their cocoon. Suppose I meet a lot of boys — why, the first thing they will hear in arriving in N. Y. is 'Chapman is a malicious ass.' It might be a positive advantage to know some of them beforehand.

Seriously speaking, I wish you would think about coming home. Those lectures in Scotland or wherever it was were never of the slightest importance. It makes no difference to the present or to the aftertime, to you, to anybody, whether they be delivered or not. Why, look here — to turn from those academic diversions of yours to something more to the point: about the day after tomorrow I'm going to discover the cause and theory of everything — just one plumb jot of an idea. Now you know when I have it — I may never tell anybody, and if I don't — nevertheless it will prevail. Please remember me to Mrs. James and forgive so foolish a letter.

Yours affectionately
JOHN JAY CHAPMAN

To the same

[*The long silence before and after this letter was due to Chapman's illness which so seriously interfered with all his activities for several years beginning in* 1901.]

(Dictated)

RIDER'S FARM
HAINES FALLS, N.Y.
Aug. 25, 1902

MY DEAR JAMES

Thank you for sending me your book, I haven't read it because I haven't read anything for eighteen months, but I am sure it is a good book, and I am sure it is having a great success, because two people this summer have been reading it with enthusiasm, my sister-in-law, Margaret Chanler, and a friend of mine, Jane Russell. Now these are about the only people I have seen from time to time, but I can tell from their state of mind, and their desire to make other people read the book, that the book is going to get read widely. The quotation from the *Political Nursery*,[1] bowled me over. 'Another profound moralist' is good. I thought to myself, so that's what I am, is it? Why of course, why certainly, why not? But it really is a jolly idea in one way, because most people who have heard of the *Political Nursery*, regard it as a malicious and unnecessary squib, and will sit up hard when they glance at the footnote. I laugh every time I think of it in this light.

I am getting along finely though I can't walk yet but a few steps a day, and expect to be very slow about it generally.

I long to see you and shall come on sooner or later, perhaps a year from now, and stay about Boston and Cambridge for a while and revisit the place. Meanwhile I am

Yours affectionately
JOHN JAY CHAPMAN

To the same

BARRYTOWN
DUTCHESS CO., N.Y.
Sept. 28, 1904

MY DEAR JAMES

I don't think I ever got a letter that gave me so much pleasure as yours. I've been thinking about you often — and expected to see you at Commencement time, but was not up to the trip. My recovery is perfectly steady but slower than it is conceivable to understand — and I am content. Six months ago I began studying harmony — which all my life I had longed to know something of. I began with a few minutes a day and now I do a couple of hours. If algebra or chess had a sensuous and spiritual meaning — that's harmony. Being a sort of branch of mathematics, it's like a game where you always win — and really it's fine tonic. They say one can't learn music after one is grown up — but if every one of ten million German fiddlers knows it as a matter of course, it's extremely unlikely that a grown person can't learn it. At any rate it's an immense enjoyment and leaves no rack behind. My powers of locomotion are very

---

[1] In *The Varieties of Religious Experience* (p. 324) James quoted at some length from an article, 'Luxury,' in the *Political Nursery* for April, 1900, and characterized its author (Chapman) as 'a profound moralist.' This came at a time when he stood in the deepest need of encouragement.

limited, and if I overdo them it's no joke for anybody within miles, but they go forward. The thing that is most disastrous is being socially agreeable to people almost strangers. If some one comes to dine, I go into a cold sweat — lie awake after it and resolve never to see anybody. Then of course I can't help it and it does happen again and the bosom of the family and lots of neighbors force my hand and boost and discipline and kick my invalidism back to life.

I tell you all this not to talk about myself but because I want to tell you — I have no doctor. When I first got sick three or four years ago I had one for a few visits. He wanted to give me small quantities of strychnine — but he didn't know what was the matter with me, or what effect the strychnine would have. Who does? But strychnine and other poisons may be digested and the stomach is a natural place to put such things and has resources of its own against them — but the injection of anything under the skin really sounds horrible. I hope you will give it up before you have done yourself real harm. Why, nothing in the whole kitchen of pharmacopoeia ought to be put *under* the skin. Milk would be injurious.

We are building a house — and one of our ambitions is to get you and Mrs. James to come and visit us. Your references to the wife's share in nervous prostration seem to go to the right spot in my wife in a most remarkable way. She is almost more responsive than necessary. You see no one else has made the point, and I suppose there is something in it.

I am going to send a letter to Mrs. Frances Parkman for you to forward if you will. I have not her address.

I feel the same way about Boston. I can no longer find it, in my imagination. Boston is no more, youth is no more, a whole world and society and legendary stratum of time is gone.

Other such romances for others and the young will not want for them, but I might search the streets in vain. But you see this is really not true. I shall come on there and see you — and when you are gone I shall see — somebody's children — or my boy's friends — or strangers — and they will seem valuable and rightly in occupation. Were we to stay forever? Really I hope I shall not hear you are dead. These first knocks in middle life make me dizzy and expect all things. But I hope better. Thank you for your letter.

Affectionately yours

JOHN JAY CHAPMAN

To his Mother

Oct. 9: 1905

MY DEAR MAMA

... I send you some lines to Carlo Dolce which I wrote this morning — hardly real poetry, you know.

Your affectionate son

JACK.

To Carlo Dolce

Sweet Charley, if each waxy flower and saint,
That you faked in your life-time in canvas and paint
Can make you immortal — I'm damned if you ain't,
   Sweet Charley!

Fame plants in her children perennial seeds
Of deep human passions and deep human needs —
How deep in all breasts are the germs that she breeds
   In thine, Sweet Charley!

So long as mankind shall eat treacle on bread,
And mix sugar with rum for a cold in the head, —
While biliousness lives, thou canst never be dead
   Sweet Charley.

To Owen Wister

Wed. 3, *Dec.* 30: 1905

DEAR DAN

... We have been reading the H.[ouse] of Mirth. Half through. It is doubtful how much further we shall get — owing to the lack of bass strings in Mrs. W.'s harp. It is fearfully clever and for the first hour quite satisfactory —

but there is no stomach to it — and it's all reiterated — and it's thin and no reverberations of circumfluent atmospheric good feeling. It is becoming a weariness. No one could have given the beginning a more glad reception than I — I was so glad to have this social set torn to pieces. I was prepared to think every word masterly — and to explain all deficiencies — but I am worn out with one third of the book — damn them all, there is no saving your interest in these characters — they defy you, they rush to the wastepaper basket. After all one must have benevolence somewhere in any book.

Yours

J<small>ACK</small>.

All the same I have read more of it than all the passages of H. James would piece out to — if put end to end the times I've tried to read him.

V

New England Memories
Interlude

IN PREVIOUS chapters of this book there have been extensive extracts from Chapman's unpublished 'Retrospections.' They were introduced at the points, in the sequence of events, to which they were most nearly related. One portion of the reminiscences cannot be so definitely placed, for it concerns the Harvard and Boston which he knew first in his youth and continued to visit to the end of his days, with that mingling of pleasure and irritation in which the irritation becomes a part of the pleasure. Twice in the summer of 1900, passing through Boston while his wife was at Gerrish Island, he made characteristic expressions of his delight in the place. Once, on a sparkling 17th of June, it took this animated form: 'Charming town this on a day like this — all smiling, gay, cool, cheap, and cheerful, like Emerson in a straw hat on a steamboat landing.' Again in the same summer, failing to find a special delivery stamp at an apothecary's, he reports giving a 'letter and a tip to one of those men of science who for some reason choose to drive hacks in Boston and who give an atmosphere of virtue to the town. Most of them remind me so much of Mr. Brimmer I almost ask them for news of the Assos expedition.' These were the brighter moments — yet even when his Boston friends annoyed or disappointed him, he could write, 'The Bostonians are the stupidest people in the world. I believe that's why I like them.'

The portion of the 'Retrospections' to be inserted here, in the interval, as it were, between the years before and after the illness that cut his life into two parts, may be taken as looking both backward and forward. We have seen that in his opinion all autobiography is dated by the time of its composition rather than the time with which it is concerned. This, like the rest of the 'Retrospections,' was written while his life was nearing its end. It is, however, so characteristic of Chapman, even in its mistakes, and so illuminative of a vanished Boston under a piercing scrutiny from without, that it must be preserved.

Harvard

It was a good day to be at Harvard in the eighties. The Professors, Norton, Goodwin, Lane, Royce, James, Shaler, Palmer, were domestic and approachable. The examinations were easy. I should now be declaring that examinations meant little to me, but that in my breakdown of fifteen years later I dreamed every night that I was passing an examination. The tension, however, came from my own nervous disposition rather than from the rigor of the work.

The studies were prescribed for the Freshman Year, and after that, one had a large liberty of choice under Dr. Eliot's 'Elective System.' The elder tradition of a University as a place where a man could get an education if he wished one was given its chance. In those days the professors had a leisurely and social relation to their classes, partly because the classes were comparatively small; partly because the students had chosen their own teachers and wanted to learn. The old Medieval System was in force and there was life in the work. I chose my courses — somewhat at random — one under Goodwin in Aristophanes, one under Lane — I think it was Horace — one under Child — Chaucer, and one about the British philosophers, with Palmer. As for Norton, he had a sphere of his own, and every one came under his influence.

Our Charles Eliot Norton was a man of remarkable force, of remarkable goodness, of untiring public spirit. I have been running across traces of his activity ever since leaving college. For instance, in the Memoirs of John Hookham Frere, the translator of Aristophanes, I find Norton quoted as one of the early critics to praise Frere's work, about which Norton wrote an

article in the old *North American Review*. Now Frere's translations were published in 1847, when Norton was twenty years
old. The other day I walked into the Athenæum Library in
Boston and asked, 'But how did you acquire that large case
containing the library of George Washington?' The custodian
replied, 'Professor Norton many years ago raised [1] the money
to buy it and present it to the Athenæum.' Norton was a man
who started things, and must be thought of as a citizen of the
Franklin type rather than the Ruskin type — in spite of the
preciosity which came over him later. This preciosity represented a reaction against his theological inheritance, and he
became, as it were, a puritan turned aesthete. He retained the
battling qualities of his origin.

In the eighties Professor Norton was in his academic bloom
— an institution. His personal eccentricities and his habit of
articulate speech — every consonant a triumph, every vowel a
jewel — combined with his function as the prophet of culture,
led him into extravagances that delighted everyone. A younger
contemporary of his, Frank Sturgis — probably a cousin —
used to give a lecture (unfortunately I never heard it) in imitation of Charles. Sturgis would dress himself like Charles,
walk on like Charles, take his seat on the platform with the
care of a character in a play by Ben Jonson, and begin in a musical, modulated, deliberate voice — 'I purpose this afternoon
to make a few remarks on the hor-ri-ble vul-gar-ity of EVERY-
THING.' Norton attended the lecture and enjoyed it as much
as anyone. He was indeed crusted all over like an armadillo
with comfortable scales, and he would have patronized Michael
Angelo. His mission was to promote beauty in its every form,
beauty of manners, of thought, of conduct. He was the Bal-
dassare Castiglione of his day. But let us not forget that he
was also the friend and helper of all classes of men. At his
country house in Ashfield he used to give an annual harvest-
home dinner to his country neighbors,[2] and on every Christmas
day at Shady Hill in Cambridge he gathered to his board such
students as he believed to be far from their homes and in need
of the comforts of a friendly household. His sister, Miss Grace
Norton, was quite as remarkable as himself, a quiet, old
dowager, who lived in a large house of her own, and by her

---

[1] It would be more accurate to say *collected*.

[2] The 'Ashfield Dinner' was in reality a local festival in which George William
Curtis and other 'summer residents' also bore an important part.

manners, brains, and experience of the great world always suggested the dowager — the dowager of diamonds and real lace, the dowager of the elder world. She had known every one of importance for fifty years and corresponded with the great men of her times. She was at home with old and young, and in her later years became the cynosure to whom intellectual foreigners brought letters, and with whom she struck up friendships. There was a naughty side to her; indeed, there was a *bad little girl* side to her, an unexpected savagery and out-rageousness which made you angry for a minute, till you saw that she was good granite. Both she and her brother Charles were first cousins of President Eliot, and all three were as tough as boxers, and sometimes gave you an unexpected uppercut which was not quite within the rules.

I somehow came to know Miss Norton quite well while I was an undergraduate, and I recited to her in her parlor my Ivy Oration, the conventional pasquinade of Class Day, in order to be sure that I had not over-stepped the limits of pro-priety in my sallies. For many years after graduation I cor-responded with her, and I used to lay traps for her in literary criticism, into which she plunged like a walrus. For instance, I made use of the word 'suppliance' (in the sense of something supplied) in a note to Miss Norton, and received an avalanche of contemptuous abuse in her reply. Thereupon I produced a large piece of wrapping paper a yard square. In the centre of this I drew a rectangle two inches by two and inscribed in it the words, 'Ham. I, 3, 9. I folded the paper up small and mailed the missive to her. In order to solve the riddle she was obliged to unfold the thing and consult a copy of Shakespeare.

To show the kind of savage she was, during the Great War I wrote some extremely gloomy verses called 'May, 1918,' which were to appear in the *Atlantic*. One of her cronies, a reader of the Riverside Press, showed her a proof of my verses, upon which she wrote me an outrageous letter, a savage and impertinent diatribe. Miss Norton's rare interest in my ex-cursions into different fields of writing was of great importance to me, and her sometimes boisterous frankness an inspiration. I have read in the books that a friendship between a lady of the great world and a young aspirant in any field of art has a good sort of spiritual influence on each of them.

Professor George Herbert Palmer was a kind, a holy, and a gloomy man. He followed up the students who took his courses.

His rooms had low ceilings, were walled with books, and darkened by large, distressing steel engravings of the great philosophers — Locke, Kant, Hegel, and the rest, into whose company Palmer lured the serious-minded youths and charged them with capsules of religious poetry — Wordsworth, Herbert, Vaughan, etc. He told me once that Wordsworth was 'the fashioner of his soul,' which seemed to me a dreadful way of saying it. He used to give readings from his translations of the Odyssey in a lyrical falsetto monotone that suggested that peculiar limbo of moral feeling which foreshadows suicide. He was an anchorite, but there was a wellspring in him — hidden, blocked up, and subjugated, filled with the junk of philosophic thought and moralism. This wellspring broke out later, as we know; but it could be felt even in the days of his first widowerhood when I was at Harvard. Palmer had not only a wide but a lasting influence upon his scholars, and he kept them in sight after they left the University. There was a power in him. The course I took with him was on the English philosophers, Locke, Berkeley, Hume, etc., and I owe to Palmer a philosophic experience that left a permanent trace in my mind — an impression, a preoccupation, that I never quite got rid of. It came about in this way. We had polished off Locke and were making a flight over Berkeley in order to reach Hume. In dealing with Berkeley, Palmer outlined Berkeley's paradox as in the nature of the human intellect, and how we possessed no acid or touchstone that could test the validity of our own Reason. Our explanations of any problem were, for aught we could find out, merely a part of our dream. This was news to me, and I said to myself, 'Very well; until one can get past this barrier, I do not intend to burden my mind with philosophy.'

This idea has been with me — you might say — every minute since then. Palmer gave no explanation of the paradox, but stated it clearly; and it was worth while having gone to Harvard to hear the case honestly stated. From time to time in after years, when I met a competent metaphysician, I would enquire of him whether any progress had been made in the solution of Berkeley's riddle, and received always the same reply, that no answer had been found. It was due to Palmer that when at the age of sixty-eight, I ran across Lucian's apostasy as to the validity of geometry, the idea was familiar to me. The strange point was that between the dates of these two philosophers, no one else had noticed this discovery.

Palmer himself passed into my dream with Berkeley — Berkeley as the smiling saint and philosopher, Palmer as the sad figure on the barometer that comes out when it is going to rain. He was a good old boy, and after his marriage with the famous Alice Freeman, he became rejuvenated — or at any rate juvenated — for I doubt if he had ever been young. With the proceeds of his book about her and of his Odyssey, of which two hundred thousand copies were printed for use in the public schools — he sent me one — [sentence uncompleted]. I always sent him copies of any books that I wrote, which he would acknowledge with monosyllabic comments on postal cards — occasionally with longer homilies, growing greyer with the years till they became, as Jaques says, 'mere oblivion.'

My experience with Professor Child was disappointing. He was an old-fashioned, caustic, witty little fellow of the Scotch type, the headlight of modern Teutonic scholarship in America, and his subject was Ballads. His attitude toward the students was Pecksniffian.

I once showed him with some pride a few folio pages of a broadside of Charles II's time. I had bought the thing at an auction in New York in my Washington Square days. Child glanced at the thing, dashed it with the back of his hand and returned it to me with scorn. (One would think that he would be pleased to find a boy who bought such a thing.) He became for me the symbol of the German school of documentation, classification, and footnotes. Kittredge was his pupil, and Kittredge was an iron man who would be seen stalking about Cambridge with a vicious looking small bag filled with burglar's tools and footnotes on Othello. I looked with a shudder on both Child and Kittredge and to this day feel that between the commentaries of such men and the works of genius to which they tag their notes, there is a deep gulf fixed.

Social Boston

In our day there was a well-organized social system for the young in Boston — a Friday evening dancing-class for the young at Papanti's, the son of the original Papanti, a gaunt Yank who was master of ceremonies. This seeming-casual circumstance of a dancing-class was almost more important than the University, for it made one a citizen of Boston forever after. I met last summer a woman whom I hadn't seen for fifty years, and we were both quite moved, though our acquaintance had been of a 'chassez, croisez, ladies' chain' variety, with a final bow to the mothers on the platform.

I am no philanderer and I hate to open up these old drawers; but I was always in love — a great many times anyway — and, Oh, my! how I did suffer from a sense of responsibility and inferiority. I can today block the north light of my studio and turn on various side-bulbs and dentist-probes and see my youth as a continuous torture chamber. The dancing class, however, was a symbol of the social system of the town itself; for the town was a genial hum of interlocked families who had come down from colonial times with their *lares* and *penates*, ceremonies, festivals, traditions, and passwords, local oracles, stock-dignitaries, and licensed characters.

The rest of America laughed at Boston for being over-educated; but the rest of America, including New York, was under-educated. In Boston there was always humor, and after all it is humor that makes social life agreeable. In Boston, there were *bons mots* that circulated and dinner parties that were interesting. One was always hearing of the quips of Dr. Holmes, Dan Curtis, Tom Appleton, Mrs. Bell, or Mrs. Dorr. True wit is a blossom of sophistication. I recall one of Mrs. Bell's sallies. She had been taken to Cambridge to attend a Greek play, and on being asked about it, replied, 'Oh, it was one of those Greek tragedies where one of the characters on the stage says to another, "If you don't kill mother, I will."'

Tom Appleton was a middle-aged man of pleasure with everything handsome about him. In talking about canvas-back ducks, he said, 'They say that their exquisite flavor is due to the wild celery on which they feed, and that farm-yard ducks would taste the same if fed on wild celery, *but damn 'em, they won't eat it.*' Does not that give you the portrait of a rich worldling in a club window? Methinks I can see his burnished exterior and his handsome watch chain.

Mrs. Dorr was intense, a heart-to-hearter, and extremely indiscreet in revealing the heart-secrets of others whom fate had thrown in her way. She lived in the heart-secrets of others. She had been one of the original transcendentalists, a friend of Emerson and Margaret Fuller. She gave large dinners and caused her guests to change places in the middle of the meal, called all women by their first names and all men by their last names. She had a low-pitched, authoritative voice, and was a tyrant; but dear me, what social talent! Mrs. Bell —

quite an old lady in my day — one of the Choates, and a real cut-diamond in wit — used to say that if the Virgin Mary should come to Boston, Molly Dorr would drop in at the Bell household and say (here she imitated Mrs. Dorr's growl), 'Helen; dine with me tomorrow. *Mary'll be there!*'

Mrs. Dorr would call from her seat down a long dinner table, 'Edith Everett, you have talked long enough to Lowell. Let him come and tell me about his experiences in England. Royce! tell me your story about the snake-eaters.' The persons addressed would be ruffled; yet the heat generated by an interruption would pass — Lord knows how — into social exhilaration. Mrs. Dorr was highly educated, had lived in Europe and known the *literati*, great prelates, scientists, British countesses who drove about in phaetons. She loved fine bindings, religious essays, old Roman prints, good china, India shawls, and rosewood. Her pose was that she had known everybody intimately.

Of course all salons arise out of the ambition of clever women and the vanity of clever men whom they subtly flatter. Yet salons arise only in deep-rooted civilization, and there existed such a civilization in Boston.

Mrs. Howe was an institution — only perhaps too much so. The shades of Dr. Howe and the Blind Asylum flanked her, and the 'Battle Hymn of the Republic' was chanted around her. Her very numerous descendants made the most of her eminence and somewhat explained Boston's attitude toward her. Boston society was tired of her. Nevertheless, she was unspoiled and benignant, enjoyed life intensely, was poor, had the habit of literary work, and was indifferent to society. I came late in life to know her well, for she was the sister of Samuel Ward, the famous raconteur, wit and international man of pleasure who married a grand-daughter of John Jacob Astor and was the grandfather of my second wife. Mrs. Howe was the daughter of Samuel Ward, the banker, and used to relate how she had seen the kegs of bullion unloaded when they arrived just in time to save the State of New York from repudiation in the thirties. It is curious to remember that in her girlhood she had taken lessons in Italian from DaPonte, the librettist, who had written the words of 'Don Giovanni' and the 'Magic Flute' for Mozart. The thought makes one feel near to the Eighteenth Century. Mrs. Howe was for many reasons an outsider in Boston Society. She had enjoyed the ostracism meted out to the anti-slavery people before the Civil War and had travelled abroad with Dr. Howe, the opener of the eyes of the blind, when all the philanthropists and scientists of the Western world flocked to do him homage, and Boston Society meant little to her.

At the time I was at Harvard and for many years afterward there reigned a *sanctum-sanctorum* in the air when Boston or Boston's gods were mentioned. I once wrote a conventional literary paper about Charles Norton and took it to William Roscoe Thayer, the editor of the Harvard quarterly journal of the period. Thayer laughed genially in my face in referring to it. He said he had his lesson in the past as to papers like mine, and they simply couldn't be printed in Cambridge. When my mildly humorous article on Charles was printed in a book of my miscellanies, Miss Norton wrote me a meat-axe and scimitar letter about it. She was especially indignant at my having called Charles a 'satellite' of the pre-Raphaelites. After her death, however, Mrs. William James wrote me quite casually that Miss Norton had said to her that 'What Jack Chapman had said about Charles was true — all true.' I remember causing a chill that could be felt to run round a stately dinner table by a casual remark about Hawthorne, and Walter Page, while Editor of the *Atlantic Monthly*, positively struck out some words of mine about James Russell Lowell that hinted at the idea that Lowell was not as great as Milton. My brother Henry used to say to me, 'But when you write such things as that you are pulling a brick out of their monument. Of course they resent it.' Massachusetts had a sort of miniature nationalism of her own.

The first time I ever saw Henry Higginson was at our dinner table in Washington Square, New York, when I was a small boy. I asked him how he got the scar on his face, and he said that a very fine gentleman in a very fine uniform on a very fine horse had given it to him. The great services that Henry Higginson did the country were due to his congenital, frank, overmastering emotionalism. On the other hand, his great business talents led to his becoming a tyrant, and in his later years he became something — what was it? — well, something that faintly suggested King Lear. The unity of his life was magnificent. His generosity in public benefactions of all sorts made him the father of the town. He did not belong to the era of agitations for reform; he came later. I remember being shocked by a story told me by a lady who had sat next to Alexander Agassiz at a lunch party. Agassiz was Higginson's brother-in-law and a large owner in Calumet and Hecla, the bonanza copper-mine of that day. Lee, Higginson and Company were, I think, the bankers of the company. Agassiz had said to the lady, 'Why, if it were a question of bribing a State Legislature, I should regard it in the same light as the removal of a bank of sand.'

Mr. Higginson's earliest ambition had been to become a musician. In default of this, his determination became to give music to his countrymen. His instinct told him that this must be done tyrannically — and his instinct was right. Not by propaganda for music, but by music itself, must the taste for music be instilled. The most striking illustration of this law — even more striking than the history of the Boston Symphony — was the influence of the Kneisel Quartet. Thomas's Orchestra had somewhat blazed the way for orchestral music, but the taste for chamber music did not exist. Mr. Higginson toured the land with his Kneisels, who played the stiffest kind of classical quartets and inculcated the taste for chamber music into the hard-minded, ignorant American public. He gave them ears and they began to hear. His example comes to my mind every time I hear mention of one of our crying needs — a literary weekly of the first order, like the Supplement of the London Times. The passion for letters and the money to support the project till it becomes self-supporting must be found in one man; and it will take ten years to establish such a paper. At the end of that time the critical taste of the country will have been sharpened and its literary standards improved.

I had a correspondence with Mr. Higginson apropos of Dr. Eliot's Five-Foot Bookshelf. It was at a time when I was putting things to rights in the world, and I objected to Harvard's name being used as a trademark for a commercial enterprise. Mr. Higginson wrote me a long reply in which he appealed to my better nature and called on me to recognize the character and attainments of Dr. Eliot and the Managers — technically called the 'Fellows,' who were then in charge of Harvard's destinies — (they were a fairly representative group of upper-class State Street financiers) — and asked me what I could wish or hope for more. I showed this letter to Owen Wister, an intimate friend and all but a confessor in the Higginson family. Wister recognized the touch of old age in the epistle and said to me, 'You must never show that letter to a mortal soul.' Well, I didn't, and I recall it *en passant*, because it was an appeal to my 'loyalty' — to that sentiment which takes the place of good sense and intellect in appeals for support made by our schools and colleges — an idea, a phrase, borrowed from politics which has no relation to education.

Mr. Higginson's rather simple philosophy of life was once expressed in my hearing at a lunch-party at Mrs. Whitman's at Beverly Shore, where the question was asked, whether he would give orders to the members of his orchestra as to how they should vote at election-time. He replied that he certainly *should*. Now consider what an ingenuous and spontaneous nature such a remark implies.

I wish myself back at those lunch- and dinner-parties in Boston. In those days we were searching for truth. No doubt a large element in this feeling is the glamour of youth. And no doubt this was true in the case of Talleyrand when he said that no one knew the meaning of happiness who had not lived before the fall of the French Monarchy.

It will be seen that I have been digressing and retrogressing, not following dates but memories and visions; for all these recollections are parts of Harvard. The academic part was only the gateway. My friendship with William James and my acquaintance with Josiah Royce were of a later period, though both of them were circulating in the heavens above when we were in college. A lecture on the sexes was given before each Freshman Class and James performed the function in my first year. He looked quite young then, and very severe. But after all, what can the poor wretch of a lecturer say upon such an occasion? He becomes coldly philosophical at his peril; he can't be humorous; he can't be religious; he can't be purely scientific and medical. James left on me a strong impression of stoicism — a thing at variance with his nature, as I afterwards knew it. If you compare the early photograph of him published in his Letters with the photographs taken in his later life, you will notice a great change in the size and shape of his head. This was due to the enormous quantity of technical philosophy that he had laid up in it; for he had not only gone through all the great classics of the subject, but had followed the European developments of it in his own day. He had hundreds of feet of them on his book-shelves. He could not only talk their languages but translate them into a lingo of his own, which was comprehensible to the younger generation and to the professional thinker who took psychology very seriously. He expressed his own religious faith in the symbols of this passing pseudo-science.

I had some passing correspondence with him in the early days of our New York civic agitations, and at a later period, when my wife and I were in England and James was lecturing at Oxford, we persuaded him and Mrs. James to take a small tour in the Cotswolds, which became the foundation of a real intimacy for us all. Mrs. James was the equilibrator and regulating power of James and the only person in the world who understood him.

I once made an attempt to express to James the consciousness which a simple-minded person might have of the presence of God as the *causa causans* of his own anatomy. I forget where the interview took place; I think we were standing in the corridor of a Boston hotel. At any rate, the surroundings were dreary in the extreme. At the close of my fable I said, 'Can you not imagine that such a creature under such emotional conditions should cry out, "Abba, Father!"' James started like — not a guilty — but angry thing surprised, and a trap door opened under the interview.

So also with regard to Free Will. In the shipwreck of the elder conventional philosophic system — Reason, Emotion, Will, etc., James had preserved the Will. He believed in Free Will, and said that without that we had a 'Solid Universe,' which he thought very undesirable and therefore untrue. My own feeling has always been that the more one's will dissolved in the Will of the Universe and the nearer one could come to the feeling of a personal relation to God, the better it was. But like a well-trained lawyer who comes to believe in the reality of legal principles, James had accepted bits of the old philosophic machinery — a lever here and a turn-table there. The Will was to him a reality.

Another bout with him was over the word '*concept*,' which, as I understand, was one of Kant's contributions to thought. I opened a book at random and asked, 'What is a concept?' Of course, he couldn't reply that a concept is a term whose meaning you can only come at by seven years of technical, professional study, and it somewhat resembles the Knight's move in chess; you must know the game. After a pause I said, 'There ain't no such thing as a concept.' James said, 'Yes, there is such a thing as a concept.' This was the close of the discussion.

I must have been as much offended with James as he was with me, or I should not remember the incident so clearly. I ought to have said to him, 'My dear James; whatever religion may be, it is a *passive* experience. If a man is booked for it, it will come to him. Let him not try to assist or foment it. Religion is a thing that encloses, envelopes, and unifies, affects both the mind and the muscles, the inner and the outer — the digestion and the dreams of a man. The only way to assist religion is to be passive, indifferent — all the bars down. Every snare you set to catch it scares the bird.'

James himself was the child of Christianity bridled by the languages of historical, metaphysical theory — a saint in chains. He finds a chink here and there in the walls of his jail-psychology, and shows the sky to his followers. You can find his jail at night through the light that streams out of his chinks. The light is the light of Christianity.

My experience with James suggested an idea that has dogged me ever since; namely, that the progress of man's thought has been constantly arrested by the crystallizations of the finest intellects. We are the victims of their avocation. I once had an experience of this sort — trivial yet significant. I had for a year been writing humorous articles quite regularly for *Vanity Fair*; and I sat down to write a paper on Shakespeare. It took me a month and a half and filled many waste-paper baskets before I could get near the subject. Everything I wrote turned under my hand into a skit for *Vanity Fair*.

Since writing the above I have looked into James's Letters published by his son. I find that James wrote to James Henry Leuba in April, 1904: 'My personal position is simple. I have no living sense of commerce with God. I envy those who have, for I know the addition of such a sense would help me immensely. The Divine, for my *active* life, is limited to abstract concepts, which, as ideals, interest and determine me, but do so but faintly, in comparison with what a feeling of God might effect, if I had one. It is largely a question of intensity, but differences of intensity may make one's whole centre of energy shift. Now, although I am so devoid of *Gottesbewustsein* in the directer and stronger sense, yet there is *something in me* which *makes responses* when I hear utterances

made from that lead by others. I recognize the deeper voice.
Something tells me, '*thither lies truth*' — and I am *sure* it is not
old theistic habits and prejudices of infancy. Those are Christian; and I have grown so out of Christianity that entanglement
therewith on the part of a mystical utterance has to be ab-
stracted from and overcome, before I can listen. Call this, if
you like, my mystical *germ*. It is a very common germ.'

The progress of Faith on the earth seems to consist in evap-
oration of the capsules into which minds great or small continually strive to enclose it, and the same is true of all varieties
of historical research, poetical theory, educational theory, etc.
Poetry and the fine arts alone seem to survive the crystallization.

I cannot think that anyone ever met James without feeling
that James was a better man than himself. His altruism and his
regard for Dr. Eliot led him to make one mistake which I
knew about by accident. James had fished up in Berlin a brilliant, philosophic adventurer called Münsterberg, and had
planted him in Harvard. Thereupon the place began to heave
and surge with Münsterberg. Münsterberg had a head shaped
like a watermelon and about as large. He spoke and wrote
teutonically like a zoölogical monster. I once said to James,
'Why do you stand for the self-advertising of that adventurer,
Münsterberg?' or words to that effect. James said, 'He's useful.
He's ready to go to San Francisco and deliver a lecture at
twenty-four hours notice.' This view accorded with the general
policy of Dr. Eliot. All the same, James came to dislike Münsterberg. James had caught a Tartar.

Then came a grand, philosophic ceremony at the opening of
Emerson Hall. The college authorities passed a self-denying
ordinance to the effect that none of the Harvard professors
should speak — only distinguished guests. But — O madness!
— Münsterberg was appointed to introduce the speakers. Of
course, he made a self-glorifying harangue between each one
of them. He danced upon the lid of Harvard, while all the professors gripped their umbrellas and ground their teeth.

James, on leaving the hall, went home and wrote to Münsterberg such a letter as made the retirement of one or the other of
them inevitable. All this was told me by Henry Rutgers
Marshall, the psychologist, a gentleman of the old school who
lived in New York, wrote books about Consciousness, and was
an intimate of James. At this time I happened to meet Marshall,
who showed me a letter he had received from Münsterberg,

enclosing a copy of an ample apology by James to him. James had let slip the chance of getting rid of the incubus that not only sat on the stomach of the university, but had become James's own *bête noire* — Münsterberg.[1]...

The saintly side of James appears to a disadvantage in this episode, for even a saint ought to know his world and accept a scuffle when the clock strikes. Besides, James had, himself, introduced the snake into Cambridge, and there would have been an especial fitness in his driving it out.

James, Palmer, and, I think, Royce, too, had a feeling of loyalty to Eliot, the sort of dog-feeling that great leaders inspire in their followers. Milton had it for Cromwell; Roosevelt inspired it; Wilson inspired it. A friend of mine, who, as a younger man had lived through those Princeton University struggles which first brought Wilson into notice — told me that there were at that time sixty men, professors and else, at Princeton, who were Wilson-mad, and would follow him to the death. Some of them didn't even *like* Wilson.

There was only one man at Harvard who fought Eliot in faculty meetings — George L. Kittredge, the Shakespeare scholar — who was a terror. It was Yank bite Yank. There was one occasion when Kittredge's onslaught was so fierce and continuous that Eliot bent forward and covered his face with his hands. Some contemporary described the scene to me. The delicate-minded Henry James doesn't give this side of Eliot in his life of him. The era of Eliot was the age of big business reorganization and the genius of the age controlled Harvard. Her managers were hard-minded business men, and Eliot was their great white paladin.

The Tavern

There were a lot of agreeable men, old and young, in and about Boston at the time of my graduation and of my years in the Law School, and a group of them turned by degrees into the Tavern Club. I vividly remember one of their early meetings in the rooms of Frederic Vinton, the painter. It was a dinner given to Salvini — at which the great actor recited the death

[1] To keep the record of this episode clear it should be noted that on the day after the opening of Emerson Hall James himself wrote to Henry Rutgers Marshall, as follows: 'I learned today that [Münsterberg] had not jumped in... to boss the show yesterday; but that Palmer, Dewey and the President had all urged him to preside. So I did him injustice and take back my blame. It is our own fault. If we are too lazy to do any work ourselves, we are estopped at carping at the way in which he does it.' See Ralph Barton Perry's *Thought and Character of William James*, Vol. II, p. 152.

scene from La Morte Civile and managed at the climax to dispose himself on the floor with the grace of a gigantic serpent — the serpent of the Laocoön.

As time went on, the Tavern came to play an important part in the history of Boston. The group was always made up of old and young, distinguished and undistinguished, artists, actors, musicians, literary men, amateurs and professionals; and it has always retained its informal, spontaneous character. Almost all complimentary dinners tendered to public characters are tedious. It was not so here. So warm and general was the welcome of the Tavern Club that if one of its former guests passed through Boston again he would look in on the Taverners. I shouldn't wonder if more unforgettable dinners have been given at the Tavern than in any other club in the world. The club-house itself had a good deal to do with this influence. It somewhat resembles a converted tavern. It is an old brick house on a side street, has been made over many times, is full of odd objects and mementos, all of them casual and unobtrusive, and is crowned by a large open loft with rafters above it. Here plays, operettas, and burlesques are given by the members. The house contains three or four bedrooms, a billiard room, a dining room, a library and a second-story open-air veranda for meals in summertime.

I was not an early member of the Tavern, for after leaving Boston I lived in New York for many years and had neither time nor money for excursions; but I had known the original group before leaving Boston and was almost counted as a member. For many years I have used the Tavern as a nest, a secret habitation, a refuge in times of crisis, tragedy, or fatigue. Everybody welcomed me, nobody bothered me. I have been part of the place, and the place of me, and its rooms are full of memories — scenes with my sons while they were at college — some of them almost tragic, many jovial. After Victor's death I stayed at the Tavern for ten days and read Plato's Republic, and in the intervals resorted to the Public Gardens and took tours in the Lohengrins. In more recent times when I have had some particularly hard job on hand, something that required an astronomical abstraction of mind varied by the relaxation of familiar faces, cups of tea, pipes of tobacco, and no appointments to keep, I have moved on to Boston and roomed at the Tavern.[1]

[1] This passage has been used in my *Semi-Centennial History of the Tavern Club.* (Privately printed: 1934.)

VI

Middle Years
1905–1914

THE establishment of Chapman and his family at Sylvania marked the beginning of a period of domestic felicity lasting till the end of his life. In all that time the tragic episodes of earlier years had but one counterpart, in the death of the first-born son, Victor, as an aviator in France. The deaths of other members of his family fell more within the inevitable order of nature.[1] The winters in New York, at the Eighty-Second Street house close to Riverside Drive, excursions abroad, and the midsummer months of about ten years on Seven Hundred Acre Island at Dark Harbor (Islesboro) on the Maine coast, afforded frequent changes of background, but Sylvania became, and remained, the base and symbol of home. Here the married state, the nurture of children, the cultivation of friendship, the extension of human relations in many directions, had their fullest exercise.

With respect to the married state Chapman held positive views of his own. He believed in it heartily, though admitting that 'certain remarkable natures arrive at an equilibrium at the age of fifty-three.' Marriage, he maintained, 'merely does the thing *quicker*, or in, say, two seconds and at an earlier age — say seventeen'; this from a letter of July, 1897, which continued: 'As for me, my private self, I could never have got there alone — and never wanted eternity, immortality, or even mortality, alone. Wouldn't take it on

[1] His brother Henry's in 1913, his mother's in 1921.

205

any terms — take no interest in it — desire to be excused — and always felt so.'

To his primitive belief in marriage as a necessity of self-fulfilment he added the conviction that, of all relations in the world, marriage is that in which absolute frankness, untouched by any poison of diplomacy, is imperative. 'Only in the sharing of thought lies truth,' he could write before his second marriage; 'all things are half things, dead or crooked, till looked at with the beloved.' In the same letter he exclaims, 'All things that were ever told to you from the beginning of time were told with the promise and distinct understanding that as between you and me was to be no privacy, no wall, no retention. No other than this is the union, or the understanding of it, among all tribes, nations, polities, where monogamy prevails.' As with the interchange of sympathies, so with the conflict of wills, the strivings of one against the other for supremacy, and the consequent need for the highest faith and unselfishness at every turn. In moments of conflict he would declare, 'marriage is hell' — and so often that it became a family adage. Another pet announcement was, 'I pray God every time I leave the house to keep me from falling in love with the first woman I meet on the street!' An assumed cynicism is far from a perfect disguise. It amused the impish Chapman to put it on. The man himself spoke in the words of 'Both Choruses' in 'The Treason and Death of Benedict Arnold': — the passage would not seem an intruder in the 'Book of Proverbs':

> Who shall praise a woman, save He that made her, save God that understandeth all things?
> I will sing a song of woman, and magnify the wife of a man's soul. His goodness she has discerned when no man else can find it; his crimes are known to her, yet is he not in them: she seeketh his soul among many.
> She divineth salvation out of hell; and bringeth water from the desert. Who shall praise a woman save He that made her; save God who understandeth all things?

Before his second marriage Chapman faced frankly the perils involved in an amplified mode of life. 'The first thing you know,' he wrote to his future wife, 'we'll be drowned in possessions and then by thinking of our horses' health.' He had seen good men degenerate through ease — he would not degenerate. 'It is not so easy to keep the keen vision which an empty stomach lends, if you have footmen. I fear a footman. I tremble before a man with hot water.... Let's keep the New Testament open before us. The losing of wrath is to be feared.... If I become classed with men at ease about money, the Lord protect me. It is a steel corslet against the heart of mankind and the knowledge of life.' An empty stomach had in reality never much affected his own keen vision, yet certainly, and inevitably, the background of his existence underwent a large amplification, especially through the occupation of Sylvania seven years after his second marriage. There remained uninvaded, however, 'a hidden ground Of thought and of austerity within,' not merely shielding him from the dangers he had so feared, but holding him free to exercise his own powers according to his own bent.

As those powers returned after his long illness, his old taste for dramatic writing afforded a natural outlet for them, and between 1908 and 1911 he produced five books of plays. Two of these contained four plays each, all for children. The simplicity and directness of the young always had a strong appeal for Chapman, and never more than through these years when he was winning his way back to health. The re-espousal of an arduous cause, like that of political reform, would have been quite beyond his depleted nervous and physical resources. The writing of plays for children was not.

In the Preface to the first of these little books, 'Four Plays for Children' (1908) he wrote: 'The following miniature plays are the outcome of an interest in children's recitations, children's theatricals, school exhibitions etc. We have had

207

a series of these things at Barrytown, in which the children of the neighborhood, including my own and those from the village school, have been engaged. The experience has left me with the belief that all children, however differing from one another in natural endowment, can be equally counted upon to learn their lines thoroughly, and to work with unflagging enthusiasm over the production of a play.'

Chapman's plays for children were thus produced at Barrytown, Islesboro, the University Settlement in New York, at Philadelphia under various auspices, and at schools in several places. The music written by Philip Goepp, a Harvard classmate, for 'The Lost Prince,' may well have contributed to its relatively frequent production. It was not merely the appeal of simplicity in children — for its very oppositeness to Chapman's own complexity — but an habitual element of pity that warmed his heart towards the young and helpless. Instances of spontaneous kindness, in countryside and town, might be related at considerable length — the bestowal of unsought alms, the provision of healing measures and continued care otherwise beyond the reach, for example, of a boy with tuberculosis or another in need of orthopedic treatment. There was, besides, his sharing of poetry with the 'shut in' and the young, of which more will be said on a later page. 'The gift without the giver is bare,' and with every gift Chapman gave prodigally of himself.

There can be no question either that Chapman believed confidently in his own powers as a playwright or that he must have been disappointed in his failure to win any substantial recognition for his plays. Three of them, obviously designed for adult actors and audiences — 'The Maid's Forgiveness' (1908), 'A Sausage from Bologna' (1909), and 'The Treason and Death of Benedict Arnold: A Play for a Greek Theatre' (1910) — never received the test of production by a wholly professional company. The last of these must nevertheless take a high place among Chapman's writings.

A quality of nobility, in which poetry and historic imagination are joined to admirable purpose, marks it as 'closet drama' of a distinguished order. It had an outdoor representation at Katonah, in which Chapman's brother Henry enacted Benedict Arnold and Ben Greet Father Hudson, and another with Walter Hampden as Father Hudson at Mount Kisco in the summer of 1911. Chapman's own reading of it was something not to be forgotten. 'The Maid's Forgiveness,' a mediaeval play of serious intention, and 'The Sausage from Bologna,' a rollicking farce in four acts, once produced by amateurs in New Orleans, fail to convince a reader that they would prevail on the stage, or that in writing them Chapman was proving himself truly a dramatist. The personalities he imagined paled beside his own, and the 'tricks of the trade' eluded him. It is one thing to live drama, another to create it.

That the plays for children were acted, and with success, is not surprising. Humor, sentiment, and a gay fancy brighten many of their pages. They were in general, however, primarily pastimes for Chapman himself, as author and coach, as for the children who performed them, and it is not to be expected that between the covers of a book they can produce any such impression as they seem clearly to have made when endued with the graces of living childhood. Yet here and there a poetic passage of enduring beauty offers the reward of repeated reading.

His interest in children led him far beyond the writing of plays. In daily life he could not encounter them without overtures of friendliness, often in the form of little gifts from his own pockets. At Barrytown, up to 1912, the children of the Public School would troop to Sylvania on Friday afternoons, and Chapman in his library would read to them the poems he had read to his own children. It was a sad day for host, hostess, and guests when it was felt that these pleasures must come to an end.

Then for two years there was a more difficult experiment

in New York. The Chapmans took a store on Tenth Avenue below Forty-Ninth Street, in a district known as 'Hell's Kitchen,' furnished it as a club-room for young people, provided teachers of basket-making, sewing, and chair-caning, and bade the boys and girls of the neighborhood welcome. They flocked in, chiefly Irish and Roman Catholic, of ages from about seven to twelve. They were not an easy lot to handle. Mrs. Chapman recalls the whole experience as 'like heavy surf-bathing with a bad undertow.' Another such club had adopted the motto, 'No praying and no cursing in this building.' Chapman, on the contrary, began the evenings with the Lord's Prayer and a few verses from a Psalm — which may have accounted for a surrounding hostility to what seemed too Protestant an enterprise.

One episode must be recounted. Two unruly boys were ejected on a certain evening and forbidden to return. Chapman expected them back the next night, and back they came. He was awaiting them outside the door, prepared for the scuffle which ensued, but not for this piece of deviltry: the boys filled their mouths with kerosene, sprayed it on his beard, beneath which they lighted matches. He did not take fire, but when the boys' eyes and mouths became so inflamed that they could blow no more, he said in a friendly way, 'Now rub your hands on your coats and get them as clean as possible, then take this pocket-handkerchief and wipe your eyes.' They obeyed quietly and walked away.

When he reported the matter the next day to Mrs. Chapman, then in a hospital, he was much discouraged — unscathed, but in sorrow for Tenth Avenue. His wife asked him if he had not felt as he stood there that his patience was doing some good to the boys. 'No,' he replied, 'I felt that I could be of no use to them, but' — this as if to himself — 'that I might possibly be doing good to somebody in China.' The next winter the venture was discontinued, on the orders of Mrs. Chapman's physician that she should not resume her part in it. The enterprise was not one which Chapman could conduct alone.

The solitude adapted to his powers was that of individual thought and expression, and, as the period now under observation proceeded, Chapman's writing turned more and more to prose — a larger production of verse (some of it for the stage) was to come later. In 1910 he produced a prose volume 'Learning and Other Essays,' containing papers that had appeared in the *Atlantic Monthly, Harper's Weekly*, and other periodicals, even his own *Political Nursery*. The shortest essay in the book, 'Norway,' occupies only three pages, and may be taken as a touchstone of appreciation of Chapman's humor. For another touchstone, there is 'The Doctrine of Non-Resistance,' already mentioned: here is a test of response to Chapman's religious faith. 'A man ought to follow truth,' he declares, 'and when he does this, he will find that, as he gropes his way through life, most of the light that falls on the path in front of him and moves, as he moves, comes from the mind of Christ. But if one is to learn from that mind one must take it as a lens through which to view truth; not as truth itself. We do not look at a lens but through it.' This thought, expressed before his illness, was fortified by that experience, and reaffirmed by his including it in the 'Learning' volume.

The nurture of his children has been mentioned as one of Chapman's preoccupations through these years. This had many aspects and angles. A letter to one of his boys, at school, illustrates clearly his fashion of seeking to help a son through the lessons of one's own experience.

> ... I am rather disturbed at finding how sensitive you are to being criticised. It is unpleasant to discover that one has not acted in the noblest manner — and yet the willingness to concede this seems to be the beginning of honesty — intellectual honesty with one's self. Every body is apt to be caught napping in some way; and it doesn't mean that you are a lost soul because you now and then look too sharply after your own interests in some way. You are full of generosity and

regard for others and accuracy and honesty in a hundred other ways; and the mere fact that you should sometimes be found not enough interested in some one else's rights doesn't alarm me. The thing that does a little alarm me is your tendency to defend yourself so eagerly. This used to be called *pride* — and was one of the deadly sins, etc. I don't of course know what it *really* is. None of us know what things really are. But this pride or self-defence, or unwillingness to admit one's imperfections, comes from avoiding the unpleasant. It's extremely *unpleasant* to think that one has done a mean thing (or a stupid thing, or a flighty, unwise thing). The people who don't bear the pain of seeing themselves look ugly get farther from truth all the time.

A good wholesome discomfort, a willingness to admit that one has *very likely* been guilty, is the only safe or strong attitude. Even this attitude is extremely unpleasant — especially at the beginning. Now we are all of us being pushed hither and thither by the forces of life; and I notice that the people who can't bear the unpleasant are shoved to one side and gradually sloughed off till — when they are 50 years old they don't amount to much. Society conspires to side-track them, while the people who can stand pain are constantly enlarged and strengthened and adopted by the world — till they are made into great characters and strong intellects.

The tendency to avoid facing one's own weaknesses is like a smooth surface that sheds off the salutary life-giving, tingling force that arouses shame and honor.

Now inasmuch as you are going to be confirmed, and, as this is a period when you are examining yourself to try to find out what your faults and dangers are, I thought I would tell you about this....

It was in this period that Chapman began giving expression to two antagonisms to which he was yet to devote much thought and utterance. They were the menaces of business-mindedness and bigness at Harvard, and of Roman Catholicism. The announcement of the 'Harvard Classics' — President Eliot's 'Five-Foot Shelf' — drew forth an emphatic letter, in *Science* for November 1, 1909, denouncing the spirit of commercialism represented in the authorized use of the word Harvard in connection with a money-making venture in books, however serviceable they might prove to the half-educated. A paragraph in this letter should be read for the light it throws on this and many subsequent criticisms of Harvard by Chapman.

> It is with a kind of joy that I attack Harvard College, knowing that Harvard supplies the light and liberalism — hardly elsewhere to be seen in America — by which I am permitted to proceed. I should grieve to have this freedom extinguished, as it would be if the alumni were forbidden to take a critical interest in the institution.

It was not until Chapman became openly critical of Harvard that his *alma mater* began to recognize his existence. In a private letter he once tossed off the term 'alma-matriotism,' to define an obnoxious sentiment. It was a sentiment against which he delighted to inveigh, and once he caused a good friend in the Century Club, Henry Osborn Taylor, to write to another, Edward S. Martin: 'Jack has put me all four feet on Harvard's side. I care for her most. Years ago I told Jack that he shouldn't kick his mother in the belly every time she annoyed him.' Chapman's indignant response, reported by Osborn, was 'Yes, I will; yes, I will.' When the episode was related, in lines of bantering verse, to Chapman, he gave them the terse endorsement, 'Our Intellectuals.'

It was at the request of the Intellectuals at Harvard itself that Chapman delivered his 'Phi Beta Kappa' poem on June 17, 1912.[1] Harvard was its theme. He wondered if 'his subject' might be 'himself disguised.' . . .

> 'His own heart by his own heart criticized —
> The thing most worshipped seeming most disprized.'

That thought must be remembered for its bearing upon Chapman's antagonisms. One 'thing most worshipped' by him was certainly learning, another religion. The manifestation of learning, as he conceived of it, in Harvard College, and of religion, as embodied in the Church of Rome, es-

---

[1] On April 7, 1923, Chapman delivered a Phi Beta Kappa oration at Princeton.

pecially with reference to education and politics in America, did not square with the ideal view in which he held these two objects. The speaking of one's own mind was a cardinal principle with him. Unhampered as he was by the responsibility of putting his ideals into workable forms and administering them, he could, and did, speak his mind with complete freedom. He was bound to give offense — he wanted to give offense. In his letter on the 'Harvard Classics' he referred to letters previously written to President Eliot and Henry L. Higginson, and declared, 'At this time I can realize, in re-reading these letters, that there was a good deal of desire to give pain, to see the worst, to nail the claws of the offenders to the ground, to state facts in such a way that the Harvard officials could not answer without making humiliating confessions and without, in effect, acknowledging that I was more virtuous than they.'

It was through giving offense that he believed it possible, in the parlance of Stevenson, to stab the spirits of the offended broad awake. Policy and compromise held no place in his philosophy, nor did sweet reasonableness enter often into his methods of persuasion. Yet underlying what often seemed perverse and mistaken there was a fundamental principle, an integrity of purpose, that could not be ignored. His own declaration, already recorded, 'It is an accident when I *do* right, but I *am* right,' carried with it implications — justifications if you will — more inclusive than he could have imagined. These are to be borne in mind especially in relation to his bitterest antagonisms. His opposition to the Church of Rome will be considered on later pages — also his criticisms of Harvard in some detail.

If slavery had not been abolished before his day, the mingled Jay and Chapman blood in his veins would have been sure to make him one of its most flaming foes. Though he never identified himself with the organized cause of the Negro, there was one instance of an outrage upon a black American which roused him to action at once unique in its nature and completely characteristic of himself. What was it that so moved him, and what was his action?

The newspapers of August 14, 1911, were indeed enough to stir a man of Chapman's sensitive fibre to the deepest feeling. From the New York *Tribune* and *Evening Post* the hideous story from Coatesville, Pennsylvania, of a Negro variously called Zacharia and Ezekiel Walker may be reconstructed. According to the *Tribune*, Walker, when caught on Saturday night, August 12, in the act of holding up and robbing a foreigner near the works of the Worth Brothers Steel Company, shot and killed Edgar Rice, a special officer of the Company. The Negro tried to escape but was himself shot and was lodged, under police guard, in the Coatesville Hospital, from which a frenzied mob dragged him, and burned him just outside the town. The *Evening Post* added details lacking in the morning paper. Walker was reported to have confessed at the hospital to having drunk too much on Saturday and, in his exuberance, to having fired three shots near the Worth mills. Rice, he said, came to arrest him, and when he asked 'what for,' he was told 'for carrying concealed deadly weapons.' '"Then I won't go,'' says I, trying to pull away. He drew his club and reached for his revolver and it must have been then that I shot him.' Rice being dead, this story could be neither confirmed nor refuted. The Negro's fate, however, is a matter of record. After his killing of Rice he was caught in a tree in some woods near by. When his armed pursuers began shooting at him, he shot himself in the mouth, fell to the ground, and was taken to the hospital. As the mob dragged him thence to his death, he declared that he had shot Rice in self-defence, and pleaded, 'Don't give me a crooked death because I am not white.' It was truly a crooked death that waited him, bound with ropes to his hospital cot, which was placed, with the victim, on a pile of rubbish as his destroyers, their faces bound, for concealment, in handkerchiefs, lighted the pile. The ropes burned, Walker made a dash for liberty, tried to climb a fence, but was dragged back and hurled into the flames. The *Tribune* of August 15 printed a Coatesville despatch of the day before, saying, 'For hours today the scorched torso, the only thing left of the Negro Walker, was kicked around by children on the highway a short distance from where he met his death.' At length it was put in a box marked, 'To be claimed by relatives,' and taken to the morgue. The fury of the mob was feared even there. The immediate attempt to identify the lynchers was met by the denial of every suspected person that he knew anything about the affair. According to the *Evening Post* an astonishing number of citizens were out of town or early in bed on that Saturday night. Even a year later it does not appear that one of the savage murderers had been brought to justice.

The grisly story is retold here not for its own sake but merely to recall what Chapman found in those August newspapers of 1911 that led him to the action he took. Thus he described it himself:[1] 'I was greatly moved at the time the lynching occurred, and as the anniversary came round my inner idea forced me to do something. I felt as if the whole country would be different if any one man did something in penance, and so I went to Coatesville, and declared my intention of holding a prayer meeting to the various business men I could buttonhole.' So he appeared, not for condemnation but for intercession. The town had already achieved a notoriety which it did not at all enjoy, and the local writers for the press may well have felt, a year after the lynching, that a pall of silence was the best covering for any revival of so shocking a subject. Fortunately there are letters from Chapman relating to it all — and there is his speech at the prayer meeting.

Mrs. Chapman was in Islesboro at the time, much concerned for what might befall her husband in this adventure. On August 14 he wrote to her from New York that Miss Edith Martin, one of those 'children of the New Testament'

[1] See *Harper's Weekly*, Sept. 21, 1912, and *Memories and Milestones*.

who had fortified his spirit, was going to Coatesville with him — 'which puts my mind at ease as if I had a big bull-dog to guard me, not from lynchers but from — I don't know what. I feel as if she understood this sort of thing. She liked the address and approved — rather to my surprise, so my mind is at ease.' On the next day he wrote from Coatesville: 'Very hard to get a hall — the prejudice against the subject. I have hope to get the *City Mission* (sort of salvationists) but naturally can't get it Sunday, therefore try for Saturday.' Then on Friday, August 16, two missives were mailed, one containing the following notice cut from the *Coatesville Record* of that day:

In Memoriam
A Prayer Meeting will be held
on Sunday morning, at 11 o'clock,
at the Nagel Building.
Silent and aral [*sic*] prayer:
Reading of the Scriptures:
Brief address by John Jay Chapman.
In memory of the Tragedy, of August 13, 1911
O Lord receive my prayer.

The second missive of this day was the following letter to Mrs. Chapman:

By good luck the local newspaper is a daily which appears in the afternoon, so — having hired my room by 9.40 this morning — (and most grateful to get a room — which I succeeded in by slightly changing my policy. It occurred to me that it was *not necessary* — nor morally right — to *burden* the conscience of the real estate men with my plans and purposes. By not knowing them *they* remained innocent). Curious experience in the backward working of principles in moral force: — I was a little afraid last night that perhaps I wasn't quite sincere — and really was after an agitation and not a prayer meeting — so I resolved it must be real, and drew the notice so. Well, at the newspaper office there was some doubt and trouble and the head man was called in. (Everybody says he's a tremendous shouter for peace and not an honest man.)

But as I stood waiting for him to decide I thought to myself —
'If the *Record* refuses to print that notice — the Philadelphia
papers will give Coatesville such a hammering as they have
never received' — (the hammering by the press of the country
is what has injured them and pained them) and I was just
going to suggest this when he saw his way to print the ad.
He somehow saw it. He must be an able man. The room will
hold 20 people but is very conveniently situated. If there
should be a crowd, we can always move to a larger place.
What I mean about principles is that by really abandoning
politics I had bungled into the astutest thing I could have done.

No one who has not been up against it can imagine the
tyranny of a small town in America. I believe a good old
fashioned Medicean, or Papal, or Austrian tyranny is child's
play compared to it. There's a dumb, dead, unlistening decision to do what it *has been decided* must be done — what business
demands — e.g. to not raise the lynching issue in Coatesville
today — by Jove, it's amazing! It doesn't irritate me —
as the old political tyranny and hatred of opinion. Merely
because the battle is won. It's a joke, this idea of Coatesville —
whereas there was a good deal of seriousness in the successful
way they used to put down independent ideas in New York.
The great men of Coatesville are not so heavy....

I haven't suffered from either fatigue or change of climate.
I got into a nasty old hotel yesterday — didn't like the morale
of it either — filthy room and no air — piazza in front, and a
bar room as big and desolate as a dream. My, what that long
dreadful stretch of stinking bar implies — one hundred men
could drink there — fifty anyway, and what ruffians! Now,
I've come across the street to an airy, clean, large, comfortable
room and have nothing on my mind and nothing to fret about.
I have sent for Miss Martin, though I *almost* didn't — because
it's so long a journey — and then I thought after all that was
her mission.

Yours

J<small>ACK</small>

On Saturday, the 17th, there was a shorter letter, calm,
and confident that 'people will come to that meeting tomorrow, but it's all right if they don't.... I go to bed very
early — I am extremely well. I have not had a moment of
worry since I secured the room. I think the inhabitants

rather like the idea of a prayer meeting. I get this in the air. "Who's back of this?" said the editor of the *Record* fiercely. "No one," said I; "at least I am." This satisfied him as he didn't know what kind of a feller I was, but I looked meek.' By this time Mrs. Chapman's anxiety was relieved by a telephone talk which Victor, in Maine, achieved with his father.

Chapman's notion that the Coatesville people liked the idea of his meeting and would attend it was entirely mistaken. As he himself described the audience,[1] 'A friend of mine [Miss Martin] came over from New York and we did hold the meeting in an unused store — a prayer meeting with Bible readings, addresses, prayer, silent prayer, and a talk on the whole matter. Two persons came: one an antislavery old Negress, who lives in Boston and was staying in Coatesville; the other a man who was, I think, an "outpost" finding out what was up. We held the meeting just as if there was a crowd, and I delivered my address. There was a church meeting going on opposite to us, and people coming and going and gazing, and our glass front windows revealed us like Daniel when he was commanded to open the windows and pray.'

What passages of Scripture were read to his audience of three, what prayers were offered, there is now no means of telling. The address remains — brief (only seven small pages of print in the 'Learning' volume), written with austere restraint and tragic beauty. Some sentences from it have already been used to set the scene. So poignant was the whole brief address that one who has not already seen it in print should make its acquaintance through the Appendix [2] in which the greater portion of it is given.

Having thus delivered himself of the burden upon his heart and mind, Chapman joined his family at Islesboro, quietly returning to his habitual mode of life so strangely interrupted. Through all of this Coatesville episode he appeared in his chosen rôle of the solitary reformer, free from all danger of

---

[1] *Memories and Milestones*, p. 226.   [2] See Appendix B, p. 473.

finding himself outvoted by fellow-members of a committee.
The rôle was more nearly that of an Old Testament prophet
than of an American of the present day. The prophets, in the
light of immediate results, were often mere voices crying in
the wilderness. So indeed it was with Chapman in this
instance, but in all his life there was no better illustration of
his own words, 'I am saying things which will some day be
thought of, rather than trying to get the attention of anyone.'

Such was Chapman's theory. In the earlier days of his
extreme activity in agitations for political reform in New
York, his theory and practice were often at variance, and his
written and spoken words were uttered, as we have seen, for
instant effect — for today, not for 'some day.' It happened,
however, that only a few years after he went to Coatesville
he recalled in a brief paper, 'Memories of Paul Fuller' some
of the experiences in which he and that fellow-worker for
honesty in politics had shared, and from this paper a paragraph on 'the philosophy of agitation' well merits a salvage
from oblivion:

> A life of agitation does not always make men bitter, but it
> is apt to make them rough. They feel that they must shout
> and dance in order to be heard. Let us suppose that your pro-
> blem is to bring to the attention of a rich smug merchant the fact
> that he is half unconsciously allied with some sinister abuse,
> for which he is morally responsible. In Voltaire's time you
> might write a clever satire upon the man, which every one
> would read. But in New York in 1890 no one would read a
> satire: one might as well feed bon-bons to a hippopotamus as
> expend wit upon the American business man. On the other
> hand sharp abusiveness hurts his feelings, and stings him.
> They did not sting him much, but a little. If you waylaid him
> and beat him half to death, he would avoid you for six months
> by going down a side street when he saw you coming. And if
> you continued to smile pleasantly on him, the time might per-
> chance come when he felt safe in your company, and then some
> day he would ask you, 'Do you mind telling me why you beat
> me on such and such a day?' Aha, you have prevailed! Now
> at last you have the man's attention. Such, reduced to words
> of one syllable, is the philosophy of agitation.

At the time of the Coatesville tragedy the Negro was occupying a large place in Chapman's mind. In the spring of 1911 he was planning a drama, never accomplished, with John Brown as its central figure. In 1913 his 'William Lloyd Garrison,' the most substantial single biographical study in all his writings, was published — obviously the fruit of extended preparation. The 'Benedict Arnold' play and the Garrison book can hardly be read without raising the question why Chapman, with all the wide range of subjects on which he touched, did not produce something about a character which would seem so peculiarly made to his hand as John Brown. His letters to Mrs. Chapman in the spring of 1911, immediately after their return from Europe, with an excursion to Algiers, reveal his having gone so far towards such an undertaking as to visit Harper's Ferry. On his way thither, late in April 1911, he wrote to his wife from New York that he would content himself with the two books he had on Brown — Sanborn and Villard. 'You know I've never known the literature of the subjects I wrote on. I never knew the Emerson literature — except Emerson himself.' At Harper's Ferry the Hillton House — 'the coffee is made of peanuts, but the eggs are very good' — and the surrounding country seemed to interest him more than the object of his quest. Besides the physical distractions there was an enthusiastic reading of Butcher and Lang's Homer, and before long he was writing of his possible return. 'If by that time I have started my play, it will be all right. If not, it will be time to give up this job (for the time at least), and go and dig at something else.' The battlefields he had meant to see could wait: 'My struggles over the John Brown drama are not of this kind, but are thoughts over the dramatic setting, the artistic framework and convention and device, the spirit and the means and the essence. I could do it as well at Barrytown, I believe. It is in its nature a difficult, obscure matter and must come by nature or not at all.' Alas! that it came not at all, for the spirit of Chapman and of John Brown had enough in common to make the failure to accomplish this piece of work a lamentable loss.

To offset it, however, there was the 'Garrison,' published in 1913, and therefore presumably that 'something else' at which he was planning to 'dig' should the 'John Brown' come to naught. I have called it his most substantial single biographical study, and so it was; but it is hardly to be called a biography. On one of its own pages he refers to it himself as 'this essay.' He might even have called it a series of essays. While the book was in the making, he wrote about it to his mother (December 25, 1911): 'The idea of the book is to put something into the hands of the young person which will be an introduction to the whole subject. I intend the volume not as the end and summary, but as the opening up of a field of historical research.' Most of the facts of Garrison's life are to be found in it, but slight regard is paid to proportion, chronology, or any other conventions of biography. It is rather a philosophical study of a great movement, with brilliant generalizations on agitation and reform in their larger aspects. The career and character of Garrison of course provide the basis for the discussion, but much of its value lies in its revealing of Chapman himself. In no other place does his concern for decency and honesty as between human beings declare itself so fully. Nor did he make any other study of society so tellingly designed to show the timidity and slavishness of the supposedly unenslaved in America.

The danger of beginning to quote from it would lie in not knowing where to stop. A single passage beyond one already cited must, however, be given. These are the final words of the section, 'Garrison and Emerson':

> Garrison set a great brazen trumpet to his lips and blew; and the walls of Jericho fell. Garrison dies, and his trumpet sounds no more. Nevertheless, the small, inner, silver trumpet of Emerson caught and sounded the same note; and it continues to sound the note, shaking down the walls of inner Jerichoes in men of later and ever later generations.

The diversity of Chapman's interest through the period reviewed in this chapter has been suggested in the preceding pages. The letters now to be quoted will illustrate it still further, and will touch upon three journeys abroad. These were in the spring of 1909, the winter of 1911, and the summer of 1914. The outbreak of the war found him in Germany, whence he made his way instantly to England. The experiences then encountered belong to the next chapter, but it is a happy circumstance that almost the last of the letters to be quoted in this section — from Fulda on July 28, 1914, to Langdon Mitchell — presents in a vein of humor the attitude towards Germany and the German mind which was soon to become so vitally serious a matter in Chapman's own way of thinking.

Letters

To Owen Wister

DEAR DAN

I've been here for a week staying with George Dorr and revisiting the glimpses of the moon — Porcellian, Somerset, and Tavern, etc. Really I have enjoyed myself. What a world it is — of friendship and tie. There are twice as many people about here that I know and care for — ten times as many — as there are elsewhere all over...

Yes, I should be sorry to see Roosevelt President of Harvard because I do not regard it as important to keep Harvard to the front — in the ordinary sense — that is in numbers, popularity, and general notoriety. This he would probably do — but as an influence on young men he is about the opposite of what we want. He represents, you might say, the reigning vices — glorying in being seen, Hurrah for us, Americanism of a magazine variety — (alas, you are not free from it) — and the settlement of questions by a sloppy emotionalism which turns to anger when confronted with world-old, world-deep, and world-near moral alternatives. (Which tendency I must say you are entirely free from.) In one way the question who is president of this or that institution is not so important as it seems — for it seems to me that the importantest things are never taught by institutions at all — but come straight out of individuals and go straight into individuals, and these are born and appear in unexpected places, and while we are quarrelling over who shall lead our sewing circle the real leader has been born and died, and the thing is controlled by him.

But if you descend into the visible and the talkable and insist on taking an interest in America as distinct from Europe — what does America need? It needs men whose minds are not in America but who are willing to sink America where truth is concerned and who have no desire for anything except truth — truth often which makes us seem cheap and horrid and compels us to admit that we do not know — that we do not know a damned thing about the whole business — or only one thing, viz., that Europe is ours also — that is, it is all one concern. To return to the visible. We see a marked inferiority in intellectual fibre, in training — in our American scholars as compared to Europe. Average for average we are not in it anywhere. For a good many years past I have asked each specialist I met — 'Now tell me how we stand in your particular subject' — nowhere. Well, scholarship is a sort of branch of religion — a form of self-sacrifice, a form of worship, an interest in something for its own sake. . . .

To William James

BARRYTOWN, N.Y. *May* 29, 1906

MY DEAR JAMES

I have been desperately hoping, and do still, that somehow you and Mrs. James will spend a week with us before we all die. And now if you are getting so old and contemplate that form of suicide — living abroad — I am going to lay wires, use influence, and take steps to bring about some sort of reunion soon.

Why, of course, of course — I wonder how you have stood it so long in the treadmill — how you have kept free from the shackles of pedagogy, institutional life, Cambridge, Boston, Massachusetts, and the era, which is eating up all these and transmuting them into corncobs? I have always wondered at it and wondered whence you drew the vitality to do it. And now that you have borne the burden and heat of the day and shined your light abroad — and it has been a real light — and has helped many and steadied much — why, now you can be turned out to browse and live peaceably at Oxford or Florence or where you will, with the respect, gratitude, and affection of everyone who has ever heard your name following you to your grave.

I do not suppose that with your active mind and an unimpaired vigour, you will really escape the fate that seems to fall on Americans who go to live abroad — the fate of coming to regard small things as important. Were you worn out, you would be safe, but your energy will destroy you. But it is folly to talk like this. You have never been influenced at home — then why abroad? And I don't care what you do. Go and lead the brigands — go and give your sanction to the Pragmatists — you still cannot stay the sweet influences of the Pleiades which will be in your work. But if you do not — if your destiny leaves you still bound — like a sort of only half-inspired Prometheus — you will hear before you die the strains you have waited for so long — and stopped your ears to so earnestly — and which are heard only when search is exhausted and curiosity is dead and stillness follows because there is no power of motion left. Then the wind from without blows upon the soul and having blown it out — or seemingly out — blows it to a new life, steadily, and the old is seen to have been but a blustering and beating of the same power, and to have been a part and origin and necessary stage leading to the exhaustion, and all the past has been controlled and ordered — and we have come from the beginning, as a calf is made to go into his stall. . . .

To the same

325 West 82 St.
New York City, *Feb.* 13: 1907

My dear James

I found I had a dinner party and so cut your last lecture — and, by the way, I afterwards met a lady — not one of your auditors — who says quite seriously, 'Ah, Fragmentism — such a good name too.' So you see you and your footnotes are making a big inroad into the metropolitan consciousness. . . .

James Croswell is my candidate for President of Harvard. But he is not worldly enough to suit. He'd get fifty blackballs out of fifty-one votes. A College President *must* be worldly. You said so yourself — though not in those words. Well, it's not true. I used to care somewhat about Harvard College; but since those circulars about Eliot's seventieth birthday and the three million fund, and all that bombast and vulgarity, I cannot go it. I cannot bear to be called 'a loyal son of Harvard.' This chest-thumping, back-slapping, vociferous and cheap emotionalism, done to get money and land money, is too much like everything else. I felt so clearly that the whole age's decay of scholarship and decent feeling could be shown from the Eliot circular, that if I hadn't been sick (and sworn off anyway) I should have come to Boston and given a lecture on the *English* of the document — the mere tone of it. Everything seems to be a base-ball team — jollying, rough good-feeling, and a thoroughgoing belief in money and *us* — and it's bad form to be accurate about anything except cash. Harvard is a base-ball team, and they'll bid high to get the best man they can, even if they have to out-bid the Sioux City Nine. The truth is, I don't know much about Harvard, and don't doubt there's much else in it — only I always happen to meet the boom-side of it. Eliot has boomed and boomed — till we think it's the proper way to go on. He *must*, or lose foothold. Well, why not a man who does not boom? Is boom the best thing in life? Is it all boom? Is there now and to be nothing ever but boom, boom, boom? Is there not something that operates without money — not anywhere?

Why, my dear fellow, Eliot and the crew of howlers have wasted and destroyed more by their buildings and their gates — they are submerged in their improvements. It will take hairshirts to get the sky clear. It is no one's fault. They done the best they knew; and the next generation can pick up the pieces and painfully recover and reconstruct the idea that a university is a place of thought, truth, religion.

Pierpont Morgan is the actual apex as well as the type, of the commercial perversions of the era. The political corruption, etc., the power behind all.... Now then, at the dedication of the New Medical School, Eliot goes about in a cab with Pierpont, hangs laurel wreaths on his nose, and gives him his papal kiss. Now what I want to know is this — what has Eliot got to say to the young man entering business or politics who is about to be corrupted by Morgan and his class? How eloquently can Eliot present the case for honesty?

Can he say anything that will reverberate through the chambers of that young man's brain more loudly than that kiss?

If Eliot is a great man, I want a small man.

All this sounds to you remote — because you never, perhaps, were in an office — but in the offices of men entering the field, comes one form of the struggle between light and darkness, and it comes very quick, within a month or a few days — and it always comes; and it is always elementally the same — lawyers, architects, engineers, doctors are up against the commercial forces just now — very distinctly. Well, they are daily doing better, seeing more clearly, understanding the thing more clearly, but they need light, not fog, from the headlights of humanity and progress.

Of course you will say, 'Yes, but they never have got it from them in the history of the world.' That's all I mean.

Yours affl'y

J. J. C.

To Elizabeth Chanler Chapman

MUNICH, *April* 14, 1908

... I like the Bavarian women — I saw four thousand of them at the music. Of course it is an exaggeration — but I will say that I never saw a Bavarian woman that I wouldn't willingly marry before sun-set.

But I am old. Why should I talk of these things? Candor compels me to question their mode of dress. They are not ashamed of the body. They have never reflected that the average female is not physically beautiful. When very young she is skinny. In middle life she is baggy — in later life she is bulgy. The Bavarian women accept all this, and simply wind or lay thin stuffs against the body — nothing stiff, nothing pleated — in youth they lay them on up and down; in later life round and round but always thin. The stomach appears as a stomach — the breast as a breast. They are completely unconscious and simple. I like them better than any women I ever saw anywhere. They are educated — equal to men? no — but clever and nice. The most, best womanly women in the world. They are like Eve. *All* of them are so. The old and the young. . . .

To the same

ROTHENBURG, *April* 28: 1908

Next to San Gimignano this town beats all. It's 300 years later than S.G., has pointed roofs, a complete old wall with turrets — my window is over the wall and looks down the valley — a dear old inn. Everybody ought to come here. It's beautiful and complete. The whole town. It ought to be put under glass.

Later.

Well, it's less powerful than San Gimignano, but more beautiful, and equally perfect. You must come the next time you are in Europe, even if you give up the trip to getting here. I like it about as much as any place I ever saw or dreamed of. It's one of those bird's-nest towns — not a house has been taken down or put up since 1650. All the towers and all the walls are here — and the place is full of healthy people and lovely children. No matter where you are in the town, you look down a street and — and lo — a view of fifteen miles — valleys with churches and bridges and poplars and streams. O my, it's a wonderful place — and this inn is wonderful. You walk into your room without going up stairs. It is a big double room and out of the window — you find yourself four hundred feet above a bend in the river which you can hear rushing — birds are singing. From this window, in the valley below, you can see a mill, a gothic chapel, a double bridge (like an aqueduct) and then as the rampart winds you see a half mile of winding turretted city-wall, with pear trees and market gardens below it on the steep slope and red roofs, spires, angles, nooks, gables — and all old — why, it's an incredible place — and a great big clean kitchen on the same floor.

You must not die without seeing Rothenburg.

I've seen it enough now. I lie on the bed and just *think* about it. I want to go away and come back to it. It can't be as beautiful as I think it.

To the same

... I was bored with Oxford till I found this place — and stumbled on a Wesleyan church last night — where a very nice man was preaching to six people about the Holy Ghost — a very short sincere talk. There was no choir, and he wore no surplice ... I hate Oxford, but can stand this inn and the Wesleyans. If I lived here a week I should join the Wesleyans. If you subtract the picturesqueness and historical — I mean external and internal — picturesqueness, I believe Oxford is the emptiest town in Europe. I'll tell you what, Wesley was a pretty great man — to put up a fight against this gigantic piece of furniture, the Church of England — in Oxford too — and have churches going in his name 150 years afterwards — and he never would leave the church. He always called himself the church....

Went to Magdalen to a service — twenty-four people at least — the doors locked — and various kinds of wooden images intoning the service. The singing bang-up, but the music insignificant, except Bach's chorale — *O Haupt voll Blut und Wunden*, one verse of which was sung without organ, O sacred head once wounded — and very beautiful. Imagine drilling a lot of small boys to intone the Lord's Prayer. The whole thing is done with hearty gusto — without any element of reverence or intelligence. It's bad form to read the lessons in such a way that a listener can catch the drift. It might as well be Latin. There's a certain religious possibility in the drone of the Roman Catholic service — if you are far enough away. But this is like a shooting match.

Cushions for your feet. Heavily bound prayerbooks tied to the stalls — you sit in the apostles' stalls — a big fat velvet cushion for each book — attention! fire! they wheel and say the creed — I must get to a service in Keble — if that's the high church one....

To the same

[*William James at this time was delivering at Oxford his Hibbert Lectures, published in* 1909 *as* '*A Pluralistic Universe.*' *The* '*Frenchman*' *of the ensuing letter was Henri Bergson.*]

BADMINTON
Friday aft. [*May* 22, 1908]

... James's lecture was very good — I hardly know how much it was understood. I wrote him a note about it. It seemed to me to be a destruction of all authority in philosophy — and that it ought to be called 'A Defense of Poesy.' I cannot be sure that he so meant it or whether he sees the consequences. But I got more impression of dawn than I ever had before at one of his lectures. The form of the thing was very peculiar — a close and *long* discussion of Achilles and the tortoise — which paradox proves the futility of logic and philosophical reasoning. Because Achilles does, you know, in real life overtake the tortoise — all this treated very dryly and gingerly, with a tongs. Then a sudden plunge to the suggestion that we must treat the whole living character, heart, body, soul, and being together — as it lives — all dissection is misleading.

One step beyond this — i.e., treating of all of them — of everything together as it lies — would be mysticism and religion. I think James would resent the name of mystic and yet he is coming to be what I call a mystic. He didn't take the step in the lecture. He is very happy in himself, I think — just now. He talked a great deal about a Frenchman and seemed to think he was delivering a lecture about this Frenchman. He was rather dull about the Frenchman. He says the Frenchman is a crackerjack. He quoted long, confused things — at least he lost the point in giving them — O, but James says the Frenchman is way up.

The Frenchman's idea seemed to be the Wordsworthian idea of inner will — only James didn't put it so well as this. He called it pragmatism, but said you needn't call it pragmatism. Well *I* don't — no matter what it is.

JACK

231

To Mrs. William James

PORTCULLIS HOTEL
BADMINTON, GLOS.
May 25, 1908

MY DEAR MRS. JAMES

... Strange world. I go to Oxford. I hate Oxford and yet find there what I was long seeking, the key to the Pragmatists. The name has bothered me. And, apropos, I meant to write to Professor J. suggesting this: If you produce a pumpkin you can name that Pumpkin — e.g. 'Sloper's Punkin.' But if you produce a philosophy you must call it *The Truth*. The world at large will call it 'Sloper's Punkin.'

To William James

39 CLARGES ST. PICCADILLY
LONDON, *June 2, 1908*

DEAR JAMES

It's too bad I didn't know about this before the lectures are over — I'd have posted down to Oxford, and got to you to leave ten minutes at the end of the hour and invite questions. Then I'd have opened up with — 'Well, Protagoras, I understand you to maintain,' etc. — we'd have shown them what a philosophical lecture ought to be like. But it's chiefly 'good form' as you say, that is choking them. I ran across a very over-educated, finical, cross man called Robert Brydges [*sic*] — a poet — who was full of curiosity about you and spoke of your vast following. He is the sort of man who has lost the power of admiring and is used to having the last word in a circle of ladies — yet a good fellow at bottom. He had gone so far as to go in to one of your lectures — and came out again because he said the air was bad. He said you had the face of a sage which shone as you talked — but not when you were reading. I felt he was about to hesitate dislike about Pragmatism so I knocked him down first — and then gave him a lecture on what I understood it to be (Lord forgive me) and rather to my surprise he ended with, 'I quite agree, I quite agree.'

Well, if you have aroused this degree of interest in this world-weary Oxonian sceptic who has always had money

enough to pick up culture with a tongs — and who goes out
of curiosity because James is in the air at Oxford, you have
prevailed farther than you know.

We meet you and Mrs. James at Bibury on Wednesday,
June 10th, Swan Inn. We can stop for one night only and
I'm not sure of our route — but somehow we shall make it.
Yours affectionately

J. J. C.

My wife says she now sees why I desire to see you. It is
because we both desire to lock arms and groan.

To the same

[*The Chapmans had been motoring with the Jameses in the
Cotswolds, after the completion of James's Hibbert Lectures at
Oxford.*]

CHARING CROSS HOTEL
June 13: 1908

MY DEAR WILLIAM

For to this it must come. We seem to be about to embark,
though I will not believe it till it happens. Well, I went to
see an old lady, sort of second mother to Elizabeth. I thought
it would be a gracious act to say good-bye to her — especially
as I have been rather eccentric and almost rude in avoiding
a host of dear people. Well, I got through it I thought very
creditably — and this morning Elizabeth tells me I went on
like a cross child railing at everybody — nobody good enough
— nothing to suit me. And she who had been nursing the
tradition that I was a lofty prophet whose seclusion was
merely the necessary shroud to a beaconlike benevolence.
It's too bad — and the cause was barber-shops and the buying
of umbrellas — fatigue. There are certain conditions when
fatigue is a crime — and the only crime. You made a tremendous effort at Oxford — be content. I was under a great
temptation to read you my play at Bibury, but it would have
spoiled a rare occasion — and besides — *cui bono?* A play
must speak from the stage — and, if it can be managed, from
the page, but an author's reading is no fair and reveals nothing.

I also had a temptation to open up a sort of Platonic suggestion that philosophy was only an inexpressive form of

poetry and that you would end by teaching poetry if you make philosophy speak. It becomes poetry. But while this seems to be true in theory, and while you gain fullness of expression in a certain sense — I question whether it be not the dry thought that gets farther in the end, changes people more — like dropping a compressed watchspring into somebody's mind which expands at last — and functions of itself, becoming part of the life. The excessive abstraction of the thing you were getting at in your lectures only became plain to me when I began to give an account of it to others. I found I was remaking it — or it me — in the exposition. I question whether poetry does this. It is too emotional and posed. It says, 'Stand here and you will see this.'

As for my own poetry — it is not poetry but clever verse — and this play could or might only have the importance of showing that the stage can very easily return to verse. If the lines are properly recited no one need discover that they are verse, but merely feel that language has become more expressive. Plays in fact must be in verse in order to get into the region of natural human feeling.

We must start doing this in order to give the poets a field when they come.

Yours affectionately

JACK

To the same

On board the Kroonland
June 20: 1908

MY DEAR WILLIAM

I have read a little in Aristotle's Ethics. It seems to be a rapidly-written book and to deal with age-old topics. One is not so much in contact with Aristotle as with a thousand years of talk. It's pretty shop-worn — and classroom-worn — I don't mean *now* — but in its substance. Was so in Aristotle's day. It's like a game of dominoes — old, smooth, yellow. But the thing that strikes me is the remoteness from life of all of it. I suppose the Greeks were as profoundly indifferent to ethics as any people could be — and as enamored of conversation — and polite culture. But really, you know, this is pretty cheap stuff. It has no actuality. It reminds me of those pass time romances the Heptameron, the Cortegiano — the parliaments of love or conversazioni among triflers. I know that, of course, you will say that as soon as a thing has actuality it ceases to be Ethics. It becomes religion or poetry or politics and I think this is true. 'Ethics' is the old box of dominoes — the same box. Which is part of the historic possession and toy collection of the race. On the Steamer it comes in handy. Now I like Aristotle, and think him a nice man and a very clear thinker and able arranger, but he would have been greater if he hadn't accepted the old categories of education and felt himself bound to write an 'Ethics.' If he had frankly said 'to hell with Ethics' I should have admired him more.

I have been reading plays by some of Shakespeare's contemporaries. I can't understand their reputation or make sense out of what the critics say in their prefaces. I believe it is all a vast illusion and unconscious conspiracy, revealing the non-critical character of the English mind. It must befog the young. The plays are for the most part incredibly dull and ill-planned — showing every cheap device of lust, murder, incest, madhouses, torture, etc., which yet fail of effect on account of their crudeness and lack of preparation. There are good lines now and then and bad ones very often — and how people ever sat through them becomes the main question of interest. I wish I knew where to turn in English for sensible, well-instructed criticism. If I had a wider reading I could do it myself — just unpretentious attempts to prepare people for what the thing is — like Sainte-Beuve. It requires enormous knowledge — that's the trouble. The Mermaid Series — probably represents English scholarship. It is perfectly useless, misleading, and ignorant. I know less about an Elizabethan poet after I have read an essay by Swinburne or Symons or Havelock Ellis, or Charles Lamb, or Hazlitt or Saintsbury or Chesterton — or any of them — than I do before I read it. I am exceedingly glad I never read these plays before — or at least at an early imitative age — for they seem to me to be as bad as bad — as far from true drama, good sentiment, natural expression, competent or comprehensible workmanship, honest understanding of their craft, as they can possibly be — and, though redeemed by strokes of genius, the very most dangerous models either for playwriting or poetry in general. We have had a most smooth uneventful voyage and are almost at land. The old nurse is doing very well. Please remember me to Mrs. James. Elizabeth sends her love to you both.

Yours Affly,

J. J. C.

To Elizabeth Chanler Chapman

BARRYTOWN, *Aug.* 6, 1908

... Strange law of spiritual growth. You rise after a period of prayer — *weak*. The cistern is empty. You think the water has run away, but it has been drawn up into the clouds. I believe this recurring feeling of mortal weakness endures to the end — even to Gethsemane. It is an illusion because you are really stronger. We are redissolved at every step into elements — almost to chaos. The fear grows less — the fear as to the outcome — and yet the experience remains severe. Then it goes away and leaves you serene and able....

To Mrs. Winthrop Chanler

October 25, 1908

MY DEAR DAISY:

... I am voting for Bryan. Not solely for the purpose of annoying my respectable friends, but because I sorter like Bryan.

The first edition of 500 copies of the Children's Plays is exhausted. Is that much or little? To me it seems very large. I thought it would take three or four years to sell 500 — and does it mean that the plays are really liked? Then why shouldn't 2,500 be sold? Nobody knows these things. Nobody knows who reads a book. I know that my essays were only read by very *intelligent* people, of whom only 1173 exist in America, but I have better hopes for these plays. Servant girls ought to like them. Now let us suppose that the average public school teacher liked them: There you have 1,420,000 right away. Don't let's get excited....

To Gordon Abbott

BARRYTOWN, N.Y.
Oct. 25: 1908

MY DEAR GORDON

... And who is your candidate for President of Harvard? My own is J. G. Croswell — you will say it is my passion for voting alone. I have heard serious talk of Jim Storrow. (If he could only read and write he would be splendid, so moral, so rich and successful, and so benevolent and able. After all Charlemagne couldn't write — or very little.) Then I have heard of Richard Cabot — really I think he would be excellent — only too Boston — and yet I sympathize with the idea of a Massachusetts man — (though this is against Croswell). I rather like keeping Massachusetts alive as long as possible and by any and every means.... What I want to know is this, Who pays for all the postage stamps and expensive circulars with which Tommy Cummins [1] makes the life of his classmates miserable? It cost somebody $8 in stamps to ascertain the middle name of my grandmother for the benefit of posterity. There is gross malversation somewhere. One cannot buy stamps on credit. Tommy must have some large funds at his disposal. It ought to be looked into. Also — is it a discretionary matter with a class secretary how far into the past he shall probe — or is it governed by statute? Can he indulge a taste for genealogy (which we all know is a disease) without any restraint? Aren't there statutes in restraint of such things? It seems to me that a great many evils have been got at on the theory of the 'Use of the Mails' for improper purposes — and something might be done in this line to curb Tommy.

Yours affectionately

J. J. CHAPMAN

To William James

BARRYTOWN, N.Y.
Feb. 27: 1909

MY DEAR JAMES

I shall certainly send for those books. I always imagine H. G. Wells as a man with eleven children and his rent un-

[1] Secretary of the Harvard Class of 1884.

paid. Nothing less would excuse him for writing so much. But this is not quite fair — for in artistic matters — and sociology is sometimes a field for artistic expression — the people who have written most have written best.

I have been and indeed am, laid up with a broken arm — luckily the left upper arm. Everytime I have an accident to that arm, it means — whatever it means. I have been exceedingly miserable — but this, it appears is common with broken arms. But I am getting more comfortable and *à l'ordinaire.*

(I fell on the arm while holding a pony — with a long pair of reins. I was standing up on solid ground and doubled up my left arm under my back.)

Many thanks for your thought of me.

Yours affectionately

J. J. C.

To the same

[*The date of this letter indicates that 'the sausage' flung at James, according to the postscript, was a copy of Chapman's play, 'A Sausage from Bologna.'*]

SYLVANIA
BARRYTOWN-ON-HUDSON
April 25. [1909]

MY DEAR JAMES:

The 'Pluralism' has come and I am reading it with real pleasure, at least the essay on Hegel, (I have temporarily dropped the book out of the carriage on a drive and am getting another copy). The trouble is, I lost it just as I was beginning to be convinced I had some good ideas.

You said something about a *concept*. Now what is a concept? Where does it begin and where does it end? *Are you sure that there is such a thing?* If you were sitting in your capacity of President of the Society for Psychical Research and the story of one of these concepts were brought before you, would you not put it down in the name of science, quench and dissipate it, and show it to be a mere mist and vagary and never-twice-alike will o' the wisp — in the name of modernity and evidence and intellect and X-rays? I can just imagine your polite 'not proven.' But when you get on your tripod, you go puffing out these things at the top of the smoke-stack in perfect unconcern, in perfect belief that you are in good society and that no one will find you out.

Modern Philosophy since Kant is a game and so many thousands are in the conspiracy that almost any one may be tempted to throw a few *louis d'ors* on the table as he passes through the gambling hell. With three years practice I could play it myself.

I have recently been reading Thomas Aquinas (in the notes to Dante) and I find that he is a very serious man and has meanings that any man can understand — at least any man can feel the reality in Thomas Aquinas. The same is true of Kant. Kant was not playing a game, he was inventing a language. But all you fellows since Kant, and including Hegel, are living on Kant and haven't the initial force to use him, as for instance Dante uses Thomas Aquinas — simply quarry out of him or take words which you reinfuse with your own meaning. You are using words at second hand and are dabblers. I got several ideas out of the essay on Hegel and when the book turns up —

But can't you see you ought not to encourage this Volapük society? Let it alone! Don't call attention to it! Then it will die out. Thousands of young men are yearly ruined at your gaming table — their intellects gone forever. Desist, desist!

Yours

J. J. C.

I thought to spare you my own not very happy follies. I have lost confidence, and no longer presume. But I herewith fling my sausage at you. The modern taste is so jaded — pickles and paradoxes — jamhog — over everything. Why, my dear fellow, do you not see that the pessimists live on negation? Bernard Shaw, Nietzsche, etc., manage to tweak morality and get a sensation, but you can't go on living on jokes, parodies, and reductions ad absurdum.

[*In reply to this letter James wrote, April* 30, 1909 (*see Letters of William James,* II, 321): '*A certain witness at a poisoning case was asked how the corpse looked. "Pleasant-like and foaming at the mouth," was the reply. A good description of you, describing phi-*

losophy, in your letter. . . . There are concepts, anyhow. I am glad you lost the volume. It makes one less in existence and ought to send up the price of the remainder.']

To Evelyn Ames and Frederick Hall
[*On their engagement.*]

SYLVANIA
BARRYTOWN-ON-HUDSON
May 18: 1909

MY DEAR EVELYN AND FRED

I congratulate you both and am overjoyed. Elizabeth and I could not help suspecting something of the kind in January and I have been tempted ever since to write you to go ahead and plunge and don't fear your fate too much, etc. I was only restrained by knowing such things must come of their own force and power. So I am relieved to hear that I may tell you how much we both liked and believed in Hall and hoped it would come off. As for happiness the less you argue about it and concern yourself with it the better. Any marriage may be unhappy and all marriages contain terrible grinding difficulties of character. Marriage demands the utmost of human virtue. That's why it is valuable. You will suffer immensely and would have suffered immensely no matter who or when you had married. What of it? We cannot escape it — ought not to seek to escape it. Rather we ought to prepare for it as necessary to our and all men's fulfillment. Happy those to whom it is not denied.

Yours affectionately (I mean both of you)

JACK

To William James

[*This was written six days after the installation of President Lowell at Harvard.*]

BARRYTOWN, N.Y. *Oct.* 12, 1909

DEAR JAMES

It's all a question of getting the reality of the mysterious side of life before the public. No discussion can do more than end by suggesting — what everybody knows — that we are surrounded by goodness and power flashing about and we must not get in the way of them. Here is Harvard, a bean-bag, a money-bag and a wind-bag — Eliot, Higginson, and Bishop Lawrence — and they are delighted with themselves. But there is more in life than that. The Lord was not in the whirlwind. What I ought to have said was — 'How wonderful that such a board of Trustees has done so well — (for there are several good things about Harvard) and now — wonder of wonders, these young idiots, the Fellows of Harvard, have chosen a scholar for President! It's the millennium.' That would have been more just and philosophical — but I didn't think of it.

Well now, since Lowell is in, the cat's cradle is in a new form — and what Lowell will need is *support*. As so often happens, the support he needs can best begin by punching his head. He needs protection against the pressure of the old machine and he needs play for personal impulse. The Harvard professors must fight out their own standing ground — no one else can do it for them. At present they are cowed by false ethics, and are like a pack of hounds to be sold on the death of a tyrant. They laugh on only one side of their mouth when Eliot is mentioned. They fear the roof will fall. This is a service *you* could have done — and would have done if it had occurred to you — years ago — standing up for ideas against the oppressor. And, by the way, your influence in the community is, I think, largely due to your public fight — on healers and doctors. You have an extra-University following. That's what every professor needs. The fight for ideas must be done by men in the university. They will have to risk their jobs of course. Higginson is a practical man and would follow an enemy to California to keep him out of a job. But fortunately these idols are old and tired. I've been talking to younger professors and I find them cautious. Their career — their specialty — they do not see that here is a career and a real one. The great public must be relied on always, not the small public. You must always be on the sea.

I was at a loss to know why you wanted your letter burned. It is no more foolish than your other letters, and then I remembered the accurate and subtle characterization of your two former colleagues. Well, I have deleted their names — will that satisfy you? It is too much to pay out such magnificent approbation as your letter contains to one who shall be nameless and ask him to burn it. Human nature — woman's nature — revolts. If I don't lose the letter, as I undoubtedly shall, I shall leave it to my children.

P.S. Perhaps your point is that what we want on the Boards of Trustees is not so much scholars, as scholar-finders — men with an enthusiasm for genius in others.

This is very likely true. The distinction hadn't occurred to me — and I'm not sure that these last-suggested men would not be the rarer bird of the two, counsel of perfection to require them.

What I really had in mind — there is a sentence in Lowell's inaugural that expresses it — 'every student should, at least in one subject, know the sources of opinion and the manner in which professionals deal with them.' Eliot — Higginson — Charley Adams — Perkins — (at a guess) Walcott. None of these men would know the meaning of that sentence.

I rather think that Dr. Cabot and Judge Lowell would.

All this is a mere sample of the general state of the U.S. You and your notion of 'what people want' for education are a horrid exhibit. Ghastly. Every man should teach what he wants to teach — not what others want to learn.

There is no allowance to be made anywhere in the universe or in the system of the university for what somebody else wants. That is the devil. That is corruption. That lies.

Pick up a school English primer (perhaps in Mass. they are better — but come to New York and pick one up.) This book has been put together by a man trying to give what somebody else wants. The whole wealth of English Literature is lost on him. He is rushing and shoving down hill to chaos — rubbish — degradation — because he is filling a want. *De te fabula.*

That is — as a side-light on pragmatism.

I have a notion that I could tell you what is the matter with pragmatism — if you would only stand still.

A thing is not truth till it is so strongly believed in that the believer is convinced that its existence does not depend upon him.

This cuts off the pragmatist from knowing what truth is.

J. J. C.

To Mrs. Winthrop Chanler

SYLVANIA,
November 29, 1909

DEAR DAISY:

If Mrs. Wharton is in Paris, give her my love. She's a dear old thing — and tell her I wrote her a letter a year ago; but it became so long and encyclopedic and so really terribly profound and inclusive that I had to destroy it. It was no use of having anything go on at all after such a letter. Poor world! Give it a show.

I wish I could read her books. The Roman important politicians used to have a nomenclator whose business it was to know everyone's name. The nomenclator, who was always a slave, whispered the name of everybody. Of course it implies slavery, and good old classical slavery, of the highly educated class — but I wish I could have a book reader — somebody whom I could force to read any book I had a curiosity to know about. Elizabeth won't do it. I find one can get a good deal out of buying a book. I suppose the soul of the author gratefully reveals itself through the covers. Very often I buy a book because of living in the country and fearing someone like you might drop in and not find anything more recent than Samuel Johnson. ...

Yours affectionately,

JACK

To William James

SYLVANIA
BARRYTOWN-ON-HUDSON
Dec. 19: 1909

MY DEAR JAMES,

I have not been quite at ease about you since hearing, a month ago, about your trouble with your knee. I hope it did not develope into anything serious. If you are in the mood to glance over a few pages of typewriting on 'The Comic' — a sort of old-fashioned genteel essay, I will send it to you on its way to Royce, for I am going to send it to the Hibbert. I will enclose stamped envelope addressed to Royce so as to give you no trouble. It isn't quite finished — just a little varnish — and blowing the dust off the high lights. Then I have an ambitious essay on S. G. Howe, which I began last summer as a chore, at the request of Laura Richards, and sweated over and didn't much like, and put in a box — for two months, and then found it in the box and put some modulations into it and I am delighted with it. But I won't bother you with it till it is in a volume of some sort. If I had the eyesight to do the necessary reading I should be under temptation to write a whole volume of portraits of Howe's contemporaries — from George Ticknor down. But the muse has taken away my eyesight without giving me a sweet song, so I shall be put to poetry and plays. I have another child's play and Christmas Cantata — and should like to write enough for another volume of children's things. My eyes are all right for writing — and good enough for glancing into books; but for the all-day sort of reading and running through volumes, I can't do it.

Our prohibitions are just as valuable a part of our destiny as anything else. Do tell me how your delightful children are. That youngest boy is a most dear person going through the hardest part of his life — one has to take it sometime — and perhaps it is well to have it in early youth. I had a sort of hope that Victor and he would strike up a friendship.

Yours affectionately

J. J. C.

To the same

12 MOUNT VERNON ST.
BOSTON, *Jan.* 24: 1910

DEAR JAMES

... Academic honors! I don't count it against you one bit. You are a natural target for these things — a spiritual law of some kind shies them at you. Represents weakness, of course — moral weakness. Any one who takes an academic honor trades upon the baseness of others — or a decoration from a King. What are these French Institutes but the refuge of royalist national sentiment? Bergson feels toward the Institute as Joan of Arc felt toward the royal line. It is the ark of the French covenant. What rot! I say truly, seriously, in soothest sadness — and looking deep into your eyes — how can you help build up this rubbish?

Old Bryce of the bushy eyebrows was made a very fine order of Elk by the King. He said the King had made it a personal matter, poor old deluded man.

Why, it's putting incense on the altar of Baal. It's condoning, and smiling, and playing priest, and sipping and simpering, and selling out the gift of prophecy for a seat in the synagogue.

It seems to me that if you had had an ounce of manhood in you you would have replied to Bergson when he announced your election as one of the eight non-resident honorary members of the Corpse of Moral Sciences and Inscriptions —

'Sir: The first principle which morality inscribes upon the heart of man is contempt for institutions. You think you are inscribing my name on your walls, but in reality you wish to inscribe your darned old institution on me.

Yours, W. JAMES.'

Most of my closest, oldest, and dearest friends take no interest in the things that interest me. If I accidentally allude to such things I regret it.

This is the normal thing, and by it we are forced to learn the secondary nature of our interests. They are bosh anyway. Here we treat them as bosh. I am just about to solve the whole problem of the world and finish up a matter that has vexed humanity since the time of Job — when Ropes Trask says 'hello' to me and this hello supplants the problem — is more important than the problem.

J. J. C.

[*It was after this letter that James wrote to Chapman:* 'You, dear Jack, are the only reincarnation of Isaiah and Job, and I praise God that he has let me live in your day. Real values are known only to you.' *See* 'Letters of William James,' II, 329-30.]

To the same

DEAR JAMES

Many thanks for your splendid letter. I take all the good as true and all the bad as not true. Compliments make me happy — disparagement makes me very nearly happy. But I want to tell you something: — writers of essays and writers of philosophical stuff always seem to want to do too much, claim too much, prove too much. For instance, I think this Frank Harris book about Shakespeare is on the whole the best Shakespeare book I ever read — and on the whole he makes his point. He convinces you that Shakespeare was that sort of a man and that you have always felt it anyway. As to details I am against him on almost every page — especially in his apparent ignorance of the fact that Shakespeare was writing plays. Many things are really to be explained by the fact that *they sound well on the stage.* Neither ethics, nor truth, nor self-portraiture are at the bottom of them. When Shakespeare found a thing went well, he did it again — either a character, a device, or a remark.

Henry V is a perfect stage-dummy of a king. You and I don't like him, but the popular consciousness demands that sort of thing in a stage king. *Voilà tout.* So of a hundred places in Harris's book: if he had not taken his theory so seriously I should have believed in it rather more.

By the way — does a man describe best what he is? I rather think he does. Though Kipling is a coward — and yet loves bloody courage and excels in the descriptions of it. All the same this is the best book about Shakespeare I've ever read, and makes its point. Writers of theory almost always carry their theories too far.

Why not drop a hint like a fire-cracker and run away? That's *rather* your method, I believe. Santayana is lecturing in a rich, cheesy voice on Goethe (I take the words of a brother-in-law who went to bring back his seventeen-year-old girl from the show).

Goethe never crosses the Atlantic so far as hits me, though

years ago I used to read him and hate him; and lately, on looking into Nietzsche, I have longed for him.

Yours ever gratefully

JACK

To the same

325 WEST 82ND STREET
March 28, 1910

Villain! to flee away and give no time for notes to catch
your ship.

I've a good mind to go to Nauheim. I have heart trouble;
and somebody once suggested Nauheim. You leave nobody in
this country except Dickinson Miller. I am just writing to
him to ask him some questions — but alas, what does he know?

The great need is to get information without reading
books.

Reading books is so injurious to the mind. I am thinking of
you and of many other great intellects. That is the problem,
how to get what is in the book out of it without reading it.
A good but dangerous way is to live with it. Buy it and leave
it on a table and talk about it. Then in three months — write
about it. After this, information will begin to come in.

Yours affectionately

and to MRS. James too and much love from my wife to you
both . . .

JACK

To the same

['*The Amsterdam gentleman*' *mentioned in this letter was Benja-
min Paul Blood, of Amsterdam, N.Y. James's article about him,*
'*A Pluralistic Mystic,*' *appeared in the* Hibbert Journal *for July*
10, *which contained also Chapman's article* '*The Comic,*' *included,
virtually unchanged, in* '*Learning and Other Essays.*' *The same
volume contains a brief paper,* '*The Jesters,*' *in which Chesterton and
Shaw are presented as* '*the Max and Moritz of the present epoch.*'

247

THE CENTURY ASSOCIATION
7 WEST FORTY-THIRD STREET
June 19: 1910

MY DEAR JAMES

Well, I came to town to get away from the lawn-mower and immerse myself in the deadness of this club.... Read your most satisfactory article on the Amsterdam gentleman in which you and he arrive at the unknowability of anything. I just felt as if I were meeting a friend at the railroad station. I felt as if I had been waiting for you and you arrived with all your bags. You may imagine that I only was examining the Journal to see my own article — by the way, they cut out the attacks on Shaw *through error*, and I'm going to put them back — Shaw is a ruffian. But what I mean is that if you take a human brain which vibrates as a unity in its conscious parts, that brain will believe in a monistic universe. If it vibrates in one part and also in another part, but is not conscious of the link of force between the two — that brain will believe in a pluralistic universe. I don't see what else can happen. It seems to me we ought not to use such terms as the universe. They are sure to mislead somebody.

By the way, I took your advice and added a tail-piece to 'The Comic.' You may not remember that you told me to put on a tail-piece — and one day it occurred to me — and the strange thing is that it seems to have been there always, as the main end of the article. This shows — I don't know what it shows. Elizabeth is extremely well and in good spirits and would send you and *Mrs.* James any quantity of love if she could. What a fellow you are for health. You are always about to die of overwork; and yet you enjoy life, and produce and skate about and support and inspire and prevail. And I'll bet you are roaming over hills and dales and discovering new genius in Germany now.

Yours with love from us both, for I shall report at any rate that I have written.

JOHN JAY CHAPMAN

O, but you have done harm too. D. Miller exposing Palladino — under sofas — newspaper talk. Who was it set this fashion in higher philosophy? W. J. Miller was sick with excitement, and all of them together — who started the spook hunt as a scholars' recreation? W. J.

Germany, is it? I have it. I have it. I have it. You will come home with a Teutonic decoration. Shame — and *dreimal* shame!

To Elizabeth Chanler Chapman

[*After a reading of ' Benedict Arnold' in Cambridge, Chapman stayed on for a few days in Boston, visited the new Art Museum building, which he found ' utilitarian, uncharming, grim ... just like the soul of Charles Eliot,' and amused himself in Boston and Cambridge, not least through the Harvard philosophers.*]

12 MT. VERNON ST.
BOSTON, 17 *Nov.* '10

... Then went to Emerson Hall — the philosopher's building — had a talk with Royce. He says James shortened his life by fussing over his heart — not that he wanted to live, but that he thought it somehow a disgrace to have diseases and was always trying to cure himself — by physicians, by quacks, by healers, etc., etc. With all these people he talked about his case and had theories about it. If he had only let it alone and thought of something else, R. believes he'd be alive today. (By the way I called on but didn't see Mrs. J. on Monday. But I *did* see and took Victor to see Miss Grace Norton — who was *enchanting* to us both. She afterwards went to the lecture and came to me at the end of it and pointed to her streaming cheeks — 'It isn't only these tears — but I have other things to say to you about it' — or words to that effect.) On leaving Royce I went across the hall and attended a lecture of Palmer — just the same as twenty-seven years ago. He had to go to a meeting, so I left him and went to the Porcellian where rested and read half a play of Euripides in Bohn, then food with the boys. Then back and paid a long call on Palmer.

He talked a great deal and most interestingly about everything — mostly old Eliot whom he idolizes — but, as he *used* to hate and oppose him for many years, he is sympathetic to the hating of him. A most curious psychological puzzle how so many things can be true. The bottom truth, however, is that Eliot is a bad man (though very powerful and extraordinary) and Palmer a deceived person. I could explain it if I had a blackboard.

Then to Emerson Hall where Morton Prince was giving a lecture on Memory and so came home in the cars with him in great spirits.

Also saw Santayana but not to talk to. He is a very agreeable man, with good manners. I have never known him. He makes the impression on me of not knowing more about life than a kid-glove exposed for sale in a shop-window. But I like him. . . .

[*At another time came this quatrain:*]

OUR SANTAYANA

George is a skeptic who confutes confusion:
　　His thought is clear and logical and brief.
But George believes all thinking is illusion,
　　And therefore disbelieves his own belief.

To the same

[*While the Chapmans were abroad in the winter of* 1911 *Chapman left his wife for a few days at Naples, to visit their life-long friend Etta Dunham, married to Count Antonio de Viti de Marco in Rome. Two letters to Naples recount a warm-hearted reunion and the splendors of Roman society. The following gay passages are, however, the most characteristic.*]

Saturday
IL POGGIO
4, VICOLO CARCANO

P.S. I am having some gold fringe put on my pants and I have assumed the title of Monsignore. It is amazing how easily gentility sits on me. I believe some people are just naturally swells — you know what I mean — and fit well in palaces and eat good food naturally and without effort. I remember the first royal palace I saw — seemed to me — gave me a feeling — just like the old homestead. I often think that Grandma Jones used to say, 'the Chapmans were once Kings.'

Dear old Grandpa, with his old cotton socks, wouldn't he be proud if he could see me he-hawing and chaw-chawing with Roman princes!

Sunday morning
Feb. 12: 1911

I begin the day with breakfast in bed — as I know the Vitis don't get up early and I feel as if this were more restful to the household, I am so unselfish in small matters. Also: — the second man-servant began talking about *my bath* as soon as I arrived yesterday, and whether I would like it wet or dry or hot or on toast, and that he would prepare it. He began again at dawn. Well, I did a very mean thing to that man. I took my bath and never told him about it till afterwards. But I can't help feeling that *by taking breakfast in bed* I regained his respect and love.

I am reading old Florentine lyrics in the book I got at Spithöver's — and may rake up a Theocritus — though S. didn't have any. I didn't spill any egg in the bed — (or very little) and to show how one ill act leads to another I ate my eggs out of my coffee cup — so had to drink my coffee out of the water glass by my bedside — so, now that they have taken the tray away — I have to drink out of the water bottle all day — and every drink I take, I say this shows! Let this be a lesson to you!...

To Victor Chapman

[*In March of* 1911 *the Chapmans made a motor trip from Tunis to Biskra and Algiers. Victor was then a junior at Harvard. The following passage is from one of the few letters from the father to this son that seem to have been preserved.*]

ROYAL HOTEL
BISKRA (ALGÉRIE)
Mch. 27: 1911

DEAR VICTOR

This is a big enormous large good hotel in an oasis. The real Sahara is fifty miles away; but there is a very good imitation desert — undulating sand hills and bad land — the red sandstone hills towards the north — and clustered palm trees of the oasis are just what they ought to be and they look like the geography pictures. It's a French winter watering-place — small shops — an Arab bazaar — Moorish dances at night. The desert looks exactly like the sea — you'd swear it was the sea. But I wish it *were* the sea. The sea is more interesting, and the desert as a sensation is something of a fraud. People pay large sums to guides and tents and camels and go for three days into the desert. I haven't got imagination enough to be thrilled by it. You couldn't get *far enough away* to thrill me. Perhaps in a month you might. But a month would be an awful bore . . . .

Well, the Moorish dances are a dreadful fake — poor old slobs of various degrees of blackness contorting their unseemly arms, head, backs, in stupid trances of convulsive and meaningless gesture. A buck nigger beating a drum — an old scavenger of hell collecting francs in a brass plate and guides — O, guides, who pursue and maul and grab and surround and chatter you to death, and fight each other. It's like running the gauntlet to leave the hotel. And no guide is needed because there is nothing to see — except these bazaars — which you couldn't miss unless you were blind and deaf and went in a black maria. A guide approaches you and points with his hand and says, 'The mountains — look at the mountains. Behold the mountains — very fine — want a guide, Sir? two francs.' (Of course women travelling alone, of whom there are hundreds, DO need a responsible guide as a sort of body guard.) I very nearly murdered one guide out of sheer anger — My! but they must have little brains, these Arabs. The Arab is better than the American Indian, but resembles him in many ways. I prefer the Arab, but I could willingly never see another Arab. Some Arabs work — they make wonderful linen — hand looms — wool, and leather goods. The women weave in the mud villages. But the Arabs you see don't work — they avoid work. They sit and loaf — they play checkers, they dream and moon. They love talking and bragging. Conrad gets on with them — and is generally seen with a crowd of Arab peddlers about him who are trying to sell him fossil shells and Roman coins and knicknacks of silver and beads, etc. The bargaining goes on in French for hours — great gaiety, screams of laughter. And Conrad, who has just the same temperament as these loafers only more education and wit, sold one of them a broken fountain pen for a franc yesterday — and we had to interfere and protect the rascals from Conrad's superior game, because really the pen was worth nothing. He had explained that it was broken and couldn't be mended; but he had somehow fascinated them with it. The ruins of Timgad are worth the journey, and the situation and sight of Constantine is the most wonderful sight in the world....

To Mrs. William James

[*William James died August 26, 1910. His posthumous volume of essays, 'Memories and Studies,' appeared in October, 1911.*]

SYLVANIA
BARRYTOWN-ON-HUDSON
Oct. 21: 1911

DEAR MRS. JAMES

The new essays came just as I was leaving Barrytown yesterday morning. Thank you ever so much for them. What a rate he was writing at during those last years. He could not stop. He had the public ear and a surge of facility — long files and cues of waiting utterances, like the box-office when Sarah Bernhardt is coming. I shall read them with mingled feelings, and shall ever believe it's dangerous to look forward to writing or doing. Perhaps our work is finished now.

Yours sincerely
JOHN JAY CHAPMAN

To Mrs. Winthrop Chanler

On the train Thanksgiving day, 1911.

DEAR DAISY

Henry Taylor lent me H. Adams' big book about his Education which I read half of. This reminds me of you. You are a sort of pupil — and castaway, drowning, clutcher at the piping Adams as he sits on his raft at sunset and combs his golden hair with a gold toothpick.

There ought to be people like you in the world — and I hope there always will be.

But what I wanted to say was how amusing and delightful

the book is. Why, it's quite a Social fan and Horace Walpole sort of book. It has the social point of view. Bon ton — if that's how you spell it — is the altar, and instead of throwing a rotten egg at it I ought to welcome it as you do. Surely life is large or — so small rather — we ought to be grateful for this type, and I'm a great ass even to criticise him.

Did you hear what Howells once said to a boring author who was trying to wring a compliment out of him? 'I don't know how it is,' said the author, 'I don't seem to *write* as well as I used to do.' 'Oh, yes you do — indeed you do. You write as well as you ever did; — But your *taste* is improving.' I swear this is as good as Voltaire. It's too good to be new — must come from Alexandria. Only Alexandria was dull, I think....

Yours affectionately
JACK

To Rosalind Richards

[*Miss Richards, a granddaughter of Julia Ward Howe, and a cousin of Mrs. Chapman, was for some time a member of the Chapman household.*]

BARRYTOWN, N.Y.
January 15, 1912

... I have been writing all this last autumn a book on Wm. Lloyd Garrison — which is just finished and will be about as big as Learning: — and in it I have put everything I ever thought about the Abolitionists — and which has been bubbling and stewing in my mind for years — (incidentally I have read *through* the four large volumes of Garrison's life — and I am probably the only man who ever did this). Well, this volume of Follen I had read and marked long ago — and I always felt there were things in it I wanted to look at again. Now it arrives just in time.

It's a good thing for a writer to live in the country and have few books. I have manufactured this Garrison essay out of very few books — and I know very little about the subject. This is the only way to keep your ideas clear and in proportion. It won't do perhaps for the historian — but an essayist is a free lance and is pardoned for all licenses. He doesn't

pretend to be giving history so much as suggesting something
that may or must have been somewhere concealed in history.....
Yours affectionately

J<small>ACK</small>

To his Mother

[*Written three days after reading his Phi Beta Kappa poem at
Harvard.*]

June 20, 1912

... I got off my Φ. B. K. poem all right. It wasn't much of
a success *as a recitation* — though I did my best for the darned
old thing and recited it well. But it didn't have the popular
carrying power — and of course the mourning-over-Jerusalem-
as-a-hen-gathereth-her-chickens attitude which I assumed towards Harvard in it isn't ever received with enthusiasm by the
party who represents Jerusalem. You see — I was so afraid of
being a shrew and critic — and everybody had told me ' do be
careful,' etc. — so I was so awful careful — so awful tender —
so confounded gentlemanlike — and so *patronizing* — unin-
tentionally and sincerely, you see — and I say, serve 'em right!
They are a lot of old stuck-up hens in the rain *any* way, and
President Lowell, who listened carefully and didn't applaud,
is an umbrella folded up wet. He means well, that man.

Your aff. son

J<small>ACK</small>

To Elizabeth Chanler Chapman

[*This concludes a letter begun on the train from New York, to visit
Mrs. Chapman's cousin, Mrs. Maud Howe Elliott, at ' Oak Glen.'*]

N<small>EWPORT</small>, R.I.

Sept. 9, 1912

... Newport is by far the most charming town in America
— and the only one worth talking about. The journey here is
made very agreeable by the hour on the boat — so cool and
the low romantic shores of Narragansett Bay — so friendly,
wide, dreamy, and full of leisure — are always dear to me.
Then the harbor of Newport — quite enchanting. You know
when I was a boy we spent nine summers at Narragansett

Pier; and all this landscape and the feeling of the place is familiar and yet far away. Maud very handsome and very quiet. She is bull moosing but not moose-mad. After all, suppose I knew about Roosevelt what she does — I should feel as she does — e.g. I have just read an article about Johnson (Roosevelt's vice *president* and who has been a reform Governor of California,) which makes me think Johnson is a fine man. Strange, that destiny decides that that utter thief Roosevelt shall get votes of this just and good, though late-coming, religion. But *so it is*; and you can't stop it — you can't explain it away. You can't say 'Hi hi! — you fellows over there! First, you should have found out these things fifteen years ago — and second you are hitching your star to a wagon! Can't you see this man is not your man?' It's all a fatal game of blind man's buff. I can't express how senseless and grotesque it is. Somebody ought to be laughing at it somewhere — Gods or devils.

Maud very mild and docile....

By the way — most of our papers are without humor. But I do think there is lots of good humor in this: Roosevelt's speech at Chicago — goes by the name of the Confession of Faith. You see he is whispering it — as *confession* should be whispered. The phrase 'contract with the people' is, I suppose, one of his phrases at Chicago — and the *innuendo* is to his broken promise not to run.

To Owen Wister

SYLVANIA
BARRYTOWN-ON-HUDSON
Nov. 17: 1912

DEAR DAN

What terrible books we do read! Jane Addams all about prostitution — and more. Booker Washington — the man farthest down — tuberculosis — arbitration. I draw the line myself at arbitration, but Elizabeth subscribes to the Societies and they send a cubic yard per week of Conference talk. I really long for a ladies' annual. Last night I read a paper before our little local College — about Harvard and Eliot and the dreary folly it all was. Every year I do some stunt for the

College, just to be friendly — by reading something I have on hand. By the way, and historically speaking — do you know there has never before been such wickedness on the globe as today in big American cities? It's a new record. Poor old darling little Antioch — and its fountain built by the prostitutes — and its domestic charm. Poor harmless middle ages with just a few sharp pinches of Inquisition — or a murder or two — poison — an oubliette — chiefly the necessary discipline of church government. But in America we have constructed various machines — as big as the nation — seventy million soul-power machines — for destruction of humanity. The most heartless people in history — that's what we are. But I think we are changing for the better. Love feast at St. Paul's — also at Groton — where Amory Gardner took Elizabeth and me in for five nights while we tutored the boys in a play. Groton a splendid place to start a school of speaking. It can spread to the other schools afterwards. Groton so small — no reason why the whole place should not speak like good actors. . . .

To James G. Croswell

[*Chapman's friend, Croswell, was at this time headmaster of the Brearly School in New York.*]

325 W. 82 ST.
Nov. 26: 1912

O JAMES, O JAMES

I looked into that asphalt palace and saw a great crowd of enthusiastic women; and raised up on the platform I saw J. G. C., covering his face with his hands; and a strong-browed, middle-aged woman was evidently speaking to all the surging, hatted women. It was like the French Revolution. But what she said I couldn't guess; for the noise, and the footmen, and the automobiles, and the elevators, and the electric lights, and the surging, surging enthusiastic women. So I went upstairs and saw the open-air playground and the cage; and then I saw a floor of patent desks, with patent boards; and on every board was a lump of patent, deodorized clay; and I thought about art. And as I looked at the boards behold they were kitchens, and I saw chemicals, and I thought about

257

science — and then I saw some patent, stuffed, deodorized antiseptic, hygienic samples of animals and animated nature. They were fixed on the walls; and I thought of the wonders of nature. And I wondered how any brain of a child could withstand the knowledge of these things — and what would have happened to *me* if I had known them in early life. Persons ought not to know of the existence of such horrible things as high-school fittings till they are adult. And I thought of the shouting and the French Revolution going on below, and of the instruments of torture on the upper floors; and I wondered what would become of Humanity — and all was being done in the name of James Croswell. It was a ghastly dream. O James, can't you think of the *next generation*, before you do these things? You live so happy-go-lucky and in the present — never a thought of tomorrow. *You* can stand it, yes. But think of the *young girls* who must come within these walls.

Yours

JOHN JAY CHAPMAN

To William Rothenstein

BARRYTOWN-ON-HUDSON
Dec. 21st, 1912

MY DEAR ROTHENSTEIN

... The boys have come back from school and we are here for ten days. Having a boy come from school is one of the gifts of life. It is a wonderful experience, and has all the joy of both ages in it. It's forty times as happy as being the boy. We have been a good deal relieved at Chanler's metamorphoses. First he got so bumptious and unmanageable that we had to send him to school. *Then*, at school he got so good and sleek and polite that we were sure he would die with a pious ejaculation on his lips, and we should have nothing left but the memory of his sanctity. *Now*, after forty-eight hours at home, he has broken out into riotous spirits and regardlessness again. So we feel he is all right. Early holiness in boys goes with pneumonia. It's not only in story books that those very good little boys die. My wife had a brother of this kind who died at thirteen or fourteen. There's something about the careless kind of boy that's very reassuring: dirt, and pleasure,

and food, and lawlessness are what you want in a boy. So
when the horse play began we sang a mass. Chanler has a
deep place in him which may be music; but which had better
not stay with ethics just now.

We are in the middle of a big snow storm and the multifarious small details of Christmas in a community where we are
the patriarchs, and the children of the second gardener have
to be counted and checked off. My wife always almost dies
over it, for she does it with the passion of Catherine of Siena,
who didn't dare to fall asleep till daylight; for she felt that
her prayers were preserving the city during the dark pest:
perhaps when the light came the Universe could be trusted to
run itself without getting off the track and all up for an hour
or two. All the same we all enjoy the hurly-burly. . . .

To the same

[*Near the end of this letter Chapman refers to the death of his brother
Henry Grafton Chapman, which occurred January 16, 1913. This
brother, two years his senior, graduating at Harvard a year before
Chapman, possessed brilliant gifts, imperfectly realized in his pursuits of law and letters.*]

March 8th, 1913

My dear Rothenstein,

I have been so very busy that I've not had time to drop you
a line, to say that I saw Tagore and was most interested in
him; and I would have heard him lecture, but was telegraphed
back to New York from Cambridge (where I happened to be
staying at the time of Tagore's lecture) by the news of my
wife's sudden seizure and operation for appendicitis. (This
was three weeks ago — and she is doing finely and has had a
model recovery.)

I went to see Tagore with reluctance.[1] He telephoned me
with reluctance. He doesn't want to see *anyone*, and I don't
want to see a man whose seclusion is so self-conscious and
who is a little *afraid*. But both of us 'done noble' for the sake
of Rothenstein, and come together, and bore with each other
for half an hour — and I am extremely delighted to have

[1] Rothenstein had provided Tagore with a letter of introduction to Chapman.

looked at him, and profoundly moved with the reality of his power and his relationship to the unseen. He is a little unhealthy. His voice is falsetto and his moral being, *hot house*. I speak as a fool, of course; because, what do I know?

Abdul Baha — if that is the right name, the Persian — happened to be here in the autumn and by some accident I went to see him. (It's a funny business to be in — visiting prophets — and was accident in both cases.) Well, I liked Abdul the better of the two. He could sit in the sun and talk to children. He reminded me of the Book of Job — one of Job's counsellors, the sort of old man that has always been sitting about in Syria and the land of Uz. A great and good man. But this Indian was *specialized*, and corresponded so wonderfully with everything I ever heard about India, or read, or dreamed. It's a land of special powers — special controls, special miracles, insights, tricks, illuminations, divinities, devilries, and special learnings. I looked upon him with wonder and enthusiasm, but with a little repulsion too — not that either, but rather as one feels towards a very luxurious invalid.

We have had a mixed up winter, owing to my mother's long and serious illness, my brother's death, some new sociological experiments of our own, and the unquietness of the Universe which will not let us alone; but keeps thrusting itself in and booming and banging. It never leaves the room without banging the door or enters except by falling into the centre of the room and raising a howl.

My wife sends you her affectionate regards. She says that Chanler's picture is a constant source of happiness to her.

Very sincerely always
JOHN JAY CHAPMAN

To Henry Osborn Taylor

[*Mr. Taylor had recently reviewed H. S. Chamberlain's 'Foundations of the Nineteenth Century.'*]

March 26, 1913
325 W. 82

MY DEAR HARRY

The review of Chamberlain is excellent — full of benevolence, humor and discrimination: and manages to convey your detestation of the man and his work without saying anything Except Good. This is fine. I wish you would take occasion to write things less serious and responsible than your bookish endeavours. It's all rot, this dishing of things out of books and into books. It's apothecary's work — examining labels and tasting messes. Do write an essay on swill barrels — or nurses and babies — or some comic essay on things in your bureau drawer. Write about women's foibles or men I know at the club. Write an attack on Somebody — why not write poetical epistles about Morgan, J. P.? There's an idea for you. No literature is in existence on the subject. I am keeping the review to show to my wife. If I *lend* it to her, she will lose it. So I have to wait for an opportunity. If I thrust it on her, she bites. Yet she wants to read it.

Yours sincerely
JOHN JAY CHAPMAN

To Langdon Mitchell

[*Alluding again to the death of Chapman's brother Henry, early in this year.*]

325 W. 82 N.Y.
Easter [1913]

DEAR LANGDON

I have just got your splendid letter, which comes, stalks in like Prisca Fides, or the antique age when servants worked for love and not money, Dante's Grandpa's Florence, or any other imaginative epoch of virtue and the simple life. What you say of Henry is extremely true and mysterious. I put together the same ideas into a notice which I shall send you. It's only a few words long. I wonder what it was that happened to him — that he never went forward. Was it an illusion that he ever was so remarkable as we all used to think him? He was, I believe — or, would he, in another age, and if puffed and padded out with fortune, position, some decorative value, have continued to satisfy the demands of his contemporaries all his life? I don't know. It's a pretty killing age and climate over here. And the society of it was at its worst just in our time. The, e.g., Philistinism in Strong and Cadwalader's office when you were there — probably registers the *lowest ever in the world* — highest I mean. Many years of study make me believe this. Things are better now.

I can't tell you how delighted I am by what you say of the 'Neptune's Isle.' Of course not three people read such a book and I have — *had* — pretty well concluded there is or was nothing in it, or in my poetic attempts, except time-honoured ambition, and going through the motions — (which has its value). But your letter is most thrilling. I am ever so glad you wrote....

By the way, Harry Sedgwick did a jolly thing the other night — at a solemn conclave of fashionable boarding school masters — Peabody — Croswell, Miss Spence, Maria Chapin — the heads of the swellest New York schools and their clientèle who met to discuss how to keep the young folks away from the theatre in vacations — and rot — utmost twaddle — considering the whole lot of protesting parents and schoolmasters had spent their lives keeping in the swim and being friends and servants to the swell mob. So after a most senseless lot of suggestions as to how the mothers should get together and pass laws to keep their college boys out of mischief, while they were in New York at holiday time, etc., Harry gets up and demurs and doubts and wonders and talks of the complexity of life — and reminds them that the *greatest modern moralist* — had spent his youth with gypsies and champagne — Tolstoi. — Sensation! Bully for Harry! Then everybody jumped on him and made him write letters the next day to explain how he didn't mean to imply that gypsies and champagne were *de rigueur* in early youth, etc., etc....

To S. S. Drury

[*Many letters to the headmaster of St. Paul's School, Concord, bear witness to Chapman's unremitting interest in the education of his three sons. In the week before writing this letter Chapman had visited St. Paul's School, and had brought his son Conrad home with him. On December 3 he wrote to his wife, 'In all these days at St. Paul's I have spent two or three hours a day in silence and prayer. I have read Drury's report. I should never gather anything from it*

about either St. Paul's or D. It seems to me like a fussy, pettifogging,
mean-spirited sort of document. This shows how little you can tell
about anything anyway. I must write him a comic letter. He's
coming to speak before the Cosmopolitan Club. This drags the school
in the dirt.... Happy thought — tell him this!' The 'comic letter'
was written two days later.]

BARRYTOWN, N.Y.
Dec. 5, 1913

DEAR DR. DRURY
DEAR DRURY

I read the blue Report in the train yesterday. I read it hastily and while thinking of other things so as to get a casual,
unprejudiced sort of impression, and I'll just tell you in a
dreamy way how it struck me and what sort of reflections it
awakened. I know you won't be offended and that you laugh
easily. It struck me as a pettifogging and conciliatory document. No one could get from it any idea either of the School
or of S. S. Drury. One would get a much truer idea of both if
you had written nothing at all — for that would suggest the
idea that the school must speak for itself. All I seem to remember about that report is that the financial condition of the
School is good and then some Grand Questions: I, Shall
chewing gum be allowed in Chapel? II, Cheque books. III —
O yes I do remember your saying that the school should be
like a home — which is perfectly untrue: if it was like a home
I never would send a boy there — also that St. Paul's must become the best school in the country. You ought to be too
proud and too subtle to say a thing like that — but never
mind — and you said you were going to New York to lecture
before the women's Baronial Daughters of America. I do hope
you will feel foolish when you get there. The N. Y. parlor
business was started by Peabody twenty years ago in order to
hold his New York trade. As a preparation for it he used to
have Grafton Cushing stay with the Whitneys and walk on V
Ave. and 57 St. every day for two weeks. He had another man
in plain clothes walk on the opposite side, and point out to
passers — 'See him over there? That's a master at Groton
School!' By these and other devices St. Paul's School was

263

saved and Groton was rather ruined. St. Paul's stood in the direct line to receive all the New York rich — and would have done so in the inevitable course of events. But Peabody drew the poison on himself and saved us. The outcome has in it both justice and injustice. For Peabody has been punished with an avalanche for pulling the string.... Well, there you go! *Qu'allez vous faire dans cette galère?* So of Conferences. The age is Conference-mad. A conference is the devil — always. It brings in Uniformity — the very thing we don't want.

Recently I had an experience that brought the philosophy of the matter home to me. I am very fond of the Groton masters — except one who shall be — well — one of them asked me to come and talk at a teachers' club. I told him that teachers saw too much of each other, and that they needed each a cave, and not a club and let each one do what he thought right, and never consult anyone else. Consulting is cowardice and timidity. If a man has an idea let him apply it — not talk about it, and if others are interested, let them go and see it operate. He said — 'Well, come and tell us *that.*' I said — 'I won't be accessory to any such meeting. I can say all this better by staying away.'

De te fabula.

A man who spends his whole time in writing — as I do — knows its futility. Writing is for people who believe that what they say is true and that their analysis is the thing. For people who know that all statements are gross illusions it's almost *fraudulent* to talk....

Yours sincerely

JOHN JAY CHAPMAN

Don't waste your time in answering this letter. I know all that can be '*urged*' on every side of this and all other questions — and the tongues of men and angels wouldn't persuade me — or illumine. I'm only writing to entertain you and Mrs. Drury — to whom please convey my regards. I found a most splendid atmosphere at the School — an atmosphere of intellectual freedom which exists in no other place — and is more so now — much — than it was before, also the boys look more carefree and healthier. There used to be a slight strain — I don't know what — the masters also, and I had a good many talks with a good many of them, are on the top of the wave, and not critical. I almost believe it is getting to be a good kind of place to send a boy.

To Dickinson S. Miller

[*Dr. Miller was at this time Professor of Apologetics at the General Theological Seminary in New York.*]

325 WEST 82ND STREET,
NEW YORK CITY.
February 21, 1914

MY DEAR DICKINSON

If you will only hold out till the 28th I will tell you all about it. I cannot get there at 6:30, but shall enter the chapel by the window at 5:43 and pass through the sacristy and chapter room in search of the refectory. I suppose I shall see a few acolites, vergers, and lay-brothers distributing complines. I like your cheek in thinking I haven't travelled and read books enough to feel quite at home in any place where theology and the use of Baedeker are required. My strong impression is that after I have looked over the plant I shall put everything into one word, so very awfully profound that you and the Archbishop will fall flat — something like — well — 'More O give!' or 'outer edge.'

We went to the Fancy Ball and the ungrateful world never put us in the papers. Elizabeth needs saving, like all those saints who never have had paint and powder when they were young. Now she pricks up her ears like the war-horse. It is pathetic. You will have me yet down there. It is the only place for a gentleman to live in New York I always think — your cloister — (you self-pleasing Sybarite.) But if I could save that woman from the Everlasting Bonfire, the rest would be easy. Look within, I say. Look at the dressing table covered with psalm books and rouge — *masks*, by the mass! The fatigued eyes of pleasure — and breakfast in bed. If this could not stir to passion — if the visible pile of vanities once burnt by Savanarola and now — lutes and fans — red slippers and the smell of Arabia, pervading this Christian home — do not move a man, I will speak such words will turn Ninth Avenue to repentance.

O Dickinson, Dickinson, you should be preaching here, not we in your desperate little lost stronghold of thought.

Yours,

J. J. C.

To S. S. Drury

May 18, 1914

O Thou Schoolmaster!

— I never got a mark higher than 75 per cent in my life; and I have a strong prejudice against any boy who can get such marks. It means low ambitions. An endeavor to please the elders is at the bottom of high marks and of mediocre careers.

I know that distorted natures are needed by the world. Society requires them. The schoolmaster, the editor, the picture-dealer, the perambulant Jew who buys calves and broken horseshoes, all are useful in the operations of cosmic force. And great mother nature puts forth also anti-toxines against them — poets, parents, artists, and men of heart.

J. J. C.

To Rosalind Richards

BARRYTOWN, N.Y.
June 8, 1914

My dear Rosalind

You are a spunky little devil. Who would have thought you would carry such hot fire for so long — to remember all these points. Besides, you are right about all of them except perhaps about Emerson, which is the sort of question that is temperamental and essentially bottomless.

As for Mrs. Howe, I have written a splendid sketch — but it is entirely due to Elizabeth. I couldn't have begun to do it alone: and as it was, I had to redraw, erase, and sweat over it like a Trojan. Your instinct was *perfectly right*. And besides, I don't deal with the side of her you knew. I couldn't do it. I just evade it — a sketch is a nothing.

As for my grandmother, a life of her would be dull, I think.

There wasn't enough variety. She was just one thing. Some-one sent me a lot of family letters, but they were mortal dull, and written in such a fine hand that I couldn't have read them if they'd been by Isaiah. The man who could have stood a volume was Quincy; [1] who was a wit — and every letter of his in the Garrison life casts as much light as a bush-burner on the queer crowd of enthusiasts he spent his life with. He and Anne Chapman had a daily correspondence for many years which would have made a monument of the epoch — for it would have been *amusing* and some cussed idiots of the next generation destroyed them. Such are men: especially Ameri-cans. They want to be tidy and respectable; whereas life is a scramble.

I certainly should never have written to Mrs. Richards exactly as I felt about the life of Mrs. Howe — because you should never write just exactly what you think about any-one's book unless you think nothing but good things. But Mrs. Richards asked me to and I said I would; and I got deeper and deeper into it and more and more determined. The proper thing would have been to rewrite my letter to Mrs. Richards — toning it up and down into the proper vehicle. Whereas I sent her the *memoranda*.

As for mere love being enough to make a memoir — there you have a subject for an essay. I should say love was a danger in artistic matters. The extreme case of a biographer who felt that it was a danger and did his best to avoid it is Palmer's life of Mrs. Palmer. This book is a monument to the idea. And really I think Palmer did the maximum that could have been done for Mrs. Palmer — who was a woman singularly difficult to deal with because her power was personal, not of the intel-lect. She had a commonplace mind — in a certain sense. Her whole mission was personal. Even as it is, I doubt whether the book will be expressive in later years to people who have only the book. But it is a *tour de force*. Any other method would have made people think that after all Mrs. Palmer was not so remarkable as her reputation.

Palmer, through his perception of the matter, has done all that could be done. His intellect perceived just where love

[1] Edmund Quincy, 1808–1877.

began and he let intellect, not love, do the thinking. The impersonal is what counts in the symbolic world and one must see things in terms of the languages of the world and hitch our pictures into the existent world of letters. You can't do anything else without drawing attention away from the subject and exhibiting yourself rather than it.

I am overjoyed with all your joy about the Garrison. You can't imagine how much so. That whole epoch is a great possession of the American people — if they ever come into their possessions. Someone ought to devote his life to writing the history of it from the only point of view which unravels it, and unifies it. My idea was only to give the spot on which one has to stand, and to which the lines converge. There is a dualism in any less remote spot. There was a man whose name I forget who refused to vote for the Constitution because it sanctioned slavery, but retired to New Jersey or wherever it was. Well, that man was right....

Yours affectionately,

JACK

To his Mother

On board the Provence
June 21: 1914

DEAR MAMA

I never enjoyed a voyage so much; and I think the French are the only people who understand ocean travel. The arrangements, customs, food, and service are infinitely better than on the swinish German steamers or the brutal Britons. I'd rather go to the bottom with the French than float about eternally with the beastly Teutons. Although the ship is or *must be* so full, it doesn't seem crowded. The stewards and stewardesses are polite, and efficient. The sea is calm — that's a great point and much to the credit of the French. Scarcely any one drinks anything. When I consider the cork-popping on the German line — the hours over swilling tables of odious food — the gross salutations and imprecations from unwiped lips — calling a blessing upon the indulgence — I shudder. The boys are extremely happy and do lots of work every day. I have taken the time to read Bright's Life with more care than I should have given on land. It gives me the best glimpse into English politics that I've ever had. Bright himself was so bored with the fictitious character of the English system — the fact that it is all *a game*. But I think he was the greatest figure of the century in English politics so far as enduring interest goes. The rest are so mad about ephemeral details that one forgets and confuses them. Bright has always in mind something that *remains true*. Just now the Jingoes are on top and it may be a long time — before the little-England point of view comes to the front again. One would think from reading this life of Bright that Disraeli had made a failure. But if you go to England you find Bright forgotten and Disraeli their *great man* — their George Washington. I say this to their shame: for I think Dizzy was a humbug and quite properly stands for *all the humbug* in British life — which under the present Imperialism is particularly rampant....

I shall go so far as to encourage their industries by purchasing two or three light flannel suits later in the summer and perhaps a tweed sporting suit. The absurd fondness for sport has this good in it that it produces wonderful men's clothes. At the sacrifice of all reason art is produced — as usual. Umbrellas too are good. I shall call on the Laugels and Ferays of course — and immediately — as we hope to leave Paris almost at once.

Your affectionate son

JACK

To S. S. Drury

June 24, 1914
LA PROVENCE

MY DEAR DR. DRURY

I have been reading 150 lines per day of the Iliad with Conrad and think we can increase it very soon. He has to work up the grammar himself afterwards; as grammar is a subject I cannot feel any interest in. It's all humbug anyway....

Apropos of Conrad's becoming a professor I recommend him to forget it for ten years after leaving college — go out into the world become a part of the great world — *then*, teach if he likes. What schools and colleges need [is] to have men of the world in them.

What schools need is not to be schools, but just part of life. Arnold's idea is baby. The notion of influencing boys is baby. Let us all live in the real world; there's no more to it than this.

Yours sincerely

JOHN JAY CHAPMAN

To Mrs. Winthrop Chanler

HOTEL NATIONALE
FRANKFURT-AM-M.
July 24, 1914

DEAR DAISY:

This is the railroad hotel just opposite the Bahnhof. It's like Charing Cross Hotel, whose only merit is convenience — and in this case cheapness. We go out and *bummel* and see things and eat at Rathskellers. The Opera and Theatre are closed. But we did succeed in falling on an extremely funny farce, musical affair (much the best I ever saw anywhere) last night. I hate musical comedies and never go to them. But Victor and Elizabeth have low tastes, and this time for once I was rewarded. We move on the Thuringenwald Sunday — day after tomorrow — after spending four nights here. Our previous stops were Rouen, Paris (a week and a half) Beauvais, Compiègne, Laon, Luxemburg, Trèves — whence we came down the Moselle, a divine trip, to Coblenz — then St. Goar, and then here. The boys have been very agreeable, though maddening in their habit of wandering off and doing as they please while Elizabeth and I were kept waiting. Young people seem to be quite selfish and un-principled. I dare say you have observed this. There has generally been a moment during the day when I hoped not to see any of the boys for a month. Fleas we had. One *must*, in travelling properly in Europe, and one might as well accept them. Chanler has suffered the most and is a sad spectacle. We affect small towns, second-class inns, and third-class carriages. We eat at very foreign places — and fleas are a part of this tradition. In this particular hotel we are free from them. We are having a wash-up — sitzbads, large, expensive, two-mark baths. But this is very exceptional. I think Elizabeth must really be rich with all the money she must have saved; but it is not her policy to admit it. She admits only that she is barely holding her own, etc. Conrad, by the way, is the courier. He does *everything*: tickets, payments, transportation, fees, cabs, customhouses. I never had such a luxurious feeling. In all other journeys I have ever taken in my life, I've had to attend to things. Now I just do nothing but walk through the gate....

I have read almost all of 'Faust' aloud to the family — Goethe's house and museum most interesting. How beautifully the Germans do these things. Such good taste, such simplicity. I dote on Germany and the Germans — (except Bismarck and Goethe) and I am beginning to find out why I don't like these two personally. But I must write an essay about it. Nor Wagner. I never could abide him personally. But the German *Geist* and way of life is very agreeable — most full of heart. *They say* that the German doesn't jump into the water to save a woman's life, and is a selfish brute generally. And that Englishwoman says a lot of bad things about German men; but I can't help it, as I see them I delight in the people and in German life, and I've always done so. I believe they *would* save your life.

Yours affectionately,

JACK

We have bought an Empire iron stove today in an antiquity shop opposite the Goethe house. It is to warm the top room at 325 to which I am driven by piano playing. I shall write over the door of my room

> Hinter den Ofen gebannt
> Schwillt er wie ein Elephant

To Langdon Mitchell

FULDA, *July* 28: 1914

DEAR LANGDON

I wonder if you've ever been to Fulda. It's about the charmingest small town on a hillside I ever was in — eighteenth century schloss and gardens — now occupied by retired officers and public Seminaries. Eighth century church — eighteenth century palazzo, turned into a first-rate hotel — great big rooms with stoves in them, pension 7 marks a day — lovely wine — excellent table. The *Frauen-berg* hill (with views of the plain) rising like a sugar loaf just behind the town — you go up it by steps of the cross — and a monastery of rubicund German Franciscans on top who look as if they had enough to eat. I'd like to stay here *forever*; and I did succeed in getting the rest of them to stop for several days. We go to Cassel three or four hours north of here to see my German cousins — and then to Weimar, Leipsic — and finally to Bremen whence to England for a week or two before returning. I have been reading German somewhat; and I think if I lived here for a year or two and gave my attention to it, I could find out something about Goethe and his talent. The thing that annoys me is to have him classed in with the unconscious artists — whereas he's always a little self-conscious — and more clever than poetic.

It's a strange fact that I read Balzac when I want to enjoy myself — he's more unconscious and more objective and more Homeric; more carried away with enthusiasm by the subject — more everything a poet ought to be than Goethe ever is. I say this as a paradox — to catch your attention; but I also propound it as a deep truth. Goethe is never quite the thing-he-preaches; but always a drawing-room edition of it.

I find the English poets more naïf. The matter is so complicated by race differences that it is hard to get at. I should have said, for instance, that Goethe had a very *ungerman* nature. But the German has (beside his lyric side) a distinctly dogmatic side — and this dogmatism I feel in Goethe, a very intellectual, highly romantic thing, and yet, categorical — I feel the iron railing in 'Faust.' What is it? I don't know. Virtuosity?

By the way — with all the wonderful cultivation of modern Germany, isn't their mode of writing a give-away? — that multiplication of qualifying clauses — and then the *Erlösung* of them by verbs and participles. It is closely connected with a dogmatic habit of mind. The German *believes* in the possibility of accuracy; and he thinks he has *got* the *thing*. So he sets it out with accuracy. He will not state anything which he is obliged to qualify afterwards, as e.g. 'the horse is white in his legs.' He regards that as sloppy. The German must say the white-as-to-his-legs horse.

This sentiment for accuracy leads to those piled up sentences which we all know. But the psychology at the bottom of the whole procedure is *totally false*. For in real life one apprehends things in the vague; and then afterwards senses them and perceives details. Now I say that no highly developed, well-rounded, intellectually experienced person of any race or time would write as the educated, highly educated German writes today. Goethe and Heine didn't do it. I don't remember whether Schiller did or not, but I'm sure he didn't. I thus attack the major part of the contemporary intellect of Germany, and show it to be *undeveloped*. So there! There you are. I do enjoy French books.

By the way, I am going to see my very nice but through-their-attachment-to-the-Court-and-the-Necessity-of-moving-always-in-the-Circles-of-the-Nobility-upon-a-small-Income somewhat intellectually contracted first cousins tomorrow. Their into-a-principle-erected economic Necessity of Personal-opinion-suppression is to me of a certain Dulness, or Mind-over-growing Stupidity, often thought to have been the apparent Cause. (You perceive the need of capitals.)

Now there is no exaggeration here. These are mild specimens. Now you and other *apologists* for Germany are in the habit of thinking that all this introversion of language is just the German way. But it's a *bad way*. It's a hob-nailed, crass-cultivated way — for boor-minded, hob-minded people. Posterity will not stand it. All books written in this language will perish, all such books have always perished. Immanuel Kant will perish. Human nature won't stand for it.

Well, thus, too, also in addition, moreover, will I add: — that the self-conceived and, in every-modern-German-consciousness, secretly nurtured Ambition to leave an-however-small, accurately-stated-monumentally-important Book about Something or other, which shall have had at one time an Influence of Significance for the to-be-thereafter-written

books upon the same subject, is, and, by-the-inner-nature-of-
its-mode-of-being must essentially remain, a heart-and-mind-
somewhat-contracting (in spite of its contributory advantages
from the point of view of Character in relation to Humility)
ultimate Influence.

Yours affectionately

JACK

Please remember me kindly to Mrs. Langdon.

To his Mother

[*From Fulda, at the end of July, Chapman went to Cassel, to visit
his Jay aunt, the widow of General von Schweinitz, all of whose sons
were immediately involved in the war. Chapman's letters relating
to the events immediately following the visit to Cassel belong to the
ensuing chapter.*]

CASSEL
HOTEL ROYAL
July 30: 1914

DEAR MAMA

The war scare is on. People are surging in the streets.
Anna is off to Berlin (probably tonight) to see her sons
before the next thing happens. If Russia gets involved
Germany must go in. This is an immense bore to the Germans, for they had no sympathy with the Servians, and would
enjoy seeing Austria discipline the Servians. At any moment
the wires may announce that Germany is at war. All the
Schweinitz boys have been summoned to their regiments
and even van Nott has been called to headquarters together
with the rest of the ministers. We saw Anna for an hour and
a half, also Maria — also three fine small boys of Wilhelm.
Anna had spent all the morning at the railroad station seeing
people off — and at the dentist — but was quiet, controlled,
and pretty gloomy. Eleonore is to come to lunch here from
Bebra, where she lives, tomorrow — unless war events intervene.

All these things have destroyed our visit and we shall
probably leave for Weimar tomorrow afternoon. I suppose
the professional soldiers enjoy the chance of fighting; but

no one else does. They say that the bottom of the danger is the fondness of the Russian people for the Serbs. The Czar and his administration may be rushed into war. No one believes that Russia — the officials — want war.

Your affectionate son
JACK

VII

The World Ablaze
1914–1918

It was not for one of Chapman's nature to stand detached and philosophical through such years as those from 1914 to 1918. The conflict in which millions were to die became at once for him an intensely personal affair. The whole period was for Chapman a time of deep travail and suffering. Half way through its course the death of his eldest son in France made his personal relation to it all only the more intense. Visiting his aunt at Cassel at the very moment when her military sons were beginning their service for Germany, finding himself in London a few days later, in close touch with persons of the highest responsibility there, he faced the gigantic facts of a hideous time. From the first his heart and mind were completely with the Allies. The relation of the United States to the war, both before and after April, 1917, was a matter of supreme moment to him. Though hostile in general to the course of President Wilson, there were times when the policies of the Administration and the character of its chief met with his warm approval. If Wilson's actions were subject to variation, so certainly were Chapman's opinions. How positive they were, even when contradictory, we shall soon see.

Chapman's days in Germany and weeks in London during August of 1914, and his September weeks in America, yielded him experiences and charged him with thoughts, both fully chronicled by himself, which are peculiarly worthy of record. His letters and a diary, begun in London August 18 and continued for several months, are of remarkable substance, with respect both to events and to ideas, all so closely interrelated that they belong to the more strictly narrative portion of this chapter and will be used accordingly. It was through the earliest weeks of the war that circumstances of uncommon significance call for recital in special detail.

A long letter to his mother begun at Boxtel, Holland, on August 1 and finished in London on August 3, gives a vivid picture of the Chapmans' escape from the Continent. It tells first of leaving his aunt, Madame von Schweinitz, at Cassel two days before, starting for Berlin to say good-bye to her sons. It describes a railroad journey from Eisenach on a 'howling, shouting, crushing, mob-train to Bremen,' whence they hoped to sail to England. 'But *State of War*. No boats at all.' Hence a railroad journey to Flushing: 'Took a bawling overcrowded train — most people standing up — at 4.30 P.M. Saturday, and rode in it for twelve hours.' Reaching the middle of Holland — Boxtel — they left the train to rest before proceeding more comfortably to Flushing. On the train, he wrote, 'I lay on the floor of the passage way in the car with Chanler on top of me from 12 to 3.30.' He described the 'farce of passports' at the Dutch border: 'You produced any paper — return tickets, letters of credit, etc. — and they let you through,' and proceeded: 'My disgust at the German idiocy about small matters and incompetency in everything except *routine*, makes me hope they will mismanage their war. Some case will arise which is not provided for in the manuals, and then everyone from the Kaiser downward would behave like a muttonhead.'

The letter was continued at Flushing and on the steamer to England, with vivid and penetrating observations on a state of affairs that seemed 'like Jules Verne — and the Imaginary Romances.' There was one clear foreshadowing of an interest that within two weeks was to plunge Chapman into a vigorous endeavor, in which no statesman was far-sighted enough at the time to join him. 'I cannot imagine,' he wrote, 'that this experience should not be followed by a convention rearranging the laws of warfare. People will see the necessity. The whole weight of the world must be turned against a nation who begins a war — just as the whole weight of society is turned against a street fight.' The fourteen large pages of the letter were brought, with infinite relief, to an end at 'London 5 P.M. [Monday, August 3] Artillery Mansions Hotel.'

Chapman turned his first day in London to account, for on August 5 appeared over his name in the *Times* as a letter to the editor 'An Appeal to Americans.' A portion of it reads as follows:

> *Sir* — The Americans who have come from Germany during the past few days are the only people in England who have already experienced the awe-striking brutality of actual war. . . .
>
> On reaching England we saw the smiling fields, men and women playing tennis — welcome everywhere, affection, comfort, the inexpressible relief of personal safety — the kind world again. Yet we were haunted by a terrible sentiment — namely, that England did not understand the depth of the Continental disturbance, or the size and nature of the convulsion. In any case England is wisely holding back and husbanding her power — it is all going to be needed. France now holds the fort of modern civilization; but the whole power of England is needed to buttress her.
>
> As for America, our history and our policy force us to stand outside the conflict; though every American who understands the conditions will feel the appeal so strongly as to make him almost desire to enlist under the British Flag. That we cannot do. But one thing we can do — namely, we can use our personal power to explain this war to Americans at home, to the millions of our fellow-citizens far away, who may think that this is an ordinary European war with which we have little to do — a European diplomatic imbroglio which will settle itself. The understanding sympathy of one hundred million Americans is no small power in European affairs. It is for us through our influence at home to educate America. . . .

Through the following fortnight he wrote with great frequency to his mother. Here are a few passages from these letters:

> *August 6.* I have telegrams and letters of congratulation on my Times letter — one from Henry James, quite to my surprise as to his fiery approval.
>
> *August 7.* . . . In the meantime my wife had bought the last ten pounds of chocolate in Selfridge's store to give to my son [Victor], who having read that the American students in Paris are volunteering, is trying to get across the Channel to enlist under the French flag. After all, this is one way to serve the cause of architecture. . . .
>
> During the last month many persons of gentle breeding in Germany, and high up in military circles, have seemed to be under an obsession. They are like people under a spell of some sort. The religious zeal of the Emperor is not personal, but tribal. We are in the presence of a military fanaticism which reminds of Mahomet. I have been a little terrified for some years past in meeting individual Germans. A gleam like hatred or like insanity would flit across their personality, and give me a vague, queer chill which could not be seized or analyzed. This element was in a German tutor who spent the summer with us a year ago. The chill was a message from the Great Secret.
>
> *August 8.* I saw Victor off at Charing Cross at 2 today for Paris, where he is going to enlist with American volunteers under the French flag. I don't suppose there is much chance of their getting to the front, but it will be a great training and experience, and is a splendid thing for both France and America that the movement should be made. I really envied him a good deal.

Then came a break in the daily letters, but a passage in the Introduction to 'Victor Chapman's Letters from France' preserves the continuity of record: [1]

> Just before his enlistment in August, 1914, there occurred a scene between Victor, his stepmother and myself, which was our domestic part of the great war drama. No doubt millions

[1] From 'Victor Chapman's Letters from France.' By permission of The Macmillan Company, publishers.

of families on which the wheels of fate were then turning, can recall similar little dramas in which the dies of life and death were thrown for them. We were all in a London hotel, having fled the Continent at the mobilization. The English people were singing the Marseillaise in front of the Parliament Houses. Victor had been prowling about in a lonely way for twenty-four hours, and he now, with a sort of hang-dog humility, suggested that he was going to enlist. I reasoned with him. With that stupidity which is the natural gift of parents, I probed his conscience and suggested that perhaps it was merely a random desire to see life and get rid of his serious duties that led him to the idea of enlistment. He concurred, with dumb diffidence, and said: 'No doubt this must be it.' My wife says that I called him a quitter and held him up to the scorn of just men. But my own idea was that I was only preventing the lad from doing something which was not fundamentally his duty. He submitted. I supposed he was merely being rational; but there was a something in his voice and manner, something, I know not what, of a soul-tragedy, that struck his stepmother and gave her a vision of a ruined life. And as soon as Victor had left the room, she said: 'He has submitted through his humility and through his reverence for you. But I had rather see him lying on the battlefield than see that look on his face.' Within a week, he was in France.

The letters to Chapman's mother take up the story:

August 12.... What with Victor's going off to the wars in France and the other various odd things that have been happening in Europe, I have been neglecting you.... My own opinion is clear that Germany will go down after a year or two. She is crazed, and will fight like the Southern Confederacy, but she won't win out. The world is too wise to make a truce with her. America has as much to lose as anyone. Imagine what America would be like with Germany *in control of the sea*. America will be drawn into the struggle if it grows very severe.

August 14.... I read Balzac. Balzac is the only writer, from Homer to Kipling, that I can always read. The other writers have to fall in with my mood, but I fall in with Balzac's. In times like this, where the danger is of getting excited, it's a great thing to have a big novel to read as a child reads it — like a big cake which you dig through. I don't know what it is about Balzac that dominates me. I could show him to be absurd, and yet he's one of the very greatest writers of the world.[1]

August 17.... I have been too busy to write — about things I'll tell you of afterwards. I spent Saturday and Sunday at Wittersham (where Elizabeth has been all the week) with Mrs. Lyttelton's family — a whole houseful of them. Then Elizabeth and I went to Rye, and lunched with Henry James, who asked after you and wants to be remembered to you. He is a dear old thing. I told you, I think, that he had written to me commending my *Times* letter. Was there ever such luck as to get the letter in, in that number of the *Times* which contained the declaration of war!... H. J.'s house at Rye is wonderful — a garden, an old house, a mulberry tree of 1600 at least, the most charming old Queen Anne, irregular, respectable place.

The 'things I'll tell you of afterwards' were things of which little was said at the time, but that little was said to such persons as Balfour, Haldane, and Grey in England, and Wilson and Bryan in America, and the things themselves were of an importance, in their truly prophetic foresight, which entitles them now to a significant place in the annals of war-time thought. The visionary Chapman, as so many would have called him, must be recognized now as one who saw from the first a real objective for the war — an objective still sought, still unrealized, but so fundamental in its purpose that the failure of ruling statesmen to adopt and further the plan which Chapman laid before them must be counted among the untested opportunities from which — who shall say? — some betterings of a distracted world might have proceeded. A 'Memorandum on Compulsory Disarmament' speaks for the working of Chapman's mind during the first twelve days of August. The date of its composition should be borne, fixedly, in mind. Thus, in part, it ran:

... In the present war, if Germany is defeated, there will be an opportunity for a Congress of Disarmament — compulsory disarmament — a thing to be carried out quietly, and enforced

[1] See Chapman's paper, 'Balzac' in *Greek Genius and Other Essays* (1915): 'I myself often finish a book of Balzac's almost wishing that I had never begun it. His books add a new duty to life. To read one of them is like having a live crab entangled in one's hair: there is no quick way of getting him out.'

by gunboats. Any policy which England, France, and all the smaller powers of Europe (together with the United States and the smaller Powers of America) may agree upon, can be enforced in Western Europe. The danger is that between now and the end of the war, these Powers may disagree among themselves.

We are all very virtuous just now. But I suppose it is impossible that Germany should retain Alsace. It might be that Alsace and Lorraine should be established as an independent government under the Suzerainty of France — like Poland under Russia. In any case, that course should be taken which will leave the fewest wounds behind it. We must exclude from the area of our thought all ideas of national aggrandizement. If the Allies once begin to think about national aggrandizements, the antagonisms will recommence, and the world will be booked for additional unpleasant experience.

One might prophesy with boldness that such will be the outcome; for Government is a slow growth, and World Government has not yet begun. Nevertheless it is worth while to consider the whole problem at the present time; for the moment we admit that Germany may fail in her ambition, we are face to face with these questions. In any event, we ought to consider them now, while we are still virtuous. The possession of firearms is what makes war — not colonies, not trade, not mere ambition. If Germany had had no Army and Navy, she could not have made this war. To deprive her of colonies will not cure her; but to police her land, and prevent the recreation of armies and navies will cure her.

It will be said offhand by everybody, that this suggestion is impossible of execution. But the thing does not seem impossible. France and her Allies will, if they win, dominate the Western world. With their congregated power they can compel the gradual disarming of all other Western nations — doing the thing slowly, and in such a way that their own congregated power remains ever predominant, while all Powers diminish gradually. In other words, Europe and America must consolidate for police purposes. It is likely that many attempts will have to be made before the law and order of the Western world is established; and that the East will make the matter of world-peace slow in coming. It remains true, however, that our comprehension of the process will accelerate it. . . .

The fact is that Great Britain can retain her greatness only by pursuing the very opposite policy to that through which she gained her greatness. She grew great through an unconscious power of self-aggrandizement: she can remain great only through a conscious avoidance of self-aggrandizement. Have her statesmen the subtlety of mind to perceive this? The average Briton, at the present moment, reasons thus: 'Of course we want nothing from this war. But if we win, we shall of course take the German colonies.' Such reasoning is natural but, if acted upon, it will prevent Great Britain from doing a great service to mankind — a service so great as to belittle her whole past history and to make her the star of the world.

It may be that military necessity will require that certain things be taken from Germany during the war; but as little as possible should be taken and as much as possible restored at the close of the war. The disturber of the peace must be restrained, not pillaged; and the hand of the constable must receive no part of the thief's property.

The Congress of Disarmament ought to follow the War quickly and act quickly. There will be a moment at the close of the war, in case Germany's ambitions are defeated, when the public feeling in favor of disarmament will be overwhelming. Plans should be matured now which can be carried out before the new world-sentiment evaporates through delay, or dribbles away in diplomatic controversies.

London, *August* 12, 1914

To this should be added a single paragraph from a shorter paper, 'The Practical Aspect,' produced at the same time:

If Great Britain could decide *now* that she would annex no land at the end of the war (though she may be forced by military considerations to seize land during the war) such a decision would make her the hope of the nations so far as Universal Peace goes. Such a declaration would arouse a wave of enthusiasm among neutrals, and make the war into a crusade. I confess that the war is a crusade already. Let us say, then, that such a declaration would tend to prevent the war from degenerating — as crusades are apt to do.

For more than a month after putting these sentiments into words Chapman made every effort to transfer them to the realm of fact. He was not given to the keeping of diaries, but at this time he must have felt that his daily experiences

were of more than common moment, for many of them are
recorded in a journal begun on August 18, continued with
few interruptions for a month, and then falling into the
irregularity that precedes the common fate of diaries begun
by non-diarists. The final entries in this one were made
on January 28 and March 6, 1915. Thus it began:

> *Tuesday, August* 18, 1914. — On Sunday had a talk with D D
> [Mrs. Chapman's life-long friend, Mrs. Alfred Lyttelton] and
> gave her the Memorandum on Compulsory Disarmament, also
> read her the Practical Suggestion. She is going to see about
> getting the ear of Sir Edward Grey.

Before this came about there were many general observations
and a few personal encounters to be recorded.

> *August* 25. — To S.S. [office] and bought tickets for Lapland
> sailing Sept. 1. Got telephone from D D (whom E and I
> visited last night after seeing Page) saying we were to lunch
> with her and meet Arthur Balfour 1.45 tomorrow. 9 P.M.
> D D telephoned for me to come round. I had a long conversa-
> tion with Lord Milner.
> *Aug.* 26. Most satisfactory talk with Arthur Balfour, a long
> lunch, the whole field covered. It couldn't have been better.
> Elizabeth is afraid it may evaporate in talk — in the way of
> the moony educated English — in the socio-intellectual draw-
> ing-[room] field of their existence. But I don't think so.
> 7 P.M. Lodge was interesting. He gave me a letter to Haldane
> — whom I am to see at 2.45 tomorrow. Lodge quoted Haldane
> 'This fight is to put an end to Prussian Militarism and if we
> win it must mean disarmament.' This is all we need — spoken
> solemnly by the whole Administration. Lodge is not satisfied
> with Wilson and Bryan — too much German in it. Wilson
> still says he will buy the boats. If he does Lodge will attack
> him. So will I. L. says he couldn't get me an interview with
> Wilson — a letter from him would be waste paper. He will
> think up *how to do it* — probably by a letter to Olney in Boston —
> perhaps by more strings. . . .
> On the whole Elizabeth is right: the English don't under-
> stand the idea of acting for the world. It doesn't thrill them or
> mean much to them. To act for themselves with resultant bene-
> fit to the world — (because on the whole their methods were

more liberal and gentler than those of any other nations).
This has been their destiny. If you ask them to do something
for any one else — they answer — 'Why, England always
does that.' They cannot see that the present fact that they
want no more land is a novelty. Their feelings are hurt if you
ask them to make plain their intentions. According to themselves they have always been lovely people. My friends here
think that I am just coming to understand England — (after
years of attack on their Boer war). They think that my eyes
have been opened to their virtue — 'now I see what England
is, etc.'...

Aug. 27. Saw Lord Haldane for half an hour. The four
points the Cabinet has in mind as the outcome of the war are,
1. Independence of Belgium. 2. Promise to Poland of racial
organization under Russian sovereignty must be performed.
3. Alsace to France. 4. Disarmament. He said that the time
to announce these had not come. I distinguished — certainly
not as to some of them. But as to disarmament — the policy
ought to be announced at once. I put it as a personal quandary of my own in returning to America. How can I announce
that England favors disarmament any more than Russia or
Germany? Can I say 'O, that's the way the English I've met
seem to *feel?*' I must have an authoritative declaration somewhere. The same thing would raise the troops in Yorkshire —
put the case so that the nonconformist and the peace-man sees
it is a war for peace — and the economist for the saving of 500
millions annually in armaments (this last point is Haldane's).
But we need them now. He said first catch your hare. I explained that it worked the other way. If we once catch him
we'll eat him. We want to promise we won't before we catch
him. This repartee is of the escalier, but is good. I'll get it off
on Sir Edward Grey whom I am to see at 2.55 tomorrow.

Haldane says they are satisfied with both Wilson and Page,
and has no fears of any German influence at the White House.

I had a smile with Haldane over the British feeling that
their aims in this war were so lofty and unselfish that it was
superfluous to ask them to say that they were not out for aggrandizement. Considering their past — a respectful interest
in their *intentions* is not untimely or illnatured. By the way,
I opened up the conversation with Haldane by recalling Lincoln's unwillingness for two years to declare his intentions
with regard to slavery — and telling Haldane of the quandary

which this threw Bright, W. E. Forster, into; and the rest of the British Friends of the North. The moral support of England was only enlisted by the Emancipation Proclamation. Well, we want such an emancipation proclamation now. I explained the need throughout this was of a *publicity campaign*, a University extension end of the whole movement. If they don't attend to this they'll have a barren victory. They won't be allowed to carry out their disarmament. He evidently had not thought of this.

Aug. 28, 3 P.M. Twenty minutes leisurely talk with Sir Edward Grey. Much the ablest man I've ever met. The conversation couldn't have been more satisfactory. I made two practical suggestions. *First*, that he should give an utterance on Disarmament as the object of the war — as soon as possible — and that this should be the beginning of what the Americans would call a publicity end of the war — a thing as important as the battles, i.e. continuous explanation to the grand public of the aims of the Allies. *Second. Wilson.* If Wilson really understands the war, then it is a trifle what he may do or not do about the purchase of ships. He may make mistakes — he may be pigheaded or perverse. *It will make no difference in the end.* He will work out of his errors as he did in the Mexican situation. I went so far as to suggest a personal note from him to Wilson. He didn't shy or poohpooh this. He said — 'What one thinks about it — is that it would be so unusual and how it might strike Wilson,' etc. I said the unique greatness of the occasion allowed anything — which he silently seemed to concede....

7.15 P.M. Saw Cabot Lodge and reported. He gave me a letter of introduction to Richard Olney in Boston. Thanked Lodge and called on Henry Adams who is staying at the same hotel. Delighted to see Adams in London. Fifty years ago he was here as his father's secretary. This man has known England better than any other American has known it. All his old pals gone — only one rag left — Lady Somebody — 'And you, the other rag,' said Mrs. Lodge. This has been the most remarkable month of my existence, perhaps of most people's.

The diary continues with many comments on inserted clippings of press reports upon matters that rapidly became history. The temptation to quote them at length, in evidence of Chapman's instant response to the largest issues then sharply facing the world, must be resisted. One passage, written September 1 on board the *Lapland*, is typical:

> The modern world is increasing the speed of reactions. Telegraphy and newspapers make things occur in a few days which one hundred years ago took ten years. It required twelve years for Napoleon's unimaginative conduct to evoke the forces that overthrew him. But it has taken only twenty days for America to understand the Germans. The latest American fugitives left Munich in special drawing-room cars with flowers and fine speeches from the Emperor. This is due to the awful fuss the earlier fugitives made about their atrocious ejection.
>
> Since the destruction of Louvain — a week ago — the American press is urging the introduction of rifle practice in our public schools. The press is right too. If Germany should win America must arm. All this illustrates the extraordinary celerity of modern social reactions. It may be that in order to be melted into modern Europe America must go through with this experience. My ideas of disarmament, etc., may be like reaching for the moon.

Arrived in New York Chapman makes note that on September 10 he is to lunch with Cleveland Dodge, with whom he must, according to a subsequent note, have discussed approaching Wilson on his disarmament project: 'The result of my interview with Dodge was to convince me that Wilson knew more about the matter than I did. So I shall not go to Washington for the present.' Yet only a week later he did consult with Wilson, and meanwhile had presented his letter from Lodge to Richard Olney. Both interviews are recorded in the journal.

> *Sept.* 13. Sunday — at Falmouth Mass., where I came to deliver a letter of introduction from Lodge to Richard Olney. Olney is exactly like a Frog-King in a fairy tale. His face is ugly, hard, shrewd, grotesque: his person monstrous — and yet he is not a bad fellow. He's the 'solid men of Boston' type, no interest in cultivation, a house bare of objects, a mind of impressions. He was sitting alone in his arid little parlor like a big spider when my card was sent in. He came out of

his parlor — 'Well, what's this?' 'It's a letter from Cabot Lodge.' 'I see it is; but what's it about, what's your business?' I shoved my way in and sat down. He couldn't read Lodge's letter; and he is one of those men who screw up their eyes and hold the paper sideways instead of putting on glasses. He sat in his chair contortionizing over Lodge's letter at the same time bidding me 'go on' — and was the veriest picture of a fat old worried ogre. I gave him a lecture for half an hour, punctured with — But what do you want *me* to do? — Why do you tell me these things? He became a little more like a gentleman towards the end of the interview, but not much. He refused, of course, to give me a line to Wilson, in which he was right. Wilson is sick, frail, staggering under this task and should be spared. I wouldn't have missed the interview however for anything. I have known so many Boston men, college boys and else, that his intonations, language, and tone of mind were familiar. His savagery was shocking, but so picturesque as to be amusing. His face, skin and waistcoat wrinkled and rolled about. His eyes twinkled, appeared and disappeared when he was listening with interest as he did at certain times. *Suspiciousness* was at the bottom of his conduct. He really thought that I wanted something out of him or would make some use of the interview. In this, how far below the English. Yes, socially speaking we are far below them. I hate to admit it. In some sort of social development which has got rid of *suspicion* they are out of sight.

Well, besides this, Olney's an old siege-gun abandoned on a rampart. How should he understand?

Washington. Sept 17: 1914. Yesterday at 8 P.M. had a talk with President Wilson. He looks a little rocky but then enduring. He is all religion and feeling. I told him of my English interviews with Grey, Haldane, etc., and of the subordinate position that *Disarmament* occupies in the European mind. He was very quick and very sympathetic — much more so than I expected — and not at all surprised. He seemed to know all I told him — but not to know it so definitely as I do. He did nothing but assent; but perhaps I was so moved and vehement and the time was so short that this was the easiest thing for him to do. He had been seeing the Belgian Refugees. He had been obliged to dismiss them without speaking as he really felt, for he could not have shown his sympathy without seeming partizan. As he described this his face became drawn

Sunday, Sept 27. 1914.

Barrytown. Had a long talk with
Nicholas Murray Butler last
night at Ned Vanderbilt's party.
He says that the letters written
by Eucken & Haeckel are
undoubtedly written under
pressure. Similar letters
have been extorted from
all the German exchange professors
who have been in America
& a supposed therefore to
be influential. German
propaganda has been
declining since 1880.
The State has appointed
all the professors & crushed
the least sign of inde-
pendent thought. Butler
said that the moral
power of the U.S. in all
the present crisis was
entirely due to the Repeal
& the Canal tolls Bill.

A PAGE FROM THE 1914 JOURNAL

with feeling. The inability of the English to state that they are fighting for Disarmament is partly constitutional, partly political. I told W. — what was just suggested while we were talking of the matter privately in England — that perhaps the time might come when the English Statesmen might willingly answer a question of Wilson's on the subject. I spoke of necessity of internal agitation in America — to formulate our ideas, told him of how I had warned Grey they might reap a barren victory unless they kept educating the public and especially the American public as they went along — to all of which Mr. W. gave an assenting attention. We spoke of Sir Edward Grey. W. had known nothing about him and didn't understand him till Grey sent Col. Somebody over here and Col. Somebody turned himself inside out to Wilson and Wilson turned himself inside out to Col. Somebody and since then he felt he had a good understanding of Grey. You see Wilson is a hot and natural person. Imagine his doing these things — and then telling me in this simple way. I asked him about John R. Mott — 'Why, he was here today. If I had only known I would have brought you together.' Wilson was in favor of my seeing Mott. But the notable thing is that Wilson saw I didn't want anything and that I understood the complexity of his position. He was really quite as frank as the Englishmen — so perhaps I have maligned my countrymen — (except that crocodile Olney). I asked if I might send him the *Mem.* and have done so. It is an immense relief to have this long prayed for interview over — and to have the president's ear, in case I need it.

The diary does not record a second interview of September, but it is recorded in a letter Chapman wrote to his mother before leaving Washington.

... I did call on Bryan, to whom I took a letter, and I like him. He is a big, benevolent man with a musical voice, who consoles and comforts everyone. He was refusing, in the most sympathetic and fatherly way, to endorse a poem which an old gentleman from Georgia was trying to get him to recommend. Bryan sat down and talked like a family doctor, encouraging and consoling the old gentleman in a sincere way. He is big, beaming, brilliant-eyed, and handsome; and in all he said to me was very ready and very intelligent. I tell you he's a fine figure of a man.

After the first few months of the war in Europe Chapman's activities in direct connection with it differed from those of thousands of other Americans on the eastern seaboard chiefly in the intensity of the feeling behind everything he said and did. Whenever a good occasion arose he wrote or spoke in burning words, the true expression of himself, on behalf of the Allied cause. Such deliverances were too many even to enumerate. Yet before the strain of the desperate period was well begun he achieved one piece of work which must be mentioned. This was the publication, in November 1914, of a volume, 'Deutschland über Alles, or Germany Speaks,' made up of letters from German statesmen, scholars, and others, with comment by Chapman on the hatred, power-lust, and self-exaltation apparent in them. Chapman could present this damaging illustration of the spirit of Germany at the beginning of the war with more first-hand knowledge of the German mind and character than many of those who contributed to the formation of American opinion at this time. As that opinion, and his own, increased in violence, one passage in the book must soon have seemed of an astonishing mildness. Today it may be read as an early milestone on the road along which even so vehement an anti-German as Chapman travelled:

> We must not, however, allow ourselves even to feel annoyance, far less to take any cruel reprisals if we should have the power. The antidote to war is peace, to unreason, reason, to mania, sense. If America can remain neutral without violation to her self-respect, it is far better to do so. If America should enter the war, the world would lose the benevolence and common-sense which we now possess, and which is a strong factor in the whole situation. You and I would, in that case, become partizans, cruel, excited, and bent on immediate results. The unfortunate sick-man, Germany, would have a double pressure put upon his brain, and the solution of the whole world problem would become a little retarded.

While the problem was working itself out, Chapman, consciously or unconsciously, was keeping his balance by interesting himself in other matters than the war. Shortly before going to Europe in the spring of 1914, he had produced a small book, 'Homeric Scenes.' This could hardly have excited much attention from the American public at any time, and in the infancy of its first few months the affairs of the world deprived it even of the notice it might have commanded. Its sub-title, 'Hector's Farewell and the Wrath of Achilles,' defines its substance. Its method was to present in dramatic form seven scenes from the Iliad, with no attempt at literal translation, but with a resulting effect of Homer seldom found in English verse. A typewritten list of 'Books and Publication Dates' preserved among Chapman's papers, has a note about 'Homeric Scenes': 'This I printed myself, and I have bushels of them. I think it my best thing; never noticed or reviewed anywhere.' A few friends, on whose good opinion of such a book he placed a special value, thought well of it. Langdon Mitchell was one of them, and nearly a year after the book appeared Chapman wrote to him (March 22, 1915):

> Two people besides my wife thought well of the Homer sketches — three: you, Croswell, and G. H. Palmer, the old Greek Professor — Philosophy — at Harvard. But it's enough. It's a bull's-eye. Croswell is a terrible loss to many. He had the most wonderful understanding of what anyone was driving at. It's a form of genius.... I always had him in mind in writing, and especially in excursions into Classic mythology, for he was a scholar and had read everything at the same time that he had a completely non-scholastic point of view....
>
> Old Palmer is a funny little dried up old acorn, and it took some courage to send him the Homer, because Homer is his subject. He translates it, and reads it aloud, and lectures on it, and, besides, he has generally written me nasty little notes about my most ambitious enterprises — condescending Massachusetts notes.

In the spring of 1915 appeared another book, 'Memories and Milestones,' quite unrelated to the war, and later in the year two others, 'Greek Genius and Other Essays' and 'Notes on Religion.' These were cumulative products of the years before the cataclysm. In Chapman's shipboard diary of September, 1914, he is seen reading, with his wife — a vigilant collaborator in all such matters — the proofs of what he then called 'Memorials and Milestones.' 'It is a soothing little book,' he wrote of it, 'and will not do harm to anyone. How different are my ambitions to those of Nietzsche. My hope is to write what everybody sees to be true and everybody thinks he always understood.'

Because this book is so personal in flavor, through consisting so largely of individual memoirs, it is also most characteristic of Chapman. The subjects of them and of the less personal papers contained in the book may be found in the Bibliography on later pages. The best things in this volume are so good that the book should stand among the first to be read by those who would savor the essential Chapman. Quotations from it have already been made at several points in this book. Yet here must be one more, in which Chapman, writing of William James, says very much what James might have said about him — and rather as James would have said it:

> In general talk on life, literature, and politics James was always throwing off sparks that were cognate only in this, that they came from the same central fire in him. It was easy to differ from him; it was easy to go home thinking that James had talked the most arrant rubbish, and that no educated man had a right to be so ignorant of the first principles of thought and of the foundations of human society. Yet it was impossible not to be morally elevated by the smallest contact with William James. A refining, purgatorial influence came out of him.

'Greek Genius and Other Essays,' like its immediate predecessor, is a collection of papers which had appeared in various periodicals. 'Memories and Milestones' contained a chapter 'Greek as a Pleasure,' and a considerable portion of the new volume illustrated this theme. Chapman counted himself but an amateur in the classics — as in other fields of learning — and such, in the best sense of that word, he really was. He resented dry-as-dust scholarship, though glad to profit from some of its results. 'Euripides and the Greek Genius,' filling nearly half of the book, revealed both the profit and the resentment. This was centralized upon Professor Gilbert Murray, not as the critical scholar whom Chapman admired, but as the poet-translator who 'sheds a sad, clinging, Tennysonian morality over Dionysus,' and represents the 'whole school of limp Grecism in England.' Letters of later years show no trace of a surviving personal rancor on either side. Indeed in 1929 Chapman wrote to Mrs. Frederick Winslow: 'Last year I met Robert Nichols, the poet, a great friend of ours. He said, "By the way, I met G. M. coming down a flight of steps at a reception, and I said, 'How about Jack Chapman's attack on you?' and G. M. replied, 'He hit me very hard. But he's a great spirit.' " And since then I have exchanged books with G. M. and we are friends.'

'Shakespeare' and 'Balzac' filled most of the remaining pages of this book, each essay, like the first, the work of a veritable amateur of its subject; and of course there is plenty of self-revelation. In view of the stupendous number of written pages in which Chapman recorded his own existence, these sentences from the Balzac paper, like the passage on William James that has just been cited, have a reflex bearing upon their writer:

> Your complete literary man writes all the time. It wakes him in the morning to write, it exercises him to write, it rests him to write. Writing to him is a visit from a friend, a cup of tea, a game of cards, a walk in the country, a warm bath, an after-dinner nap, a hot Scotch before bed, and the sleep that follows it. Your complete literary chap is a writing animal; and when he dies he leaves a cocoon as large as a haystack, in which every breath he has drawn is recorded in writing.

One of Chapman's liveliest essays, 'La Vie Parisienne,' brings 'Greek Genius' to a somewhat surprising conclusion.

The essay was written 'in the hope of saving a favorite niece, who thinks of making a plunge into the vortex of Paris.' It is a humorous, yet serious, study of the disintegrating effect of Europe upon American expatriates. 'The cult of cultivation,' says Chapman, 'which is merely a becoming sort of fashionable cough to thousands of Europeans, runs straight into scarlet fever and typhoid with the American visitors.' Only one who knew Europe so well as Chapman did could so persuasively exhort Americans to cultivate their own garden.

The second book of 1915, 'Notes on Religion,' was a small affair, only a hundred pages. The first half of the volume was devoted to 'The Roman Church,' the second chiefly to a series of twenty-five brief 'Memories and Half Thoughts.' Although no more, indeed, than 'Notes,' these flashes of comprehension are of greater worth than many sermons in bringing the modern mind and the spiritual core of Christianity into that speaking distance of each other in which working relations may exist. On the 'Roman Question,' which was to engross a large share of Chapman's thought and energy for ten years to come, his concern was more for the political and educational results from a growth in the power of Rome in America than for its effect upon individual lives. In a letter of 1922 he wrote: 'I myself am conscious of an antagonism to Catholicism which goes back to the Wars of Religion and which philosophy cannot eradicate.' It was in his Huguenot blood, farther back, in point of time, than the antagonism to slavery which could be traced to both Jay and Chapman grandparents. Yet his expression of it in the positive, often violent, terms which prevailed with him for more than a decade did not begin until 1915. In 1895 he wrote to his mother about the articles his brother was writing for the short-lived magazine, the *Bachelor of Arts*, of which he was the editor: 'Henry's articles are certainly very good. The R. C. one bores me because I don't think the subject important, but the beginning of it is as clever a piece of writing as I ever saw.' And again, 'He reads and writes easily, and out of his bookishness he gets himself interested in wholly insignificant subjects like the Roman Catholic Church and its attitude towards science.' The time was yet to come when Chapman would appear as indeed the grandson of the John Jay who in 1879 produced an uncompromising Protestant pamphlet, 'Rome, the Bible, and the Republic.' This grandfather's grandfather, John Jay, the first Chief Justice of the United States, in sympathy with discriminations of the English law then in force against Roman Catholics, had gone so far, in the discussions of a constitution for the state of New York, as to propose — according to his latest biographer, Professor Frank Monaghan — 'that Roman Catholics should not enjoy civil rights until they had sworn in the Supreme Court that no priest, pope, or foreign authority whatever had authority to absolve them from their allegiance to the state.' The anti-Roman bent of Chapman's mind, a manifest inheritance, will be clearly enough revealed in pages to follow.

In one of the 'Notes' headed 'Speech and Silence,' Chapman declares: 'It seems absurd to abuse anyone for any reason; and yet the righteous indignation at the bottom of certain kinds of abuse does good. A whirlwind of seraphic influence is behind it. Neither speech nor silence is important. If you speak with the power of God, the power of God will be expressed. If you keep silence with the power of God, the power of God will be expressed.' In relation to the Roman Church he wrote in this very book, 'Our duty is to break silence at once, and to break it with a mace that is heavy and calm.' What disturbed him most deeply in the whole matter was the conflict between 'the idea of the direct union of the soul with God' and 'the idea of the authority of the church.' To him it was an irreconcilable conflict illustrated in special force by the Jesuit order. 'The Catholic,' he said, 'is precluded by dogma from conceding true holiness to Protestants. But the Protestant has no excuse for looking with a jaundiced eye upon the saints in the Roman Catholic Church.' His own eye, here and elsewhere remained unclouded with respect to individual saints, but for ten years, as if under a vow of speech rather than silence, he strove, in public and in private, to bring his countrymen to share his view of the peril in which America seemed to him to stand.

When his friend and fellow-reformer, Paul Fuller, died in 1917, Chapman, greatly admiring, wrote, 'I never happened to talk religion with him, though I always felt that religion was the guide of his life. The impression survives in me that God made only one Paul Fuller, and that now he is gone. I can never find out whether it is possible to be a good Catholic and yet not want to build up the Catholic Church at the expense of private judgment.' If he ever found such another, the discovery was not announced — nor was there anyone else, Protestant or Catholic of whom he could write; 'If I should name the prominent citizens whom Paul Fuller has laughed me out of murdering the list would serve as a directory of Fifth Avenue.'

Chapman's books of 1915 gave no intimation of all that was stirring beneath, and upon, the surface of his days. The war in Europe was paramount with him. His private correspondence, his letters to the press, his occasional verses, glowed and burned for the cause of the Allies. While he and Mrs. Chapman were abroad, chiefly in Paris, from April to July 1915, she wrote to their son Chanler, 'Papa, of course, reads and writes hard all of every morning. He would do that whether he lived in the desert of Sahara or on the Acropolis at Athens.' Through these months in Europe they were deeply concerned with Victor's transfer from the Foreign Legion to the American aviation unit then in process of forming. Looking back upon this change, when Chapman came to write the Memoir of his son, he said: 'Victor's entry into the American Aviation was, to him, like being made a Knight. It transformed — one might almost say — transfigured him.' And if anything was needed to intensify Chapman's own commitment to the defeat of Germany, here it was. While Victor was still in the Foreign Legion, Chapman wrote from London to his wife in Paris: 'I do hope the Americans will get into this war, for I feel business training and enormous prestige as practical people has fitted them for the job. But they must get into the game by spilling their blood.'

Meanwhile the favorable impression that Wilson made upon him in September of 1914 had undergone sudden changes, usually for the worse. Only two months after their interview he was writing to Lord Haldane, 'President Wilson is rather wearing out our patience.' As time went on he seemed a 'mendacious coward,' a 'putty-faced, untruthful person,' a 'President who rowed with one oar and backed water with the other,' a 'hopeless jackass.' At one time Chapman was considering, with congenial spirits, 'a scheme for making a register of Wilson-Haters all over the country,' for the purpose of keeping them supplied with the best anti-Wilson editorials and leaflets. This was long before the United States entered the War. When that happened, and the daily irritation from the President's slowness to act was diminished, there were many mitigations of Chapman's anti-Wilsonism. There were also periods of intense gloom during which Chapman gave way to forebodings that the war would last indefinitely. Even as late as July, 1918, he was writing that Hoover predicted two more years of war, and 'I am still for about five to eight years, which is a great concession, for my view originally was twenty.' The November, 1917, issue of the *North American Review* revealed a more hopeful mood, in his 'Ode on the Sailing of our Troops for France: Dedicated to President Wilson.' A letter of gratitude from the President saying that he had read the Ode twice to his family — 'and all approved highly' — was received with obvious satisfaction.

There was still time, however, for many variations of feeling, and as late as 1920, when Wilson's course in one respect gained Chapman's approbation, he wrote to his mother,

'Who'd have thought that Wilson would ever do what I'd be grateful for! It's a puzzling world.' Just as the war was nearing its end he wrote, also to his mother, more steadily out of sympathy with the President than Chapman, 'You, by the way, are a little mentally enfeebled by contact with Wilson. I'm not sure that I haven't been touched myself.'

Among Chapman's activities during the period of neutrality was the writing and rehearsing of 'Washington and Lafayette,' a play for children produced in a pageant, 'The Children's Revolution,' at the New Century Theatre in New York on March 4, 1915, for the benefit of the Lafayette Fund. More than two hundred children, many of Revolutionary descent, took part in the affair, Chapman's youngest son among them and two of his Chanler cousins, in the characters of Hamilton, Washington, and Lafayette. More than a year after the performance Chapman wrote, in reference to it, 'If one can keep one's temper through private theatricals, one is fit for heaven — no use trying to improve.' It may be inferred that he did not keep his. There was a reward in store, however, in the translation of Chapman's little play into French by Émile Legouis, the French historian of English literature, for production in Paris at the Théâtre Français.

Quite apart from the war was another by-product of this period which should be recalled, if only as a token of the high spirits to which Chapman might yield himself at almost any time. On September 21, 1915, the New York *Sun* printed an editorial, in its characteristic tone of amusing banter, 'Is New York Only a Railway Station?' It was based on Chapman's remark, in the preface to the revised edition of his 'Emerson and Other Essays,' that 'New York is not a civilization; it is a railway station,' and brought him to book as an admirer of Boston. Here was a challenge which Chapman could not ignore, and on September 24 the *Sun* contained a letter, dated 'Barrytown, September 23,' nearly all of which follows:

To THE EDITOR OF THE SUN — *Sir:* I was wrong. There is such a place as New York. I have discovered it. I have been in the old, ancestral, historic, picturesque, traditional New York, where Bryant sang and Irving mused and N. P. Willis wrote articles for the *Mirror*. In fact I wandered into Trinity Church at Professor Van Amringe's funeral. Van Amringe was a friend of mine and it seemed a decent thing to attend his funeral, especially as he was a professor, personally poor, certainly old, perhaps obscure; and I thought it might please the family if a few respectable friends should turn up and show that the old gentleman was not completely forgotten.

So I went down to Trinity a half hour before the service and sat in the shady churchyard, beneath the liquid shadows of the morning which the high buildings and the large sycamores were casting over the quiet old gravestones....

By the time the funeral began I had forgotten all about Van Amringe, and entering the church mechanically I perceived a large and murmuring crowd. I thought I must be in a dream, for the scene was like the Day of Judgment — everybody was there. The church was packed. Pretty soon it became like the Book of Revelation. A procession of elders appeared in the western triforium and wound its way down round toward the eastern portal, carrying crosses, robes, symbols, maces and croziers. Then choristers, old men and striplings, decent, glad faces, the faces of men who spent their lives in pacing cloisters and in copying manuscripts and who were now interring their dead master with all the pomp of ancient learning. Next came certain apostles and church dignitaries. I was told that they were trustees of Columbia and vestrymen of Trinity and vergers from the Century Club; but I rather think they were early and obscure Christian saints, the kind that foreign parish churches abound in. All of these men had visages of stern piety.

The effect of seeing so many of them together, so unexpectedly — and so dramatically, for the procession stretched a mile — was to stamp their type in my mind. It was the gargoyle type. The New York worthy, the patriarch and revered city fathers, is a distinct person, and he is not dying out — he is multiplying. There were not only seven hundred of them in the celestial procession which moved slowly to meet the bier on that day, but the church was filled with others exactly similar to the robed and vested ones. The reader will perhaps remember that in Trinity Church the aisles are wide and that on great occasions the sexton brings out little truckle pews and fills up the aisles. These pews are emergency pews. They are undersized things, but on the occasion of Van Amringe's funeral every one of them was filled with large Manhattan gargoyles, any one of whom could have replaced any figure in the procession, and all of them resembled our great antique New York figures. I saw William Cullen Bryant, Robert Lenox, John Bigelow, Washington Irving, John A. Dix, and men innumerable. Young ones too, I mean men of seventy who by the time they are ninety (the New York age of greatness) will be exactly right to replace the great men of old.

The whole affair was to me not a funeral but a resurrection of immortal old New York, indelible, indestructible New York; unmistakable, peculiar, serious, stiff and very religious New York. For just imagine how impressed any mediaeval monk would have been if he could have peeped his fat nose into the church and seen those august goings on. What zeal, what fervor of worship, what unanimity would he have observed!

He would probably not have enjoyed the music, at least the Chopin march would have puzzled him. For Chopin in his march walked but a step or two, piano, pianissimo, tremolo; and then violently flung himself upon the ground, and wallowed foaming. Then Chopin would raise himself with slow pain and next quite unexpectedly sprint for twenty yards, then stop as if he was shot. No, no, Chopin on that day behaved in a disturbing manner. They say that Trinity Church supports a school of organists. If this is true it would be a splendid thing for Trinity to catch the organist who played the opening voluntary at Van Amringe's funeral and put him in the school.

I left the ceremony before it was really well under way, partly, I confess, because of the organist, partly because I saw that my benevolent assistance was not needed, but chiefly for fear lest my fresh and wonderful impressions as to New York should be disturbed by some afterclimax in the proceedings.

A city that can bury a leading citizen as New York buried Van Amringe — and from such a sanctuary — is a home of traditions and a vessel of civic consciousness. I shall never call New York a railroad station again.

JOHN J. CHAPMAN

Thus he could rise at times above the sorrows of the world, his own impatience with the administration at Washington, and a haunting anxiety for his son Victor, since the mid-

CHAPMAN (RIGHT) AND J. S. SARGENT, YALE, 1916

summer of 1915 a member of the Lafayette Escadrille. In May of 1914 he had written to Langdon Mitchell, when the son of a friend of theirs had died: 'I lost a boy once. It's more terrible than anyone can have an idea of. You have to be re-made in seven years and come out another man.' He knew too well what such a loss meant. Yet at this time his pride in the spirit of his son Victor was paramount, and this must have fortified him for the writing of a mythologic play, 'Cupid and Psyche,' for production at the fiftieth anniversary of the Yale Art School, June 16-19, 1916. The music, by Horatio Parker, the settings, and the admirable performance by New Haven amateurs, all supervised by Chapman's friend, William Sergeant Kendall, Dean of the School, combined with the poetic text to give the occasion a memorable beauty and charm. It was capped — not to say gowned— for Chapman by his receiving the honorary degree of Doctor of Letters at the Yale Commencement on June 21, when John Singer Sargent was similarly honored as Doctor of Arts.

In the midst of the happiness of this week of achievement and recognition, came a message that on June 17 Victor had been wounded in France. The injury, according to the report, was slight, and Mrs. Chapman, confident that the daring aviator would survive all dangers, could not understand the grave faces of those about her. Chapman himself, at the Tavern Club in Boston a few days later, is remembered as coming down to breakfast with a letter from France and saying, after he had read a fellow-aviator's praise of Victor's extreme intrepidity, 'That boy will never get through.' What he did not put into words was his profound belief that every such demonstration of American sympathy with the Allies as the members of the Lafayette Escadrille were making was of infinite value to his country, and that any private grief which might come was not to be measured against the public good.

With such a heart for any fate Chapman returned to Barry-town before June 23, the day on which came the news that

Victor had fallen, killed in combat at Verdun, within the German lines. The message had come by telephone from a reporter at Poughkeepsie, asking, with all the enterprise of journalism, for comment by Victor's father. The head farmer on the place took the message at his farmhouse, and delivered it to Chapman who soon passed by. It was received with no visible emotion and only the words, hard enough of comprehension even by one who had known all the workings of Chapman's mind and heart, 'That's good.' This was Chapman's way of saying Amen to the will of God. He came at once to Sylvania with his tragic burden, more concerned for Mrs. Chapman's sorrow than for his own. Looking up and seeing his face at the library door, she hardly needed to hear his words, 'Victor has been killed'; the quiet and matter-of-fact tone in which they were spoken could not belie their meaning.

Amory Gardner, Owen Wister, and Chapman's brothers-in-law, Lewis and Robert Chanler, came at once to bring the sympathy and courage which such friends, who had loved Victor and were passionately devoted to the Allied Cause, could impart. The Fourth of July was near at hand. In Paris a memorial service in the American Church gave expression to an extraordinary public sentiment of sorrow, gratitude, and admiration. To Frenchmen and Americans alike this first American aviator to fall became a symbol transcending all personal feeling, and speaking for a unity of spirit against which nothing could prevail. This overflowed from son to father, and Chapman soon found himself vicariously an heroic figure. As such he had already taken part in another memorial service, nearer home — in Trinity Church, New York, on June 30. The Marseillaise was played, the congregation standing. When the service was done, and the people filed out to the strains of 'Le Chanson du Départ,' Chapman stood by the door shaking the hands of friends, with tears in his eyes, but a look in his face which bade them take heart and prepare for victory.

302

There was a long tradition of family prayers at Sylvania, and in a Prayer Book there, opposite the Sixty-sixth and Sixty-seventh Psalms, is written in Chapman's hand, 'Read at Sylvania, family prayers for Victor, July 4, 1916' — the day of the service in Paris.

> O come hither and behold the works of God; how wonderful is he in his doing toward the children of men.
> For thou, O God, hast proved us: thou also hast tried us, like as silver is tried.

Thus the father ratified his acceptance of the loss of his first-born son. When the United States entered the war it was a profound satisfaction to him that his son Conrad sought and secured an Ensign's commission in the Navy. His first service, highly dangerous, was on an escort to troop-ships. He would appear in West 82nd Street between these voyages, stay a night or two, and then disappear as suddenly as he came. The lines, 'Our Sailor,' in Chapman's 'Songs and Poems,' describe these visits. Conrad Chapman was transferred later to the Pacific service, in which he remained, at the request of his superior officers, until after the Armistice, thus foregoing the pleasure and stimulus of returning to Harvard with his classmates, though winning a full measure of his father's pride and sympathy.

It is easy to see that such a father, with the special flame of Chapman's nature burning within him, would resent any expressions of sympathy, real, implied, or imagined, with Germany. Chapman's resentment flashed forth when the Corporation of Harvard College on November 27, 1916, voted, at the request of certain alumni, to receive contributions for a fund 'to establish at Harvard University a fit memorial to the Harvard men who gave their lives in the European War of 1914, at such time and in such form as shall later be determined, with the approval of the Corporation, by a Committee consisting of President Lowell, Major Higginson, Dean LeBaron R. Briggs, Messrs. E. S. Martin, G. D. Markham, W. C. Boyden, M. A. DeW. Howe, W. C. Forbes.' Three

Germans, former students at Harvard, had already fallen, fighting under their own flag. The United States had not yet entered the war, and unofficial suggestions had been made that the future memorial should honor all the men of Harvard, irrespective of nationality, whose lives were sacrificed in the war. It was not even then a generally popular suggestion, or likely to be acted upon. But the fact that the resolution of the Corporation did not definitely repudiate it roused Chapman's ire. He wrote at once in protest to President Lowell, and received in reply an assurance that the Corporation was not committed to any particular memorial, and an expression of confidence that the Committee could be trusted to do the wise and proper thing. Chapman was not thus to be turned from his wrath. On the day after Christmas he wrote a letter to the *Harvard Alumni Bulletin*, which appeared in the issue of January 4, 1917, under the heading, 'A Monument to Zero.' In the course of it he wrote: 'It may be that I am overinfluenced by personal feelings due to my son's death in France, or to an ineradicable sentiment that I am bound up with Harvard and that her fair name is my business. In either case you will be able to discount any extravagance of statement which I may fall into.' It was certainly an extravagance to have said just before this, 'The Harvard Corporation on November 27th voted to include in one memorial both those who fell fighting for the cause of Germany and those who fell in the cause of the Allies.' It was no extravagance to argue as he did on monuments in general:

> If you should erect a monument to any two ideas that are mutually exclusive, e.g., to Theseus *and* the Minotaur, to St. George *and* the Dragon, to the Greeks who fell at Thermopylae *and* the Persians who slew them, to George Washington *and* George III, your monument would become a symbol of Zero. No matter what you intended to express by your monument, it would express Zero on the issue.

Such a monument as he now prefigured would announce to the world, as he went on to say, that Harvard sees no difference between conflicting forces and has no interest in the cause of France. Then why erect a monument? 'The Corporation's resolution of November 27th is at this moment a little enduring monument to Zero erected with the sanction of the Corporation — Zero on the moral aspects of the war.'

For some time after this letter appeared, the *Bulletin* received and printed many communications, pro and con, relating to the question which Chapman, with greater force and passion than any other correspondent, had raised. The editor of the paper, who happens now to be writing this book, was taken to account in April, 1918, for printing, without any reference to a monument or memorial, a list of all the Harvard men who had fallen in the war up to that time — a year after the entrance of the United States — and for including in that list of fifty-eight names, the names of the three Germans then known to have fallen. It may be held a mistake, in the state of feeling then existing, to have called the list the 'Harvard Roll of Honor.' The plans for a memorial were then far from taking form, and when they did, neither the omission of the German names nor the decision upon so pacific a monument as a University Church averted another flood of controversial letters. Chapman had fired his last resounding gun on June 17, 1918, in some remarks he made at the Harvard Phi Beta Kappa luncheon, an occasion traditionally immune from report in the public press. The resolution of the Corporation nearly two years before was still his special grievance, and when his remarks were printed, their vehement objection to the course of the Harvard authorities came to a mild conclusion: 'For these reasons I very respectfully suggest the need of formal action rescinding the resolution as having been inadvertently equivocal in its form.' The resolution was not rescinded, but when subscriptions to a War Memorial Fund were invited, one of the first to be received was a generous contribution from Chapman, in memory of his son Victor, whose name is inscribed with 372 others on the walls of the narthex of the Harvard Memorial Church.

Each year, moreover, a student from France, nominated by a committee of French scholars, benefits at Harvard from the Victor Emmanuel Chapman Fellowship, established in memory of him whose name it bears.

In the volume of 'Songs and Poems' which Chapman published in 1919, when much of his best verse was still unwritten, a sombre poem of much beauty, 'May, 1918,' ends with the lines, speaking for Chapman's prevailing mood at this time:

> Alas, when all is done,
> What shall the dayspring find to shine upon?

It was truly a time of turmoil and suffering, yet there was that within Chapman which the world did not see. The Rev. Dr. John R. Atkinson of Christ Church, New York, of which Chapman was a devoted member, and a vestryman, has told of his habitual attendance at the Quiet Hours in the Church. 'Often he and I,' the rector said, 'were the only persons in the church. For months he never failed to attend, all during the war and after it. He assured me afterward that he derived the greatest comfort from the peace and quiet and sanctity of the meditation.' Through the torrents of Chapman's utterance a clear, separate stream held its course: 'If you keep silence with the power of God, the power of God will be expressed.'

Letters

To Lord Haldane

BARRYTOWN, N.Y.
Sept. 18: 1914

MY DEAR LORD HALDANE

I greatly fear that more of German *Kultur* is going to fall than you or I imagine.

Their ethics and ethnology, their *Philologie* (which means any sort of whimsical raving), their metaphysics of thirty years past — will all be found to be infected. On examination they will all have to go into the disinfecting Bucket of Oblivion. I doubt German esthetics and astronomy. Their whole fabric is a house of cobwebs. Mommsen is a pamphleteer. I had a most satisfying talk with President Wilson; and upon my word I believe he understands the war better than anyone in America. He has a kind of genius for understanding men and for using the symbols of government, and within him is a furnace. He has during the last few years controlled the American mind; and this war with its intense and unified feeling everywhere aroused, has given him, somehow, the attributes of a mythical ruler. There must be some good in the American people or they never would have chosen such a man. Indeed the rulers in France, England, and America are the best the nations have. This is the most fortunate accident of the whole situation; for this war was predestinate and *might* have broken out at a time when Jingoes were in the Ascendency in England and America. The French Jingoes are going to give trouble later, see cutting on Clemenceau, which tallies with a newspaper interview given out by Delcassé at the beginning of the war.

Can't you send a quiet big Englishman in plain clothes over to Paris to button-hole this kind of man and tell him it *won't do*? There are things that formal diplomacy can't grapple with, where a hint and a nudge given at an early stage of the game can change the whole atmosphere.

American Education — that wretched flimsy thing — is showing up on its strong side just now — the practical side. Our press is surprisingly able, and the capacity of the average man is seen to advantage.

Yours sincerely

JOHN JAY CHAPMAN

No answer.

To Edward S. Martin

[*After the funeral of James G. Croswell*]

March 16, 1915

... The funeral was a sort of apotheosis. Not having anyone saying anything, but leaving the service to say it, was so valuable, and so rare. ...

It was an extraordinary funeral. Everyone was thinking the same thought — and that was Croswell. He appeared to each as a sort of luminosity, with his humility and his understanding and his position always in the beyond. Whatever you said, he was beyond, the other side of it, waiting till you got through talking — with his charming grin. I can't believe he is dead! ...

To Langdon Mitchell

325 W. 82, *Ap.* 1: 1915

DEAR LANGDON

... Our uncles seem to be dying freely. We are becoming the oldest generation. How do you like that? It's not so bad. The only subject I avoided with Dan was Unitarianism. But I could write a critique on Dan's relation to it. What is Unitarianism? — and the worst is the hot Unitarian. There has only been one hot Unitarian.[1] This kind is filled with the fears of the ethical person in regard to dogma — and the ardor of Torquemada in regard to head sauce of his own kind. There is pepper in his head sauce. There's the surprise of it. Goepp who is a disciple of the *1st* Unitarian Church set one of

---

[1] Chapman's definition of Mrs. Owen Wister.

my child's Xmas dramas to music — and struck out Holy
Ghost and put in 'See the pretty birds' with the zeal of a
Jesuit. There is matter for a profound essay somewhere
here. . . .

To Mrs. Winthrop Chanler

April 22, 1915

MY DEAR DAISY:

We had a dream return as from a dream, and are now
diligently sending flowers to old ladies and exerting ourselves
horribly to finish off New York and go by motor to Barrytown
on Saturday. Elizabeth has just given me a half-hour curtain
lecture, prologued by objurgations and exordiums. I took a
pencil and paper and was going to write down my duties. All I
had to write down at the end was: 'Do not curse and swear'
— i.e., when I find out that a lot of certain things are going to
happen. I have forgotten what they are — more old ladies, I
suppose.

The war makes me sick. Are we still fighting for the salute
or what? How can we tell when to stop?

This sort of thing ought to make me tolerant of the outrageous conduct of England, Italy, and other governments in
the making of unjust wars. I'll never open my head about
them again. I don't see a soul who doesn't feel in the same
way; but yes — William, our coachman. He says we ought
to have licked Mexico long ago — it's what they need. I am
shocked at him. He has a Christian home and two boys of his
own, and a great deal of intelligent conversation from me
during many years.

Consider that Mexico must live in traditional fear of being
gobbled by the United States. It's human nature that she
should — consider history. Also, it's reasonable in her to do
so.

But we behave first with abject humility, then with sudden
ferocity. It will take generations to correct the impression.
At least it would seem so.

By the way, isn't the notion of *honor* of nations, I mean as
distinct from rights, always a humbug?

Suppose a Japanese gunboat enters the harbor of Cadiz,

signals a salute to every nation except our own — why should we care? But this is what people care most about.

With most affectionate recollections and love to Winty.

Yours

JACK

To his Mother

[PARIS] *May* 17: 1915

DEAR MAMA

... A friend tells me that a Frenchman is going to review my 'Deutschland' in the *Revue des Deux Mondes*. By the way, what a deadly stupid thing the R. de D. M. is. It may have been good back in the time of de Musset and Balzac — but I have never seen anything I could read in it and I've *often* tried at the Century Club. There's nothing like the stupidity of a magazine when it goes in for being dull. It gets its readers trained, you see, to expect a certain type of dullness and then it deepens and blackens and adds laudanum and lead and every one gets to needing *more* laudanum and *more* lead, and at last the thing becomes a mystery to the outsider — like the bottom of the deepest parts of the sea — darkness and the waving of sea weed.

Your affectionate son

JACK

To Elizabeth Chanler Chapman

[*In another letter of the same day Chapman extolled the English to his wife as 'too brave — only stupid.... I like them all so much better than I like any other people that it's silly. They are the most darling people in the world. I confess that they seem to me very incompetent.*']

LONDON, *May* 25: 1915

... In comparing the civilizations of France and England it should never be forgotten that the Continent presents no cheese that competes with Stilton. Enough has not been made of this point. The general claims of France on the side of food predominate. But there is this weighty monument of England's greatness in Food. I had a piece of cheese at lunch — in

this unemotional inn — that was like Agincourt. It was
sonorous, undying. The food in this hotel is mere fodder.
The coffee is tasteless and harmless, the puddings are straw and
treacle — the meat is canned meat, the bread is seven days
old — and suddenly in all this prose the Stilton cheese blows
a blast of poetic power like Roland at Roncevalles. Fall
France, kneel cows of Switzerland and Italian formaggi, and
the Greek Islands — cheese was a mere pastime and a peasant's dish till Britain came. . . .

To Mrs. Henry Copley Greene

PARIS, *June* 21: 1915

MY DEAR MRS. GREENE

Think of any one's being young enough to have babies —
that is the chief reflection that your letter brings to me. I have
given it up long ago — and that belated Harry Greene who is
really a contemporary of mine — whatever he may pretend —
and whatever underhand devices he may have resorted to to
get himself married into a younger generation. All the same I
envy him and you and the babies. Your letter reaches me here
and gives me great joy. Indeed I have had more fun out of the
'Memories and Milestones' than out of any other of my writings, perhaps because it is less ambitious, and more like what
any book *really* is, and only can be, a memorandum. Even
philosophies and histories in twenty volumes are no more, and
ought not to pretend to be more — but *they always will*.
Thank you ever so much for writing the letter and give my
love to Harry. It is, by the way, all the grossest error about
Victor's being decorated. All those letters in the American
press written by Rader, a newspaper man who was with
Victor in the trenches and wrote about the Foreign Legion —
are according to Victor horrid fictions. But don't tell anybody
— for, you see, they represent *ideal* truth. Victor swears he is
going to leave the Legion and come to America to confute
them. But as he can't get out and can hardly read and write
anyway — he is not very apt to succeed. Just now he is in a
quiet corner of the line, though during the winter he had a
good deal of fighting and lost a great many of his comrades.
I have some hope that he may get transferred into the Ameri-

can Aviation Corps which has been formed during the last six months and is not yet entirely in action — though I dare say that he is as well off where he is.

We are sorry to be missing so much of the excitement at home — and of course nothing suits us except war — and Wilson seems a slowpoke and a pro-German temporizer. But I admit that the whole movement of everything in America seems in exactly the right direction. Stupid of the Allies to bombard Karlsruhe — What can we say? — Very stupid.

Yours very sincerely
JOHN JAY CHAPMAN

To S. S. Drury

MORGAN-HARJES, PARIS, *June* 24: 1915

... Victor has been growling like a dog all winter because he was not getting killed. It appears all soldiers do this. He is being transferred into the Aviation American Corps — where he will be trained to fly. It appears there is a big movement on in this line and we may expect hundreds of Americans to flock to France, to become aviators. I have long ago given up worrying as to Victor's destiny. He is extremely well so far, and some flyers (who don't get killed in learning), may be expected to survive the war. It doesn't seem likely, I admit, but these things must be allowed to take their course and he is very clear as to his desires. I think that we shall probably get a chance to see him *in transition* in passing from the Légion to the *Corps Aviatique*....

To André Chevrillon

At Sea, Aug. 6, 1915

MY DEAR CHEVRILLON

They say Warsaw has fallen. This will encourage the German civilians. Perhaps if we knew all we should be content to have the war go on as long as necessary to the total exhaustion of Germany and the killing of the bacillus in the German people — no matter at what cost.

Nothing else could have extinguished the slavery craze in America except something that almost amounted to extermination.

It is very unpleasant and makes literary things hard to think of — but all the more reason that some one should keep alive the normal life of society. I read *La Petite Fadette*. It seems to me very great — greater than 'Hermann and Dorothea,' 'Vicar of Wakefield,' 'Silas Marner' — and all the rest of the peasant-life fiction. The form of it, and the language, are epic — in their weight and in their perfection. I don't know anything like them.

By means of the archaisms natural to peasant-life she creates a vehicle which suggests the *conteur* — the mythic, original, old Frankish, Gothic, Languedocian fairy-tale and household tale — and yet her archaisms are so natural, so unexaggerated, so happy — that you forget the *conteur* most of the time and only remember him in that he gives a touch of realism.

I think *La Petite Fadette* is one of the most remarkable things in modern literature. But I don't think it has Balzac's passion for innocence. I think it is to be classified under the sophisticated pictures of youthful passion. Only how beautiful!

By the way — talking of peasants — I don't like Millet's pictures — nor his disposition. If you're going to leave out the hope that keeps life going, you will make deadly pictures.

I'm sure that these villagers of George Sand — for all they are *poussés* and arranged and lighted and posed and subdued and glorified into the frame of fiction — I am sure they are somehow truer to life than Millet's deadly, hopeless, sad, awful, gloomy disgusting *peasants*. There was something the matter with Millet. He relapsed and returned to his wallow. There is something damnable in Millet — though I don't know what it is.

My wife protests against all this and says that Millet is like Michael Angelo, etc. I admit the likeness: but here is a whole side of Michael Angelo — a world — which is not in Millet — the world of conventional myth and beauty, cherubs, sibyls, prophets, forms of imaginative power — always unreal — and this is the side of Michael Angelo that I like — spite of his gloom. O no: Millet is not *very much* like Michael Angelo after all. He's a *fin de siècle* sociologist and rather belongs with Tolstoi. I think I should put him in the same bolgia with Tolstoi — and Sisyphus — compliment enough.

Lots of unpleasant conversations on the ship as to war with Japan. Unpleasant world.

Yours sincerely

JOHN JAY CHAPMAN

Later — on board ship

I have been reading your Sydney Smith. It's the best book I've read in seven years. I wish I could have read it in 1884 — before it was written — as a guide to England. You are wrong to call it or think of it as a College Thesis. It's *immensely interesting* — all of it — every page — at least as far as I've got. I read three-fourths of the *Souffle d'Islam* [1] at a sitting — and this is not the way to read that book. It's like eating a pound of candy — and there! by accident I have hit upon the word by accident — which expresses the weak side of the book. It is — I mean it strikes my mind — as a little too much what the French mind would expect to find in a book about the East.

The title itself is a little *précieux*. The beauty of the descriptions and of the writing is extraordinary (a good deal of this sort of writing is lost on a foreign public — which does not even know the language well enough to really appreciate word painting — I think yours are wonderful) but I miss something. By the way, two Americans — rabid admirers of yours — are on the ship. They have been living in Geneva — a place where Chevrillon is a great name. They had all the India, Holy Land, and Egypt by heart and — *chose curieuse* — they greatly admired the Egypt — were really in a wonderment over it. Not so much the Holy Land or India, but — here comes the point — they *have been in Egypt* — but never in India or Palestine.

By the way — you are too mild and gentle to those crude brutes who wrote the *Edinburgh Review*, especially to Jeffrey. If you ever come across Harriet Martineau's Reminiscences — written in 185-, see what she says of meeting the aged

[1] For *Un Crepuscule d'Islam*.

Jeffrey — and his own descriptions of how they used to squeeze vitriol on the bones of the young poets in 1812 — and *loved* to do it, and enjoyed the pain they gave. Instead of serving literature they were hypocritical penny-a-liners.

Mem. You give the wrong implication in translating 'cultivate poetry on a little oatmeal' — as POUR *un petit pain*: — though the meanings tie so close together.

I've always thought this suggestion of Smith's was the best classic pun ever made.[1]

What stupid old creatures the whole of the English are. There is more perception in this Sydney Smith book of yours than in the whole cubic mile of British Biographies from Southey to Chesterton. Has England ever produced one intelligent man?

To his Mother

[*After a visit to Plattsburg.*]

THE WESTPORT INN
WESTPORT ON LAKE CHAMPLAIN
N.Y., *Aug.* 28, 1915

... We were at the camp the day Roosevelt was there; but we were so tired with running about to see sham battles and reviews that we cut the speech-making — though I had a talk with him on the train on the way up. O my! if he only had a little more *mind*, how he could cut up this administration. But he has only a bludgeon. He needs a scalpel. Humor, sarcasm, pretended sympathy and stilettos are the only thing for the situation. I myself am so spoiled by philosophy and a desire to get at the truth that I am no good as a controversialist. Whatever I write turns into an essay, and, by the way, I wrote an article on the Camp — which I sent to the *World*. It is very impressive — the camp, not the article. If they publish it I'll send it to you. Of course no end of people you know are there. By the way, forty-three men from the Porcellian. This is very remarkable. The Porcellian is a small club — and when 1400 men volunteer out of the 100,000,000

[1] Sydney Smith made the suggestion that '*Tenui musam meditamur avena*' ('We cultivate literature on a little oatmeal') should be the motto of the *Edinburgh Review*.

in America — forty-three of them are from the Porcellian. This seems to my mind to show that the Porcellian does really amount to something — which I have never believed.

To the same

DEAR MAMA

I had a long talk with Colonel House. He is *extraordinarily intelligent*, very frank, very quiet — meets every point without evading it — and all but told me he agreed with me. I of course was polite and intellectual and indulged in no railings — but set out the matter of Wilson's cavings in and pudginess — and the honor of the country idea, with all the calmness I could muster.

Everything House suggested by way of qualification and excuse was a true idea — not overstated — not taken in the spirit of a partizan. It was a delightful lunch....

Your affectionate

JACK

To Mrs. Winthrop Chanler

325 W. 82 STREET
NEW YORK, N.Y.
October 19, 1915

DEAR DAISY:

I think the reason why I make a moral problem and cast moral aspersions on H. James, Mrs. Wharton, and the dwellers abroad, is a certain jealousy of our loss of talent. We are so impoverished that we need every intelligence at home, and these people *seem* as if they might do good gardening at home instead of being wasted abroad. This is, no doubt, all an illusion on my part and represents a tincture of practical politics — very foreign to true science. I ought to point out all these things, but without ulterior purpose. It would be more effective if I could do this.

As for the Republic coterie, I dread and hate them, yet I believe they represent a normal, healthy movement which will get seriouser and hardier and realer; — and later, and in other hands, will grow into a cultivation. My early life in politics and reform keeps me looking at things with the reformer's eye, and wanting to water and push and weed and prune. Your true scientist or your true poet is more purely receptive, more purely *voice* or eye (but it's harder to do, this pure science and pure poetry — takes more intelligence)....

J. J. C.

To S. S. Drury

THE GREYLOCK
BERKSHIRE HILLS
WILLIAMSTOWN, MASSACHUSETTS
Oct. 19: 1915

... You preached too long on Sunday and disappointed Chanler — who has a high opinion of your preaching and had been bragging of you — hoping you would do your best and 'give us a good one.' This is Chanler's almost only intellectual interest and quite surprises me. Anyway, you ought to be preaching by a sand glass — everyone ought. In the rising interest of his theme, the preacher doesn't hear the unconscious, automatic feet-scuffle that follows the thirteenth minute. He's just warming up — and they are *warming down*. I saw the whole thing. All the more noticeable because the substance was all exceedingly good and well aimed at boys....

(P.S.) Elizabeth says I am *wrong* as to Chanler — who thought the sermon was 'a wonderful sermon.' This shows what a liar I am.

To Rosalind Richards

BARRYTOWN, N.Y.
November 8, 1915

DEAR ROSALIND:

You and your mother are too good to me — about my writings. Still I need it, and it bolsters up my mind. E.g. I sent the *Notes* [on Religion] to Daisy Chanler.... Then, on general principles, and somewhat in a Christian spirit, I sent her the Greek Genius book — which she likes and praises — but interweaves some vile phrases about my religious book —

317

which she says is like a monkey hanging by his tail and doing tricks. I am keeping calm and reading Emerson. 'Hit hard; but never get into a *controversy*,' that's what he did. I commit her to the Universe — and let her blows fall upon the solid ether which will, no doubt, repercuss them against her own cheek bones and (I hope) hurt her a lot. Nothing like trusting the Ether. No man can hurt anyone except himself — (excepting of course the wicked — who *ought* to be hurt.)...

To Henry Osborn Taylor

[*Chapman took his candidacy for the National Institute of Arts and Letters, for which he refused to be nominated, quite as he would have had William James take his election to the Institute of France.*]

SYLVANIA, *Nov.* 11, 1915

MY DEAR HARRY,

This is just to make you laugh — as the whole thing is only worth a laugh. There was method in our sudden elevation into dazzling recognition by the representatives of posterity and R. U. Johnson.

You and I (being about the only persons among our social acquaintance more or less fitted to join an Academy) were known to be shy birds. Therefore they got our intimate friends to put us up. Adams is undoubtedly entirely innocent. Somebody wrote him and suggested it, and of course he did it.

Wister and Ned Martin who nominated me are much less innocent — as I have been seeing them and they never let on.

My wife's strenuous hand is all that prevents me from giving a guffaw which Martin would not mind but which might upset a lifelong intimacy with Wister who has less humor.

To hell with them. I'll bet that if you wrote a letter to H. Adams saying what 't hell, he'd say, 'Why, they came to me.'

Of the two birds they got one — which is a good record. Surprise is the principle at the bottom.

O Johnson! O Ripley Hitchcock! O Academe!

Yours
JACK

To S. S. Drury

325 W. 82, N.Y., *Feb.* 11: 1916

DEAR DR. DRURY

I have been groaning a good deal about St. Paul's School. The place is running still on the impulse of Henry A. Coit and is, I fear, going the way of all flesh.

Buildings, Endowments, Alumni Associations have crushed out education in America. There's not a man of the alumni who won't praise the faith of the old Doctor in neglecting such things — and write eulogies and make after-dinner speeches — at dinners got up to raise money. In the present stage of the world and trend of things in America St. Paul's School is absolutely sure to get enough by devises and gifts without this hellish hurrah boys.

I can understand the position you have got into — because naturally, in getting hold of the school and machinery and sentiment, you wanted to know the alumni and play in with them and lead them. But it's a juggernaut. They'll give you buildings you don't want and color the place with sentiments not yours. You have the awful warning of Harvard — and Groton. There's no leading alumni — except by the blow on the head which the life-saver gives to the drowning man. You can't stop 'em — they'll do these things anyway; and your only hope of controlling in some degree is to be outside them — a thing with which they have to deal and the more masterful and unapproachable you are, the better. Why, my dear Sir, you're playing with an avalanche.

I had thought there was one place in the world that didn't want money. Do you think you can get it in this way without being changed by it? It's never been done in the history of the world.

Yours sincerely

JOHN JAY CHAPMAN

To Victor Chapman

SYLVANIA
BARRYTOWN-ON-HUDSON
May 26: 1916

DEAR VICTOR

Your letter of May 12 — pretty quick — came May 25. You will see by the enclosed that your exploits get properly chronicled. The American Aviation is becoming a pet of the public. The effect on the public and on public opinion is what I care about....

Grandmama is really getting pretty old. She nods and falls asleep after dinner. Nothing interests her very much or long. She's *dead game* and determined to walk her walk and knit her knit — but it's a great struggle against the conqueror — and very sad. Old age is a bad arrangement. I cannot approve it. It is dreadful — like slow suffocation....

To his Mother

[*Written on the day after receiving the honorary degree of Litt. D. at Yale, and just before the Harvard Commencement, at which he 'thought it would be fun to wear my doctor's gown and very pretty blue hood, and show the Harvard Hoodlums how we do things at Yale.... Darn Harvard anyway.'*]

TAVERN CLUB
BOSTON, *June* 22, 1916

... The ceremonies at New Haven yesterday were wonderfully staged and conducted — much better than at Harvard — so far as ceremonial drama goes. Of course Hadley is a genius at happy speeches — just as Eliot was. Eliot used to confer degrees with the real dignity of a Thomas Aquinas — and fitting words. Hadley has not the manner — for he's a jumping jack in his gestures — but he gets there all the same. He's so clever and so earnest. Then, yesterday there was also the *Orator*, Theodore Woolsey — who presents the candidates for the honorary degrees — with a few words about each. My, I had a full box. You needn't think I am going to die undiscovered. I've been *discovered*, by Jove! Well, Woolsey was as handsome and as beefy and as urbane and a great deal more witty than Cardinal Wolsey would have been. They had a mace as big as a Lord Mayor's and gold chains and robes. John Sargent looked like Titian at least. It was all very noble and as such things should be. Then lunch — with speeches — then president's reception — and all sorts of minor things — one third of the attendance was absent owing to the war-scare — and this made things agreeable, for there was no crowd. . . .

To D. B. Updike

BARRYTOWN-ON-HUDSON
July 10, 1916

MY DEAR UPDIKE

Many thanks for your good words. All that is going on, even the Mexican muddle, is tending to put the views of courage into us and Victor's death and the way [it] was received shows that something is working in us — the result of all the last two years' struggle of the civilized part of the world against the great new Slave empire.

The U.S. made a false start in her relation to the whole matter, but I feel that we are swinging round to the right side. It's going to be a long struggle. It's true that Victor was a rare mystical person — but his appearance, and the sudden recognition of it, is no accident but a national apparition. That's its importance. All the work of the young Americans in Europe is at the back of it and he is getting a credit they all deserve. I suppose this is part of the natural law of it. At any rate we are very happy and proud.

Yours very sincerely

JOHN JAY CHAPMAN

To André Chevrillon

BARRYTOWN, N.Y., *July* 20: 1916

DEAR CHEVRILLON

Just reading your Shakespeare paper — very interesting. Just the way I feel. N.B. *en passant*, I think Taine is more remarkable than is generally understood. He falls between two stools. The French don't understand him — he's too liberal — and the English naturally wouldn't. I never take up his English Literature without being astonished at his perceptions.

321

My brother used to say of the English, 'They are all brutes — genius they have, and natural goodness and all that can be claimed for them; but if you forget that they're brutes, you'll run into it; even Browning and Tennyson and James Bryce are brutes.' Something true about this. I think it comes from insularity and lack of contact with neighbors.

In this war, e.g., they are just fighting their own old hand. They don't know anything else. Vide Rupert Brooke's fine poem — it's Frobisher and Nelson and Kipling. It makes me laugh. Letter about Victor's death from a dear, true, typical, English school friend of my wife's — she thinks Victor was fighting for the mother country — i.e. England — 'the dear old mother across the sea.' Shades of George Washington and the Alabama Claims! At the outbreak of the war I went to see Sir Edward Grey, and several leading Englishmen to try to get them to say or do something that would put the war on a universal basis — (this so as to appeal to America). They were too *honest* to try — and too stupid to understand.

The astonishing contrast of the French — of all classes, all equally thinking and expressing themselves in terms of universal idea.

The problem of Great Britain's future is whether she can really care for anything but herself. No doubt the need will bring and is bringing a change. I seem to feel it in their outer crust. It might sink in gradually.

This is only a mem.

Yours affectionately

JOHN JAY CHAPMAN

They also are jealous that the best book on English literature should have been written by a Frenchman — indeed the *only* good book on it.

To Langdon Mitchell

TAVERN CLUB
4 BOYLSTON PLACE
August 8: 1916

MY DEAR LANGDON

I got your very dear letter just before leaving Barrytown. For three days I have been living here quietly waiting for my youngest boy to turn up from his training camp at Plum Island and go with him to Camden, Maine, where the rest of the family is. It's a wonderful thing to get off by oneself and after a month of so much emotion, excitement, and writing of letters and telegrams. Victor's death had every element in it to make it a death that one could not grieve over. It came at a time and in a way that was not only glorious but most useful in France and here. All the American Ambulance drivers, soldiers, surgeons, nurses, and aviators, who have been active in France have shown the world that there was heart and brains in America — and men and women who knew the meaning of the war and their own stake in it. Victor's death dramatized the French feeling and became a sort of symbol of the emotion aroused by all the Americans' aggregate work. This has changed the standing of the whole country in France, and its effects upon our own slow-blooded ignorant people will come by degrees and hereafter.

The consolatory feature of it is that the individual has so much power — a few insuppressible individuals change the reputation of a hundred millions. As for affecting the character of the hundred millions, that's another matter. The thing we need is depth of feeling, and this is religion, and it only comes through itself and straight from God and there's no use trying to convey it or punch people's heads for not having it. The real cure must come without means and out of the ground, as it were. I don't doubt that it will come and that people who feel as you and I do are sort of premonitory symptoms of a religious age — which will, among other things, invigorate the intellect of the country.

The last infirmity of noble minds is to take a sneaking interest in your own country — or your own college — greater than in any other. This is absurd of course — and, so far as colleges go, I've pretty well suppressed my leanings towards Harvard — (assisted by the obtuseness and general wooded self-complacency of the Harvard gang), but I have stupid yearnings over the American people — most absurd. There has been after all a great awakening in the last few years and I take great hope from seeing some of my boy Conrad's friends, who are of a serious, literary and old-fashioned cast, that there's going to be a batch of living and interested persons. Middle life is apt to take gloomy views — so here's to the future.

Yours affectionately

JACK

To André Chevrillon

SYLVANIA

BARRYTOWN-ON-HUDSON

Oct. 28: 1916

MY DEAR CHEVRILLON

I have thought of you often but have not had time to write — and suppose that I shouldn't be doing it now, but that one can't print a private letter without asking permission — or giving notice — so please take notice that I shall print almost the whole of one you wrote me about Victor. It not only shows the French feeling — I mean France's feeling — but gives the best picture of Victor that exists. So much for being a literary man. We are going to publish some of his letters — a short memoir — by me — and a miscellany of addenda — and I've just been through all the mass of letters and notes. They are full of fire and feeling, but for the most part add nothing to the picture of Victor.

Besides — a college boy is not much known, and Victor only began to live at the period he met you. In that year of aviation he went from the grub to the dragon-fly.

His earlier letters are half-growl, for he *wrote off* his megrims; and most of his most amusing passages are abuse of somebody — (during the year in the trenches) — and of course can't be published — but there are enough of a lyrical and descriptive kind — anecdotes and reflections to make a small volume — and it's a deuced job to comb it out — as he writes half in *argot* — with spelling of his own — and on tissue paper and with aniline pencils. Also some photographs. Luckily the Kodak era has left us with a very good collection since his early years.

I shall send you a copy as soon as I get one; but of course it won't be for six months. . . .

I am taking your book to my mother, who is a voracious reader — has an English son-in-law.

VICTOR CHAPMAN, AVIATOR

CONRAD CHAPMAN, ENSIGN, U.S.N.

Your account of the psychology of the British during the waking-up period is the best thing one nation ever saw in another. But then *you* don't count; you learned these things in youth and by contact (which is the only way we really learn anything). Some day I'm going to write an essay on Byron and show you the other side of the British — which you know equally well.

But I've told you all this before.

I have been lecturing — and am too old for it. It's too fatiguing.

Did you hear that the Lafayette Fund people (i.e. Mrs. Chanler) have bought the palace (in Touraine) — where L. was born, and are going to use it as a secours or hospital during the war — and thereafter as a Museum of Franco-American Memoirs?

Yours affectionately always
JOHN JAY CHAPMAN

To Henry Osborn Taylor

Nov. 25th, 1916

MY DEAR HARRY,

You really must read Santayana on 'Egotism in German Philosophy' and make Mrs. Taylor read it. It is most entertaining, original, witty and full of little spontaneous unexpected blossoms of *irony* — which is the rarest thing in English literature and one of the greatest things in writing. No other attitude than the one he writes in could be so effective in dealing with the subject — he *effleure's* it. It's all any one could do and it's marvellously well done. I bet the book is enjoyed in France. I wrote to Santayana. — I never before could see what any one found in him, for I couldn't finish a page. I was taking him too seriously — perhaps he was taking himself too seriously. But in this case it is admirable fooling.

JACK

To S. S. Drury

BARRYTOWN, N.Y.
Nov. 26: 1916

MY DEAR DR. DRURY

Do you really think that if I *had* any ideas on the parent and child question I'd waste them on you? But just now I am taking a loaf and trying to forget the whole subject. Is the education of the young the whole of life? I hate the young — I'm worn out with them. They absorb you and suck you dry and are vampires and selfish brutes at best. Give me some good old rumsoaked club men — who *can't* be improved and make no moral claims — and let me play chequers with them and look out of the Club window and think about what I'll have for dinner.

Yours faithfully

JOHN JAY CHAPMAN

To Mrs. Winthrop Chanler [1]

325 W. 82d Street
Dec. 17, 1916

CHÈRE DAISY:

... En tout cas je suis content que la Société des *Gens* de Lettres, en me décernant cette médaille, soit tombé sur le nom et sur les prénoms que je porte à tître juste. J'ai débuté en France sous le nom supposé de 'James Joe' Chapman le célèbre, etc., appellatifs qui m'ont beaucoup plaît, d'ailleurs. C'est toujours un peu comme ça quand les médailles sont à la volée.

Langdon Mitchell il y a quinze ans m'a raconté que l'Université de Padoue célébrait alors pour la cinqcentième fois sa fête anniversaire, et qu'elle distribuait ses doctorats aux hommes d'éminence qui y affluaient de tous les pays. Dr. Mitchell fit le voyage en Italie et eu pour compagnon de voyage, James Russell Lowell. Tout les deux se félicitaient de leur renommée. Au moment suprême de la cérémonie on annonçat un doctorat qui vint d'être décerné à 'William

---

[1] Letters of Chapman's in Italian and Spanish might have rendered this volume polyglottic indeed.

Henry Lowell' — le susceptible Lowell se sentit tout soit peu abbatu. Mais il faut empoigner les médailles sans trop se casser le tête en les déchiffrant.

Mille amitiés.

JOHN JAY CHAPMAN

To S. S. Drury

BARRYTOWN, N.Y.
Sept. 10: 1917

... Your school English is monstrous. I say 'your' just to be disagreeable — as one says — 'your' railways, 'your' climate, etc. — to foreigners, for I know you can't do anything about it.

Elizabeth and Chanler have been spending two hours a day for a week on a Rhetoric book over *shall* and *will*. They have memorized forty rules.

Now I will engage to teach anyone — from a Hindoo slave to a Pittsburgh boy — to use them correctly, simply by making him learn by heart ten phrases out of the Bible and Shakespeare in which the words occur — till his *ear* demands the correct uses.

But these awful abuses must go on. Slowly, slowly, and amid the constant destruction of bodies and souls the world grinds upward — or else we can *delay* it as it goes downward or *think* we can — which is the main point. Besides, there's a lot of good even in the abuses — mixed in....

To the same

BARRYTOWN, N.Y.
Nov. 11: 1917

DEAR DR. DRURY

Elizabeth's account of St. Paul's is like St. Francis' idea of heaven — all glowing and jolly, merry, joyous, and the boys at play, on the field, and at meals, and in their rooms she describes — like the Elysian fields — no that's too solemn — well, at any rate, she is running on like a mill-race. All this social element, and free talk and development, at St. Paul's is your influence. At any rate the gaiety of it is due to you — for, while it existed before, it was a little sad and embryonic.

327

The mass of old St. Paul's boys always strike me as the stupidest men on the earth, good they are — and honourable and successful — but O my, how dull! I was saying this to one of my non-St. Paul's brothers-in-law — and he asked if ——, my contemporary, was a sample — I said 'perfect.' He said — 'But he fell on his head years ago, and has been a little stupefied ever since.' I said 'That's just what made him perfect. He was too clever before.' Well — all this social badinage, and angelic humor, at St. P.'s will certainly make the next lot less *abruti*. You know, after all, the old doctor thought that if a boy smoked a cigar he was a 'worthless fellow' — I've heard him use the expression often — and furthermore, the old doctor thought the cure of the soul of that boy — (in not-hopeless cases) lay in St. Paul's Epistles and *nowhere else*.

Now you can't say the old doctor wasn't a jackass in many ways.

You know, the best scientific opinion nowadays is — (it must be wrong of course) — that St. Francis and his joyous influence was at the bottom of the Renaissance, and of the revival of learning, etc., etc. — including Luther — Loyola and everything else.

My own independent studies long ago convinced me that *social life* was at the bottom of every form of art, and that the deadness and feebleness of our social life in America was the cause of our artistic incapacity. So perhaps you're getting a good cold-frame started, and perhaps in 400 years something will emerge — pictures or something.

Yours affectionately
JOHN JAY CHAPMAN

To Mrs. Henry Copley Greene

325 W. 82, N.Y.
Feb. 21: 1918

MY DEAR MRS. GREENE

... The Fourth of July religious celebration is a splendid idea — though just what to attempt, and what scale to do it on, and what part to do, is a separate problem for each person. There are managers and propagandists and I don't think one can control what they shall do. The thing must be a growth — and the people must appear out of the times and do it.

My own instinct, I mean so far as what I do myself, is to keep out of the organizing part of things. I don't want to bother you with talk about myself; but I want you to understand. After a good many years of organizing clubs, meetings, demonstrations, etc. — I retired from this kind of work. I had a temptation at the time of the Coatesville incident — to get up a vast, national annual prayer meeting at Coatesville — to which every town should send suppliants — a sort of penitential pilgrimage. The country had been so shocked by the episode that I felt as if the whole country would respond to an appeal, if made by a group of leading men and women of all sorts — perhaps build a chapel at Coatesville and have the name come to signify *expiation*. Well, I ended by seeing that the thing to do was to go there alone: — and my wife, who had fears for my life — which, by the way, were quite fantastic — insisted on my taking a friend. I asked one man, and he wouldn't go — so a very remarkable woman, sort of healing priestess of the New Thought kind, went with me. So you see prayers on a small scale and in a back room seem to me the way to begin — and without waiting for the Fourth of July. Though if some Fourth of July ceremonies come out of it — very well.

I am not saying any of this as advice or suggestion to you or to anybody. There are so many kinds of people and modes in which they require expression that one ought not to try to direct them — least of all to repress them. The thing at the bottom of the desire — must and will create its own machinery. It's an invisible thing....

To Elizabeth Chanler Chapman

ROCHESTER
Feb. 25, 1918

[*This was written after a diatribe, in a letter of the day before, against a sermon to schoolboys, a sermon ' of the O-you-boy-are-you-religious? variety — and O-boy-do-you-love-God — and you just better — that's all we want you to do.'*]

... P.S. The matter with the clergy is perhaps that they

profess to *teach Christ*. Can you imagine anyone being such an ass? They think they have got the thing and that they can hand it round. I know this illusion goes back to Christ's words — 'preach the Gospel.' But Christ meant preach to the people who didn't have it. He surely never intended to set those robustious fellows bellowing at the world *forever*.

At any rate the *preaching* of the gospel is played out or at any rate over done. Do you know I sort of wish that Christ had never made the suggestion. Suppose he had said — Be ye my Gospel, but preach not often. Something that was *humane* — (for of course they'd bust if they didn't preach) and yet a curb. Strange fact: — piety without intellect doesn't make a good preacher; and intellect without piety sometimes does. . . .

To S. S. Drury

325 W. 82, *May* 5: 1918

DEAR DR. DRURY

I dare say my wife will be dropping in on you to look at her peculiar chick and see whether he's more likely to turn out a crocodile or an ostrich. Of course you educators in the boys' schools have the job cut out and do your duty to preach war to the boys — show 'em cinemas, horrors from the front, tales of glory and romance — elder brothers dying for mankind and the Church of God — and when the seventeen-year ones are loaded — fired and exploding — you add calmly, 'My dear boy, the greatest need of the present times is that boys of your age should know Cicero and algebra. It's your duty to continue the excellent peace curriculum which we follow here. Floreat St. Paul's.' Well — I don't see how the schools and schoolmasters can do anything else. But you've got to look out or the seventeen-year-olders who are really matured by the crisis, and are quite able to enlist, will jump off and go their own gait. I should rather bet on the boy who did so — rather than on the one who took your advice and buckled down to Cicero. You must somehow head them towards service in the army, or near it. As for Chanler — I haven't seen him for some time and don't know just how his desires will work out. If he's intelligent enough to want to get at least *into* college before the new era begins, I shall rejoice; But I don't believe in any boy's taking such a course because his father wants it. Fathers are generally damn fools; and any boy who is pious in such a matter is somehow weak. It is the boys who violate their parents' plans who come to something. It wasn't till Victor began taking his head that he amounted to anything. As for the schoolmaster, he is an unfortunate being who must talk out of a book — and utter platitudes. I wouldn't be in his place for a farm. But I admit that a peculiar genius goes with the place and am mighty glad it does. . . .

To Henry Osborn Taylor

[*After Chapman's speech at the Phi Beta Kappa luncheon, mentioned on p. 305.*]

TAVERN CLUB, BOSTON,
June 19, 1918

DEAR HARRY

I find your note here. Most sorry to have missed you. The *resolution* repays study. Apparently the College is collecting money for a monument to those who fell in the war — and the Committee and Corporation will decide later when, how and *to whom* the arch is to be raised. The public pays its money and the Corporation makes the choice. Was there ever a monument so planned before?

It was the original purpose to include Germans — for I received a letter about the matter from an insider in 1916. At present, however, the Corporation is grieved, shocked, and hurt at the suggestion that they should do such a thing as include Germans. Nevertheless they don't say they *won't* include Germans. They ask us to show confidence in them — confidence that they won't do what they openly proposed to do. They disavow the *Harvard Bulletin* — which editorially favored the German plan. It appears the *Bulletin* is not an official organ — only — I don't know just what — an *enfant terrible*, perhaps. The Corporation is a very innocent, well-meaning, kindly lot of men, not very astute about finance. Of course it would be worth ten million to the German interest to have German names on a Harvard monument. Mr. Busch and other big German-American business men who were in consultation with the Harvard people for years as to financing the Germanic Museum might subscribe. The Germans in America would assist. The Imperial Government, which helped with the Germanic Museum, might exert quiet influence. But the Corporation never thought of these things. They are amazed, grieved — good souls that they are — that any evil-minded person should have rooted out such recondite suggestions. — Unholy — profane — *unworthy*. I love these men for their sweetness and light. They just do the duty of the day — sturdily, simply, trusting in Providence. I love the way they cluck to the distinguished graduates and Harvard men — saying, 'All is well, trust the dear old mother. Have confidence, have confidence!' — and the chicks run and cuddle and chirp in concert, 'O profane! O base suspicions of our dear mother!'

All the same, from a purely worldly point of view the Corporation has got the University queered and is evidently going to stand still over it. Whether the parents of Harvard boys killed in the war will deposit their urns in the Harvard Library I don't know. I fear the cinders would get mixed with some German cinders during the next twenty years.

Especially the *dépouillés* of the volunteers, which represent pure hostility to Germany — (with no patriotism mixed) — would be apt to have smaller and smaller labels as time went on — nobody's fault — a mistake — for who could doubt the honor of the Librarian? But the trophies will be removed a little later to a safer place. The era of good feeling for Germany will dawn at Harvard sooner than elsewhere. Gus Gardner's sword — Norman Prince — my boy — Sill, etc. I have in mind a circular letter or memorandum on this subject addressed to the parents of future Harvard heroes, for I don't feel safe, and I think I should be a damned fool to feel safe. There is such a thing as a non-Harvard brain, a just ordinary human intelligence which looks at the facts as if they had occurred in some other college.

Your aff.

JACK

332

I am keeping a copy of this, for I think it gives the idea more *quickly* than I could do in a serious argument and I think I'll enclose it in writing to William Lawrence — who comes nearer — at least in my imagination — to being a halfway sensible person than the rest of the Corporation. The people of whom you are a type show the brain effects of this college patriotism tomfoolery, which is one of the banes of American life. I must confess however that you are *not* a coward. I apologize for calling you a coward. You displayed perfect *sang-froid* at the moment you thought I might be going to make a scene, which would have somehow been fierce. — Also, the *lunch* was splendid — (I name this first as it was much the most important event of the day.) The rest of it was managed wonderfully well and everyone says it was a brilliant meeting.

To his Mother

[BARRYTOWN, N.Y.] *July* 29, 1918

DEAR MAMA

Reading Burke all day and Trevelyan's 'American Revolution.' The English seem to have had a sort of madness that reminds us of modern Germany. They were resolved to punish and subdue. They thought to starve Boston — and thought the rest of the Colonies would sit by waiting for their turn (as the Germans thought about England and America). They passed bills to *hang* the Americans as *pirates* — to drag them to England for trial. I really hadn't remembered how senseless they were. It's a bug. They regarded Burke as a foolish person and his speeches as sentimental rubbish. They were led on by a sort of *ignis fatuus* — and blew the whole trouble up out of nothing. They did it themselves. The history of the American Revolution is a sort of mystery play — showing one form of the way ambition defeats itself — also the way the larger interests of humanity take care of themselves — for it would be a bad outlook for the world today if America were British. All these wars are new phases of the same struggle. The English *people* (not the Government) were more liberal in

1776 than they were in 1900. This is a very curious reflection, but the Boer War shows it.

Your aff
JACK

To the same

[*Chapman's sister Eleanor, Mrs. Richard Mortimer, had recently lost her son, Richard Mortimer, Jr., in the war.*]

BARRYTOWN, *Aug.* 7, 1918

... I hope Eleanor will later on get interested in some sort of work — as otherwise she will get bored to death. When you lose a boy in the war and at a time when everyone else is losing them and it's part of the age and of value to the country — this is very different from having one die of disease in ordinary times — and there's a natural law which alleviates the grief. Otherwise it would be intolerable. Every one would be in despair. But the French and English are not in despair and we shall not be....

Your aff. son,
JACK

To the same

BARRYTOWN, *Aug.* 21: 1918

As for Wilson's being a Frankenstein — he is more like a cypher. His power is due to extraordinary circumstances — like that of an ordinary ship-captain, during a mutiny. It rests upon everyone's consent, the consent of intelligent people. The moment he tries to use it after the emergency passes — he'll be disregarded and ridiculous.

His dictatorship is certain to wane — and then will be the time to see what he is made of. Fate has made him a power — — a preponderating, unnatural power in European politics. If he tries to retain this world position for the U.S. we shall have trouble. If he lets the power evaporate as it were un-ambitiously — and lets the U.S. get out of her unnatural position — and lets Europe run herself — then he will really have been very great. To tell you the truth I have, on this score more confidence in a Democratic administration than in a Republican one.

334

The Republicans, as you can see by Davison, want to right things through party. They have a tradition of expansion, centralization. They take Panama and the Philippines — and are much more jingo than the Democrats. I hate Wilson personally as everyone does. He's a mean man. But he has qualities — and it's ridiculous to judge him by one's personal antipathies.

Yours
JACK

To S. S. Drury

SYLVANIA
BARRYTOWN-ON-HUDSON
Sept. 22: 1918

DEAR DR. DRURY

I always knew you were a donkey — the only thing is, you are a different kind of a donkey from what I used to think.

All rot writing your letters by hand — it's as if I should cook my own food. You'd better get a young woman who knows a little typewriting, or a poor boy, the son of a widow. This Simeon Stylites business is not the way to fight the war. Hoover says so himself. It's one thing to joy-ride and eat always at Delmonico's (the last time I went there I got heart trouble — and now I slink past the place — groping my way — and clutching for my bank on the opposite side of the avenue), and quite another to take a cup of coffee, two eggs, some peaches and cream and a few doughnuts and half a pot of jam before a hard day's work. I am sending you *Vanity Fair* — which Chanler says is an excellent magazine — and read by all people who know what's what, and much better for me to write in than the hypocritical high-brow periodicals like the *Atlantic*. I do hope that boy is going to behave halfway decently. He went off in the wildest spirits at the prospect of getting back, and my wife says that it has at last got into his mind (through the conversation of our old coachman) that really nobody wants him to go to war this year and that to do so is a senseless idea anyway.

Yours sincerely always
JOHN JAY CHAPMAN

To Owen Wister

BARRYTOWN, N.Y., *Oct.* 8: 1918

DEAR DAN

... You will be amused in reading my *North American Review* article to see that we have both hit on the same metaphor — the victrola for Wilson, but I take a more abstract view than you do. I almost died of the man — as we all did, and he gave me so much pain that for a long time I was pinched and bleeding inwardly. But what with the relief of getting into the war — which was so great that I didn't even care whether we lost it or not — and what with present conditions, and prospects, I've come to look upon Wilson as an interesting phenomenon operating in an environment which is essentially mystic and incomprehensible — a weather-cock to invisible currents — a super-politician — and *pro tanto* a great genius — the *genius of the moment*. But you see the moment has struck, I *think*—it's going to be a continuous moment — so far as the American people goes — and he won't have any temptation to spoil his record — record in two senses — for some time. I confess that if anything should throw the American people into the doldrums again, I should expect Wilson to go into them. But if this is the true view, nevertheless it's not a matter of calculation with him but rather of response to currents.

The other side of it is — that this talent for expressing the will of others has made Wilson into a great genius. He has, as Elizabeth says, given restatements of Democratic idea, freshly, attractively — spontaneously — and gained an assent from Europe to things they couldn't say themselves and *don't really understand*. Your idea that Europe is jollying him and flattering him is to my mind quite erroneous. If he don't do anything to spoil it, he will go down in European history as the greatest sage of the modern world — and one of the greatest ever. And his words will bear him out. There are enough of them already to write on pyramids and columns — quite as quotable as Lincoln's. Wherever they came from — (they really come out of the brain of one hundred years of America) — Wilson uttered them. The Hungarian peasant already knows them.

Of course everything depends on what a man does. It is his death that made Socrates and his talk interesting. If he had broken jail, we should never have heard of him; and if Wilson should do something foolish the inscriptions would not be put up.

In the mean time my effort is to stand back from the canvas as far as possible. He is got into such large water and such foreign seas and alps and islands that there's [no] knowing when he may get home again and the whole thing has become the greatest show there ever was on earth. Perhaps in time it will lose its unity, but just now it is stupendous.

Yours affly

JACK

To Émile Legouis

BARRYTOWN, N.Y.

Oct. 19: 1918

MY DEAR LEGOUIS

Your boy was with us for two nights. It was the greatest good fortune that we were in town when he called — as I should have hated to have him return to France without our seeing him. He is an enchanting youth and we enjoyed seeing him immensely. He seems the picture of youth and more a poem than a soldier. I never saw so poetic-looking a young man and with such a charm. I should think every woman would fall in love with him across an opera house. Well, I'm so glad we saw him and he takes our love and messages to all of you, and by the way I also sent Harper's 'Wordsworth.' What a blow to you that book must be! — *ought* to be — for you know Emerson says — if a teacher have a particular tenet which he studiously conceals, that tenet will be as much in his teaching as anything else, and here are you who never realized that a dark mantle of early peccadillo hung over the life of Wordsworth — and stiffened him into the old Scotch hypocrite he was and set the world maundering over him — and he never got found out. But *you*, why you ought to have seen the thing in his verse. I'm sure *I* should, if I had given him all that study and written the best book — any man ever wrote. O, I'm not going to read that old book now — I'm disillusioned.

337

You know Professor Palmer of Cambridge — he's the only real Wordsworthian left in the world (for I don't call intellectuals like you the true thing, no matter how many books they write). Palmer was pale about the gills — and wouldn't quite answer my questions. Palmer's an ethical person, probably is more versed in the subject than any one since H. Sidgwick. I suggested that no one could ever read the Prelude again — take it seriously. It pretends to be a history of the poet's soul (you recollect the poem I refer to) — very intimate, you know, the sacred deep experiences — heart laid bare — that sort of thing — noble emotions. Poor Palmer — I hate to say 'Poor' anybody since Carlyle — but it is right, here — I'll be saying Poor Legouis next.

I found my wife this morning quite worried about the possible advance of Socialism after the war. People get so in the habit of worry that if you save them from drowning and put them on a bank to dry in the sun with hot chocolate and muffins they wonder whether they are not taking cold.

My own fears about the future are in another direction and are not very strong anyway. I think there is some danger of our becoming imperialistic in consequence of military success — wanting to run Europe, etc. I confess I don't as yet see any signs of it — but fear it because it is a thing that *generally follows* military success in any nation. I am in consequence delighted with Wilson's message to Austria (October 19), saying the Austrians must settle their own squabbles. This gives the key. If we only hold to this in all the muddle that is to follow we can get out of Europe with credit. Of course Wilson is not dependable. He seems not to understand the meaning of words. On September 27 he called Germany an outlaw with whose rulers no one could deal. On October 4 he invited an explanation from the same rulers. This threw America into convulsions for two days.

Everybody wrote to the newspapers and telegraphed madly to Washington. Wilson braced up. No one knows today why he thought fit to give us the shake-up. Perhaps he wanted a plébiscite. He got one any way.

But what I count on is not Wilson or any man in particular, but the common sense of our people who will want to get out of Europe with credit — and will see that the way to do this is to leave all these European boundary questions and infant nation questions for Europe to settle herself. The note to Austria gives the cue. It is a valuable paper. It is short. It contains no puzzles.

With many kind regards to Mme. Legouis from my wife and myself

Yours very sincerely

JOHN JAY CHAPMAN

VIII

Banked Fires
1918–1929

EACH decade of Chapman's mature life up to the time to which this chapter relates had taken its toll, its heavy toll, of him. In the eighties of the last century he lost his hand; in the nineties, the wife of his youth; in the first ten years of this century, his health and his son Jay; in the second his son Victor. It was time, indeed, for a respite, and, in so far as the tragic strokes of fate were concerned, the respite came. Yet it did not bring tranquillity at once: that was to come by degrees through the post-war decade and the few years that followed. Far from dropping the weapons of a foe to the evils he feared, he fulminated in these years against Harvard and the Church of Rome with all his powers — and only the more vigorously when he fancied them in collusion and could bring them together for a single attack. In politics he battled against the ascendancy of Alfred E. Smith, on the score of his Roman affiliation, and, turning from the admiration of Jews which he had felt in the days of his close association with Isaac H. Klein, joined with those who shuddered at the 'Jewish menace.'

In matters of education his intense preoccupation with the development of his two younger sons, as students at St. Paul's and Harvard, brought into his thought a personal element that strengthened his opposition to things as they were in our schools and colleges. Heaven knows that in many fields the discrepancies between the actual and his ideal for it had provided him, through the years already passed, with abundant grounds for complaint. Now the 'brave new world' that filled many aging men with dismay confronted him, and various changes from conditions he had always deplored appeared to him, as to so many of his generation, changes rather for the worse than for the better. 'The chief thing I see,' he wrote to his friend Émile Legouis as 1926 was nearing its end, 'is a general vulgarization of everything, due to the increase in the world's population and the outcomes of science.' Even earlier, in 1920, he had made his lament to Edward S. Martin: 'It's a horrible world, no matter how you put it, and just now it's particularly so, and any endeavor in letters, art, intellect, or morality seems always to be in a skiff washed and wallowing and about to be submerged. Would it were a hundred years hence and all well!'

A 'Sonnet on Middle Life' found among his papers, and dated November 7, 1918, struck the note of that vast perplexity in which the war had left a multitude for whom Chapman could speak:

> The Sibyl paused, her pen above the leaf
> Large as an atlas that before her lay,
> While the dim plunge of waters far away
> Wafted upon my brain their cool relief
> From cavernous distances, as who should say,
> 'Trouble thyself no more. The time is brief.
> Thy mind is harvested: its little sheaf
> Stands in the granary of yesterday.'
>
> Abashed I spake not, but observed her then,
> Watching to see if she would turn the page
> Or write the caption for some newer age.
> And next, the god inflamed her, and her hand
> In a poetic fury wrote amain —
> Strange symbols that I could not understand.

The period was one in which Chapman was to express himself more fully, and more memorably, in verse than ever before. There were moments of misgiving, recognitions of 'strange symbols that I cannot understand' — none more impressive,

perhaps than the noble lines 'No Pilots We,' which appeared
in the *Atlantic Monthly* for March, 1925, and began:

> Would I were one of those who preach no Cause —
> Nor guide mankind with meddling fingertips;
> But let each star that moves without a pause
> Shine as it list.

But he was not yet of that silent company, and in verse and
prose continued to pour forth those certainties of his own
which a changing world had not yet shattered. These found
their way especially into 'My Secret Journal,' a long series of
Byronic stanzas, many of which were printed in the *Forum*. 'I
think,' he declared in one of them,

> I think that every man should keep a journal
> And jot from time to time his passing fancies,
> Or airy plunges into Truth Eternal;
> In fact, let ready writing take its chances
> And save the husk, although it lose the kernel;
> Writers are ruined through their audiences.
> And now I draw the curtain, take my tea,
> And write what nobody shall read but me.

Of course he wanted, and found, many readers besides himself. Byron was one of his topics:

> To me he seems the master of the crew
> And type of all who swear they won't be bored; —

the theme and the medium, both congenial, yielded a penetrating criticism in verse. 'Education,' 'Letters and Patriotism,'
'Our Architects,' 'Regeneration' — these and other topics
provoked a long array of stanzas, printed and unprinted.
'Speaking out' was still, for Chapman, the panacea for the ills
of the world:

> Speech is the cure — plain, honest, open speech;
> Expensive, hateful, downright, crude opinion.
> This great elixir is within the reach
> Of every man, this key to the dominion
> Of courage and of intellect. Let each
> Address the demon that on sable pinion

Soars in his cowering mind, and plainly say
Just what he thinks. I've finished for the day.

If there was one subject more than any other on which
Chapman desired, and cultivated, freedom of speech, it was
the Church of Rome, in its broader relations to American life.
'My Secret Journal' was obviously the medium through which
he could give untrammelled utterance to his inherited and
individual opinions. In 1928 he produced and distributed
broadly a pamphlet, 'The Roman Catholic Mind: Extract
from My Secret Journal.' One of its twenty-four stanzas revived a thought expressed in some earlier verses, 'To a Roman
Catholic Friend' (his sister-in-law, Mrs. Winthrop Chanler).
They read as follows:

> Shall we sit and talk it over?
>   I can tell you what I mean;
> Yet not break the glassy cover —
>   The divide that falls between.
>
> Any thought I hand or slide you
>   In your cage, you take and toss
> Towards the priest that stands beside you,
>   To appraise for gold or dross.
>
> As a croupier you receive it,
>   Not presuming by yourself
> To believe or disbelieve it,
>   You arrange it on your shelf.
>
> Fearing it implies perdition —
>   Hoping it may prove a toy —
> You await the great permission
>   To abominate or enjoy.
>
> Honest talk is true and hearty,
>   Headlong, careless, debonair;
> I'm annoyed by this third party,
>   Listening ever on the stair.
>
> Yet you long for conversations
>   With the thoughts they leave behind —

343

And the blessed broken rations
Of the topics of the mind.

Honest talk is sweet as honey;
But, dear person, it is rash
For you who pay out paper money
To ask of others ringing cash.
November 19, 1920.

'The Roman Catholic Mind,' as a whole, deals with philosophic generalizations extending far beyond the personal, and at the last present a clear-cut bill of particulars with respect to Boston, reaching a climax in the following stanzas:

The Bench, the Bar and Business; Politics,
    The Press, the Clubs; Chapel and lecture-hall
Have all agreed that one must never mix
    Religious questions with the vote. That's all!
Meanwhile One Hand holds up a crucifix
    And thick as autumn leaves the ballots fall
While every voiceless voter finds some reason
For thinking frank discussion not in season.

Silence enslaves them — silence and the cant
    Of Tolerance. 'Tis almost past believing;
And yet 'tis very simple, so I sha'n't
    Expound in words too hard for your conceiving
What everybody knows: — The Protestant
    Who braves the Roman Power can't make his living.
If *fear* be all Rome needs to keep her steady,
    These Protestants are Catholics already.

Yes, Boston has been conquered and subdued.
    Her monuments are meaningless; — her dome
That seems to shine in heaven's solitude,
    Is but a symbol of the Church of Rome.
Gone is the race that once embattled stood
    For Liberty — for conscience, hearth and home,
The stars and stripes wave on, o'er souls that quail.
    Take heed, my country. 'Tis no fairy-tale.

Before these lines were written Chapman had contemplated seriously coming to Boston, hiring a hall, and delivering a

344

lecture on 'The Roman Catholic Church.' 'Sounds terrible, don't it?' he wrote to a friend. 'But the substance of the lecture might prove an anti-climax — I mean to those who expected Wendell Phillips on the slave trade.' This project was dropped. Meanwhile incidents had occurred to stimulate the feeling behind the lines just quoted. The tearing down of a British flag on the Union Club by Irish-Americans coming out of St. Patrick's Cathedral in New York after Mass on Thanksgiving Day, 1920, was one of them. 'The Union Club Incident' was the subject of a vigorous letter from Chapman in the *Evening Post* a few days later. Here, however, his condemnation of the incident was offset by the praise he bestowed upon those men and women of local importance who signed and published a letter to Archbishop Hayes beginning, 'As Americans and Catholics we protest against the infusion of politics into our beloved church.' The signers of this letter, Chapman declared, 'have set the whole Roman Catholic question upon a new plane, and lifted it into a place where it can be discussed without rancor.' Before long another incident provoked ample discussion with more of rancor than Chapman had contemplated.

It all began with a speech by Cardinal O'Connell, in October, 1924, at the dedication of a Roman Catholic church in close proximity to Harvard College, when he was quoted as saying that 'some centuries ago some of the great schools of Europe, like Oxford and Cambridge, forgot their duty to their mother,' and as deploring the separation of Harvard from 'the old faith of Christ.' These remarks provoked Chapman to write an open letter to Bishop Lawrence, of the Harvard Corporation, quoting the Cardinal's words and asking for comment upon them, especially with reference to the election of James Byrne, a Roman Catholic, as a Fellow of Harvard. He asked also whether the demands of precedent and liberalism would require the appointment of another Roman Catholic to take Mr. Byrne's place when it should become vacant, and how any free discussion of the relations between the Roman Catholic Church and American education could be held in the Corporation while one of its seven members was a member of that church. Bishop Lawrence did not answer the letter, but many others did, and for several months the daily and weekly press resounded with discussions of the matter, generally adverse to Chapman's position. That well-tempered clavichord of opinion, the editorial page of *Life*, conducted by Edward S. Martin, declared that everybody 'hates to think, and dislikes to be punched up to that exertion. Such people want the world so quiet you can hear a pin drop, and when a man like Chapman comes along and drops a dumb-bell they think it is awful. But it has to be done now and then.' Whereupon Chapman dropped his dumbbell on the toes of Mr. Martin himself as 'the shepherd of a compact flock of all-wool Americans,' declaring that he 'would permit himself to be nailed to the cross and his readers would rather see him nailed to the cross than have him admit anything so low-minded as, for instance, that there was any line of connection between the Pope, Cardinal O'Connell, and the Harvard Board of Fellows.'

By way of parenthesis it should be said that Bishop Lawrence was a member of the Harvard Corporation who stood high in Chapman's esteem. On January 20, 1923, he wrote to me: 'Do you know I think Bishop Lawrence's little book called "Fifty Years" is a shining, inspiring little book. I read it because some clergyman chanced to say that this book was at the bottom of the Episcopal Church muddle. — Yes, perhaps, but in about the same sort of way that Christ is responsible for the Spanish Inquisition.' Before addressing his open letter to Bishop Lawrence he had said in another letter to me (May 29, 1924), touching upon an unexpected display of openmindedness at Harvard: 'Well, I *shall* try to be proud of Harvard, but I know it will kill me if I succeed.'

As in education, so in politics: the honesty of Chapman would not have been what it was if, before the nomination of candidates for the presidency in 1928, he had not produced a pamphlet, 'The Honesty of Al Smith,' assailing his contention that 'there is no such issue in American politics as the Roman Church.' For the silence which Chapman so delighted in breaking he blamed the Protestant intellectuals. 'These men,' he declared in a published letter incident to the discussion of Harvard and Rome, 'should give articulate warning of the danger that confronts the republic. They leave this to be done by the Ku Klux Klan, whose undiscriminating violence discredits a cause that is real, profound, enduring — viz. our duty to think and act seriously with regard to the aggression of Rome.' His fear of the Jewish influence never mounted to the height to which he was lifted by the Roman Church, yet there was a time when the two dangers united in his thought, and for the expression of it in print, through a sonnet 'Cape Cod, Rome, and Jerusalem,' he resorted to the columns of the *Ku Klux Kourier* — perhaps because no other journal would become his medium in this instance.

Whether Chapman was right or wrong in these and other agitations, his own desire, set down at the very beginning of this book, to be shown wrong on every question of his time rather than to be erased into a cypher by his biographer is always to be remembered. The reality of his convictions and the skill and force with which he uttered them cannot be erased.

There were other aspects of Harvard than the religious which distressed him. The exclusion of Negroes from the Freshman dormitories brought his anti-slavery spirit into play. In the *Boston Evening Transcript* for March 12, 1924, moreover, he printed a skit, 'Alma Mater,' poking fun at 'Brodignag [*sic*] University' for its bigness, its pumping-up of alumni spirit, its College of Business. Chapman reprinted both this and an earlier *Transcript* article, 'Our Universities,' in separate leaflets, and distributed them broadly. 'Many years ago,' he wrote in 'Our Universities,' 'the story was current of the American who was buying a ticket for Oxford at the Paddington Booking Office and who, upon the clerk's asking him: "Which class, sir?" almost shouted: "Princeton, '77!'" The creation of an artificial 'loyalty' to class and college was the thing that seemed to Chapman quite apart from the true purpose of a university, especially his own. It pleased him well, soon after the appearance of 'Alma Mater,' to receive an invitation to speak at the annual dinner of the *Harvard Business Review* on May 8, 1924. There he made a trenchant talk, shot through with wit, amplifying his exhortation, 'My friends, the truth is that Business is not a profession; and no amount of rhetoric and no expenditure in circulars can make it into a profession.' Just before leaving home on this adventure, he wrote to his young English friend, Robert Nichols, that he was going to Boston, 'to deliver a lecture to some erring Harvard idiots who have been heading the University toward the ditch for a generation, and are going to land it there sooner than the most accurate philosophy could hope or wish.... A good sign of the times is that there are signs of possible humor in the air. For three months ago I printed a skit about "College Spirit" in America and the constant Drives for money, and instead of taking it in dudgeon the Harvard Business College invited me to their annual dinner. If we can laugh, there's hope for us.'

In spite of his belief in laughter, and his practice of it, Chapman himself could not always laugh. It was with anything but mirth that he greeted a speech and some poems of Siegfried Sassoon at the Cosmopolitan Club on a February night of 1920. Sassoon had dined alone with the Chapmans on the night before, and Chapman had sought in vain to dissuade him from carrying his gospel of disillusion and war-weariness to American youth. This gospel was the burden of Sassoon's message to the women of the Cosmopolitan Club. It was more than Chapman, on fire with the heroisms of war, could stand. When Sassoon stopped speaking, Chapman, urged by ladies who shared his indignation, mounted the rostrum, and asked — as his words are recalled by one who heard them — what would become of the world if the

philosophies of fear and self-pity were to prevail, what
Washington's soldiers would have thought of a young man
who went about after Valley Forge preaching 'no more
bleeding footsteps in the snow.' Some of Chapman's best
friends joined in hissing him, and there were outraged de-
partures from the room — even as there were those who stood
with Chapman in the whole affair. Afterwards he commended
the Cosmopolitan Club as a place where people could hiss if
they wanted to. At the time he wrote (February 25) to his
son Chanler at Grenoble in these terms:

> Well, the poet Sassoon made such a speech and read such
> verses about the nature of war, and the war, and how the men
> were sacrificed, and didn't know what they were fighting for,
> and committed suicide in the trenches, and were in an abnormal
> condition of excitement when they went over the top, with hits
> at every good influence in the war, church, patriotism — in
> fact the most painful talk I ever heard — that I had to call
> him down.... The audience was surprised and grieved at my
> denunciation of Sassoon, and thought it very ungentlemanly.
> But really, you know ——

That was not quite the end of it. A letter from Mrs. Chapman to the sons in Europe tells that their father called on
Sassoon on the day after their encounter and, finding him out,
left a card: 'Of course if he had seen him he would have
removed the few remaining hairs on his scalp. But... the
card had just the friendly affectionate expression lying on
Sassoon's hall-table that represented Papa's true impulse in
leaving it.' More than that, Chapman wrote later in the day
to Sassoon:

> Sorry to miss you this morning. It was a suffering occasion
> last night. I think I suffered as much as you did. If you will do
> it, why, you must: and I suppose the universe will not be
> wrecked by you or by my trying to stop you. As for the wreck-
> ing of a ladies' club or two, it's not of the smallest consequence.

The note went on to warn the visitor against allowing himself to be exploited: 'The pro-Germans will try it politically,
and the women will do it emotionally.... There's nothing in

it — except wayward motherliness. (I don't see how the universe stands the women in it!)'

There was no explosion either of rage or of laughter over one matter on which Chapman must have done some inward chuckling. Many of his friends felt that Harvard, like Yale, should bestow an honorary degree upon him. In November of 1927 he received a letter from a member of the Harvard Corporation saying, 'I have duly protected you, as requested, someone having suggested your name. If you have any vanity you would have been much pleased by the attitude of the others, which was also my attitude.' In sending this note to his wife, Chapman annotated it to the effect that he had asked this friend on the Corporation, in the event of any proposal of an honorary degree, that he 'should finally sidetrack the matter.' In the following June, according to another letter to Mrs. Chapman, he fell in with a second member of the Corporation, who 'was friendly and amused at my refusing a degree, to which matter he referred in an oblique and discreet way. I said I was afraid I'd lose my utility if I became good-natured — or words to that effect — and that I was softening anyway, to my alarm.' At least he was standing by the principle he had expounded to William James nearly twenty years before and not 'selling out the gift of prophecy for a seat in the synagogue.'

In correspondence with editors and publishers there was no thought of selling out the gift of prophecy — if prophecy be the proclaiming of unpalatable opinions. Like many spirited authors, he held these middlemen of letters in low esteem. 'And yet you say editors are human beings,' he wrote to George Dudley Seymour in 1923. 'They are more like the underlings of undertakers — slinking shadows seen with a bag of chemicals after the doctor has gone for the last time. They answer you with their tools. You meet them at lunch, and the next day they write you, "Thanking you for the privilege." My God, what ghouls!' Whether the editors happened to be his personal friends or not, he told them precisely what he thought of them and their ways. To the credit of their fraternity it must be recorded that all of his objurgations were not taken "lying down." Many of them were half humorous, yet not without a sting which provoked response. This might come from even so true a friend as Edward S. Martin, who once wrote to him: 'You have no judgment. You see a little and not the rest. You complain of me because I sometimes suspect that the nose is not the whole face. You have ingrowing sight. The nose is all you see. The really important things that are going on you pay no attention to. You are full of learning and most of it is old stuff — not operative. Really I wonder that I bother with you at all.'

Nearly a year later another editor, Thomas B. Wells, of *Harper's*, resenting Chapman's charges of timidity against his magazine, wrote a letter taking him more elaborately, less light-heartedly, to task. In an *argumentum ad hominem* he pictured Chapman at the bar of Heaven, silenced by a charge of inadequacy in representing what should have come to him, by inheritance, from the first John Jay and, by education, from John Harvard. It was not a letter out of which an inter-change of banter, as with Martin, could proceed.

One editor with whom no clashes seem to have occurred was Frank Crowninshield of *Vanity Fair*, to which Chapman contributed more than a score of miscellaneous articles from 1918 onward for several years. Editor and contributor had a congenial meeting-place at the luncheon-table of the Coffee House, an informal club in which Crowninshield was the moving spirit and Chapman the only honorary member. He held a strong belief that good conversation was the basis of good writing, and towards the end of his life planned a book to be made up chiefly of his *Vanity Fair* papers and to be called 'Coffee House Talk.' It would have contained some lively pages on contemporary letters, art, and affairs. There were also three 'Imaginary Obituaries' of living persons, Edward S. Martin, the Reverend Percy S. Grant, and Major George

Haven Putnam. The last was wholly in praise of a friend; the second a scathing comment, with anything but praise; the first a mingling of admiration for a friend indeed, with sorrow over his incapacity for righteous wrath. Chapman had qualms about this sketch — as well he might — and wrote to Martin, 'I am beginning to have remorse, which they say is the most horrible of the passions.... This writing business is the devil — much flash and vanity in it. Glad it's you anyway. It might have been somebody else.' Of course Martin took it all with perfect equanimity. At first Chapman was disturbed because there were no angry letters from Martin's admirers: 'It almost looks,' he wrote to Martin, 'as if I had been too mealy-mouthed. "What don't bite ain't right" is my motto in writing.' But soon he was encouraged and wrote again; 'By the way, I've got a big opinion of your obituary. Will Rogers praised it as a work of art. I like that thing. Your aff. Jack.' It is easy enough to see why he could never stay long out of favor with his best friends.

It made no matter how critical or abusive Chapman's letters were — they were so often signed 'Yours affectionately, Jack' that these words might almost provide a title for his correspondence. The fitness of it would appear in his frequent solicitude for his friends. 'Go slow,' he bade one of them, who gave evidence of weariness; 'refuse invitations' — 'that's the whole thing. Whoever opposes — slay them.' An invitation to visit the Chapmans might carry with it a cheque to meet the expenses involved — 'I wish such had been the practice when I was young.' An older — and cherished — friend shows signs of advancing years, and receives this: 'If you want to beat that surety company, you've got to stop dragging your feet. I have the same tendency — it's the old man's tendency — and it's the quick road to the grave. You've got to get so that you *hear* it when you drag them. Whereupon you straighten, stretch, raise your head, and *lift your feet*. My Jove! you shuffle like a nonagenarian — I can hear you a block off on Sixth Avenue, and I can see you half a mile —

and in a club I'm afraid you'll *fall* on me — Yours affectionately, Jack.'

In other journals than *Vanity Fair* Chapman published
many other essays in this period, and of course did not fail to
express himself on Prohibition — especially in an article in the
Independent, 'Why not Speak Out?' in which he urged all men
to follow his example in saying openly to what extent they
observed the law. 'To-day,' he declared, 'I will buy wine
made by a neighbor, or I will buy pre-war stock from a friend.
As yet I cannot quite bear to deal with a bootlegger, and
certainly not to swear falsely.... Who knows what I may
come to tomorrow?' He never came to the bootleg traffic.
Besides a mass of fugitive writing in print, there was a flood of
correspondence, all in manuscript, of which so much has been
preserved that imagination reels at what all of it must have
been. As if this were not enough, there were the several books
of which it remains to speak.

In the summer of 1929 Chapman wrote to a correspondent,
'All my books are essays,' and proceeded to cite as instances
several which appeared in the decade then nearing its end.
'My Life of Garrison is an essay,' he said, and that was
revived through a new edition in 1921. 'Shakespeare is an
essay,' he went on, and, touching on other titles, described
'Letters and Religion' as a series of essays, 'Dante' as containing 'a lot of little essays... Even the small volume of translations of Two Greek Plays has little essays about Greek literature in the form of memoranda.'

His definition of these books was quite accurate and Chapman, in his prose, was, first and last, an essayist — and sometimes a pamphleteer. Now the essay, like most poetry, is
generally a personal affair — the expression of something
uppermost in the writer's mind at the moment of its production. The man with a *magnum opus*, requiring years or a
life-time for its production, must turn away from many objects of immediate personal interest and concentrate upon the
great matter in hand. Chapman's books, made up of essays,

reflected the range and variety of his intellectual and spiritual pursuits — and also their boundaries. In the decade following the war, when many excellent brains were wreaking themselves on economic problems, on the relations between capital and labor, or such current objects of controversy as the Sacco-Vanzetti case, Chapman, like Gallio, cared for none of these things. The books of this single decade represent to a striking degree the confluence of the interests of a life-time — Shakespeare, literature and religion, Dante, the Greek dramatists.

All these books were small, yet glowing with Chapman's fervor for his several themes. In the production of 'A Glance toward Shakespeare' (1922) and 'Letters and Religion' (1924) his present biographer enjoyed, as 'book editor,' an unbroken friendly relation with him. When he turned elsewhere with his 'Dante' (1927) and 'Two Greek Plays: the Philoctetes of Sophocles, and the Medea of Euripides, Done into English' (1928), he wrote to a friend, 'The rash heroic firm of Houghton Mifflin has caught up the dying torch of my literary fortunes and goes nobly towards the abyss.' If they had fallen into it together, Chapman could hardly have written to his wife as he did, a few years later, 'Ferris Greenslet has the nearest thing to a mind and education of any publisher I ever met.' Where this avowal leaves his earlier publishers they may decide amongst themselves.

The four books that have been named ask little of a reader's time, but much of his responsiveness to their great themes. They are all the work of an amateur — in separate fields — and previous writings were preliminary to all of them. The Shakespeare essay in 'Greek Genius' was a forerunner of 'A Glance towards Shakespeare,' the 'Notes on Religion' of 'Letters and Religion.' This book had no such controversial pages as those on 'The Roman Church.' Its tone is suggested in such words as these: 'Hurry was born the day that steam was invented, and though art and letters resisted the acceleration for a couple of centuries, they succumbed at last, and are now whirling and scurrying like ferryboats packed with wide-awake people, holding watches in their hands.' The gist of his own religious thought is found, unforgettably, in the chapter, 'The Story and Sayings of Christ.' The book as a whole is the best single key to the richness of Chapman's nature, as the meeting-place of mind and spirit, of intellect and faith. Is it fragmentary and inconclusive? 'Conclusions,' says Chapman in the course of it, 'are lame and impotent, and the reason is plain. There are no conclusions in nature; nor can any round-up of ideas have more finality than the first two notes of a rhapsody. The best constructed endings are no more than time-signals, like those letters called *terminals* in hieroglyphic writing, which add no new meaning to the text but signify that a period has been reached.' In his 'Letters and Religion' he reached such a period.

Then there are the two volumes of translation, 'Dante,' and the Greek plays. 'Dante' consists about equally of prose comment and translations in *terza rima*, the earliest of which was his first contribution to the *Atlantic Monthly* many years before.[1] He made no pretensions to accurate scholarship either in his interpretative remarks, of singular understanding, or in his translations, of singular beauty. Writing about these to his son Chanler, he said, 'The bottom fact is that there are few bits in Dante that are translatable, and by choosing these I leave an impression that I could do the rest. The real translators, by undertaking *all*, spoil all.' It is the glory of the amateur to do as he pleases. So with the 'Two Greek Plays.' What he wrote about the Philoctetes applies to both: 'The following paraphrase makes no claim to scholarship. It may be likened to those sketches, studies, and copies of old Masters which painters make for their own use, and then file away in portfolios; or to a transcript for the piano made from a symphony.' In one of the 'Memoranda' at the end of the volume he speaks of translating the classics as a task 'chiefly valuable as an agreeable pastime for elderly gentlemen with time on their hands.' But here he was doing

[1] See *ante*, p. 75.

again only what he had done so masterfully in earlier days with his paraphrase of 'Homeric Scenes.'

Through the years in which all this work was done Barrytown and New York provided the chief background for it. Over all his writing for publication he labored intensely, demanding complete seclusion for the whole of every weekday morning. In New York he resorted to a room at the top of the 82nd Street house, and used to say, 'If the house is on fire, I want to be notified only by the smell of smoke.' In the preparation of his manuscripts for print the constant assistance of Miss Elizabeth Montgomery, his wife's secretary and helper in many capacities through many years, was invaluable to him. Every writer of books knows what such devoted help can mean. Then there were wanderings afield, especially to shield Mrs. Chapman's health from the rigors of winter in the north. At Sanibel, Florida, she exercised her artistic gifts in the creation of 'shell mosaics' from the seashells of gemlike colors found in abundance on the Sanibel shore. This revival of an ancient art of India and Italy gave an equal delight to Chapman and his wife.

Of Sylvania in particular one would like to render perpetual the flavor that made the place what it was to its inhabitants and their friends. Perhaps this cannot be done more effectually than by transcribing a portion of a letter from Robert Nichols after a summer visit in 1926.

> Sylvania — dear John Jay and Elizabeth, I shall always remember and treasure that visit — we both shall. You know I could hardly sleep the night before on the train for thinking of seeing you again, and I cried worse than Androcles' lion with the thorn in his paw before breakfast on the day we had to go. To think of those mushrooms on the lawn — what is a countryhouse without a stray mushroom set and forgotten by somebody on a table in the hall? — that big library smelling of woodsmoke and desultory conversation — the sort of library in which things — books, pamphlets, circulars, rose-clippers, cigarboxes, book-catalogues, Italian texts of Homer bound in queer white skin gone ivory with age, Dutch texts of Horace printed for learned pedagogues who scratched bottle noses over 'Jacobus

Hoogasomethingorother stultissime emendavit,' get piled up.
No library ought to be spick and span, garnished as they often
are in lords' houses; this kills the spirit and the books stand
mean and regimented on the shelves, dull as beaten convicts,
not like runners facing the mark or a jolly confraternity of all
choice and scampish heroes. Sylvania! Sylvania! Zion!
Zion! In heaven I think one is perpetually coming through the
garden doors to begin a judicious and wordy difference with
John Jay and Elizabeth. Dear place and darling people!

Europe, besides, remained an unfailing refuge. In 1919,
1922, and 1925 there were journeys abroad — the third for
the definite purpose of diverting Chapman's mind from its
concentration upon the Roman Catholic question. He realized
himself that a long continuance of intense antagonism to one
object might produce such another shipwreck of his health as
he had suffered after his political agitations through the
nineties. 'I have committed the Pope to God who made him
— but why? and how, how *could* he do it?' he wrote to Owen
Wister before the second trip abroad, 'and who could have
predicted such an outcome from the teachings of Christ? But
— aha! — something remains — some issue, some slough-
ing off (I hope the U.S. doesn't have to go into the swill
pail as the caustic reagent).'

When these words were written, in 1925, his opposition to
Alfred E. Smith and his 'Secret Journal' verses on 'The Roman
Catholic Mind' were still to come. But the ardors were beginning to cool, as they generally will as one approaches seventy.
It was confessed more than once, as will soon be seen, in letters
to friends. It was touched upon lightly in the conclusion of
some verses he read to his Harvard classmates in June, 1929:

> Youth was a vale of doubt and hesitation;
> Now memory gilds it with a magic touch;
> Old age was horrid in anticipation;
> Now it has come, I like it very much.

The new feeling was more fully set forth in a poem that
appeared in *Scribner's Magazine* for July, 1929; and with this

affirmation of the state of mind to which the years had brought him the chronicle of his chief activities shall end:

LAST WORDS

The breezes of returning spring
  Blow kindlier than before:
The robins hop, the sparrows sing
  More sweetly than of yore,
For O, the gliding seasons swim
And bear me on their rippling brim
  To my not distant shore.

I'll strive no more to be a man:
  Cold world, bad world, Adieu!
I've done you all the good I can
  Or ever mean to do.
In fact — I say it in your ear —
It was a grand mistake, I fear,
  To try to better you.

The more I probed, the more I found
  The Evil's deeper source.
I digged: — the truth was underground;
  Star-gazed: — 'twas cosmic force.
And as the baffling years slipped by
The streams of hope were running dry
  In their meandering course.

True, in the flashing of a spade —
  The twinkling of a star —
A light from heaven would pierce the shade
  And show things as they are
But still I felt the world was sick;
For no one else would wield my pick
  Or read my calendar.

Ah truth! whatever truth may be,
  'Tis neither yours nor mine.
'Twill shine through taciturnity,
  Through broken speech 'twill shine.
Then wherefore sweat to have one's say? —
To save what cannot pass away,
  Or rescue the divine?

Letters

To S. S. Drury

325 W. 82, N.Y.
Feb. 17: 1919

Dear Dr. Drury

It seems to me on second thoughts rather absurd for me to write to a lot of the trustees; for I only have one thing to say, and I will write it to you and you can tell as much as you like of it to the trustees, or nothing.

During the last half century all American schools, charities, and churches have constantly needed more money, and the tendency has been to put business men on their boards — successful, practical, and, if possible, rich business men. The result is that such men preponderate in the management of our spiritual affairs.

There is a free-masonry among them which makes them trust their own kind, and distrust men who don't understand money, and men who haven't got money, because they regard such men as unsafe. This process has brought Harvard University to a standstill. I don't know what is going to become of it during the next twenty-five years. Its management is today a pile of corn-cobs and this is sure to be found out. It has happened innocently. No one is to blame.

Now in looking over the list of Trustees of St. Paul's they seem to me to be a strong lot of men to run a bank, just as the Harvard Corporation is a strong lot of men to run a bank; but the purely intellectual or spiritual element is weak. And I know that if you try to put on a man whose fitness is purely moral — such a man, for instance, as Prescott Evarts was thirty years ago (for he's too old now) you'll find that it can't be done without a cleaver. No one is to blame for this: it's the universal condition in America.

If Harvard had made it a rule to keep one man of purely intellectual pursuits — and one of their biggest men, Royce,

359

James, Palmer — on their board of Corporators the College would never have got into its present shape. William Lawrence won't do. He's too rich and not an intellectual.

Now a school-master is the whole school in one sense, but not in another; and no matter what you do for the school you can't protect it against the future — entirely. But it seems to me that you've got to regard the Board of Trustees as part of your charge, and introduce some tradition of pure spirit among them.... It crosses my mind that someone may suggest me. But I haven't gone on any board for twenty years. It means suffering for everyone; and I shall never go on another....

To Conrad Chapman

325 W. 82, *Feb.* 23: 1919

DEAR CON:

Dear Mo [1] and I had a lovely jaunt to Boston and three nights in the luxury of Fred Hall and Evelyn's palace which you know so well, where we occupied a floor with a corridor closed off between the rooms, breakfast brought up on trays, no callers, no dinners, no duties and lots of wandering conversation, music etchings, and essays read aloud by me — one a bad one which I am destroying because it is bad-hearted. It was a review of an odious book — autobiography of Henry Adams, a cheap, cynical book by an egoist who conceives himself to be an intellectual. Well, the odiousness of the man actually got into my essay on him. The Quartet by Loeffler — which we went on to hear is *modern* — and not very comprehensible to us, but we did our best, and swore it was great and beautiful — which I believe it is in its one mode....

We came back yesterday and since then I have written 20 notes, getting up a dinner of 16 at Dear Mo's club to introduce Hampden the actor to some rich and fashionables, also raising a fund of $8000 — to help him stage his Hamlet for a N.Y. run — also booming him generally. It's been good fun because it has gone successfully; but of course it's fatiguing sort of work and takes one off regular work.

[1] A family nickname for Mrs. Chapman.

E. and I had lunch with Mrs. Gardner in her palace. She's younger than ever and seems to have an ointment or philtre, gazes at her flowers and Titians, I think, and sucks in youth. She asked us to call her Isabella. Of course we couldn't refuse; but I'm not sure I can remember to do it. I think to be called Isabella is a philtre. I wonder what she intends about her palace and collections. She says she is going to live to be 150 and I shouldn't wonder a bit, but what then? She'll do something annoying, I'm sure — perhaps leave them to the Berlin Gallery, or to the Vatican, with the proviso that a Hohenzollern or a Papal Nuncio shall always inhabit the palace. This would be a delicious thorn in the side of Boston. . . .

Your loving

PAPA

To the same

NANCY, *Sept* 16: 1919.

DEAR CON . . .

We saw at Luxeuil les Bains a good many people — innkeepers and their families who had known Victor, for he stayed in their inns and gave dinners at their restaurants — and the American Escadrille were so long stationed there just before [they went to fighting at Bar le Duc] that the village — for it is a very small town — got to know them. The landlady of the Lion Verd, where dear M. and I spent two nights, knew Victor well, for he and the rest of American Aviation lived in her villa — 100 yards away. It was quite touching seeing her, for she gave such a true picture of Victor and imitated his way of speaking and his charming manner. He was the only one of the Americans who spoke French, and so was easily distinguished. The daughter of another landlady gave us a Kodak of 30 or 40 aviators, French and English, taken in the village street — Victor among them — which we had never seen and have borrowed to have it enlarged in Paris. Rockwell and Prince are buried at Luxeuil — or rather left there temporarily — for their families are going to take them to America, they say.

Now E. and I are at Nancy for three or four nights and are going to run up to Thiancourt — the cemetery to which Victor's body has been removed — with 4000 more Americans — and then sight see Metz and Toul and then back to Paris. Our sailings are for Oct. 8.

Sight-seeing is a good offset to the tragic end of these visitations — and after a day of putting flowers on graves of Rockwell, Prince — and talking with these people who really were very fond of Victor and profoundly moved by the whole American Aviation — and the rest of the Aviation — so many young men passing through their training and dining and living and rejoicing — and whom these landladies got to feel interested in — and then reading their deaths one after another the next month — It was a wonderful experience for the Luxeuil people — and splendid people they are. . . .

Your loving
PAPA

To the same

[*The first pages of this letter describe a fellow-passenger interested in improving the Boy Scout organizations in France.*]

On the Touraine
Oct. 15: 1919

. . . The work of these uplifters is to my mind more important than the League of Nations or any merely political scheming and wire pulling — though there's plenty of that involved in it. They qualify the future — they remake France and will remake Germany. They are the influence of America — and the American Mind is the balance wheel of the world today. Behind it all is the influence of the New Testament — which, by the way, this man is reading all the time — except when he stops to chat. He's an experienced old boy, and as clever as he can be, and plods away.

There seem to be four worlds — (1) The world of official politics (Harry White), (2) the world of newspaper work, intrigue and pushing of special matters (Willy Chanler), (3) the world of causes, reforms, Y.M.C.A., Boy Scouts, uplift etc., and lastly (4) the world of thought. And all of them are interlocked. The only one that is worth talking about to my mind is the world of causes — for the world of thought takes care of itself — (one can't get out of it). These causes affect matters 100 years hence and only become visible by degrees. The invasion of Europe by America is the most important thing I can see on the horizon. When you're in Paris every one talks chopped straw and the attention is on things of the moment, next week — every one excited about things which are really mere symptoms; and almost every one despairs of any real change or any big idea — e.g., the idea of educating the peasant, giving him public spirit and some knowledge of finance. At the present moment the peasants are rich. They have billions in their stockings — all the farm mortgages have been paid off. The peasant distrusts everything except specie and land. Farm land is being sold at fabulous prices — very foolish economy and sure to bring a crash. Now the peasantry won't pay taxes. They are not taxed. It would bring a revolution. In order to get a billion of francs out of the peasants the State is organizing a lottery — 1,000,000 frs. a week is to be distributed in prizes. The chances against the peasant are seven to one. Yet they say he will pay it — in this form. Now what a ghastly system of finance.

Nothing to do but make a campaign which may take twenty years to instruct the peasant. By the time you have got him waked up — he will have children as other farmers do — and France will be saved. At present the peasant is wall-eyed about money, money, money. Time out of mind he has hidden it in his stocking till — some Panama swindle relieved him of it. It's a psychological question and nothing will meet it except the enthusiasm of a bunch of reformers actuated by a sort of religious impulse — the antidote, for the Egoist which is killing the French is unselfishness. I was quite surprised to find Uncle Willy very sympathetic with this kind of view. As we grow older people reach somewhat the same point of view by different roads.

The condition of things in France is extraordinary — incredible. Neither the rich nor the poor pay taxes — I mean higher than before the war. Rich men will tell you that they haven't paid anything for four years. The moratorium is still in existence. Americans in Paris are taxed — and their taxes have been doubled. Nobody is back at work, everybody is disgruntled. The franc dropped last month to nine francs to the dollar and is now back at seven or eight. The only remedy is for the French to manufacture and export something and they *won't begin*. We saw $20,000 worth of tobacco rotting on the wharf at Havre. The government hasn't the gumption to use it. It was in bales in the leaf — probably American stuff. There are 40,000 autos and trucks — exposed to the weather and going to pieces at Bourg near Lyons. One of the papers had a photo of them. They are badly needed in the devastated districts — but no way has been found to sell or use them. The average Frenchman is cross, explosive, and insulting. It is a blessing to get out of the land....

Even good old Harry White was so exasperated with the nation the last time I saw him — for something they had done at the peace table — that he almost roared at them and begged me to go home and write them up. You see it's now eleven months since the armistice was signed — and time for some new era to begin.

Your loving
PAPA

To Robert Nichols

[*Copied from sheets headed with the words, 'Dear Chanler, Dear Mo insists on my sending you a copy of my letter to Robert Nichols.*]

Nov. 8, 1919

... It looks just now as if, for the next twenty-five years, every body's mind was going to be devoted to practical questions — uplift and hygiene and trade and horrid, odious, useful, moral things. But then nothing ever happens that seems about to happen. I confess that this housecleaning seems to me the most imminently important thing in the world, and if you say 'What will save France?' I should answer '*Boy Scouts*.' But this can't be so. The two months we spent in France left a terrible impression of the lack of private initiative in the French. Their history lacks Lollards, Bunyans, Cobbetts, Cobdens, Brights, popular agitators and Christian stirrers-up, humanizing levelers and lifters. The French are all brains and cliques: and they all have this in common, that they lack the spirit of self-help.

Over here, on the other hand, everything is a barn-raising.
Teachers' salaries? Everybody forms in line; periodicals
appear; conventions gather; people stop you in the street and
put their hand in your pocket. The world is to be saved
tomorrow, this is virtue, this is religion. If you want to
think about something else you're an enemy to mankind.
Then, perhaps, arises the idea ' if you don't want a Revolution
you must instruct labor; — make friends, be sensible; be
humane; get together; have councils, forums, committees; see
each other's point of view; break the shock —' and every one
turns out and rubs down Bolshevism, gives it the club, then
restoratives — a trained nurse. The war got us into the drive
habit, and trained a hundred thousand very able men and
women into how to make drives.

I don't think we are either virtuous or able enough to take
charge of Europe, and I think we shall be of much more value
to Europe if we stand outside (with the capacity we have of
getting excited once in a while on the right side) than if we
sent mandatories and muddled in conditions constantly. We
should certainly get at loggerheads with England or France
over some point — one can't tell what — and then where'd
we all be? . . .

But this is only to beguile and amuse your leisure moments;
poetry's the really important thing — whatever it is.

Yours affectionately

JOHN JAY CHAPMAN

To Chanler Chapman

[*Written on the back of the type-written sheets of ' Imaginary
Obituaries: The Passing of a Rural Philosopher. E. S. Martin is no
more*' — *for publication in 'Vanity Fair.' Chanler Chapman was
then at Grenoble, before entering Harvard.*]

Nov. 26, 1919. 325 W. 82

DEAR CHANLER

This is to amuse you. It will come out, I hope, with his
picture — some months hence. I got Ned Martin to give me
a photograph and told him I'd send him a copy. It will make
him laugh. But he won't know what it's about.

365

All this reminds me that there's going to be a time in your life when you have a devilish bad time. It will be when you ultimately come back to America to settle — at whatever age you do. There's no future elsewhere, as you have an American mind, and would be an exotic anywhere else: and for any one to hook on and get planted in here, who is American yet sees what America is, is a devilish hard job. Uncle Bob did it in middle life and with his eyes open, a rather remarkable thing to do, yet the making of him. In my days I was only abroad fifteen months — and positively had to return. But I shall never forget the hardness and dryness and horror of the experience. It's so ugly and ignorant, so bleak and unresponsive — so contented and unimaginative. I rather think it's getting better — but so little. I notice already a loss in the active-mindedness which the war brought on. The newspapers are more rigid: nothing to talk of: all shop. Business shop: art shop: charity shop. Clubdom subsiding to its normal state of a bore. Last summer we were *agacé* and suffering in France. We fell into America as into a warm inn, but being here, we are here — stupid old inn. The terms of the equation are changing for the better; but its elements will remain the same for some generations — possibly centuries.

Yesterday your Mama made a speech or speeches at a three days session of a ' good speech convention' at Cambridge. At the same time I was making an address at the Hudson Theatre on the education of children. These are serious and useful activities and fill our glowing imagination with convictions of progress and service to humanity.[1] But they are not lurid. . . .

What I was going to say is this: One never can find out anything about life, because the advantages are always disadvantages and the disadvantages advantages. All the European Buffet of cultivation — as you see in Harris's book [2] — tended to overfeed and belittle the clever men — Walt Whitman did *something-or-other* just because he was ignorant. I

---

[1] A few months earlier Chapman had written to his wife: 'I have now joined the Choir Visible, and shall rank with Henry van Dyke — a platform ornament without whom, etc.'

[2] 'Contemporary Portraits,' by Frank Harris.

don't like him much — only point to him as illustrating the conquest of temperament in a particular case.

Your loving

PAPA

I read this foregoing to dear Mo — who told me the story of Uncle Bob's first night in U. S. — at 325. He saw the door knob and burst into tears — and spent a night of agony and despair. She says, however, that Europe has become dilettante and that the U. S., though rough and ignorant, has the drive and vigor of art — (this apropos of a visit to Al Jolson as contrasted with the French players here) and she says you'll be at home here — and she's pretty clever — I *must admit*.

To the same

[ATLANTIC CITY]

Dec. 29, 1919

Judea — Israel — the Lost Tribes — lost no more! found — very much found, increased — multiplied — as the sands of the sea — upon the sands of the sea — in city of the sea — Atlantic City — with cliff dwellings of 10,000 souls each — and regurgitating with Hebrews — only Hebrews. Families of tens and dozens — grave old plodders, gay young friskers — angel Jews, siren Jewesses — puppy Jews — mastiff Jews — bulging matrons — spectacled backfish — golden-haired Jewish Dianas — sable-eyed Jewish Pucks, Jewish Mirandas — Romeos and Juliets, Jew Caesars — only no Shylock. It is a heathen menagerie of Israel. Only one Christian — a big Scottish Y.M.C.A. looking man who is starter of the façade of elevators — and is out of his real job just now, for I am sure that his real job is to watch the bathers in summer and save the drowners — when the nation is in the water. For they would never trust a Jew.

Dear Mo and I lie in bed, or on the beds and read Virgil aloud — also Le Nôtre and the journals. She has her meals sent up — so far — but I descend into the amphibious theatre and prowl amid the animals. The young I like. They submit to caresses and their parents are pleased. The young have aplomb as well as the old in Judea.

Food, cigars, clothing, bien être — this people understands

367

enjoyment. They are uncritical: life is a simple matter to them: — a bank account and the larder. No, they will never rule the world. They are too easily deflected — absorbed and satisfied. It is foolish to rule the world, and the Jew knows it. They are crumbling material for the hands of their leaders and ropes of sand. They have too much sense — and will go for the glittering garments and not murder Progress. They strike me as an inferior race in spite of their great advantages. Did it ever occur to you how much Napoleon must have despised the French? He had not a drop of French blood in his veins, and was born just before or just after Corsica was ceded to France. What sort of a nation must that be that can be ruled by such a shyster? At the time of his Brumaire coup d'état — three or four men could have done for him. But Frenchmen cannot act together. He ruled them by terror and espionage, by flummery and gloire, by their vanity and their basenesses. He made monkeys of them, — and today they are proud of him! But I ought not to foment your critical dislike of the French — and their ways and vanities. You are young, and easily influenced; and something I said might stick in your mind and cause a gangrene. But to return to the Jews, my long acquaintance with Klein and his club makes me at home with them — but I'm glad I haven't *more* Jewish blood in me than I have. I don't want any more. They are losing their quality by the loss of their education. These people don't know anything. They have no religion, no customs except eating and drinking.

Imagine the job of an American Jewish rabbi. They have good hearts and charities I know, but no thrills, and O my, they *look* so grotesque that I could never preach to them.

Your loving
PAPA

To the same

325 W. 82, *Jan.* 13: 1920

. . . Curious fact. You know Alexander says that all bad functionings, stuttering, colds, hysteria, twitchings, — almost anything you please — though they show at the extremities are *really* due to a kink or hitch in the bowels. West and

Alexander — both of them men of genius in a way — have found out this by methods and approaches and lines of thought that have nothing in common. Gets me back to the wisdom of the old Jews who really know a lot — and were always talking about their *bowels*. They yearned with their bowels — not their heart, they loved and feared and mourned and fought and repented with their *bowels*. It was the Latins who brought in the heart. The Greeks used to talk about the *liver* as the seat of the passions. Prometheus' liver, etc. The profounder natures of Israel located the seat of everything correctly — by sensation of course. They felt more keenly than the Greeks and Romans and gave a better account of it. . . .

To the same

325 W. 82, *Feb.* 10: 1920

DEAR CHANLER

. . . You heard about Charley Towne's dinner to be — at the Metropolitan — ten poets — one at each table — *whose works will live*. I wonder what C. Towne thinks posterity is going to occupy itself with. Why, there won't be time for strikes or uplift or revolutions. Just making the American poets live is going to occupy every one. All the same I'm glad of the movement. It's better than business, and somebody of your age — just below the horizon — if he does write anything good will get heard. The habit of reading poetry should be encouraged. I read Sophocles' 'Ajax' all day yesterday with a translation near by. I think it is my favorite. Ovid — I bought a copy of the 'Metamorphoses' this morning in the Loeb Classics. It's perfectly easy to learn to read Ovid as easily as a newspaper. I see a work which I intend to buy which collects the places where Shakespeare has referred to Ovid. Happy thought, read it before I go to the damn fool poets dinner — and make a few citations showing famous passages in Shakespeare — which he never would have had but for Golding's translation, for I'm quite sure Shakespeare didn't read the original, — as indeed some passages show. These modern American poets despise reading, and hate the idea of being indebted to the past. My hope is that the *move-*

ment of poetry in America will continue but that the present idiots will be replaced by a generation of folks now in the nursery who know a little more. I am sending you Masefield's 'Reynard the Fox' — which is charming for its own sake and its picture of England and important as reviving narrative poetry. Sassoon tells me that Masefield lives with a volume of Chaucer open before him — (I never could care about Chaucer — very much — it's chiefly for his pictures of contemporary life that I like him. The stories bore me. But then almost all stories bore me.)

The great thing with Greek and Latin classics is to take them lightly. If you stick too close you get to imitating them and it ruins you. Merely as inspiration, reminiscence, and idea they are splendid — as influence, vague. The sentences in the 'Ajax' fall like blocks of marble — building piers and balustrades. But if one should try to reproduce this effect one would become stilted and sham-Greek — as so many English people have done both in prose and verse. The people to imitate are the great English poets, for it is an indoctrination into poetry and into the language to do so. The imitative part merges in your own talent. Not so with the Classics. Milton would have become a greater poet if he had been told this in early life. Sorry I didn't know him then.

Your loving

PAPA

To Henry James

325 W. 82, *Feb.* 11, 1920

MY DEAR HENRY

What I really think is something like this: — The great romancers of the mid-century — V. Hugo, Dickens, Balzac — clothed their extravagantly romantic fiction in vivid grotesque figures and would have regarded themselves as realists — if the term had been invented. As the romantic *souffle* died out of the world their lessons and examples as realistic writers survived — and especially the followers of Balzac continued and refined and explored and became obsessed with externals — and as most of Balzac's themes are dark and deal with defects and shadows, his followers rather unconsciously developed a theory of fiction that should consist of the analysis of shadows and defects. If you read Flaubert or Goncourt or Maupassant, H. James, or Mrs. Wharton, you visit the writer with a personal responsibility for his preoccupations — you say he must be a bad-hearted man — and of course to some extent it is true that any theory of art that enjoins a close analysis of evil will leave you looking at a viscera or a cuticle — and do you harm. But this has probably less influence on the writer or artist than the non-artist would suppose — e.g., Mrs. Wharton is probably *not* so malicious or bad-hearted as we would think. To her this manner is the true road to great sincere *Fiction*.

In H. James's case the paradox becomes positively startling, for though his essentially misguided conceptions of the art of fiction ended by shadowing his life and damaging his temperament it never affected his extraordinarily warm heart and power of sympathy, benevolence, and personal kindness of all sorts.

Something of the same kind is true of Bernard Shaw — though he did some things — in his letter on the Titanic — and during the war — that show he is a sort of albino with certain corpuscles left out of his composition. This whole epoch of blighted literary talent must be judged together — and by a glance at the cloud above it. One sees the shadow in George Eliot and one feels it more in English writers than in Continental writers — because it is such a novelty and swears so with English traditions.

Yours

J. J. CHAPMAN

Curiously enough the thesis of W. James all through his horrid medium of psychology and kindred hallucinations is — 'Feeling must triumph.'

To Chanler Chapman

[Undated — 1920]

. . . As for ennui and that sort of thing — the worm that never dies — I notice that it leaves me as soon as I am doing something that has got to be done — and comes on when I am in search of a job. If I only had a talent for verse-writing and a wife that told me that I was just the man to write the great American epic — why, I'd be happy all my days and look forward to every sunrise with impatience. If I only was a jeweller, moving from one order to the next, with a table and a set of tools. As it is, I'm a miscellaneous, not to say hack, writer — and so long as a job lasts — e.g., this Plato — I'm content, and now that I've got myself a little fatigued over it, and have to stop, I begin to feel discontented. Who can tell what he is or does, or has done or will do? We get made into something or other and do something or other. The rarest thing to do is to write poetry and every one who has the talent and ambition ought to do it, or try to, for the work itself is the best and hardest there is and will do for him what nothing else can. I used to think it was very small potatoes to be a writer either of prose or verse: but I have come to believe so deeply that good writing is one of the things we happen to need more than anything else in America — and that the mere existence of a good page of it, no matter where published or by whom read, is a useful thing. In a way I have come to take myself at other people's valuation. They always were saying, O how you write, you write so well, and I didn't want to write — and at last I say — well, I can't do anything else — write away — write the next thing — write for *Vanity Fair* — who cares anyway? It's your chore. Something of the same thing will happen to you. It wasn't till about two years ago — at the age of 55 — that I submitted — so you may expect some years of turmoil, discontent, ennui, etc., and I dare say some day in reading this [you] would perceive a great many lies in it. But I should maintain that deep spiritual truth can only be expressed through a series of lies — and besides — no one is permitted to know the truth about himself. By the way, your good words about the lines about the drifting clouds — cause me to get them out and look at them — show them to Dear Mo — and send them to *Scribner's Magazine* which is going to print them.[1] So you see how you are encouraging young

---

[1] They were printed in *Scribner's*, August, 1920.

authors already. If in the next few years you should get out
any halfway decent small collection of verse, it would be
even more so.

Your loving

PAPA

To Mrs. William Astor Chanler

325 W. 82, N.Y.
Jan. 11: 1921

DEAR BEATRICE

. . . One thing good out of your illness is that it has
turned the rest of your family into saints. Willy, your
husband, tells his beads and looks like St. Jerome, and even
Ashley is touched with something like esoteric Buddhism.
You never saw such a subdued and holy bunch as they are.
Willy and his friend Lynch talking about politics and boot-
leggers and revolutions in Cuba — but *piano, sotto voce, con
sordino.* Chanler went back yesterday — very happy in spite
of his tonsils time lost. . . .

I wish these boys would grow up. This hovering and
wishing and hatching is going on a long time. I've had
about 35 years of it. What! First, bottles — milk bottles
on journeys, that's my earliest recollection of fatherhood —
milk bottles in drawing room cars. I know that hospital
so well I almost feel that I'm there when I think of you.

With love

JACK

To Émile Legouis

325 WEST 82ND STREET
NEW YORK CITY
Jan. 25: 1921

. . . By the way, I have got the big French edition of your
Wordsworth's *Jeunesse* — though it took me a year and I
had to send abroad and buy it second-hand. I didn't get it
for Wordsworth's sake, as I am tired of the old gent, and I
know more about him than any one need or ought to know.
It's an obfuscation. I liked him better before you and Harper
took him up. Why can't you let him alone!...

373

Both my boys are at Harvard — and (oh humiliation!) I
have to acknowledge that there is some good about Harvard
— their letters are full of enthusiastic talk about books, new
and old, music, acting, people, events, discussions, and interest in life. It must be that Lowell and all his death traps
and obscurantism of commercial ignorance are *unable to kill*
the intelligence of the boys. Certainly the boys I know —
and I get a glimpse into a whole group of them — are going
on in just the right time-honored way that inquisitive ambitious boys should go on at college — and are far ahead of
anything that existed at Harvard in my day — at least that's
my impression, and I never should have got it except through
the accident of having sons there and of going on there and
seeing a little of the life....

[*These verses were enclosed in a letter of February 6, 1921, to
Edward S. Martin. 'My feeling is that James was enormously
important to his own generation' — wrote Chapman, 'by breaking
down the barriers that prevented them from giving rein to their
instinctive feelings. Whether he will do this for a later time no one
can tell.' If the lines have been published before, they have not come
to light in print among Chapman's papers.*]

LINES WRITTEN IN WILLIAM JAMES'S 'PRINCIPLES OF
PSYCHOLOGY'

The devil sat back looking musty and glum —
  Nonplussed; he was reading Lord Kames.
'If you please, by your leave, my good sir, I am come
  To enquire about William James.'

'One on me!' said Old Nick, 'I have just had a blow:
  God said he was making a saint.
Said I, "That's absurd — mediaeval, you know."
  He succeeded: — there's my complaint!

'First let me explain: — each soul has a cleft,
  Is duplex and runs on a swivel;
It turns to the right or it turns to the left;
  One's God and the other's the devil.

374

'God makes the original what-you-m'y-call
 The concept, the fluid idea;
But I have the planting and placing of all
 That pertains to the now and the here.

'"Fiat," said the Lord, and a spirit flew out
 Which I fielded — short-stopped in a trice.
"I'll place it," said I, "in my strongest redoubt
 Of ignorance, stupor and vice."

'The slums will not do — for there's General Booth;
 Nor the farm — there's a heaven above it;
If I bury him deep he will bore to the truth,
 If I blind him, why then he'll *dream* of it.

'Hurrah! I have found it, I know just the place,
 The seraphim never can spot it;
The truth shall not find him, nor he know its face,
 I will plant him with those who have got it.

'O Hegel, O Kant, you're the culture I want,
 O physio-psychical age,
A death in the desert of technical cant,
 Is the natural death of a sage.

'In a neat, shallow plot I now planted the pod,
 In a soil made of asphalt and ashes.
The American college is further from God
 Than Hell with its warm human flashes.

'Behold the young grub with his teeth in the rind
 Of Psychology — Lord, what nutrition!
And yet a queer crackling inside and behind
 Gave glints of a sort of ignition.

'It was whimsical, mystical, personal, strong,
 And more deeply religiously James
That what should have been painting and might have been song
 Was warbled in O such hard names.

'While Science was sounding the rub-a-dub-dub
 Of her black-hearted logical strife
A dragon-fly joyously broke from the grub
 In a riot of sunshine and life.

375

'He roams every province — a luminous thing
    In zigzags evasive and wise —
With the shadow of Science like dust on his wing
    And the light of the Lord in his eyes.'

The devil sat back, looking musty and glum.
    'It's amazing,' said he, 'how he does it.
The thing he expresses is just Kingdom Come,
    And by Jove, Sir, I don't think he knows it!'

JOHN JAY CHAPMAN

January 3, 1921.

To Mrs. Henry Osborn Taylor

HARPER'S FERRY, *March* 28, 1921

MY DEAR MRS. TAYLOR: —
    . . . I wish we could have accepted your most hospitable
invitation. I hate to let the winter pass without a dinner
with you and Harry, but I'm afraid we shall be pushing
through to Barrytown as Elizabeth has dismantled the house.
I have a lot of things to tell Harry about History and all
that. I think that if he could enter practical politics for a
few years so as to come in contact with *practical* life and then
perhaps go into some business in South America and *work up*,
it would give him a grounding in human nature and protect
him from the influence of books and bookishness. They say
that the merchant marine gives a splendid opening. Elizabeth sends her love.
    A party of cheerful people are singing hymns. This too is
an element which I miss in Harry's writings.
            Yours sincerely and affectionately
                                    JOHN JAY CHAPMAN

To Robert Nichols

[*On his appointment to a professorship at Tokyo.*]

BARRYTOWN, N.Y.
May 18: 1921

    ... Well, I'm just delighted about your professorship.
Why, it's perfect, gives you some money — forces you to see

376

something of the world and feel respectable and be isolated. It will do you good; especially as you have these matrimonial events beyond to look forward to. I congratulate you. Why, man, if you were Keats, you'd have to go broke and die (nowadays just as he did) to get a hearing, and you're not Keats anyway, and besides — when I read 'Endymion' all through, as I did the other day, it makes me so extremely bored and is, much of it, such an atrocious nuisance and so bad in spots that I can almost vote with the reviewers.

Happy thought. If a man will only do *one* good thing — they forgive him all and will lie about everything he *ever* did for generations. — E.g., I can't find that Rupert Brooke did more than one good poem. But he ranks with P. Sidney and Spenser. There's a good deal of circumstance in the world. The only poet I really like is R. Burns. The rest are silken puppets and lady-birds anyway. . . .

By the way, don't roar and sing the English poets at the poor Japs. It would give a man a strange idea of say Chaucer or Pope — to hear you croon and bellow and break your heart over it — or the dialogue between Brutus and Cassius — done in the tempo and sentiment of 'When the hounds of Spring are in winter's traces.' I'd like to attend one of your lectures behind a screen — and trying to pretend I was an oriental and had never heard of Shelley. Poets are bad critics — and *ought* to be — and I'm extremely glad it should be so. I don't doubt that you will give them something better than good criticism.

Yours affectionately
JOHN JAY CHAPMAN

To Elizabeth Chanler Chapman

[*After a lecture by John Cowper Powys.*]

Thursday, May 26, TAVERN CLUB, 1921

Chanler's prophet was not in his best form, and had a poor subject — Oscar Wilde — who didn't lend himself to the sort of lecture-treatment Powys deals in. Powys is a Welshman of 56 with a red wig, chiselled features, a stoop, a doctor's gown, handsome in a way and yet *manqué* with a queer

377

look as of wild man or museum freak. He is a disconnected, falsetto Anglican, not a Catholic, lives with a brotherhood who puts him up when in Boston — hates Puritans and the English Church, dotes on beauty and worship, is a dyspeptic who diets except on queer food at odd hours — likes to surprise, shock and amuse, has no money — is charming personally — frank, warm, and clever. Lectured too long, of course, and made one or two very clever remarks — e.g., as to the difference between Shaw who is cruel and is enjoyed by middle-aged people — and Wilde whose cynicism is gay and amusing and is enjoyed by the young — also while protesting against the obscene interest the public might take — he developed that side of it — furiously and over and over again — till I almost made a speech at the end — to say how that 'those of us who had come out of that obscene curiosity (so much reprobated by Mr. P.) were *not disappointed.*'

I went up and spoke to him afterwards — to tell him I thought he took W. too seriously — for W. was really an Irish adventurer whose guns weren't heavy enough to tell in the real world — so he dressed oddly and took handsprings into great houses. What W. really was was the best salon-talker in Europe. He, Whistler, Shaw, Chesterton — are all zanys *first.*

Powys was most agreeable, and said he rather thought there was a good deal in this. The trouble with him is he has become a hack. You see he's a queer dick himself, or else with his wit and brilliancy, reading, and enthusiasm he'd have shone in the church or at the bar or something — and so fate has shunted him off to lecture to barbarians — and it's told on his brains.

Chanler saw all this and developed the thesis himself. At one moment in the lecture the ourangoutang made me angry and I roared like a bull and shook the chandelier — quite unexpectedly to myself — but the episode passed and I recovered my equanimity. . . .

378

To George Dudley Seymour

SYLVANIA
BARRYTOWN-ON-HUDSON
July 4: 1921

DEAR GEORGE:

I am very sorry to hear of the death of your sister — and about the old house of which you are so fond,[1] and I know how poignant those feelings are in people who have the passionate attachment to the past which you have more than any one I ever met. But I still cannot think of you as the Last Leaf. You are more like some bloomin' lilac or magnolia tree in a New England front yard, holding its own against the trolley, and garages and Italian fruit terraces that infest the once rural neighborhood. And a most ungrateful, calamitous, squawking old tree you are too, refugiating and transplanting yourself to a Birthplace, and twining yourself about a heroic, historic figure till I swear I don't know which is you and which is Nathan Hale. You have me confused, as the Irish say.

And, by Jove, if I don't write you up some day in an essay on Early American Spoons. If I don't twine the twiner and eglantine you in the manner of Washington Irving — and make John Burroughs look like thirty cents.

Why, you're just the kind of subject that the American public never gets tired of — can't have too many of. Ik Marvel, by Jove, Thoreau — I'm going to frame you in a description of 'Old Shropshire' that will make Joseph Addison's mouth water — and hang you as the best American worthy of the century. Damn *me* — I hadn't thought of this before — but I'll do it with consummate art; for you have all the points —

And some new ones.

July 5.

My mother died about a month ago. She had enjoyed life tremendously up to about two months before her end; but since then had suffered and worried so much, and gone through so many remedies for the irremediable that her death which was painless, and unconscious, came as a release.

---

[1] The birthplace of Nathan Hale, owned by Mr. Seymour.

I haven't got used to it yet — and still find myself laying out my movements, plans, or a day in town, or letters to be written — with her in them. . . .

To Edward S. Martin

CAMDEN, MAINE
Aug. 7, 1921

DEAR NED:

Your postal recalls vague memories in my mind. If I could only recall you distinctly — and what you are. It seems that years ago, just as I was falling asleep, I was thinking of such a man, and pondering, groping — waving an idle hand in the tide — for a way of conveying to some such person what it was I meant by the Intellect. Then I suppose I fell asleep — all after that is vacancy. A lady I met at lunch today mentioned your name and I said — just to make conversation, for it was one of those lunches — 'What do you suppose he would have been like if he hadn't been deaf?' She said after a pause and a flash of intuition — 'He'd have been spoiled.' Clever, wasn't it? — though I don't agree.

Think of Dana Gibson being able to support a house, steam launches — a cow, a horse, maid-servants — a little colony — by drawing those absurd pictures — all just alike — for a greedy insatiable public that consumes and consumes. And you in those paragraphs — lucubrations — lulucubrations — and lulucucubrations. It's monstrous, but most interesting — I believe that if I could solve that I could find the answer to most anything. . . .

This here island you remember, for you once were up here. It's a good place to grow old in, too good — for it makes you in love with solitude — which is bad. My wife and I have read any quantity of Spanish novels — all of them about religion and the Roman Church — very informing — some of them favorable, some hostile. The thing I don't like in all of them is that apparently there's no privacy in Spain. Everybody's always talking about their inmost nature — just as if it was a political question — and no one hesitates to drag every possible intimate instinct to the light and have a bally-whang time over it for hours. I get the impression that this is one of the draw-backs of the Roman religion. It's *indecent* — from a Protestant point of view. I rather prefer the simple brutality of ancient Rome and the classics. You see, the R. Church must have an answer to *everything*. Every possible question has some answer. (This is very contrary to nature — for most questions have no answers.) In the finding of these answers the viscera of the parties have to be held open with tongs and examined. — Reading a Spanish novel consists in examining the viscera of people who are under the excitement of various passions — generally love — by the light of Catholic dogmas.

Now I'm going on with a new one which we are just beginning.

Yours aff.

J. J. C.

To *Rosalind Richards*

[*After the death of her sister*]

HOTEL EXCELSIOR, ROME
May 10, 1922

DEAR ROSALIND:

The memorials of Alice are the most remarkable I ever saw. The one by the school — is as good as Pericles' oration and without the touch of preciosity that is in everything Athenian — and the appeal to local vanity which one cannot help feeling in those celebrated things. And Montgomery's hymn — perfect. We are giving them to Alida, who is here with most of her family — and whom we have seen quite a lot. One cannot mourn over such a life and death. The thing that gives me most joy is the articulateness of the eulogies. One thinks of New England as conscience-bound and too inward — but here are wreaths and paeans — songs, spiritual deliverance pouring out like the streams at Tivoli. If she did *this* — among the rest of her gifts to the town — she did what Emerson himself couldn't do. Most impressive documents — and would have pleased Grandfather Howe — to say nothing of the grandmother. It seems that your father and mother have had the most happy and unclouded lives of anyone one can think of. Please give them my love.

And don't you go mourning at the thought that on your death the shops will not, probably, be closed, nor many sky-tormenting columns raised. For consider this: that should these rites be paid to everyone business could not go on; nor could the fields be used for the grateful olive and the sacred vine, for they would be encumbered with innumerable crosses, shrines, and storied sarcophagi. Therefore be content with the humbleness of your lot, and persuade yourself that the acts of the lowly reach out unseen to those ends which genius and art strive to express in lasting form. . . .

To Robert Nichols

12 CRICK ROAD,
OXFORD, *June* 21: 1922

. . . I had a Corpus Christi dinner at Cambridge, and both of us a Sunday at Eton. The latter visit very perfect in its kind — all the frills on and Eton at its best. Yet there is something about any *school* so wounding to the aesthetic feelings — that it leaves me lame for a week. I feel like a crushed thing still. (It's just the same in America.)

I think also that the helpless condition of one who is being *shown things* — towers, manuscripts — lawns — monuments — inscriptions to men killed in the war — first editions — (better than some one else's copy —) views from the window — rooms occupied by Charles I — I say the helpless ejaculation of — wonderful! Indeed! extraordinary, etc. — Something goes out of him — and deflates the soul of him. . . .

Yours affly
J. J. C.

To Elizabeth Chanler Chapman

OXFORD, 12 *Oct.*, 1922

. . . Read the Bible all the morning. . . . the whole of the Acts straight through. It certainly is a wonderful piece of narration and gives a splendid idea of Paul — whose *conduct* was always masterly. He was a master of men as

an organizer. From the Epistles one gets a much less grand-
iose impression — some of them being almost incomprehensible — especially without knowing the ins and outs of
local squabbles and backslidings, or guessing about them.
Read the Epistle to Hebrews. The congregation of converted Jews at Jerusalem — must have had the worst time
of any — they really were solitary and persecuted — and
couldn't stand the loss of their comforts. The covenants,
the Levites, the Urim and Thummim. They couldn't stand the
solitude. They began to give way. And St. Paul pulls them
together by showing in a wonderfully copious, eloquent, in-
genious review of Jewish history that they are as good as
anybody and really have a *new kind* of all these precious paraphernalia — ending up with a sublime simile 'We have an
altar, whereof they have no right to eat who serve the taber-
nacle. For the bodies of those beasts whose blood is brought
into the sanctuary by the high priest for sin, are burned
without the camp. Wherefore, Jesus also, that he might
sanctify the people with his own blood suffered without the
gate. Let us go forth therefore unto him without the camp,
bearing his reproach.'

These huddling backsliders — felt that they were *without
the camp*.

As for St. Paul's figures of speech — they were so clear
that they controlled a large part of Protestant thought —
fourteen centuries later — and caused whole communities to
adopt the old Jewish synagogue as an incubator grandmother
of their own. St. Paul kept the old synagogue alive by his
brilliance — or preserved it rather for habitation. His flight
about Christ as a high priest after the order of Melchizedek
is an imaginative piece of poetic extravagance — so out of
keeping with Christ as to be almost unpleasant. It's in his
line of 'all things to all men,' 'the unknown God,' etc.

JACK

I am beginning to see what an extraordinary man he was
— and after all this Jewish system, the legend, had been his
education. He had been impassioned for the hieratic, constitutional side of it, and his translation of it to suit Christianity had probably been done for himself and as the after-

math of his sudden conversion. They are too wonderful to
have been improvised. . . .

To Langdon Mitchell

325 W. 82, *Nov.* 17: 1922

DEAR LANGDON,

Many thanks for yours. I went back alone to Oxford on
Oct. 1, and spent a month there — gave dinners to boys and
took them auto rides — also loafed, read, and wrote, and had
a splendid time. The don is a study. His habits and nature
are well known — only he is *more so.* I couldn't believe that
he could be as much so as he is, also he is very similar. If
you see forty of them in procession at the honorary degree
ceremonies — they have the same age, same expression, *same
walk.* Their caps nod in the same way — they clutch at their
gowns in the same vague helpless way — and they have the
same mock humility — being, of course, the most stuck-up
men in the universe. Some people say they are soothed by
dons. I couldn't get as far as that, but I got so as not to mind
them.

All the same I'm convinced that they perform some cryptic
service to cultivation which nothing else could do. (I don't
say it's wholly good.) The only thing *certain* about it is that
it makes for gentle external manners. Well, that's much.
You boil alive so many gentlemen — most of whom would be
boiled anyway — and you generate this refining influence.
They are an artificial aristocracy — the result of self-per-
petuation and natural selection; and I couldn't tell why I felt
so much at home at their dinners and after dinners till it
flashed upon me — the Porcellian Club — same spirit —
same correct, quiet, effete smug, 18th century gentlemanliness.
It's a good deal like old Philadelphia — only less hearty.
The Philadelphians are in the outer world after all. The dons
and the Porcellians are in a fenced off, exotic place. By the
way — as to pure luxury — I don't think anything in the
world equals it — for a single man. Of course this luxury
ruins their intellect — but then, as I say, you never can be
sure that anything is lost by their seclusion. I am all for
them.

Please give my kind remembrances to Mrs. Mitchell and the young lady.

Your aff.

J. J. C.

To Edward S. Martin

[*The portions of this correspondence written before December 15 were answered on December 13 by Mr. Martin — thus in part: 'Ministers of grace defend us! What is Martin that such an INTELLECT as yours should be mindful of him. . . . I don't believe you have read a line of Martin's writings for twenty years. Certainly you are all off about his "success" as a writer. . . . Martin is an indolent old hack and a back number. . . . Switch your mind off Martin and read Frank Crane on the back page of the 'Globe.' Crane is still a going concern.'*]

325 W. 82, *Dec.* 11: 1922

DEAR NED:

It seems to me the consolatory reflection is that all those things we were talking about today — both the mystical ones and the practical — would be understood and substantially agreed to by millions of persons in America (they would be incomprehensible to any one else), and the land is being visited by a big spiritual vision of some sort. Whatever we do or say is somehow a part of it and furthers it; and the more detachedly, and as it were irresponsibly, we give way to its intimations the more we assist.

Dec. 11. Now the curious part of it is that all these people in America — from whatever point they started out or wherever they were trying to go — all meet at this focus of mystical belief. There never was anyone with more practical notions, or less under the belief that he was *religious* in his aims, than I. I wanted to attack practical evils — find out about them anyway, affront and examine them, understand them — and I set out by experiment and analysis to deal with them as a workaday problem. And gradually under inspection and ratiocination they turned into spiritual things, mystical elements, and went back into the envelope of religious truth.

385

Nothing else but religious truth was involved. It happened to me apropos of reform movements, to the next man in medicine, to the next in hygiene, in education, in literary work — (look at Winston Churchill). Surely all of us were toys in a shop, and were being turned by the same dynamo — we all approach more nearly all the time to a common frame of mind and temperament — a common sense of helplessness — we who were going to be so powerful and triumphant.

Dec. 12. On the other hand was there ever a man more thoroughly gone to the devil than E. S. M.? — Bound, hand and foot, and delivered to the lethal chamber of cringing popularity. It came over me at breakfast this morning. 'Why, in his cradle he must have smiled with his gums for fear of hurting the toys in the nursery' — Nurse, nurse, he has nursed his public — out of doors, gum shoes; in doors, felt slippers; in bed, knitted socks — silken. I have been wrong, wrong, about this man and given credit to miracle what was done by tact. I have always said — 'No: Ned Martin is honest; he talks what is in his mind and somehow his mind is a public average, a side-walk mind that goes and stops with the street: when the street is blocked it is blocked.' But now I see it all as a diabolical example of the worst American quality — subservience, careful slavery. This thought came to me at breakfast. 'If Ned Martin should write a book on Shakespeare thousands of people would read it. Why? Because he knows nothing about Shakespeare and don't want to know anything about him; and he would so talk about Shakespeare as to make his clients think they were exactly right in not knowing and not wanting to know. Tell 'em nothing: that's the secret.'

After all when a man makes money by writing in America it's a pretty sure indication that he's a bad man. Not to speak of best sellers and Mrs. Wharton and her flesh pots and jam pots, take Owen Wister — Ellery Sedgwick — Mark Howe has written a book about Mrs. Fields that sold 4000 copies the first month. Then there was E. S. Martin. I *knew* E. S. Martin. He was a deaf man — or else he pretended to be deaf — a much older man than I, and when I first remember him he was living at 1744 Broadway and making up a page a week for *Harper's Weekly*. He had a square yard of brown paper on which he pasted scraps cut from newspapers. The paper he stole. Nothing but the glue was his own. In this way he trained himself. Then he found he could get on without the glue — his style was the glue. He was a man of a very gentlemanly exterior. He amassed a large fortune and went to his grave respected by all. And yet at the Day of Judgment I'd rather be Caesar Borgia or John D. Rockefeller than that man. It comes over me in the night sometimes. Money is the root of all evil.

Dec. 15: 1922. Dear Ned, It's not that: it is that I have an uncertain sense of humor — which gets out of the socket. I thought that letter was a funny letter, gay, humorous — admirable fooling sort of thing. It don't make much difference with you. But I do it with other people. I am very sorry. Destroy the letter. *I will reform.*

Prophets? It's the age of prophets — and I am opening a counter at the Fair. Yesterday I went into a typewriting establishment — where I hadn't been for a year or two. They do stage work — two humorous Irishmen and twenty young Jewesses. The Irishman at the head (they had done some anti-Catholic papers for me) — grasped me warmly by the hand and cried out to his brother, 'Here's one of our sages!' The only thing I don't like is when a brother prophet — like, e.g., Richard Cabot of Boston — keeps on his Vatican manner — and herds me by his greeting in the street. There ought to be some free masonry and dropping of shop between prophets who pretend to be gentlemen.

To Elizabeth Chanler Chapman

[*This relates to the small wooden cross already mentioned. See ante, p. 162.*]

March 5, 1923

The cross is perfect: — size, proportions, and wood. I adore it — which is right. I shall keep it by my bed, as otherwise it will get broken. I was putting into my 'Letters and Religion' essay a remark about the cross — (which has been

used so much as to become a mere architectural member) —
but yet remains a symbol to people in tight places — where
the mind fails — or can't be in operation all the time — people keep hold of a cross as a humanizing — and a personal
thing. It speaks to the touch. . . .

To Mrs. William Astor Chanler

325 WEST 82ND STREET
NEW YORK CITY
Feb. 21: 1923

DEAR BEATRICE

All that you say seems to show a profoundly mistaken point
of view. For surely sculpture, as now practised among us, is
so fragmentary, half-clad, and beggarly an art — as to be
hardly an art at all, but rather a street parade by children on
Thanksgiving day, who mimic what they imagine to have
been the customs of some one's ancestors at some time in the
past.

If any Greek could have seen any bit of our unpainted,
staring, stiff, eccentric, experimental modern sculpture, he
would have asked — 'What is it for, and what do you intend
to do with it?'

Whereas *painting* is really a fine-art and the most difficult of
them all. Witness this following: — that anyone can model.
I have a niece who models — five of them, two sisters-in-law,
an aunt, and my mother's first cousin (now no more) but a
talented sculptress who made a faun so life-like that it had to
be reduced in scale and used, as a pair, for a bookrack. Did
you, by chance, ever see Sarah Blanket's statuette called the
Swimmer? — in which a bathing suit was rendered so life-like
that the clothesline reached down for it and the sculptress lost
her life in defending her model?

Very likely you *knew* Joan Scopalozzi — who lived in East
19th Street and supported herself for years by making plaques
— an American woman if ever there was one — who married
an Italian. Killed or lost the Italian and — but what I want
to say is — Do you seriously intend to take up sculpture in the
way these women have done: or merely to dibble-dabble in it?

Your true Friend

To the same

[*A bust of Chapman had just been made by the Russian sculptor, Seraphin Sondbinin.*]

SYLVANIA
BARRYTOWN-ON-HUDSON
July 3: 1923

DEAR BEATRICE

Elizabeth and I went to see the bust. It is in Scott and Fowles strong room and no eye is to view it till the great moment. It is undoubtedly the finest bust of modern times. It is rather more like Michael Angelo than like me — and where it leaves off resembling Michael Angelo it moves on to John Brown, Brahms, Victor Hugo, Euripides — (only better looking). The trouble is that people will say — 'But where are the *works* of this man?' I am having an inscription in archaic Greek incised on the neck — saying 'The works of this man perished in the Eruption of Vesuvius.' Think of poor old *père de famille* Sondbinin having done a thing like that! I must *do* something for Sondbinin — mention him in my book about Russia....

We had a house party for three days and a dance — and I was up against it — and it bored a hole through me — in the pit of my stomach — there is a round empty place that throbs like chaos and sometimes aches like echoing eternity. This will pass in a few months, I suppose.

O that beautiful Appolonia — is she at the island? — take this oak leaf and lay it on her forehead for me, and say to her that in America it is the symbol of constancy and is sent to her by one who must be forever nameless. The purest passions I have had have been for women whom I have never seen. But next to those there is a kind of love that goes out toward handsome housemaids whom the conventions, wives, children, and accidents of the world, prevent us from ever knowing — often from ever even speaking to — and so they remain images of loveliness — the inspirations from which painters build their pictures — (when they can). Something that is better than either life or art. Say all this to Appolonia when she brings in the macaroni — but as for me I am safer in writing it to you than I should be in saying it with my eyes while my mouth is full of macaroni — which (to an Italian) is love's supreme moment.

Yours affectionately

JACK

To the same

PRIDES CROSSING
July 25: 1923

DEAR BEATRICE

Our hearts go back to the little cottage and the simple life. We have expanded over a room each, connecting by a door and each room is 24 × 25 without a pin cushion, ornament or curtain, and five patent windows in each — (8 ft. by 8 in size) — with no blinds and a system of opening and shutting by bronze levers that don't work and novel wire frames that snap on the dark black rollershades and get tied with mechanical problems. It is as cold as winter — a rainstorm of the arctic kind. No fires in the vast semi-gothic fire places (10 by 6) designed for Yule logs. But — as Amory doesn't get up till 11 — I have sent for the factotum — (fac nothing) old domestic tyrant manservant, and got him to fetch andirons and wood and we are going to try out one of the chimneys. Such is the household of the old bachelor.... A dinner of eight last night, old friends of mine and very nice people — and more intelligent than you'd expect. Another tonight. At the back of the house 100 acres of gorges and glens like the scenery in Wagner — gigantic spruces, ferns and rocks — untouched forest — heaped rocks 50 ft. high and small wander-paths up and down. When I was married for the first time I was brought down by Amory in his yacht to the old house and walked in procession through the woods to the Brimmers' house next door through the woods and was married by Cotty Peabody and another priest amid the Boston princes. There's a glimpse for you of the antique world!

The idiot millionaire sons of the clever men who discovered this shore and lived on it without spoiling it — for it is wooded to the water's edge with trees as big as those on the Hudson — are moving away and all the places are for sale. The fire is now magnificent and life takes on a warmer hue.

This house, you see, was recently built by Amory — a sort of feudal palace — to leave to his niece, who will sell it to a boys' club as the Brimmer house has been sold last year to a girls' boarding-school.

Elizabeth, who was very comfortable five minutes ago — sunk in the Psalms — thought it was about time to write to Miss Montgomery and reached for a piece of writing paper — not remarking that on top of the paper was a small glass inkstand filled to the brim — the only thing furnished with appropriate contents in the room — she clutched both paper and inkstand dreamily — and turned over in bed — waving them in the manner of Barbara Frietchie — whereupon a black rain descended on sheets, blankets, pillowcases and nightgown; and her small white hand, like that of Medea, dripped with black gore. She is now cleaning the blanket *tant bien que mal* with hot water and what is left of the boiled milk of breakfast — hoping for the best. One should never give up hope. My one thought, of course, was — you divine it — 'So glad I didn't do it' — joy in the midst of calamity.

We are going to suggest to Conrad to visit Dark Harbor and take in a glimpse of the Puritan sunset on the shore here — the embers of social life in America. I had a very able, fiery, eloquent letter from him on the Prohibition question — putting me down for my views on drink — and showing that beneath his studious exterior there lives a doctrinal tyrant and reformer who means to settle things — raise up Humanity, etc. If there are more like him in his generation — it means farewell to tobacco. He is a man entirely interested in the practical world — a new, terrible demon of uplift. Poor America! can she produce but one type of virtue? But I'm not dead yet and shall pierce him with Emersonian fire. Farewell. Continue your innocent life and your domestic round. Many a poorer woman than you has nourished heroes.

Love and blessings
JACK

To Edward S. Martin

BARRYTOWN, N.Y.
Aug. 16: 1923

DEAR NED,

So much moving around this summer — boys home — guests about and serious things — that I have somewhat neglected you — and fear this may find you overgrown with weeds — and rank opinions such as sprout of themselves in deserted farm-land — and in farmers' annuals. What a compendium of popular errors are your writings! Have you ever thought of that? — an imperishable priceless record — like the fossils and the pits where antediluvian man has left his simple instruments — stone hammers and wise saws made of whalebone. One will be able to reconstruct the American of the 20th Century — with every knob and knuckle and place all his quaint idols in a row. My! it is an interesting idea — his totems and phrases of pious cant against pestilence — fever charms and college cries, his uplift and service, his war cries and peace cries — and the steady thrum of his deepest chord that says 'all's well, all's well' — when it *Wasn't*, you know.

Some day I shall head a party sent out by the Museum of Natural and Artificial History and paid for by Fairfield Osborn and after leading them up and down and round about I shall pause impressively — and say 'Dig here.' ...

Yours aff.

J. J. C.

To Mrs. William Astor Chanler

SYLVANIA
BARRYTOWN-ON-HUDSON
Saturday, Oct. 12 (about), 1923

DEAR BEATRICE ...

Sometimes I lie awake at night and think about my bust. I don't suppose enough people will ever see it. I think there ought to be a few copies made for museums and public parks, and perhaps here and there a rotunda with a copy in it.

Do you suppose — but don't repeat this — I mean do you suppose it is a little theatrical and that in seven or eight hundred years and during some period of very reticent classic taste somebody may think it *exaggerated*, and suggest that I didn't really look like that? That is what keeps me awake sometimes. Don't *write* me about this but tell me when you see me. For in writing you might say something that *hurt* me, and then I couldn't get it explained without waiting *several days*. I took somebody to see the bust the other day — I forget who it was. I forgot all about him when the store man carted the bust in (they ought to have two men) — lugged it in — and there it raged and stormed and radiated and dominated every thing like — John the Baptist or Michael Angelo or Victor Hugo in Hades.

Your affectionate
JACK

To Robert Nichols

BARRYTOWN, N.Y.
Nov. 12: 1923

DEAR ROBERT:

A *very* beautiful copy of your 'Fantastica' has come from Chatto and Windus — really, I should say, a perfect book — lovely thin paper, lovely print, and a truly appropriate red mottled smooth cover. I envy any one's having such a book and especially the author. Now in a calmer mood and soothed by all these external appeals I am going from time to time to try again to understand the *sort* of appeal the inner art essays to make upon the mind. I will read in it lying down, leaning on a sun dial, over a dying fire, with toast and muffins, in church, at the races, after Goethe, before Hobbes. I will conceal it under a copy of Thomas Aquinas and then peep into it as if I were a monk and it were stolen sweets — or put it with the new popular essays about the colored perils and general over-population of the world so as to strike into it unexpectedly. It is a humorous book — I can see that — humor of the metaphysical Gargantuan type — perhaps like Swift or Carlyle — perhaps like Sterne — or Lucian — I must give it a show, you know. My mind is destroyed by having read too many things and read too carefully. Still, that is a regulation type of mind and the book ought to mean something even to them, that kind.

We want to know about your plans and whereabouts. I still believe you are most needed in an American college — any college — male or female — just to flash some vitality into them and stir up the faculty and students. You are the element they need — except that you are still so young that you may have become modified even as I write. Perhaps I ought to *see* you again before I indorse you. Japan is a strange unknown influence — and so are earthquakes.

This summer I wrote quite a ponderous essay on Carlyle — to clear my mind. He's a rabid chimera, *bombinans in vacuo* — and I can't be sure that I've got him snap-shotted. He was once a popular writer, a being regarded by contemporaries as a classic — that's the key to him somehow. Of course no one cares a rap for him today — except perhaps a few gnarled veterans who can't get over their youth. One would have to dig them out in order to knock them on the head and say 'Ho! you there! I'm going to write about Carlyle.' Incidentally your friend Goethe comes in for a little gentle tapping and arranging of his hair.

Do write us a line and give my kindest thoughts to Mrs. Robert.

Yours affectionately

JOHN JAY CHAPMAN

To Émile Legouis

[*M. Legouis published 'Wordsworth and Annette Vallon' in 1922, and in 1923 a lecture, 'Wordsworth in a New Light.'*]

325 W 82 N.Y. *Nov.* 18, 1923

MY DEAR LEGOUIS:

Your latest on Wordsworth is the best thing that has been written in French since Pascal. I sent my copy to Professor Palmer — very reluctantly — torn by the conflicting thoughts of losing it and the desire to *tease* him. For he is shipwrecked, you know — having for 56 years taught classes and written essays about the moral greatness of our Friend W. W. Palmer once told me that Wordsworth was 'the fashioner of his soul.' It's no joke to find out at the age of 92 that your soul has been fashioned all wrong. (I laugh at nights over him.) As for you, the case is not so serious; though your endeavours in the earlier book to save the master and let him go down with his shirtfront in decent order and some expression of gravity on his brow were manful. O, the intellectual is hard to recover. A shock disturbs him like a fine watch — whereas a $3 watch can be heaved at a cat without damage. The man in the street saw at once that the Statue had had a fall, which no adjustments of lighting and drapery could ever conceal. But, in my regrets over the apparent triumph of mid-Victorian respectability, I console myself with reflecting that the peccadillos of his early days undoubtedly caused W. W. infinitely more suffering than if he had had the thing out and borne the brunt of it — for he was in a funk all his life. His poetry too would have been improved — and supplied with just what it lacks if he had played the man. Hurray for the French Archives! But the moral is: travel in Italy. (E.g., Suppose Goethe had gone on a Franzoesische Reise! — Devilish sharp fellow, Goethe. Another moral: — Avoid Crabs and Robinsons: Crabs cling and Robinsons keep diaries. They make notches on sticks — if you deprive them of pen and paper.)

An Englishman once said to me, when talking about the inevitable partizanship of mankind, that it was well known in London that when two busses collided the people on top of each bus took the side of their own driver with fervor. This has become a family fable with us; and while I was reading your paper aloud to my wife she exclaimed — 'He's on the French bus now!' ...

Yours affectionately

JOHN JAY CHAPMAN

To the same

325 W. 82, *Dec.* 23: 1923

MY DEAR LEGOUIS

Aha! Your book about Spenser has come. The only thing is — I was reading Spenser. I read him quite a lot last summer and was beginning to understand him a little, or think I did — and now comes your book interposing itself and menacing my new peace.

Legouis, I hate you. These Frenchmen make life too complicated. One of them has written a book on Shelley. Now Shelley is a curious and difficult creature — and I have never had the heart or leisure to try to understand him. But to try to unravel what truth may be at the bottom of a Frenchman's idea of Shelley is a thought that suffocates me. And yet I am surrounded by people who say, 'Such a lovely book!' These people, in their turn, become the problem, and *des Menschen ganzer Jammer fässt mich an.*

All the same, I shall be sending *you* a book in a month or two — revenge is sweet....

Yours affly.

JOHN JAY CHAPMAN

To Henry Osborn Taylor

325 W. 82, N.Y.C., *Dec.* 30, 1923

DEAR HARRY,

I hate to say these things to you — not for fear of hurting your feelings — but because I fear you may not understand them. Your night cap is so tight on. A year or two ago I began to observe that the universe was getting more comfortable — in spite of the things one saw in the newspapers. It seemed, at least, that there was one man in it who had acquitted himself fairly well, and need not alarm himself too much about assisting the whole affair any further. This pleasant sense of security was contemporaneous with a change of diet (toward lighter food in the middle of the day) — with a distinct joy in early bed; and with a new general benevolence toward the foibles of others. A sort of philosophic charity which began at home, extended itself insensibly toward others. — They too had done their best, no doubt, etc. (It hasn't yet reached your case, though I see you in a more possible favorable light than formerly.) A distinct, well-ordered and profound philosophy was settling down upon me. It was old age. And the philosophies of the world must be catalogued and understood, not according to sects and dogmas, but according to periods of short-gevity, middle-gevity and long-gevity. These are what really control us.

The rest is illusion.

Yours affectionately

JACK

To Leonard L. Mackall

325 WEST 82ND STREET
NEW YORK CITY
Jan. 20, 1924

DEAR LEONARD:

You will be wondering why we are not turning up. The reason is that I am wearing summer underclothes and we are afraid to go South for fear of the heat; and my wife has been perfectly well — never well for years — and it would be rather impious to go away in search of health — the sort of thing that is apt to be punished, you know. Every now and then I ask her what are her latest views on the subject — and get only the answer of the Sibyl — which means whatever you like.

I have been doing a great deal of nothing at all — in the trough of the sea — just where it releases you into the calm waters of old age — e.g., I wrote a lecture on the Jews — but put it aside because it's *agitation* and agitation makes me sick — brings on a hot box ever since I did too much of it about twenty-one years ago. But I don't say I won't *write* this up into a cheerful essay — which no one will print. I may end by printing a pamphlet — 25 ct. affair and peddling it through MacMahon. The use of *agitation*, of course, is that you can always get heard if you keep at it, e.g., I could hire a hall: but all that is poison. I shall let these heathen rage furiously and imagine a vain thing, and meantime I have been keeping up my scraps and rags of Greek — which I have on ice for the last stage of slippered pantaloon. The consolation is that *nobody* knows Greek. Those who devote their entire time to it have a further insight — no doubt than the triflers like myself. But they get entrapped in grammatical and psychological questions. It's a grand fairy land. Homer is the easiest — and yet you will find that no one knows the exact meaning of any word in Homer — e.g., Here's a word that means either 'very early in the morning' or else 'raise high in air.' So all the words — and most picturesque they are — describing effects of light or sound mean — darkly gleaming, or brightly blazing, a flame or a spark — or O hang it — something about fire and brightness — plain enough. They are only explained by *each other* — and occur nowhere else than in Homer, so you must read the whole Iliad for a hint on any one of them. So of the word expressing irritation, wrath, rage, annoyance. It's perfectly plain that some fellow is displeased — but just to what extent nobody knows. That's the charm of Homer. The classic Greeks didn't understand exactly and often made up sham Homeric words to suit the text (as they thought). But I get more out of him every time I read — the fluency and enormousness being the main point and in the later cantos the tragic glory. I don't want to let go of it, and whenever there's a lull in my occupations or I feel *désœuvré*, I plunge for a week or a day.

Yours affectionately

JACK

To Henry Osborn Taylor

325 WEST 82, *Jan.* 2, 1924

DEAR HARRY:

You certainly have a wonderful heart. I must confess it quick and get it over. Apropos of authorship, I this morning received two cheques from the Atlantic Monthly Press — royalties — one for $11.13 and the other for $2.81. So you see there is money in literature. I don't expect much difference in my new venture. Nor do I look on posterity with a hopeful eye. Posterity is very nice and fussy and finds more reasons for not reading a book than Chanler who has never read a word of my writing except when my wife reads a paragraph to him — which he invariably pronounces to be *very bad*, horrid, revolting, and all wrong. But who delights in your conversation — I can never see why....

Yours aff'y

JACK

To Lord Grey of Fallodon

[*In a letter of February 2, 1924, to Émile Legouis, Chapman enclosed a draft of the following letter to Lord Grey. Later he sent to M. Legouis Lord Grey's reply, saying that he was not ignorant of Wordsworth's French love affair, but had not considered it germane to his address.*]

398

325 W. 82, New York
Feb. 2: 1924

My dear Lord Grey:

As a member of the English Association I received a copy of your address on Wordsworth in December 1923. It is clear from the whole tenor of it that you have somehow missed reading Harper's Biography of Wordsworth published some years ago, in which an episode of Wordsworth's journey to France in the time of the Revolution is described — including a love affair; an illegitimate daughter; apparent cold treatment by Wordsworth of the lady, and a clandestine visit to France twenty years later to attend the marriage of his daughter. The whole matter has been much explored by Professor Legouis of the Sorbonne, through recent researches made in the *French Archives*, in the unpublished journals of Crabb Robinson, etc.

The point against Wordsworth to my mind is not the fact of his having had an early amour but that *he should never have mentioned the matter in The Prelude*, which purported to be a most solemn and testamentary confession made to Coleridge as to the influences that formed his character. He certainly was thinking of this matter all through his life, as is seen by his state of mind in his last years when some attempt was made to get him to help alleviate the poverty into which his descendants in France had fallen — without success — he being terrified at the idea of exposure.

All this casts an unhappy light on everything that we all used to believe about him and on much that you say in praise of him — e.g., his indifference to being found out, and his 'almost abnormal indifference to human censure,' etc. Indeed the Wordsworth of our and everybody's imagination and of your paper seems never to have existed. I am asking Professor Legouis to send you a little book of his on the subject, as well as a copy of his latest essay in the *Revue Anglo-Americaine* for October 1923.

I remain very sincerely yours
John Jay Chapman

JOHN JAY CHAPMAN

To Émile Legouis

DEAR LEGOUIS:

We have spent two nights in this famous club of million-aires — a simple enough place with old-fashioned comforts and no external improvements except roads of all kinds through the woods — what Lakewood used to be — on our way south for a week or two at a beach on the southern tip of Florida — Sanibel island — an unknown spot — hard to reach and said to be beautiful. Within the last three days I have read just half of your Spenser book — and it seems to me to be the best critical book I ever read about anything. The translations are *remarkable*. I didn't think it could be done. The clarity is always perfect and this, combined with the dashes of old French spelling, makes a wonderfully brilliant effect. I am going to look up the passages (for comparison) as soon as I can get a single-volume complete edition. Make a note: that hereafter, if you do any more such work, to print the *English*, either side by side or underneath in a note. The time is past for assuming that one's readers are unable to read the original — in translating from any modern language. Even in extreme cases the reader will get *something* from the original — and perhaps get a steer that will lead him to learn the language. Such essays ought to have *the young* in view.

It happens that this winter I have been reading the last six volumes of Froude, and also Sir W. Raleigh's recent volume of miscellanies, so that the epoch has been in my mind.

Spenser seems to confirm the tradition that a poet is a man without common sense. How any man of wit could adulate the fashionable world, in any age, and then revile it so heartily just because it had no use for him, is a mystery. How unchanging has been the spirit of Fashionable England from Eliza-beth's days down to the great war! and jealousy is the master passion of the English. They *all* combine against an outsider and the inner circles against the outer circles all the way up in the hierarchy. Now it is all over — for, whether or not it survives in fact, our imagination has lost it. How coherent it was! 'Gracious days of great Elizabeth,' forsooth. My, what an epoch! The stage saved Shakespeare, who seems not to have harbored any rancour against the swells. But I wonder what Spenser was after — gold chains and incense? Happy for us that he didn't get them!

Ireland was just where he belonged: it's so poetic: so Celtic: so innocent of good sense, reason, experience.

And by the way, Irish young women are not only the handsomest, and most maddeningly beautiful and womanly girls in the world, but the most romantic, mysteriously religious and unearthly. We had for two years a cook and a maid — sisters, young, small, and red haired — not especially beautiful — but good looking — elfin beings, dreamland beings, very Catholic — very quiet, very chaste. Every time I met one of them stepping demurely upstairs I felt as if smitten with a wand. I suspect there's a good deal of Ireland in Spenser's 'Faerie Queene.' Altogether it was a blessing that he was sent to Ireland. But these are mere jottings and I must go on with the book, which I have marked up till it looks like a schoolbook and, indeed, I could pass an examination on it. It is wonderfully interesting on every page.

Yours sincerely

JOHN JAY CHAPMAN

To Theodore Baird

[*In reply to a letter about ' Letters and Religion.'*]

BARRYTOWN, N.Y.
Ap. 11: 1924

DEAR THEODORE,

I am delighted to get your letter. As to mysticism, I have quite a long note from Professor Palmer — now I think over eighty — who quarrels with my form of *mysticism* and says it leads to vapor. I have no answer to him nor any theory about it, but I rather think the only proof is in the influence itself. Some mystics — like Emerson — arouse people to personal activity — some lull them to self-indulgent dreaming. E.g., To me Shelley is a type of the wrong sort.

My idea is that accurate thought always ends in something that other people will call *mystic* — and that each man develops a sort of symbolism of his own. I shouldn't even try

401

to put my symbols down Palmer's throat, and if I found out by experience that my own form of mysticism had a tendency to put people to sleep, I should say — 'Tiens, that is interesting — that is unexpected — there is a side to the whole matter that I do not comprehend.' All this flashed through my mind in reading Palmer's quite long homily. But I ended by reflecting that Palmer, being a recluse and a professional philosopher who had read too much, wasn't a fair judge of my writing — for I am an amateur and a literary gent. Such are men: they protect themselves as long as they can; and in the end come down to Mephistopheles' very wise remark to the ambitious Faust — *'Du bist am Ende was du bist.'* Something very profound and consolatory about that. It absolves us, and suggests things behind.

Yours sincerely always

JOHN JAY CHAPMAN

To Edward S. Martin

[*The 'Editor's Easy Chair' by Edward S. Martin in Harper's Magazine for December, 1924, had for its title, 'Issues that did not Show,' and in philosophizing upon the presidential election of 1924 touched — not violently enough for Chapman — upon the Roman Church.*]

BARRYTOWN, Nov. 8, 1924

MY DEAR NED

You have not touched on the Catholic question in the December Editor's Chair.

The difference between the Catholics and Protestants is that the Catholic Church claims to be superior to the Civil Government. Till you see this you can't say it. When you do say it you'll lose the sympathy of the extreme Catholics.

If ever you see the point and say it with no sweetening I'd like to see the paper.

You are quite a sophist unconsciously.

By way of pleasing every one and equalizing everything, you draw a parallel between the control of a state over the education of its citizens [and] the control of the Catholic Church over the same citizens. Now one may doubt the wisdom or justice of a particular state law. But the right of a State to control education within Constitutional limits is in-dubitable — necessary; whereas the claim of a foreign church to set an allegiance to herself above the civic duty of our cit-izens and thus create an *imperium in imperio* is a different thing altogether.

But you don't see it.

JOHN JAY CHAPMAN

You can print this if you like.

Later

Nov. 8, 1924

MY DEAR NED

I tell you what I wish you would do: Publish my last note (except the final sentence) and comment on it: confute it if you like. The important thing is to have the subject talked of and written on in a friendly way. I want the readers of *Harper's* to get a notion that the Catholic question is not only impor-tant — which they know — but discussable. There isn't another country in the world where the lid is on — as if a reign of terror was in progress about Roman Catholicism— and it's a bad augury for the best solution, *i.e.*, liberalism.

Your letters about me and my influence are silly. I don't want influence except as a wedge to get speech opened up on sane lines. To show it can be done is the best gift any one can give to the country. But your writings don't do this. They always leave the designed impression that you don't see much or anything to choose — in fact that there isn't any question.

I only ask you to print my letter so that the public shall get a plain statement of what the issue is.

The Harpers won't want even that. (You suit them to a T.) ... But they will allow you to do it, and it will do good not harm.

J. J. C.

If you won't print it, tell me why you won't. I want to see what great *doubt* you can summon....

You may put the matter thus: The discussion is coming; all one can do is to try to get the right mood.

To Elizabeth Chanler Chapman

[*It was before making the visit to Yale to which this letter relates that Chapman wrote to his friend, George D. Seymour, who had arranged a masculine dinner-party for him:* '*You know the stone which the builders rejected never enjoyed its place on the corner and regretted the old peaceful days of the stoneyard at the back of the building, where it could crack jokes about the whole enterprise. It always said to the summer visitors and globe-trotters,* 'That's enough! Now move on, do!' *and it really was a little ashamed of some black stains that just wouldn't come out, caused by some plough-chains [that] had been left on it for twelve years or so. I am studying the list of personnel like a royalty who takes a list from his chamberlain.' On this visit to New Haven Chapman read his translations of the* 'Philoctetes' *and the* 'Medea' *at two Bromley Lectures.*]

NEW HAVEN, *Feb.* 10, 1925, *at George Seymour's*

The 'Philoctetes' went off finely — the audience not large, but intent. It really was a go. The dinner before it began at 6:15 and went on till 8, a pleasant room, long table, 22 men — good food — particularly so — onion soup in casseroles, magnificent roast beef and potatoes, very good ice cream — coffee — that's all — and it couldn't have been better. I made half an hour's rambling, familiar talk — expounded the Boston Harvard situation and read scraps of old skits. I began with a lecture on *Taboo* and how all the questions were but parts of a single elemental *taboo* or mental paralysis of the American people. The only cure for the trouble was to make *men talk* — this led me up to Yale, and her secret societies (they almost fell off their chairs) for I wound into it gradually — Yale the inventor and practiser of a system that recalled Torquemada and Loyola and, considering that there were neither bayonets nor *auto da fé* behind it, was the marvel of all historic taboos — a system of torture to which our youth gladly submitted amid the religious acclaim of their families, and which, being endured for years during their formative period, entered into their blood, qualified their physique, changed the shape of the brain for life — and left a deformation in the *Bones of the Skull* — and hence its name. I said that during the great war, in cases of exploding mines and collapsing dugouts — where hundreds of men were often buried at once — the Yale bodies could be pulled out and identified instantly through this deformation in the skull — and — strangest fact of all! the deformation was exactly the same whether the sufferer had been one of the *ins* or of the *outs* of the system.

Angell, who was sitting opposite me, humorously suggested when I was entering the subject that he and I ought to leave the room, and I impart my talk to him alone — we being the only two non-Yalers. Now of course there was on the whole but faint response to my general invitation to every one to speak out — though the group was much warmer and talkativer than a similar group at Cambridge would have been.[1] One or two of them remarked afterwards that the conduct of the dinner table illustrated my thesis. But on the whole it was a very good occasion and valuable. Seymour says there's only *one* come-outer in New Haven — (who was there). Angell introduced me at the lecture in a witty and very clever speech. George and I lunch there today and tonight the president of the Sheffield S.S. dines here alone. He's the second most important official figure in Yale: but the reason he's coming is that he's very stirred up on the Catholic question. I do hope it will turn out that he's ready to abandon all, get knocked out of office, and do some real agitating in Boston. Why shouldn't he go and live there, in the suburbs — starve if necessary but do some agitating. It wouldn't take more than one man to save the Commonwealth.

Your
J<small>ACK</small>

To the same

T<small>AVERN</small> C<small>LUB</small>, *Feb.* 15: 1925

... Every one eats up truth like wedding-cake on the educational question and they will soon, I think, on the R.C. question. Boston is the centre of ignorance on the lat-

[1] Writing to Mr. Seymour, nearly a year later, about this dinner Chapman said, 'The whole occasion was splendid — or fine, and would have been splendid — if the men had not been shy. They should have thrown the dishes at me — with raillery.'

ter — but it is ingenuous, open-minded ignorance. I went to church at St. Paul's. Here's another reminiscence of Boston added to my many sentimental attachments to the town — going back to 1874 and the old hotels of St. Paul's School days, and coming down through Harvard College, Law School, courtship, marriage, visits to Beacon Street — and various dramatic episodes thereof — all recorded in these streets which have changed very little — recently *Chanler's wedding*. I spoke to Dean Rousmaniere afterwards in the vestry — being vestry-wise. He's a dear old thing and made a first rate sermon on quietude. . . . It oozed out of him. I don't like the Communion here at St. P.'s — later, and think that Christ's words should be read 'He took a sheet of rice paper and by a mechanical contrivance for puncturing produced many circular wafers — saying "This is my body, etc." ' They telescope the 'both kinds' by dipping the edge of a wafer in red ink — thereby escaping the Liquor law, I suppose. I call it a raw deal.

To Émile Legouis

BARRYTOWN, N.Y.
July 9, 1925

DEAR LEGOUIS:

After all, it's not Catholicism that's the enemy in the U.S. — it's our native materialism, which shews everywhere; and all our troubles are but forms of moral cowardice. In Europe the religious question is open, with us there's a lid on — a lid on about every subject that is vital — a conspiracy of silence in which every interest great and small concurs, and as soon as any cause shows enough strength to *be* a cause it joins the conspiracy — i.e., puts captains and agencies in the field to suppress and punish anything said in criticism *of that cause*. Thus you may take the three or four *great* interests, e.g., Big Business, the R.C. Church, the Jewish Drive — they all shake hands to control the press — nothing must be said against any of them. Below these come the various Churches, Baptist, Presbyterian, Episcopalian — all in favor of soft speech — Christian Science punishes any criticism.

And all the brotherhoods and trades unions. They all con-
cur in one thing — the American disease that no voice, no
real voice, must be raised *about anything*. But there is no
use in trying to explain this to a European. He can't believe
it. No such thing has happened in Europe as an outcome of
modern thought.

In the U.S. *thought* is taboo: that's all. I suppose that my
Protestant inheritance makes me think that the Roman
Church is the most serious and everlasting professional
destroyer of private opinion and open talk, and so I rush to
open the subject on that side — as being the side I best understand. But truly — it is the decay in the American brain
that is the real danger, and in my narrow philosophy I see
the only cure in self-expression, passion, feeling — spiritual
reality of some sort. We're about dead spiritually — that's
my illusion.

E.g., We have no anti-papal Catholics — we *have* them:
but they hide in the rocks — you would think they were
Walloons (— if it's Walloons I mean). If there existed in
the U.S. any Catholic like Lamennais (when young) — or
any of the old French crowd who were making a stand
against the supremacy of Rome, I should feel quite differently.
Our Catholics are as dumb and cowed as the rest of us. Unless the spark of personal courage, personal feeling, falls from
heaven into American hearts — we're in for a period of de-
grading slavery — we're really in it now. From the Emersonian point of view this is all very familiar....

To George Dudley Seymour

On board S.S. Celtic.
Saturday, July 19:1925

MY DEAR GEORGE:
... See an article by an educated R.C. in the July *Forum*
— very able — pouring oil and avoiding the issue. This is
the first real Catholic article and shows the pattern. To be
sure, the same vague phrases as to the *encyclicals* that I have
heard from the educated Catholics in private life. 'But, my
dear Sir, you must remember that the Pope's words are
technical and don't mean what they say' — with a rapid

passage to: 1. The idea that Christ must have lodged his authority somewhere. 2. We mustn't blame the imperfection of human instruments. 3. The American objection is really to the Irish race (this is very delicately insinuated in the paper in the *Forum*; for the man doesn't dare say it plainly). 4. A plea for tolerance. The answer would be that we only resort to their *dogmas* for the sake of explaining their *conduct*. But as a practical matter the thing to do is to go on hammering at two facts — Cardinal O'Connell's letter to all priests telling them how to vote: the church in Buffalo putting the nuns on file at the polls. Nuns voting! that's Catholicism. I judge by all this scented oil of Mr. Sands that the R.C. is a little afraid of an agitation. They don't take the high tone yet. 'Keep 'em asleep' is their true policy. It's a blessing that there are very few educated high class R.C's in America. I expect to see an importation before long. The Vatican has made an error in not having a few gentlemen ecclesiastics in every American city....

Yours affectionately

JACK

To the same

ARTILLERY MANSIONS HOTEL
LONDON, *Aug.* 20: 1925

DEAR GEORGE:

Your splendid letter reached me some time ago — but I haven't had a moment in which I could write. Now I'm alone — and lonesome, as Elizabeth has gone for a night or two to an old schoolmate's — and I do my kind of sightseeing — which is odd streets and small shops and tea rooms — where you get just the same for 5d. — same excellent bread and butter — same slops (most wholesome) for tea — that you pay 2/6 for at hotels — and I take rides on the busses — for 4d. You can go at the rate of 10 m. per hour for half an hour. These things recall London — and student days. The cheap things give one most pleasure — when one is old and rich like me. I look by the half-hour at cigars that cost 3/ apiece — and pipes at £ 5.10 with amber mouth-

pieces — (which I despise for they never are as good as the
3/6 kind —) all of which is expounded by Mr. Wordsworth
in his ode on the intimations, etc. I had a nasty illness and
cold for two weeks and all plans had to be dropped while I
was taken to the Trossachs to shake it off by sitting in the
sun and reading — or mostly being read to — out of 'The Lady
of the Lake' with all the sites mentioned in view. It's the
way to read Scott. Curiously enough, the rage began *at once*
on the publication in 1810 — tourists rushed — and have
never stopped. We went to Auchinleck in a taxi from Glas-
gow — divine afternoon, noble old estate — a ruin of the
castle — a ravine below — 150 feet down — two streams
meeting, and the whole gash filled with trees and tree tops
— *and* a wonderful old garden on the brink — yews some
hundred years old, roses of all sorts. The present Col.
Boswell and his wife are mad about gardening. The maid
at the mansion — (which dates from just *later* than Johnson's
visit — according to the Colonel's calculations) insisted that
the family were just round the corner and would be glad to
see us. They did welcome us in a noble and beautiful way
— two fine children half-grown — and the Colonel drove us
in his open small car 200 yards to the ruin and garden part —
and on our return gave us more varieties of cake and tea
than you can imagine. Neither he nor his spouse had ever
heard of Tinker — and the spouse had a very vague idea of
Johnson and had found the life 'dry.' They are most darling
people, and the place — not a gem — but a majestic, retired
manse, about the most perfect country house and place I ever
saw. The family tradition is that James B.'s widow neglected, sold, or destroyed and distributed the papers — and
I can't help thinking that they may turn up in Ireland or
elsewhere.[1] A man I met on the steamer told me that a man
he knew had been a tenant of the estate — name Mac Cabe
or Mac Something — and had carried away a pile of papers
from the cellar. But I suspected my informant of gassing.
We sent Col. Boswell a copy of Tinker's book and some time
Tinker ought to go to see these Boswells, who are the most
typical Scotch county-people in existence, with all the solid-

[1] As they did, in 1927, at Malahide Castle.

ity of English people — and with Scotch accessibility on top....

Yours affectionately ever

JACK

To André Chevrillon

BARRYTOWN *again* — *Oct.* 11, 1925

... As to Mme. Chevrillon, she seems to have the disease of this age — worst seen in the U.S. and to be reached only metaphysically — but with *what* metaphysics? The cloister and Pope are at one extreme, and Freud and his diabolism at the other — and between lie every variety of endeavor to get the patient's mind off his cause of woe — off himself. I had it myself at the age of forty for five years or so, and I was on crutches for six months *after* six months bed and spoon-feeding by a nurse. The only hopeful thing is that it's likely to get cured, I mean turn better at any moment. The point of turning comes when the *attention* turns from its problems and its preoccupations....

Now as a matter of universal fact the thing goes its course and gets worse and worse and then gets better and better. The great thing is to retain the illusion that, although it's devilish unpleasant, it is somehow all for the best. You see all the forms of cure have an element of religious truth in them, and the disease consists in an inability to accept the religious truth — (that somehow it's all for the best.) I should have committed suicide but that I somehow thought it wasn't of much importance. I was sure that my mind was wrecked — and I had a revelation as to why people commit suicide — e.g., from drink. It comes of the *certitude* that the machine is busted. 'Why live and encumber the ground?' But the machine *isn't* busted: it's only running on a new gear and will work back into the right one....

To George Dudley Seymour

BARRYTOWN, *Oct.* 27, 1925

DEAR GEORGE:

This paper is only used on serious occasions: — You are a vain old thing. (So am I, but I'm *smarter* than you and luckier than you.) I should never have been painted by a party named with such a name as Cecilia Beaux — and famous for pictures of lovely children — nor by any woman any way. But if I had done so — I would conceal my chagrin and die rather than reveal the pain of it.

You, you have been *butchered*, and will go down to posterity as 'The man with the lily,' etc., by Carola Dolci — such color — and sweetfulness. Now look at me! I refused all comers including many best friends, starting artists — till my sister-in-law comes home with a Russian Genius — and I *must* — I give way, and he leaves me as a Tartar prince in bronze — just the way I pose to my looking glass — fierce, you know — bloody — and *mouvementé*. When I think of you lying there with that chromo of Dante waiting for the Blessed Damozel, I hate that dreaded Cecilia — and if I ever see her again — the *shame* of it is what cuts me most. How God lets loose these sentimental women on the world, and provides no trap-doors for men to hide in.

I met a new kind of man on the train. A New Englander — Something Otis Something — fifty, handsome, the voice and enunciation of all the Wheelwrights, Longfellows — and what do you think he does — he has a church with a membership of 1500 and has been at Glens Falls, N.Y., for twenty-five years. *Lectures*. Lectures everywhere — on Psychology — the superconscious, the subterconscious — the will, the instincts — has the temperament of a perfectly happy, old-fashioned evangelist — and expounds the nature of their insides to classes of 200 bob-haired flappers or 1000 grimy miners — and puts it across. I never met a happier man. Not a note of the Gospels escaped him and he doesn't believe in them — or in their symbols. He has them all translated into this Choctaw without knowing it — and tells me that he thinks the young people today have a deeper and sincerer interest in spiritual things than those of his own youth. Well, I'm damned. He was extremely intelligent about all current topics and sympathetic to my — as you know — general views of the horror of everything, especially of American character — letters, politics, journalism, education, etc. His thought is based on Bergson — Bunyan coming out of Bergson. I'd like to bring him to see you — only I shall probably never see him again. Where is Glens Falls, N.Y.? I shall certainly stop in there if I am near it. By the way — do you know that the proper scanning of the line 'There are more things in the world, etc. — is to go light on the *your*? Hamlet means philosophy in general and the *your* is merely yr. and is merely a weak demonstrative — 'your so-called philosophy' — accent on philosophy. I wanted to ask him how he would express the ideas suggested by the parable of the prodigal son, etc. — but I didn't have the chance. There was a third person at the talk, which lasted two hours — a very old friend of the Psychologist — an Episcopal parson — of very holy variety, who said little but was rather on my side as the sceptic (as toward psychology). This modern world has some funny people in it.

Yours affectionately

JACK

Elizabeth says I must tell you that I really think the picture very beautiful. But, like all women, she has no understanding of irony, humor, subtlety — O my! they are all in all, indubitable — unmistakable whether in sentiment or opinion.

To Robert Nichols

325 WEST 82ND STREET
NEW YORK CITY
Dec. 23, 1925.

MY DEAR ROBERT AND NORA:
... It looks on all the surfaces as if the intellect of this country had gone to pot through the operation of the natural laws of wealth and prosperity — (and one sees no end or limit to them). I read Horace all the time and see much likeness between the luxury, riot, and folly that went on in the proconsular era, and our own epoch, but nothing of the blaze of intellect that accompanied the breakdown of the old Roman institutions — and left behind it a shelf of books.

> Damnosa quid non imminuit dies?
> Aetas parentum, peior avis, tulit
>   Nos nequiores, mox daturos
>   Progeniem vitiosiorem.

This is a good description of us — but who is there that can *write* like that?

Such reflections as all these do have the effect of making us see things sharply — and in the end lead to our remembering that we didn't *imagine* and set a-going the whole damned outfit, and if, as seems the case, it's rolling to a bust-up — why, many very serious things have happened before in the past, which we were no less powerless to prevent — not being on hand at the time — so that finally we come to this question: why do superior minds always feel so responsible for keeping Phoebus' car on its track — and that sort of thing — while inferior natures are so damned comfortable and so logical in relation to the matter?

I am dining tonight in a palace of gold plate and shall talk Jew-baiting with a very able American woman, wife of an English peer — she being a rabid anti-semite and trying to save the British Empire.... My host has a cook that was chef at the most exquisite Club in Paris and who broke his contract with the Club so that my host had to pay $18,000. My figures of speech are approximate but you see the idea. Only one thing I do believe — at a Roman dinner-party in Augustus's time one got *enough* caviare — and in modern times they're mean about caviare. Why not put a pot of it by each plate?[1] Tomorrow we go to the country over Christmas to stay with my sister-in-law. Bracebridge Hall — tenantry — a tree — candles — babies — Noah's arks — candy — cake — gifts — mottos — more gifts — useful gifts — shoes, shawls, toys, more candy, villagers, relations — poor relations, rich relations — in-laws — nieces, nephews — farm boys — old women. How I wish you both could be there! Merry Christmas from

Yours affectionately

JOHN JAY CHAPMAN

[1] Chapman took a frank pleasure in good, simple food — and plenty of it. After a fashionable dinner-party in New York, he wrote to his wife, early in 1925: 'The food of the rich is disgusting to me —... messes. Last night I had to go to Childs and eat cornbeef hash and poached eggs, which pulled me round.'

To George Dudley Seymour

CASA YBEL
SANIBEL
FLORIDA, *Feb.* 1926

DEAR GEORGE:

... The Col. House revelations are going, I see, to tell us what we know already and no more. I like House; but I never have thought that he had any influence on Wilson — except as a channel of information in which he was at first very valuable. His hand was so light, and his subtlety so great, that he was able to keep his access open, and his continual stroking of Wilson in the right way merely groomed the man into a more sleek selfhood and kept away every one else. House is probably the noblest-minded party manager that ever lived — (just as Roosevelt is the most virtuous demagogue that ever lived), but in both cases the limitations of intellect which are due to incessant attention to the practical aims of a near future are evident. House was not a humbug, whereas a demagogue is absolutely obliged to be a humbug every few minutes. By the way, neither Wilson nor Roosevelt ever had a true friend — one that would stake his relationship on a bout of truth-telling with the great man. The same is probably true of Disraeli, Gladstone, Palmerston — to say nothing of Cromwell, Napoleon, Ivan the Terrible, or Frederick the Great. A man in a position of great power won't get the truth unless he positively courts it. And, as he has always got on very well without it, and truth is always exceedingly unpleasant — why should he court it?

Why publish these things now, when everything interesting must be left out? No, no: interesting memoirs are written in later life by certain people of talent who are amused over their own recollections — and they are *published* still later. They must be seasoned with wit and not afraid of malice.

If you are interested in Napoleon read the last half of Charles Downer Hazen's volume in very large print and not long — beginning at the Chapter called the *Directorate*. This is the best portrait of Napoleon I've ever come across and gives his personalities, his politics, and his campaigns in outline — with a large brush — and so clearly you can't forget them — and it's all of one piece, one tempo, one argument — a remarkable book — or call it an essay.

Yours affectionately
JACK

To the same

CASA YBEL
SANIBEL, FLA., Mch. 10, 1926

DEAR GEORGE:

We read your letter aloud last night and it gave us great joy. You evidently are all well inside anyway, and I think the episode will have added years to your life and activities. Nothing like six months of enforced rest at sixty — if it's only deep enough. We are almost on our way north — where we arrive on the 22. By all means read whatever you like out of my letters to whom you please. Of all the American officials during the war — the man who impresses me most is Gerard. He did so at the time. The first manly American voice I heard was in a speech of Gerard's at the City Hall, N.Y., when he was here on a flying visit. He was like a strong-clawed rough bear, and the Germans were an open book to him. You don't hear him talking about hopes of aid from Zimmermann or Jagow — nor suggestions as to 'ways out' and 'doing good.' All the same House is an extraordinary being. I don't believe that he had any effect on the outcome except as a social class-influence — which is much — I mean as oil to the official amenities between England and America and France. Page was the dynamic force, and I have always thought that he would have done better to throw up his job in England and go on tour, speaking to the Americans in the U. S. — in which case he would have survived and succeeded to the Presidency. I saw him in London in Aug. 1914 — and hated him; for he was all 'loyalty' to Wilson and couldn't hear a word said against 'our President.' Handholding with Sir Edward Grey and writing letters to Wilson wasn't a big enough rôle for Page: he had something to say.

All the same House is unique. He moves like a spirit between all the elements and all the machinery — he occupies

415

no space and has no dimensions. He's like a book-louse —
a selfless, holy book-louse — the wisdom of the serpent and
the harmlessness of the dove — a superman in the manipula-
tion of vestries — votes — measures and men; but bears no
relation to the crude forces — unformulated — that are outside of his game. He's an underground character. Put him in
the sun and he blinks. But he sees in the dark. Now there is
really nothing to be done with such a nature as was Wilson's
— except smite him hip and thigh — and I hate to see House
crawling over him. They make an odious pair — say what
you will. I have just come to a place in the memoirs where
they both appear to small advantage — though they are extremely conscious of virtue. It was in 1916 when Wilson
rapped on the table and said to Europe — 'See here now, you
fellows have got to stop fighting — especially Great Britain
— or we in America will assert a few neutral rights to show
you that Germany's not the only sinner.' House and Wilson
seemed to think that the moral terror of our Name would
secure obedience — and *we not armed*. Wilson and House seem
to have thought that every one would heed America —
though she had taken no part in the fight. This shows such ignorance of human affairs — and especially of the human death
grapple then going on in Europe that I can't believe my eyes
in reading about it. Apparently this rough side of common
truth was outside both of their philosophies. They are really
silkstockings. They are asinine. The U. S. is to be a police-
man. But carry a club? oh no! If we hadn't taken part in the
war, no one would have paid any attention to us at the peace
conference. I must ask House how he sees this today. You
will observe that House sees only the wires — he doesn't see
the peoples and their passions — (except his own kind of old
maids in the U. S.). For instance, he wanted Page sent home
or taken off the board somehow — not seeing that Page was
doing wonders in preventing England from affronting the U.S.
— and giving way to her natural tendency to tell us to go to
Hell (with which I sympathize). Page counteracted this
danger by showing in his own person that there were Americans who understood the War — and saw that the U. S. *must
get into it* or die off the planet as a moral factor. But House

wanted to eliminate Page. He has no vision for the ultra-diplomatic — and there's a good deal of truth in Senator Somebody's calling him 'The Texan Talleyrand.'...

To Robert Nichols

BARRYTOWN, N.Y.
Ap. 20: 1926.

... If I were going to worry — I should worry about the *yeoman* — the man born on a farm or small country place — who as a boy has to live small and work hard — the son of the country parson or squire. I can't see how the world can thrive without this man, and yet everything is being organized to extinguish him. Canned goods and Ford cars extinguish him. Tall buildings and big business extinguish him. The movies and the press iron him out of existence before he is born. Science precludes him. Materialism will have none of him.

The Scotch, the Danes, the Dutch, the Norwegians, the Swiss — peoples that live under hard-scrabble conditions — and learn to do something that no one else can do — are the firmest fixed on the earth. The roamers and speculators and seizers of rich soils are destroyed by the ease of acquisition. See how the French people multiplied under the old Régime where everything was taken from them as soon as it was grown. Now they have the richest land in Europe and won't multiply for fear of penury. So of the Americans. — Same thing: *crescit sub pondere virtus*. People only grow while they suffer. All this nobody's fault: just human nature, you know. If this view be the true one you must by this time be about as a big a saint as any in the Roman Calendar — and as for Nora I have always thought of her as a saint, but I wish she could speak — she's like one of those sainted images that are said to speak — but don't — according to Gibbon. Give her my love anyway. I never think of you without thinking of her....

JOHN JAY CHAPMAN

To Henry James

SYLVANIA
BARRYTOWN-ON-HUDSON
June 1: 1926

DEAR HENRY:

I like your quiet philosophic interest in reforms, and whether tutors are better than lectures; and what is a University; and advances in psychology and criminology and the bacillus and the atom. But really, when you lift your brows and speak with hesitating approbation of men who are engaged in beating the robbers off your own back fence, and rousing the neighbors with their cries — I begin to think that scientific benevolence has gone far enough. It fossilizes the mind. It is fossilizing *your* mind. There are lots of people who can't think seriously without injuring their minds. Their minds were not meant for this use, and so the more they think the feebler they grow.

The cure is simple.

Speak out opinions before you think — and before the other fellow speaks. Thus you will give your mind some chance of forming them in a natural way — unconsciously. Accustom yourself to not knowing what your opinions are till you have blurted them out, and thus find what they are. That's what talk is for — and it doesn't prevent the careful summarizing of ideas upon occasion when this is in order. Your valued father went the limit in the expression of things in writing in this improvised way, for he never knew quite what was in his mind — as he told me himself — till he wrote; and it was by this course that he made his most telling cracks: for it is only in the poetic element that truth is told. For truth to be truth must be new.

If one is dealing with such simple matters as making an engine — adding a cog to it — or finding a microbe — you may reason and ratiocinate to good ends. But if you're dealing with human nature in any form, you go broke if you reason — you're an ass to reason — you must put the thing off your mind and allow the probabilities to occur to you — and never be sure then. All these developments in charity reform,

418

education, are governed by nobody knows what. They are moving clouds.

Yours affectionately

JOHN JAY CHAPMAN

To George Dudley Seymour

SANIBEL, FLA. *Jan 23*, 1927

... It is strange to me that H. Adams who in his History reveals such extraordinary powers of mind, such equanimity and patience, should in his later books have become egotistical and an amateur who dabbled in subjects. In his history he has two kinds of writing — first, an occasional page of writing for the general reader as brilliant as Thucydides but without the literary flourish of Thucydides, or the swagger of rhetoric of Macaulay — and the rest a sort of digest (for the professional historian) of the diplomatic and congressional history of Jefferson's time — most remarkable for its incredibly concatenated citations drawn from so many sources — and all of it apparently clear cut, hard, intellectual, reliable. Of course he enjoys destroying Jefferson — but he is more just to Jefferson than I could be and points to his good side and the sincerity of his soft side and really lets him off easy. Although Adams' history is in a field of life of which I know nothing, it seems to me a great book and more free from chauvinism than any other history I ever read. It makes Trevelyan's 'History of England,' which I am also reading, seem like a boys' book....

Adams is most interesting of all about Napoleon, and his scattered pages about him give me a better notion of the monster than I ever had. I suppose that all his tedious lists of Committees and votes may be necessary — to burn in the picture of the wretched American character in 1807. My! what a people — and what an epoch!

Yours

J. J. C.

To M. A. DeW. Howe

[*The first and longer portion of this letter relates to recent American biographical writing, including some of my own.*]

SANIBEL FLA.
Feb. 15, 1927

... I see by the London *Times Weekly Review*, that Trevelyan's 'History of England' has sold 66000 copies. It is a mid-Victorian book — and dates from the days of Palmerston. It is like a shoot sent up from the root of a fallen tree — a lyric from end to end, the theme being the Debt of the World to England. On every page the world is saved anew. The American revolt of 1776 is treated as an error of politicians — not as a piece of inherent national stupidity, and the release of the Alabama was due to the 'carelessness' of Russell. That careful carelessness was really due to the widespread sentiment in England that the South was going to win and that England would be stronger with two conflicting peoples in the U. S. than with one united people. Any frank Englishman who remembers the period will tell you this. As a matter of probability if the South had established a slave state, it would have backed the Germans in 1914 and they would have won. But you must put on a garland, imagine yourself a tory squire, and sit down to Trevelyan: and this is what the English have done and it shall not be taken away from them.

So also the Boer war is treated by Trevelyan as an error of enthusiasm, whereas it was really the throwing down of the half-unconscious commercial mask under which English expansion had always proceeded, and the adoption of crude ideas and methods. Cecil Rhodes was an old-fashioned marauder and the Empire backed him. The teaching of Macaulay had turned into the ballads of Kipling — (who by the way is not mentioned by Trevelyan — and that's why I call him mid-Victorian).

While Trevelyan's book is charming and very interesting, he ends every paragraph with a sweet hopefulness that makes it a boys' book, and leaves one doubting the profundity of everything he says. He simply cannot finish off an episode without an optimism as — my eye falls on — 'if we had won the Boer war too easily we might not have won the German war at all.'

See you soon.

Your aff.

JACK

To Elizabeth Chanler Chapman

TAVERN CLUB, *Sat., Nov.* 12: 1927

The Boston Authors Club was a plain but very good dinner at a sort of Community loft — with 100 or more men and women, all very chipper and agreeable and not a Jew or Catholic — a sort of fowl-yard cackling and quite unconscious of the Catholic power whose slaves they are. All the same the general temper of them was such that I shouldn't have hesitated to raise the question had it been in order, which it wasn't. It was a good occasion — good singing of Haydn by a woman of German descent — accompanied by an American woman who writes music — called Daniels — I sat next her, a very jolly sensible person. You must know that the Club was founded by Julia W. Howe, T. W. Higginson, and others and is perfectly satisfied that it is the advance guard of intellect — and all that. Every one in the room had written a book; that's essential to membership. The speeches were good — except one. On my other side was a vestal who had taken a $2000 prize for a Child's Book, offered by Little, Brown. She comes from Dakota — or some of those arid places and was quaint, wide-eyed, dry, and pathetic — and couldn't smile without a preparatory effort, but one couldn't help loving her. Grandgent is a real humorist and can gabble by the half hour à la Homer and keep everyone content.

He really was extremely witty and unexpected — e.g., told of a schoolma'am who was describing the wasteful prodigality of Nature and how 'a single salmon had five million eggs in one season' — then, seeing a small girl raise her hand — 'Priscilla, have you a question to ask?' — 'Please, how many eggs does a married salmon have?' The parched virgin from the northwest looked in torture at this. — I read them a variety of short verses, which made a good interlude. Then a most amusing editor of the — oh, one of these big old-fashioned

421

popular domestic weeklies — a well known man, Amos Wells, who had resigned after thirty-six years of continuous editorship — yet he scarcely looked so — read a most witty and not long paper — his valedictory. Then, an old-fashioned fo' de war fog-horn editor of the *Boston Herald* — locks of hair — rotund oratory — believes in the great function of the editor and his share in literature, etc.

Told some good stories and interesting facts all the same. . . .

To the same

TAVERN CLUB, *June* 6, 1928

. . . Today I lunched at the Porcellian — where I found, as usual five or six undergraduates, very athletic and respectable and respectful, but not much developed conversationally — also at the head of the table, the head of a department — a scion of the old Boston nobility whose grandmother I had known well. He wanted me to visit the Law School and see the portraits and engravings of old judges and American worthies — which I assured him I wouldn't. He had been down on Long Island at the Dudley Winthrop place (now owned by Dudley's brother) — which consists of 300 acres — surrounded by the country places of millionaires — which are all about to be rendered uninhabitable, by the enervating city. 'And then,' said I, 'they will all have to sell out — and begin over again somewhere else — having become richer and stupider than ever.' This made the athletic gargoyles laugh nervously. Then I called up Professor Lowes and went over to his house and had a good long talk with him — a splendid man — and a highly educated, all around intelligence. And lives in perfectly lovely small house surrounded by trees, lawns, and flowers — and almost next door to the Harry Greene's — the only other people I had in mind to see. They are off to Europe almost at once. . . .

Lowes said that the invention of Purgatory was the cleverest device ever got up by man — for keeping control over the living — through their concern for themselves and for their lost parents, children, etc. Antiquity knew of Hell. But Hell was hopeless — then why worry? But Purgatory —! He is very much encouraged at the changes now in progress at

Harvard both in the management and in the students —and thinks that the importation of Alfred North Whitehead made a new era — or represents a new era. Mem. must call on the Whiteheads.[1] ...

To Mrs. Frederick Winslow

[*The issue to which this letter refers was that of the Roman Church in the presidential campaign of 1928.*]

BARRYTOWN, N.Y.
Aug. 31, 1928

... As for the people who talk about intolerance in religion — let them read 'Mother India.' Must one tolerate the Hindu religion?

It's a mere glass-eye, that whole idea of tolerance, and means *nothing*. We must use our faculties. It closely parallels the old talk about Slavery in the Constitution and the wickedness of raising the issue. I may be wrong as to the *relative* importance of this issue as against the other issues — (I place it first because it is ubiquitous and permanent, enduring — sure to be with us for many years in many forms.) But I'm certainly right as to its *nature*: It is a metaphysical oppression that must be cut out like a tumor. ...

Yours sincerely

JOHN JAY CHAPMAN

To Elizabeth Chanler Chapman

UNIVERSITY CLUB — *Feb.* 21, 1929

... Discussion at the Century last night as to whether the Roosevelt Boomers could put him over in the *long run* as the Apostle of Righteousness. You know, I suppose, that R. went up the wrong hill — in disobedience of orders — and would have been destroyed unless a regiment of Negroes had been sent to save him and his Rough Riders. He never was on San Juan Hill. But he had a picture painted of himself on horseback going up San Juan Hill. The military men wouldn't stand for this; and laughed the picture into the cellar of the

[1] About a year later he wrote to Mrs. H. C. Greene: 'I have seen the Whiteheads once or twice. They are like something out of Hawthorne — but have an element of humor and light fantasy that he couldn't have evoked.'

White House. As a matter of fact — no one was on horseback at San J. It was so steep — they clawed up it on foot. Well, the man next me at table — a knowing sort of cuss — said that he knew from inside information of a U. S. Department that an effort was now being made to rename the maps of the battle ground so that the words San Juan hill should *cover Kettle Hill* — which Roosevelt ran up — as if San Juan was a term that included Kettle. One diner maintained the old paradox, that it made no difference when once a hero was established — whether he had been a hero or not. I contested this, on the ground that such a record on such facts deceived the young as to the true nature of life. Morton Prince was there and exceedingly clever and agreeable he is. He — being a great internationally known psychologist — wrote an analysis of Roosevelt — not complimentary — which was translated into several languages — and alienated T. R. from him for years. The war brought them together again. Morton said he thought of doing Mussolini. He is on his way to Italy for a rest.

Your loving
JACK

To Mrs. Frederick Winslow

SYLVANIA
BARRYTOWN-ON-HUDSON
September 7, 1929

MY DEAR MRS. WINSLOW:

I am delighted to get your letter. I thought you were away — or abroad — not hearing from you. You must remember this translation is for persons who resemble the translator in not knowing Greek and you must imagine that you know nothing about the subject before seeing it. I don't know the meaning of a single Greek word — and I have a sort of belief that they none of them have English equivalents. Any word in a language corresponds to a district in the map of the brain — and the maps of Greek and English if superimposed never show an approach to identity anywhere. The people who devote their lives to Greek get queered — (and no one can begin to know it without devoting his life to it). Jebb is an exception — having a very strong head and being unsentimental and a cross man.

In order to bring the choruses into a comprehensible relation to the text and situation on which they comment I have had to resort now to one expedient now to another. To the Greek audience they were probably a jumble of familiar names and saws, half drowned by music — or what passed for music in those days — and the tramping about of the chorus. I mean this is the sort of idea I get or guess at — as suggested by Aristophanes. I have gradually come to have a dislike for Euripides and his calculated pathos and operatic exaggerations. The 'Hippolytus' is a disgusting play — and he drags in his eternal feminism even in his Satyr play, 'Cyclops.' He's a skinny-minded man, clever — but monotonous-minded. He's of the decadence, and the brutality of the 'Medea' is all right — is just right — for him. I like it — it's very great and the play of a great mick. O Lord! Yesterday I read an essay by a very learned American Greekist about the extreme beauty of the *moral* of the 'Bacchae.' Now the 'Bacchae' is the most venomous satire ever written and the cleverest — but so malignant as to horrify me, and no wonder Euripides retired from Athens....

To Robert Nichols

BARRYTOWN, N.Y. *Oct.* 13: 1929

... The whole subject [book publishing] is a sea of ignorance; for the American public has taken to reading madly — history, biography, philosophy — old books, new books, sham books, real books. They won't read anything that is closely written and demands attention; but outside of this rule — all is terra incognita and fishing in a cyclone. They will read Galsworthy's Saga — which to my mind, after a half hour spent over the middle of it, seems dull and second rate. The Red Hook bank clerk here told me that he and his family read it aloud all one winter and were in heaven with it. Our people will read enormous, quiet, plodding biographies of Washington and Lincoln — that cost $5 a volume, for they have lots of cash. They'll buy any $2 book on a venture and leave it in the train. Their stomachs tend to become stronger as their field of information expands, and here and there you have a big 3-volume competent history of the Colonial mind — a work on the U. S. from 1620 on — which sells by the thousand as soon as printed. Chanler comes up here for Sunday every once in a while and gives us a glimpse into the game — somewhat as a stockbroker's clerk might do into finance. His people are not plungers but anglers. He is extremely ignorant and quite smart and active — and perhaps these are the very qualities that augur success just now. . . .

To Mrs. Frederick Winslow

325 W. 82, N.Y.
Nov. 3: 1929

DEAR MRS. WINSLOW:

By the way — after calling Gilbert Murray a saint — his relation to Euripides flashed through me. There is a *cruelty* in the Greek logic of tragedy — something that to us seems cruelty — even in, e.g., Sophocles' 'Oedipus Rex.' To the Greeks it was merely tragic accuracy — for they were just barely 'emerging from savagery' — as G. M. suggests — (and then forgets). But G. M. is a maidenly saint — and reminds me of Ophelia.

'Thought and affliction, passion, hell itself
He turns to favor and to prettiness.'

This is the explanation of his truly idiotic philandering over the truly grisly horrors of the 'Bacchae.' The logic of these horrors is introverted, accurate reasoning. The Greeks, a little decadent already — enjoyed it. All of Euripides is tainted with it. It's the outcome of a national sport.

Yours sincerely

JOHN JAY CHAPMAN

Murray is only the best, sweetest, most innocent representative of a whole school of modern sentimentalists. (The word is not quite accurate, but the most expressive to state the quality that results from this nature.)

IX

Afterglow
1929–1933

THE seriousness of Chapman's 'Last Words' was the more impressive for the lighter lines in his adieu to the world:

> 'It was a grand mistake, I fear,
> To try to better you.'

The world, to be sure, had not been re-made according to the pattern of all his ideals. It is never re-made in the lifetime of one man. Yet who can tell how far the unseen influences of a single life extend? Who shall say, for one example, that the politics of New York are not more decent than they were when Chapman and his friends began their labors? Who knows what lives are touched by such unremitting courage, such scorn of pettiness, such versatility and vigor of mind and spirit as the life of Chapman manifested? These things are as far beyond measuring as the influences of the stars.

In the biographies of persons who enriched their times otherwise than through far-reaching action the element of personality is of special, even of supreme, importance. This transcends the contemporaneous, for personality, flavor, individual quality, however evanescent they may be, are constant human attributes in which all the ages share. Chapman himself recognized a perennial type of humanity when it crossed his path. He was himself such a type — one of those beings, various in their individual qualities, who have this in common, that what they were, rather than what they did, is the thing that matters. This is a timeless thing, and personality is at the heart of it.

In terms of visible results Chapman's achievement is represented by some twenty small volumes in prose and verse, none of which fell into the category of 'successful' books. To the many they were nearly unknown. To the few they stood apart in contemporary letters for the penetrating originality and independence of their substance, for the vigor, wit, and mastery of the writer's art which gave them their form. In these particulars they have seemed to the few to hold a place among the very best writings produced in America. Through them all courses the bright flame of Chapman's personality.

In his talk and in his letters, so much alike as they were, that flame shone yet more brightly. The proprieties, the reticences, which never curbed him unduly in what he printed himself, troubled him not at all in his correspondence. Momentary explosions of bane or blessing found their instant way to the written page. In many activities of others he was fond of detecting a 'law of nature,' a 'religious principle,' from which there was no possible escape. So indeed it was with himself. Holding at successive times such positive opinions as he held on one matter after another, he could not help expressing himself with vehemence — and particularly in his letters — on all manner of persons and topics. This flood of expression got its unity from Chapman's unswerving search for a spiritual reality underlying all outward appearances. 'What aim?' he asked himself, in his poem, 'The Archer.'

> What aim, what purpose in it all have I?
> I draw an arrow and I let it fly
> To vanish in the invulnerable sky.
>
> Shadows there are that stalk the world of sense,
> Dissolving symbols of Impermanence,
> Through which the arrow takes its flight intense.

Naught in themselves, they brighten till they mean
Something in the beyond — a point of sheen
Piercing the blindnesses that intervene.

Thus archer after archer bends his bow
And dedicates his arrows to the glow;
But where they fall or strike — he does not know.

Here is Chapman's own answer to the inquirer after tangible achievement. It was enough for him to dedicate his arrows to the glow. This was only the natural course for one whose life was so based in religion. Like a prophet of old, he held, beyond the evils of the world, a constant vision of righteousness; like a faithful, if somewhat turbulent, apostle, he was ready at a moment to draw his sword, smite the high priest's servant and cut off his right ear.

For the few remaining years of his life his arrows were dedicated chiefly to the more intimate glow of domestic affections, of friendships, and of books. Agitation for reform no longer disturbed him. 'There must be some things,' he wrote as early as 1926 to a friend who was urging him to 'save' the Episcopal Church, 'for which I do not agitate.' At length these came to include all things.

His two surviving sons remained to the end of his days absorbing objects of devotion and concern. The elder, Conrad, after his service in the Navy during the war, pursued the life of a scholar in Oxford and Paris, attempted the establishment of a boarding-school for American boys in France, and lived more abroad than at home. The younger son, Chanler, married in 1924 to Miss Olivia James of Boston, entered upon journalism and book-publishing, in Springfield, Massachusetts, and New York. His two boys and a younger daughter, who did not long survive her grandfather, brought into Chapman's life, largely at Sylvania, a delighted renewal of contact with childhood, at once rejuvenating and sobering. 'We have a couple of Olivia and Chanler's children staying with us — aged four and two —' he wrote to Miss Frances G. Curtis in 1930, 'and this is the acme of pleasure for people at our time of life, especially as the parents are on a two-weeks' trip to Bermuda. All the same after entertaining one of them for twenty minutes I feel like a trip to Baden-Baden. Children live in armed neutrality as towards their parents, but regard their grandparents as victims, slaves, or court-fools.'

At Sylvania Chapman was to be seen not merely as father and grandfather, but as neighbor and employer. Men and women who had served him through many years — even during and before the illness that broke his life into two parts — rise up to contradict the fable that no man is a hero to his valet. 'The justest man I ever saw,' declares the chauffeur, William Rosborough, formerly the coachman, who boasts of possessing and having read every book that Chapman wrote. He will tell you also of impulsive, bewildering gifts to forlorn men and women seen from the passing motor-car, and of long-continued help to needy neighbors old and young. With such instances of pity and kindness to remember, and with personal sympathies and gratitude reaching far back into the past, the women of the household tell their tales of affection and respect.

To escape the winters of the North, demanding too much of Mrs. Chapman's limited strength, she acquired, in 1929, a small house in Charleston, South Carolina, the home of her earliest Chanler progenitors in America, and of many contemporary kinsfolk. Less remote and less exacting, physically, than Sanibel in Florida, Charleston afforded an ideal winter retreat, to which Chapman betook himself each winter for a shorter season than his wife's. His letters reveal his enjoyment of the leisurely Southern pace and of congenial surroundings. 'I have grown', he wrote to Mrs. Henry Copley Greene in the spring of 1932, 'into a mild-mannered old pantaloon who pretends he knows just which cousin he is talking to.'

Except for visits to England in the spring of 1930 and again in the last summer of Chapman's life there were no further wanderings to chronicle. Chapman himself was fulfilling the

Marion

CHAPMAN AT CHARLESTON

spirit of his 'Last Words.' Three books — of which only
the last, 'New Horizons in American Life' (1932), had any
contemporary bearing — were still to swell the number of
his publications. The first, 'The Antigone of Sophocles,
Translated by John Jay Chapman,' was brought out in a
sumptuous limited edition in 1929. Chapman's enthusiasm
for what he was doing at a given time was illustrated by his
avowal regarding the 'Antigone,' 'It is the best written play
in the world.' Alternating 'best' and 'worst' similar avowals
in his letters may be recalled. Again he rationalized his own
method as a translator. 'He is not supposed to be learned';
and his first word of warning is that 'the classical reader
will see that I have made free use of Mr. Jebb's translation.'
Scholars complained of omissions and other liberties, but the
beauty and distinction of the English verse and its power to
convey the spirit of a Greek classic stand as ample justifications of what the translator, addressing the 'general reader,'
set out to do.

Then came 'Lucian, Plato and Greek Morals' (1931).
His earlier interest in Lucian has already been noted, and
essays relating both to him and to Plato lay among his files
of unpublished writings. In this volume he turned them to
account, and took the occasion to deal with the practice of
pederasty among the Greeks. For this perversion he held the
deep loathing of a normal man. For most of his lifetime it
had been unmentionable. It was in accordance with his
principles, however, to speak of it, if at all, with complete
candor. 'I have to sail between Scylla and Charybdis,' he
wrote to a feminine correspondent;... 'But really humor
was the only path. It was Lucian that revealed this to me.
In giving the book away I sent it to a husband rather than
a wife because, among other reasons — I hope you won't
mind, it's a mere abstraction — men have a better sense
of humor than women: most men.' In a letter to J. E.
Spingarn he said, 'By the way, this only occurred to me
afterwards. This is an age when pederasty is O. K. You can't

enter a drawing-room without finding Proust in all languages. But you must not speak plainly about it — and above all not laugh, or you're an outrageous person.' Of the brevity of the book he wrote, besides, 'As long as I remember I've had only one dogma as to writing—"Small books go farther than big ones." '

Classical scholars, unmoved by the humor on which Chapman counted, took him to task for venturing into waters beyond his depth, and maintained that he did not know enough about either Lucian or Plato to warrant the book. As classicists pure and simple — where purity and simplicity were not the chief issue — they were probably right. The book cannot be counted among the few of Chapman's best, yet the light it throws upon him is significant. It was entirely like him to exalt the underestimated Lucian, the 'prize infidel,' one 'constantly occupied in destroying illusions,' and to maintain that Plato, 'the patron saint of those who sit in armchairs,' was rated too high. At least he did not pontificate. At least here, as everywhere else, he escaped the condemnation bestowed in one of his letters upon a contemporary — in private, good form, in public, disposed to show about three-quarters of an inch of ruffles. That was something to which Chapman never came. Soon after its publication he wrote to Edmund Wilson: 'Half of about forty of my social friends — (mostly old duffers of course) — have never acknowledged the gift — evidently shocked. Only one of them — (fact) — has said he read it aloud to his family and they laughed a lot over the end of it. I'm glad there's one hearty-minded family in the country.'

The final book was 'New Horizons in American Life' (1932), containing two lectures delivered at Columbia University—'Our Universities' and 'Trends in Popular Thought.' From one admiring reviewer, Lucien Price, it brought forth comments on Chapman's work in general: 'He has been a crusader without a cause. There were causes enough and he espoused them, but never *the* cause, the girl he could give his whole heart to.... For all his Hellenic culture, Mr. Chapman remains a Hebraist at heart, and an Old Testament prophet is not the person to write a book about Plato.' To which Chapman replied in a grateful letter: 'You are right about my *Hebraism*. I think I must have a Hebrew ancestor or two — and, you know, James Russell Lowell had a theory about the Jewish strain in the Yanks.' The 'New Horizons' left Chapman's stature unchanged.

That stature had always been a matter of such indifference to the public at large that certain recognitions of it which came to Chapman in these latest years gave him a delighted surprise. The first was in the form of a leading article by Edmund Wilson in a 'Literary Section' of the *New Republic* for May 22, 1929. It has been mentioned on an earlier page of this book as an evidence of Chapman's appeal to adventurous spirits of a generation following his own. Thus it ended: 'If his books were reprinted and read, we should recognize that we possess in John Jay Chapman — by reason of the intensity of the spirit, the brilliance of the literary gift, and the continuity of the thought which they embody — an American Classic.' To praise of this sort Chapman was wholly unwonted, and wrote at once to Mr. Wilson that 'the article certainly brought tears to my eyes a good many times. I thank you from my heart.'

He was soon to receive an equally unwonted recognition in England. The leading article in the *Times Literary Supplement* for August 14, 1930, bearing the title, 'An American Moralist,' contained its reservations in such sentences as 'His weakest judgments are those that owe most to sheer enthusiasm'; but a passage wrought with evident care characterizes Chapman so accurately that it must find a place in this record of his life:

> First and foremost, an American and a patriot, and as a patriot, and a man in whom ideas are action, inevitably a reformer; a man full of faith in the destiny of his race and therefore merciless in outspoken criticism of its blunderings; himself,

too, though so fearless in criticism, not primarily a critic, but an enthusiast, a poet, caught up on that high wave of hope and happiness which has turned the heads of his fellow-countrymen, and himself, from first to last, boyishly and lovably hot-headed, even to the mingling denunciation and disregard of money which is such an inadequate defence against the wiles of ever-watchful Mammon. At once candid and audacious, the rare spice of Mr. Chapman's personality comes of its happy combination of the cosmopolitan liveliness of New York, of which he is a citizen, with all those long-suffering New England pieties of which Emerson was the first and is still the most authentic voice.

Again Chapman was naïvely delighted and wrote to his friend, Mrs. Greene, 'So after years of labor by you and Robert Nichols and one or two more strenuous pioneers and trench-diggers — and buoy-adjusters — I am afloat. I am grateful to all.'

This article had for its text only four of Chapman's books. A score of others could hardly have changed the critic's estimate of his subject. Besides all the published writings in books and periodicals, there is a mass of material that was never printed. Much of it would never have received Chapman's final admission into print. Two unpublished essays of his later years — on Carlyle and Shakespeare — might perhaps have attained, under the labor of his file, the standard he set for his published work.

The writing of his 'Retrospections' was undertaken, as we have seen, with much reluctance. In a letter to his friend Charles M. Cist, of the Cincinnati bar, whom he had come to know at Sanibel, he wrote (October 3, 1932) that, after resisting the urgency of his publishers, more than a year before, to write his memoirs, he chanced on a bundle of his letters from Harvard to his mother, and in Charleston, 'last winter,' had made a substantial beginning. 'The job bored me so much that I can't imagine *ever* continuing it. But I contemplate filing it, to be found among my papers when I die — say in 1955. Well, now I wonder whether you would type — correct the MSS. for me.' To this Mr. Cist consented, and Chapman was soon writing to him, 'I'm ashamed of having unloaded all this on you; but I'm more grateful than I am ashamed.' For this help and for Mr. Cist's advice and assistance regarding many other writings of Chapman's final years, he had indeed much occasion for gratitude.

The chief labor of the last year of his life was a small book, still unpublished, on Goethe. In 1921 he had written to Leonard Mackall, 'Goethe is played out... Why chloroform a dead cat?' Yet the thought of dealing with this portentous figure kept recurring to him and at last he grappled with it. In the introductory chapter of the book there is a passage bearing every mark of Chapman's hand, and leaving the reader to wonder what he would have done with Emerson if his first book had not been written while he was in his thirties:

> For the last fifty years I have had two favorite rag-dolls — Emerson and Goethe. I keep them in a convenient drawer, and when the mood returns pull out one of them and study him — ask him questions and talk to him — and always end by mussing his hair, batting his head against the wall, and consigning him again to the guard-room. Emerson begun to show signs of wear and tear long ago; but that was because he was an earlier acquaintance than Goethe. I had found him in an old family trunk. But Goethe I brought home from Europe in my student days all fresh and fine with half a hundred changes of costume and stage properties — sceptres, crosiers, retorts, small swords; church-bells and sheep-bells, besides some apparatus for parlor magic and social experiment. Life is hard and cold in America. I felt in reading Goethe like Browning's icy fish who had thrust himself into the warm ooze of the marsh. I was the American icy fish who would thrust himself into the warm oozy marsh of European civilization.
>
> Each of my puppets came, after many years, to pall on me, Emerson because he seemed to think I was solely interested in ethics, and Goethe because he took it for granted that I cared about emotional experiments followed by a rearrangement of my feathers with the aid of a little literary unguent.

435

Later in the book he contrasts the youth of Germany, 'taught to see Goethe through a nimbus of patriotic and sentimental feeling,' with the foreigner who 'is obliged to cut a path through the jungle of lush sentiment with which the German view of Goethe is overcast.' It was to this task that Chapman set himself. He accomplished it in nine short chapters and an appendix.

Before proceeding to the final months of Chapman's life there are some characteristic letters in these years to be read.

Letters

To Mrs. Henry Copley Greene

SANIBEL, FLORIDA
January 3, 1929

... By the way, my Anticatholic interests have brought me the acquaintance of ... a two-handed engine of power who is conducting a campaign against *tax exemptions* and belongs to the most effective class in America — the grayhaired woman. Witness 'Mother India' and Mrs. Pratt. They have the freedom of Amazons and the brains of Science. They work alone and are unpurchasable, can't be terrified nor undermined nor side-tracked. It was these women who abolished slavery. They were the earliest henchmen of Garrison anyway — and there is today a band of them behind the anti-Roman movement — which, by the way, seems to have survived the campaign, and is cropping out in so many directions that the Roman Church is surprised and peevish. . . .

My wife was badly in need of a rest — not from campaign activities — but as a result, I think, of her last year's shell-decoration manufacture — which was a trying, complex, and long-drawn out business and artistic effort. But she is much rested up on this desolate island on the Gulf of Mexico — where we have a cottage. There is no village on the island — only a dock and a store and three or four boarding-houses of a kind that might remind you of 1875. We have been here for four or five winters, and feel much at home; and I occupy myself with books and studies and looking out on the unharvested sea — where there is generally bathing at this time of year. . . .

Poor old Boston — a dried nut — with a faint pulse — just throbbing and eyes all but closed — thinks it is alive — mumbles — stumbles — smiles with complacent senescent vacuity. Lowell is a good man and has a sincere desire to capture some cultivation for Harvard — thinks the small college is the way — may be the way to do it. Harkness comes along and offers him $3,000,000 — so we are to have more bricks and mortar. If he could get *money* off his brains he would see that the way to do was to get hold of an old house and garden in Cambridge — and put Whitehead (or somebody) in it and let *Whitehead* choose half a dozen boys — (somewhat after pattern of the Taine Institution in Paris). But no! Lowell can't see that *money* is the obstacle. If his first experimental house were a success, he could start others. There are some things — and they are the important ones — that can't be started on a large scale, e.g., a garden for the development of some variety of roses which you wish to improve. If you should say anything of this kind to Lowell, he would look thoughtful — but in his underwaistcoat privacy he would be exclaiming — 'What! — And let the $3,000,000 go?' ...

Yours affectionately

JOHN JAY CHAPMAN

To the same

SYLVANIA
BARRYTOWN-ON-HUDSON
July 24, 1929

... Well, I have just finished translating another Greek play into blank verse — Sophocles' 'Antigone' — and if it's ever printed I will send you a copy. It is the greatest of the Greek plays and the most comprehensible. There is a schematic formalism about everything the Greeks did — whether in art, architecture, or letters, and it takes a big human interest — a carrying universal power — which few of them have — to keep a play alive. I positively cannot get excited about a man who falls in love with his mother, or his mother-in-law, or slaughters some sheep, thinking they are the enemy, and is so ashamed that he commits suicide; and I take a faint interest in the domestic troubles of Agamemnon. But Antigone is very real. ...

To the same

... It seems rather old-fashioned and feeble-minded in you to be annoyed with Europeans for disliking America and Americans. It's much friendlier and truer to condole with them. You begin by saying, 'You know I have much sympathy for all you say — I never meet a European without feeling sure I should have felt as he does about Americans. It's all really a historic question — and due to a natural but serious error. The Europeans should have stayed at home. That would have saved the whole situation. But they *didn't*, they wouldn't. They absolutely rushed to America in Columbus's time and have been doing the same ever since. The only thing that keeps them back is when they *can't get in*. The Spanish, the Portuguese, the Dutch, the Germans, the British, the Norwegians, Poles, Slavs, Servians, Jews — just think of the Jews, and what they might have done for America if they had only stayed in Europe. The French have the least cause for regret of all the nations — for their colonizing in North America, while at one time considerable, faded out during the Seven Years' War — and their native good sense has taught them not to renew it. Their strong grasp upon those ideas which they understand is enough: it is their gift to the world. England has enfeebled her brain by colonizing and so-called Empire-building — it is perhaps more like mud-pie building — but no one can tell. But France has stuck to the classics, to reason, and in spite of some ups and downs during the last 150 years is surely the most intellectual of modern nations — and therefore, you know, must allow for the errors and weaknesses of the others.' If they swallow this — as they will — why, how pleasant it makes things for all!

So don't waste your precious strength by trying to convert a French woman — even, French men — and men as great as Taine and Sainte-Beuve and Renan are all just blowing Roland's Horn — and don't you answer with the fish-horn — Gloucester, Mass....

Yours affectionately

JACK

JOHN JAY CHAPMAN

To Robert Nichols

58 Church St.
Charleston, S.C.
Jan. 13, 1930

DEAR ROBERT:

Your letter and the translation of Turgénieff have just come. The T. is most interesting and a wonderful bit of translation — for it doesn't sound like translation. Your inscription touches me deeply. I have turned the booklet over to Elizabeth without a word — as I do with important things. She is in bed paying bills. She bought a tiny house in this tiny city last year and it is as pretty and imaginative as a doll's house. The need was to get away from the cold of N.Y. in January and February. Charleston is much like a small Italian town in climate, and livableness. The negroes call flowers in the street and bring garden stuff to the doors. Your two negro servants sleep at their own homes — and appear only to cook, etc. It is a romantic place — to a New Yorker....

To Elizabeth Chanler Chapman

[*After the funeral of Amory Gardner at Groton.*]

Feb. 16, 1930

Amory's funeral was the only real pageant I ever was at — like Parsifal, only real — every one on the verge of tears — and great majesty and beauty. I embraced all my friends and wrote to Fanny and Mrs. Monks afterwards and am going to write to Mrs. Thayer who came up to me in swirl of parting — for they dispersed rapidly — and said, 'It's so long since we've seen you — come to us! we *need* you' — and was swept past. So don't worry. It was an hour of heaven — so don't worry....

To Owen Wister

BORDEAUX, Mch. 16, 1930
At the Restaurant de Bordeaux

DEAR DAN:

The waiter has just produced a large thin chafing-dish and had transferred to it some very diaphanous pancakes which he proceeded to powder with sugar — while the dish was heating — and then to baste with sublimatic drawn butter and the odor of violets. I had all but finished a pint of Château de Beauséjour 1922 which seemed to be about the right sort of thing on top of a mutton chop — and celery braisé — when I murmured — 'I wish Dan was here' — to which Elizabeth responded, 'That's exactly what I was thinking.'

After all — what do literature and family life amount to compared to a first-rate restaurant? *Vanitas vanitatum*, I say — all this conscientious pother over one's children — e.g., our coming abroad to try to establish or disestablish Conrad and take his life on our heads. How much wiser the fishes who leave their eggs to hatch and their progeny to fend for themselves! We are reading the memoirs of Alexandre Dumas. What a man! He could write. He had no education — that's his secret. That's the secret of writing. Both you and I are rotten with learning and schooling and all that.

We shall leave nothing that will survive like Homer. I should be in despair, but that long ago I bade adieu to vanity and ambition and I live for the moment. Tomorrow — Sunday — they are giving at the Bouffes — *La fille de Mme Angot* — and Elizabeth says it will be badly done — (to show she knows what's what) — but I think it will be *well* done — finely done — just right — better than if it were better — if you know what I mean. Then she bought me a very good black rubber surtout — and in Rennes I bought myself an umbrella for 17 francs — and it appears that Bordeaux is as good as Paris for ladies' wear — and costs half. *Par dieu*, I'm so glad we came. I like Bordeaux.

Elizabeth has been buying second-hand scraps of lace at antiquity shops. She gets as much pleasure out of it as if she were picking up *primitifs*. My notion is this: — when you buy something, you have the fun. Count that as the whole matter. The number of barrels she will leave behind — the number of trunks of Minna's things that are at Barrytown in Conrad's house — all such things represent past moments of pleasure to somebody. But to find them, to undo them — to have to decide what shall be done with them — this poisons the thought of them.

Elizabeth sends you her best love and says she will give you any week you will name for Sylvania next summer. I do hope you will try.

Yours affectionately

JACK

To the same

[*After the publication of ' Roosevelt — the Story of a Friendship.'*]

SYLVANIA — *July* 17, 1930

DEAR DAN:

I've been thinking of you for the past two months continually — not so much because I have a famished curiosity about you, but because the country from end to end has been rocking with you. Now I suppose you are fastened into American history forever, and we shall never get rid of you, and I, out of mere jealousy, am peeping about trying to find myself a dishonorable grave....

I hope that you are making up your mind, if you ever come back, that you will come to see us here, as we really are beginning to miss you, and I'll be having to write another of my obituaries, for being an almost professional memoir writer of people I have known, I can foresee that I shall be forced by public expectation to write you up, and I want to have one more good look at you. It's a great thing to have been the friend of the great, and it's a *pretty* great thing to be a friend of the friend of the great. So keep it in mind to drop in and give me some material. Elizabeth is exceedingly well — never so much so before. And so am I.

Yours ever

JACK

To Robert Nichols

BARRYTOWN, N.Y. *Aug.* 28 or 9, 1930

DEAR ROBERT:

Your bombshell certainly did explode, I mean the *Times* article just arrived — but the same is true of the one you placed in the *Times* previously — and before I forget it — send me word which of my books you have and I will send

you the rest. (You must have given them up for review).
I shall send a copy of the Review to my friend Thomas
Brockhurst, a cockney manservant in the Tavern Club in
Boston — a man of the [type] Bulwer Lytton put in his
novels — the shoe-black reader of Kant and Gibbon — and
they do exist in England — for Brockhurst used to talk to
me about Omar K. Yam and Swinburne. His brother is a
distinguished painter — genius in the family — some ancestor — and he talks cockney to do your heart good. Well,
this man, on reading some samples of my writing, said —
'O, you'll be discovered by the English — like Poe and
Whitman. They'll never find you out in America' — and à
propos I have a letter this morning from an old literary
friend — saying he had advised the new Editor of *Life* — (a
rotten weekly) — to get me to write for them — and the editor
had never heard of me — thought I was English. So on the
whole the *Times* is right. I'm an international link.

Moreover — before I stop talking about myself — the
'Antigone' is in the press and is coming out in a limited edition, $10 per copy, at the expense and profit of the publishers
— Houghton Mifflin — who are bold men — and you will be
getting a copy in a month or so. I am beginning to get
letters about the *Times* article — one today from a very
eminent brain specialist — brainotomist — praising me in a
solemn 'Amen' to the article.

O, I dare say I must resign myself like Richard III — now
that I am grown in favor with myself I will maintain
it with some — anyway caper nimbly. Conrad turned up
— according to his custom, unexpectedly — and in some
fatigue and depletion of spirits, having wound up his school.
But he's rapidly vivifying. He's a dear, and good as any
man in the world; and the running of his head into a stone
wall — from which no argument, demonstration, nor be-
seechment could deflect him — will in the end, I believe,
prove a benefit. I did the same thing myself and had a five
years' illness — which, by the way, gave me so much rest
that I rather think I shall live long — a five-years' rest in
middle age is what the average American needs. The climate
has something to do with it — and the hurly-burly of con-

ditions, which seize a man and thrust him straight on till
he meets his wall.

I have just read in type-writing a book about Roosevelt —
which ought to be called the Night Side of T. R.; for it is
wholly malignant — and to that extent ineffective. But it's
true. He was very nearly mad at times — and broke down
his mind by his egotism and mendacity. I had a quarrel with
him — political, and personal, and deadly. He was a great
genius for handling a situation, and with men, in such a
way as to get credit — but he was a damned scoundrel. His
genius was to flash a light, put someone down a well, raise
a howl to heaven about honesty, and move on to the next
thing. Such a genius for publicity as never was — and our
people, being boy-minded and extremely stupid, found him
lovely. His feebleness of intellect appears in his writings —
which are dull and bombastic — and I doubt whether he will
go down as a great man. He's more like a figure out of
Dumas. Wilson, a character more odious still, will go down
to history as the father of the League of Nations. Drat him!
His writings also are dull and he also had the power of
hypnotizing men. They idolized him — even those who
didn't like him — obeyed — worshipped.

À propos — aren't great men apt to be horrid?

Yours

J. J. C.

To George Dudley Seymour

Oct. 5, 1930
BARRYTOWN, N.Y.

DEAR GEORGE:

Just found your letter. Too bad that you should have
bought a copy of Wister's book — I myself want to have
(keep) one — he didn't send it to me — for sometime I may
want to say something about T. R.

I expect his fame to fade out with the generation of small
boys living at the time of his death — for *there is no intellect
in him — he's a monster of political sagacity — force and personal
charm — all of which will evanesce with the epoch.* I read the
flimsy you sent me without looking at the end of it. I thought

it was by Roosevelt. This gives rise to a very curious reflection. Egotism looks the same in all men — *is* the same. For example — I've just all but finished a short book — designed as a school book on Lucian. My! it's going to raise the dust. You won't see anything of me hereafter except my chariot wheels. I haven't time for folks like you. I have never seen that article of Wister's about my 'Garrison' [1] — so, if it's in a detachable condition, I wish you would lend it to me for five minutes. Curiously enough, I have a note from him since I began this letter.

Yours
JACK

To Elizabeth Chanler Chapman

TAVERN CLUB, Oct. 22: 1930

Old fashioned dinner party at the Whiteheads last night — Wh. and Mrs., the daughter, a tall English don somewhat uncommunicative — George Agassiz and wife — the Harry Greenes and the de Sélincourts. I sat between Mrs. Wh. and Rosalind. Couldn't help poking fun at Mrs. W. a little — very gay — and agreeable. After the ladies left George A. and I somewhat quizzed the old gent as to whether there must be some reality — or some relation to nature about all the symbols that mathematics found it convenient to use and invent. Whitehead said he could show by simple arithmetical means that space was — O, you know what — if you kept on you would come in through the opposite window hanging upside down. George and I could not feel sure of this. When we joined the ladies — Whitehead took me firmly by the hand and retired to a corner. Said he didn't know how to thank me for my attacks on Gilbert Murray. Murray and Jowett and the Oxford people were so full of themselves — I forget his exact words. He himself had not kept up his Greek on leaving (I think) Cambridge — but of late years he had a revived curiosity in it and took the Greek text and two or three translations — and hovered over Plato to see what he could make of him. Then he proceeded to give me

---

[1] A review in the *Yale Review* for April, 1922.

a canter over Plato — hypothetical significance of the various great dialogues — very sketchy and more and more distant as he went on, and I got a chance to point out some neat work in Plato for covering up his transitions and fooling the public — and he said 'Quite so' — and that really the dialogues could not be brought to an accordance and that one must take each one for itself. This looked like thought-reading. So I ventured to give him some of my views. Then he asked me plump what I was writing and I, though I generally side-track the question — I thought being asked by such a man I really ought to tell him — Lucian. He had read L. in the Fowler translation and admired him all you could wish — wanted to know why it was and how it was done and what made a dialogue strike fire. If he had asked this two weeks ago I shouldn't have *quite* known. But I told him in three words — about the technique — and he saw it at a glance. He is either a mind-reader or the quickest-witted man in the world. I expounded Plato's obscurity as arising out of his technique, etc., and he ditto. So you see I shall have one sympathetic reader.

By the way, he spoke of the Hermotimus, the sceptic who examines the student (which he admired enormously,) and told him the upshot was scepticism as to geometry — which — (like latitude and longitude in 'The Hunting of the Snark') — turned out to be 'merely conventional signs,' with no ascertainable relation to nature herself. I asked him whether he knew if any ancient had ever seen this previously to Lucian. He didn't know. Whitehead is himself a bit groggy on the point (as our conversation at dinner seemed to indicate) but he's the open-mindedest *and the quickest* intelligence I have ever come across. . . .

To Charles M. Cist

Nov. 11, '30

DEAR CHARLES:

You needn't think that I'd be offended at anything you say. 'Homosexual' is to me a more unpleasant word than pederasty. Homosexual is a sneaking, allusive — pseudo-scientific, lurching, smirking, loathly word — while pederasty is

446

simply pederasty. You have heard of pederasty. Every one knows what it means. It conveys no falsetto modesty. It simply means pederasty and that's the subject of my chapters. I have pretty well finished the thing after endless toil and revision — and will send you a copy when it's typed — so keep me informed as to your changes of address. I can't let you keep it, for I have to send one to Greenslet — and keep one by me and need the third to show sundry people for advice. But you needn't be in a hurry to return it — as there is no hurry about the whole business.

Yours aff.

Jack

To the same

Barrytown, N.Y.
Nov. 13, 1930

Dear Charles:

Off for N. Y. and like a man after an illness — so concentrated have I been for two months — and the thing may not be right or quite right any way. I have indeed had in mind for years a notion to give a stab at the Periclean Greek influence — for I have always felt it to be false — and that pederasty is the reason of its falsehood — and that more rot has been talked about Greece than about any other subject, and I wanted to leave my own visiting card on Plato. When I ran across Lucian and found that he felt the same way — I very gradually came to see how to do it. It is not a parlor essay. It is a philosophical attack.

Two weeks ago I had a talk with Alfred North Whitehead — aged 70 — one of the greatest mathematicians in England — or they say anywhere — a Cambridge, England, man. He is at Harvard and is regarded as a sage. He spoke of my attacks on Gilbert Murray and that school — much to my surprise — with great approval, and incidentally spoke of Plato, and whether Plato really was a philosopher and what his method was, etc. Said he read in the dialogues by the aid of the memory of his early education and translations and the conceptions he could make up by the use of key words or key ideas — but on the whole he seemed delighted when

I said that the whole web and texture of Plato was insubstantial rubbish or words to that effect. So I shall have one intelligent and sympathetic reader anyway. That's the man I'm writing for: even if I have to print it myself — (which I don't expect as the times are times of liberal speech). The other class is the college student. I want to put a small cheap book or pamphlet in the hands of the class in Plato. . . .

To Elizabeth Chanler Chapman

THE CENTURY ASSOCIATION
7 WEST FORTY-THIRD STREET
NEW YORK, *Dec.* 3, 1930

Well, my fears were utterly unfounded. Greenslet had nothing but praise of the 'Lucian,' with some humorous reference to the reducing [of] pederasty to a drawing-room subject — (as if it had been accomplished) — and his 'serious' talk was to get me to write a history of my preoccupations, forays, reform movements, etc. Said he had gone through the whole set of my books recently and that the history of my education (*à la* Henry Adams) would be a record of the American people during the epoch and one of the greatest books ever written — and that I should begin the book like Bacon — whom he quoted in the line 'Francis Bacon ruminates as follows' or words to that effect.

I told him that the past bored me. But he said that he didn't look for the book till 1940 — (just tomorrow, by the way). At any rate we had a jolly lunch, including Quincy Howe whom I like.

Yours
JACK

To Henry James

[*After the publication of his life of Charles W. Eliot.*]

325 WEST 82
December 23, 1930

DEAR HENRY:

You have given a wonderful picture of Eliot and his times and conveyed him so vividly and justly that it's amazing.

I couldn't believe that I would read it all through, which in substance I did — though the second volume is rather repetitive. The fact is that there wasn't enough in the subject (for the general reader at least) for more than a one-volume life. But the survivors and educators are so many and the tradition so strong that a great man must have two, that art and posterity had to stand the expansion. But if you ever write another life take your head at the start with the family as to its *size*.

The book has, to my mind, another defect. A reader expects that a biographer will somewhere philosophize, and give his own mind on the merits, greatness and shortcomings of the life as a whole. Now you bring out Eliot's deficiencies with wonderful talent, and you summarize his accomplishments very ably, but you nowhere in a page or two show the way the deficiencies qualified his accomplishment. I don't say in the way *I* should do it, but in your own way. To put it crudely, he was a gigantic schoolmaster and thought in schedules and regulations. He had not the temperament, interests, or passions of a scholar. This resulted in the social coldness and timidity of the professional group at Harvard. They were under discipline. No such atmosphere ever arose at Harvard as at Johns Hopkins in the early days, and this spirit is the soul of a university and the idea of a university.

Then as to his *utilitarianism*. This resulted in his throwing the college into the office of Lee Higginson where it has been ever since, and a new age must if it can — but I scarcely see how — somehow pull it out of Lee Hig. All this just as it crosses my mind. There may be nothing in it.

Merry Christmas. I am off for Charleston.

Yours affectionately
JACK

To the same

[*After reviewing the biography of President Eliot for the 'Yale Review' Chapman wrote a letter in verse to Henry James, in part as follows:*]

58 CHURCH STREET
CHARLESTON, S.C.
Feb. 8, 1931

DEAR HENRY:

  I humored all your gambols and preambles,
 Your gentle gibes, your kidding and your kitting,
Charming they are — so's toast, and tea, and knitting.
  Your sail so trimly luffing, curving, gliding,
 Ever in danger, never quite colliding —
And yet there was a vacancy of background:
 I felt the absence of the sea beyond;
There was no flag or stake for you to tack round,
 It seemed that you were sailing on a pond.

  A strange child Eliot! With his giant rattle
 Of 'Education! training to the fore!'
Half of his childhood's friends were killed in battle.
 He goes to France in 1864.
A fact like this one ought not to transmography
Even in the lighter species of biography.
 You throw a cloud across the Civil War.

So of the leading part that Eliot played
 In steering and financing education
(And tying her quite firmly up with trade)
I say it should be mentioned and assayed.
Some sketch of him that should include his Age
Is needed for the portrait of this Sage —
This Happy Warrior and the course he ran.
'Ah,' but you say, 'it was not in my plan.'

Ever affectionately
J. J. C.

To George Dudley Seymour

BARRYTOWN, N.Y. *July* 29, 1931

MY DEAR GEORGE:

 Thank you for your letter. I have often thought of you —
and of running over to see you — phoning first to find out

if you were there. But what with life in general I couldn't seem to manage it. Now I'll wait till the hot weather is past and some day when I'm in the city — try it on. But I don't see that you have read my book which I'm sure I ordered sent to you — and if so I must grievingly abandon you to the tormentors. Lucian is my Nathan Hale. Does that give you the idea? — my discovery, my pet, my bull-dog. Why, he'll eat up you and Yale and the Birthplace in a jiffy and look about for more. When I say 'Rats!' he barks and when I say 'Bunkum!' he'll tackle a windmill. Owen Wister is with us for a few days — and we are having a real old man's holiday — as I have known him ever since his old she-grand-mother Fanny Kemble was alive — and would roar, or growl rather, in the library at Butler Place — did rather the only time I saw her. But Dan does not roar but purrs — and he has a good right to if you count the American people — I mean *count* them and see how many have ever heard of you — or — me — and of him, and yet you (and I) are writing for posterity and for the Eons, and our books will be treasured and reprinted long after his cow-pasture studies have turned to dust on the shelves.

Yours affectionately
J<small>ACK</small>

To J. E. Spingarn

B<small>ARRYTOWN</small>, N.Y.
Aug. 2, 1931

M<small>Y DEAR</small> S<small>PINGARN</small>:

I am learning something about the American people. I sent the 'Lucian' to about 40 of my friends old and new — and also some intellectuals, including H. O. Taylor, Paul Elmer More, W. W. Lawrence and a lot of my college intimates — and they *don't answer*. The book fills them with shame, gloom, and foreboding. I have three or four good letters — one from Gaselee, the man who did a small book — (Daphnis, Chloe?) — for the Loeb Library and who laughs. But the best one is from a college friend of my own age who for three years or more has been sitting with the rest of the family — about a brilliant son of 30, or less, who is dying of consumption, and he says — 'I have read it — and the last chapter aloud — to my two sons and wife. We enjoyed it greatly and marvelled at your learning and courage, and I think the title will attract a large class of readers and bring out of their shells many critics. I should like to see the criticisms,' etc. Well, this man and you and Gaselee have seen that the book must be read in the spirit of beer and skittles.

But no one else. We are a serious people — and morbidly timid. There will be no reviews. I have a friend on the *New Republic* — Edmund Wilson — a serious and talented young man who admires my work, and I wrote some time ago and suggested his reviewing it. But it later occurred to me that it would damage him to do so — and I wrote to him to put it off his mind.

Then it occurred to me to tell him to send it to you for review — and then, that you might not like to write for the N.R. and might not want to review the book anyway.

After all, the main thing about a literary venture of any sort is that one finds things out — things that give one no pleasure, but are interesting.

Yours sincerely

JOHN JAY CHAPMAN

To Elizabeth Chanler Chapman

THE CENTURY ASSOCIATION
7 WEST FORTY-THIRD ST.
NEW YORK
Nov. 28, 1931

Ever since reading in Rothenstein's book I have in my mind been reviewing the nineties — casually. It was an age of charades and of social attitudinizing: every one must take a rôle. Arthur Balfour — posed as a philosopher — wrote a book — living in Florence — great expectations by the elect. Gerald Balfour — Tennysonian type — Adam's-apple in marble — and great yearnings.... Everywhere the social poses — combined with searching emotions — and O — intellect! The Souls — Lady Grandby — if that's her name. The invitation to the *salon* — a mock salon — shading off into Oscar Wilde, Harry Cust, Frank Harris, Lord Alfred Douglas — (a sculptor-pose by) a bad egg.

The *Yellow Book* — cleverness, whimsies, novelties, finesse, legerdemain — but O my! all amateur. Neither John Sargent nor Whistler nor Henry James had the attitude of workaday artists toward their work. They were each doing a stunt — '*À moi Velasquez, à moi Titian,*' says Sargent as he takes up his brush — '*À moi Stendhal, à moi Flaubert, Maupassant,*' says Henry James. Whistler's aim is to produce novel effects as a *tour de force* — not as incidental to his day's work — to his nature, to his trade and craft and passion. And all these people gas and talk and attitudinize. As for Shaw, he's the caricature of a caricature — the monkey of the show. The gay part of the nineties left nothing that is going to interest later times. Shaw, the caricature of them, is busted already — much assisted towards his bust by his trip to Russia and his talk on the Fabian ideas, (which every one has forgotten) — as represented by Russia. The American people, who know something about Russia, through the ten years' work of their brilliant journalists — couldn't even laugh over Shaw's latest. They haven't bought his book on Ellen Terry. By the way, even Ellen Terry wasn't a serious artist. She was a talented, hard-working amateur — hadn't the physique of a real actress nor the metal in her — and O my, what yawps. I think Mrs. Campbell was about the only artist of the time — and I was sort of shocked at seeing that she too had gone over the edge in talking as she did the other day about a particular bunch of Shaw's letters to her as if they were different from the others —*which they were not.* So I dropped in and told her all these things — and that if she carried out her project as to Shaw's letters, she must not try to make any such distinction — and, in fact, must have only *one single note* — written in granite at the beginning of the book — saying that she was taking this way of protecting herself against his *altering* the letters when or if he prints them.

As for this project I have no opinion on it. It's too complex; but it looks as if it might work out as she designed it should.

Well, she agreed with me — I really think she *did* — about the whole age. (But it may be too late for her to get free of that age. Of course she ought never to have had such familiar

453

relations — however jocose — with such a gutter cat.) I
didn't say this, because I didn't need to. . . .

To the same

Dec. 19, 1931

'Don Giovanni' — good seat, full house, and immensely
enthusiastic. It is the acme of the human genius for joy —
the buffooners of the Mediterranean and the purity of the
Teutons — one continuous volcano of happiness. The strains
from the under world — or blasts — in the last scene antici-
pate Wagner's dissonances and are not crude, Gothic, and
horrid like his.

When one thinks of Mozart with a quill pen sitting down
before some ruled lines — and this outcome! It is about the
most divine out-come of Humanity — and somehow the
traditions of how to give it have been preserved thus far. I
was in a seat all but above the stage and with a first-rate
view of it — and music comes up. I feel as if I had taken a
bath in Elysium. 'How can I seek the empty world again?' . . .

To Charles M. Cist

CHARLESTON
Apr. 7, 1932

DEAR CHARLES:

. . . We are in the same fix as all the well to do — Sylvania
is in question — and can't see how we can keep it up —
and then what? Let the lawn grow up, discharge the farm
hands and live in the house with a cook and a buttons? And
what would the hands do? We are prepared for 'most anything
— but the subject can't be opened till sessions with Mrs. C.'s
lawyers — in which I shall not be consulted.

At any rate we are extremely glad that we didn't go abroad.
The German reading has gone on and we are nearing the end
of *Soll und Haben* — a much better book than *Hammer und
Amboss*, which we got pretty tired of. We shall take about
ten days in going north — stopping off — at University of
N.C., Richmond, Washington, etc. The social customs here
are too exacting for me — palaver and teas — every one keeping up the pace. This year I have done my duty. Next —

on one pretense or another I'm going to be very evanescent and mysterious. It's easy to deceive people. Be *very* nice when you do see them — and then cloud yourself with lies, and disappear.

Yours ever
JACK

To Leonard L. Mackall

CHARLESTON
April 7, 1932

DEAR LEONARD:

The L. T. [March 24 London *Times Literary Supplement*] Goethe article interests me extremely, first because it makes no claims for Goethe's greatness *as a poet* except what every one must feel — the lyrics and the early parts of 'Faust.' As for the rest of the article it chiefly interests me because *you* agree with it. So this is what a truly true Goethean believes — Goethe's success in taking charge of his own development, etc. Well, you know, I think it is a psychological error for any man to think he can steer his own development — and the more he thinks he has succeeded the more is he deluded. I think Goethe drifted into one thing after another as every one does.

Drifted into associations with the local gentry and into the post of grand panjandrum of a petty court — drifted into science — drifted into love affairs and the use of them for love copy.

Drifted into dramatic experiments and finally into the conception of the second part of 'Faust' as a compendium for all his driftwood.

This is the normal view to take in considering any human being. One ought to begin with the thought — of his drift.

As to self-improvement and self-education, it is a trap, an illusion, a pleasing idiocy, a brain-softening indulgence. Suppose you, for instance, to have the ambition to be the highest educated old-book-man in the world — or I to be the great American critic — the pose would shine out of us and interfere with our development. Now Goethe was a great amateur and never quite toed the mark — except as above universally acknowledged in small poems and parts of 'Faust,' and he had the Teutonic passion for self-improvement. In one of Smollett's works — I think 'Humphry Clinker' — there is a description of a young German traveller who gives his views on life at the breakfast table — among other things he will marry 'because married life is one of the experiences which a man should have to be well-roundly educated,' etc. The thing is a German invention, preoccupation, and older than Goethe — it is Teutonic and the writer in the L.T. gets it from Germany — and you do — and you ought to wash it out of your hair.

Yours
J. J. C.

To Owen Wister

Sylvania
Barrytown-on-Hudson
June 18, 1932

Dear Dan:

... By the way I have never had the experience of being able to read a book that was shoved at me with an encomium. Have you? This depression business came just in time. It has put forward the case against prohibition — stopped the bonus bill — probably ended the Al Capone era — and made everyone more thoughtful and sensible — started everyone saving his pennies and living small — showed that the greatest financiers of the world know nothing about finance — and cured perhaps the habit of the cleverest boomers in the world from playing on the weaknesses of the poorer classes with the installment plan, etc. — caused everyone to reflect on the relation between the corruptions of politics and his own income — and made everyone *suffer* — which is the only way to make anyone think.

I hope the recovery will be slow. Otherwise we shall return to our vomit....

Yours affectionately
Jack

To Charles M. Cist

BARRYTOWN, N.Y.
June 21, 1932

DEAR CHARLES:

I see what has happened. You are practising law in Cincinnati. It's the only business that has survived — and you've been appealed to to wind up something or save the remnants of something and have stayed on in Cincinnati. That shows how valuable it is for any young man to learn a trade. I wish *I* had. But I couldn't. I was on a carpenter's bench for some years — cutting my fingers and bruising my left thumb — and the more I tried, the less I could hit the nail. This Shakespeare trifle has cost me as much trouble as a life of Bacon. It has been typed and retyped — growing smaller and smaller — and isn't done yet into the fasteners. You see, my idea was to tie up Hamlet and label him and leave him where people could *find* him — and say 'John Jay Chapman fixed that feller — he *fixed* him.'

The beast wriggled and squirmed, of course. He loved his liberty and all the talk he was making. He got on the back of my chair, if I took my mind off the paper, and said, 'Here I am, old man!' But today he's in a tin container like a Strassburg goose — with a little grease round him to keep the air out — and I'm in need of a job. That diabolical devil Leonard Mackall (who is a treasure in the way of an American who knows the inside working of the Goethe-Mill) — has been trying for years to get me to take a hand in the propaganda — little knowing that what I touch I destroy — and I have been walking the fields with a butterfly net held behind my back — a Big Temptation — and my wife shouting from the window, 'Hold! Hold! Don't do it!'

All the while the bad times and the awakening of the American mind — if it *does* awaken — going on, and the insolubles spluttering in the cauldron.

We have had two grandchildren — boys — six and four, here for a month or more. They are very consoling as they have a truly wonderful nurse — all humor and discipline — the best nurse I ever saw. Chanler, who has been working for several years like a mule — has gone off with a friend

457

who owns a boat in the Bermuda Race. That's about the gayest sporting proposition I ever heard of. (I am so glad I'm not in it, all the same. Boats go up down in such an unpleasant way, and in a race one is always shifting one's seat and dodging ropes. No! not for me. Give me a pot of ink, a pad and a waste paper basket with a table that doesn't go up and down.)

Yours affectionately
J<small>ACK</small>

Elizabeth says that I misrepresent her attitude towards a Goethe essay. But women will say anything.

To his Grandsons

[*On their way to Italy.*]

Nov. 24, 1932

M<small>Y DEAR</small> J<small>AY AND</small>
M<small>Y DEAR</small> R<small>OBERT</small>:

Hurrah! Hurrah for the dashing bounding sea — whales — icebergs — water spouts — and O my, Rome! But first Gibraltar — the Pillars of Hercules — Africa! and then Naples and Vesuvius — and O my, the dear lovely Italian people, so gentle and loving and handsome and fond of children. And if you don't both come back talking and reading Italian you'll not take after your papa — who picks up languages and eats them like peanuts.

O, I wish I was along with you. No! I won't say that — it would spoil all. But I wish I could just meet you on the piazza di Spagna or in the Coliseum or in the Pantheon or St. Peter's — and watch you at a distance. Now I'll give you some great serious *Advice*: — Be Good! Go to see the Marionettes. They can only be seen in Italy and have been going on since Roman times. Also see the Wolf and Romulus and Remus — which has stood on the same spot for two thousand years. Blessings on both and all of you and your parents too.

Your loving
G<small>RANDPAPA</small>

From these letters it could hardly be deduced that Chapman had become anything other than his exuberant self. Yet there were anxieties to temper any buoyancy — the delicate health of his infant granddaughter, the straightening of financial affairs which threatened seriously the continuance of the family mode of life, the impairment of his wife's health, and of his own. In September of 1932 it became necessary for him to spend a week at the Vassar Hospital at Poughkeepsie, under observation and treatment. Before the end of October he was writing to Leonard Mackall, 'I am all recovered long ago, and only baby myself out of caution and because of the A. D. in which I was born, and the rash remark of some Old Testament chap setting 70 as the normal age of mortality.' He had already taken up 'activities suitable to gentlemanly old age.' In November, after having moved to Charleston with his wife, he wrote to Mr. Cist, 'My hemorrhage has no doubt weakened my brain, but I am so resourceful and experienced that I shall conceal this.' It was indeed his chosen rôle through all these final months to spare his wife any needless anxiety for him.

This was no simple matter, for in January of 1933 he was stricken with what he called a 'form of grippe ... which makes a man a volcano of pain, and passes off slowly.' To his son Chanler — in Rome with his wife and boys — he wrote (January 20, 1933), 'Imagine the thunderbolt and anguish it has been to Dear Mo. We are now in separate rooms, prostrated — I getting up for the day, walking in the garden and reading odd books, with the volcano *decrescendo*, and she taking treatments of a very dear and expert nurse.'

Both before and after Chapman's illness at Charleston, his wife was engrossed in plans for the building of a small house on the Sylvania place. They were to occupy it, with Chanler and his family established in the larger house near by. This interest was so beneficial to Mrs. Chapman's health that Chapman — really indifferent to it all — gave himself to the project as heartily as he could. 'Of course you understand,' he wrote to his son Chanler, 'that I have become an absolute saint — at the cost of terrible pain, hypocrisy, cringing, impersonations, sleight of hand, and ready humor.' Making a cheerful game of this enterprise, and of such diversions as frequenting a small Charleston club and speaking on Dante before the Poetry Society of South Carolina, he could even write before leaving Charleston, 'I have got so foolish and so well that I pay calls with her [Mrs. Chapman] and don't suffer. We have people to good-bye lunches with intimates, and leave cards (just like Rome) where duty calls. I seem to have become civilized, by the weeks of hideous suffering I went through.' This letter of March 3 — turning to the new plans for Sylvania — ended on a characteristic note of gaiety.

> To Dear Mo this is like the abdication of Charles V. I tell you this Chanler family is an amusing family that you have been born into — not many such families — eleven brothers and sisters in her generation and all eccentrics — and now multiplying and becoming, of course, more commonplace in the next generation, except here and there one or two who keep up the record. People like me and Olivia get a lot of good from our association with the Chanlers — sort of shakes us up, you know. That is, if we pull through.[1]

In the light-hearted spirit behind these words, the Chapmans left Charleston in April, and after a short stay in New York proceeded to London, in search of beneficial change. They established themselves, as usual, at the Artillery Mansions Hotel, and entered into a quiet enjoyment of London — tea, music, and plays in the open air, with smiling observation of the passing scene. 'Dear M. and I,' says a letter to Chanler soon after their landing, 'are both very excited and feel like birds released. She almost weeps at each familiar sight, and spends hours in old picture-shops seeking small treasures for Good Hap — (I think it's a good name for her

---

[1] Writing in 1908 to Mrs. Winthrop Chanler, after an accident to her husband, Chapman had said: 'There is always one Chanler in the newspapers....The Chanler theme dies in the bassoons and is dropped by the pathetic drum solo — but hark the flute!'

new shanty).' Mrs. Chapman's friend, Mrs. Alfred Lyttelton, was near at hand, and other friends and relatives enlivened the hours that could be spared from solitude and 'Goethe.' A letter to Chanler Chapman contains these typical sentences: 'Lunched with Ruth Draper, where also the Spicers. Ruth is perfectly enchanting — handsome, gay, vigorous, beaming. ... Well, I wish you could see her. She is a perfected soul. (I wish *I* were, though I'd compromise on the body if that were proposed — just for the sake of Dear Mo.)'

Early in August they sailed back to America, eager to establish themselves in the 'Good Hap' cottage. In their London hotel they had seen much of Basil de Sélincourt and his wife, Anne Douglas Sedgwick. In her recently published 'Portrait in Letters' she is seen to have come to London 'to fight in the last ditch, with treatments of electricity and massage by a very remarkable young practitioner who was recommended to Basil by "Jack" and Elizabeth Chapman.' The departure of the Chapmans left these English friends 'feeling like babes in the wood in this deserted London. ... It is a great bond to be facing the same sort of *ultimates* with people. He is a splendid delicious old fellow — Anaxagoras Basil calls him; and she full of fire, courage, and sweetness.' To these published words I cannot refrain from adding a sentence concerning Chapman in an unpublished letter of Mr. de Sélincourt's: 'Of course I regard him as a force and a luminary, and though on such short acquaintance felt him more lovable than any other man I ever met.'

So felt a host of Chapman's friends both in England and at home. They were no more aware than he that the end of his life was so near at hand. For two months, from about the middle of August, he shared his wife's enjoyment in putting 'Good Hap' in order. Of one result from this process he declared, 'I have never liked a room so much as this.' Early in October he was writing to his wife, absent in New York, of his delight in reading F. A. Hedgcock's 'David Garrick and his Friends,' and of his having cast out fear for himself.

Yet his health was declining so rapidly that he was taken again to the Hospital at Poughkeepsie for observation. There the doctors pronounced an operation necessary if a malignant condition was to be stayed, but, on finding him adverse to so drastic a measure, agreed to wait a while. He returned to Good Hap with a trained nurse. For a fortnight he remained there. With nurse, grandchildren, and all about him his humor and gentleness were as the leaves of those last autumn days. Knowing them to be his last, he would sit, when out of bed, with a book before him, reading little, but thankful, he said, for such an opportunity for clear thinking. In bed he would hold in his hand his small wooden cross. He spoke, as a believing child might speak, of the angels that were coming for him, and said to his wife, 'When I flit away, I shall always remember this little place.' He was in truth to leave it a hallowed place, even as if by such a translation, a place to which his spirit might still minister. About a year after his death a small card, never seen before, was found in his room, with *Te Deum Laudamus* beneath a Fra Angelico angel. On the back of it were the words, in Chapman's handwriting:

'Elizabeth came with a book in each hand. In her left hand she held the mind of the world and this book she gave first. In her right hand she held the heart of the world and that she gave me and the hand that held it.'

It was not long before his increasing discomfort and weakness proved to him that the doctors had been right. On October 29 he went back to the hospital. On October 31 an operation was performed, and on November 4 he died.

During the two days in the hospital before his operation, he was reading, and marking, an Everyman's copy of Boswell's Johnson — last of all (with dissent) the Doctor's denunciation of the 'odious wench' who had deserted the Church of England for Quakerism, and his avowal that 'we ought not, without very strong conviction indeed, to desert the religion in which we have been educated.' In this volume Mrs. Chap-

AFTERGLOW

man subsequently made a few notes so significant that it is surely permissible to copy them here:

> *Jack's first coming out of ether:* — 'This seems to me a typical period of transition.' A little later: 'I think that a period of diversion is now in order, and (shaking his finger at Miss Isobel Martin with a twinkle) if anything goes wrong it will be your fault, not mine!'
>
> Jokes were his, constantly, those two or three days, even when confused by sedatives.
>
> Jack: — 'Did you manage to eat all your chicken?'
>
> Eliz.: — 'No, I gave some of it to Miss Martin.'
>
> Jack: — 'And I gave mine to the man in the next room. *So we done good!*' This because he always twitted me with my 'good motives.'
>
> On the early morning of the 2nd, I heard him murmuring, 'A soldier lay dying, a soldier lay dying.' I bent over him to catch the words, and he repeated the first four lines of 'A soldier of the Legion lay dying in Algiers,' adding, '*But there is lack of nothing here,*' in a voice of deep feeling.
>
> When semi-conscious that afternoon, as I was holding his hand, he said several times, plucking at my fingers, 'I want to take it away, I want to take it away!' 'What?' I asked, 'the pillow?' 'No,' he said, 'the mute, the mute. I want to play on the open strings.'
>
> And that day I heard him murmuring to himself, 'Teach me, O Lord' — his constant ejaculation through life. But he was too weak to finish the verse.

Suppose him to have been borne away after the fashion of his imagining. A spear, like Ithuriel's spear of truth, might then have been placed in his hand;

> 'for no falsehood can endure
> Touch of celestial temper.'

The spear with which Chapman rushed at falsehoods throughout his life was the flame of his quenchless spirit.

Appendix A

ROOSEVELT AND CHAPMAN

MEMORANDA among Chapman's papers, letters from him, the files of the daily press, and brief references in books relating to Roosevelt illuminate the story of the relations between these two in 1898. It is a story too long and involved to be recited here in detail. Six typewritten sheets headed 'Theodore Roosevelt and the Independent Nomination: Statement and Correspondence' contain letters that passed between Roosevelt and members of the group with which Chapman was working. The opening paragraphs record the two conferences with Roosevelt at Montauk Point on August 24 and September 1. At the first of these Chapman and Isaac H. Klein laid the possibility of an independent nomination before him and 'suggested that he take time to consult his friends, promising to return after the Colonel had time for reflection.' At the second, 'Roosevelt expressed his willingness to take an independent nomination in case he received a Republican nomination, but did not consider it his duty to run on an independent ticket against a regular Republican nominee. Roosevelt stated that if he got the Republican nomination he wanted the Independent endorsement. It was agreed by Colonel Roosevelt that his exact position in the matter should be covered by a statement to be given to the press by Mr. Chapman at the time the ticket was announced.'

On September 10 the statement was issued, and the ticket, made up of irreproachable names, with that of George E. Waring, Jr., as State Engineer, and with a blank soon to be filled with the name of Thomas Mott Osborne as the candidate for Lieutenant-Governor, was announced. On the next day an apparently authorized interview with Roosevelt was published by Leonard H. Jerome, intimating that the Colonel would welcome the support of the Independents in the event of his nomination by the Republicans. The Citizens' Union, hitherto concerned primarily with city politics, was on the point of deciding whether to permit the use of its name and emblem in connection with the Independent State ticket. Meyer D. Rothschild of the Independent group hurried to Montauk Point, talked with T. R., and telegraphed to New York: 'Roosevelt stands where he did when Chapman and Klein saw him. He is all right.' On the same day Preble Tucker, of the same group, wrote to Roosevelt asking his opinion of the Independents' address to the public. On September 12 Roosevelt answered: 'That address is all right; I have just seen Rothschild.' One paragraph in the address read as follows: 'We do not know that he will decide to be a candidate in this election. We do know that when nominated by us, in case he should be opposed by the regular Republican organization, he would find it his duty to run. We expect him to be free to deal with that situation, if it ever arises, with absolute deliberation. But our duty is clear.' It was in these circumstances that the Citizens' Union lent its support to the State Independent movement.

Meanwhile another situation, imperfectly if at all known to the Independents, was arising. It was not a question of Roosevelt's being opposed, but of his being backed, by the regular Republican organization, and some details of it might remain still unknown but for the unsuccessful suit for libel brought by William Barnes, Jr., against Roosevelt nearly twenty years later. In the course of the trial a letter from Lemuel Ely Quigg, Senator Platt's political lieutenant, to Roosevelt and Roosevelt's answer to it were introduced as evidence.[1] Quigg wrote to Roosevelt September 10, 1898, giving, at considerable length, the substance of a recent conference between them at Montauk Point about his accepting the regular Republican nomination for Governor, and asking Roosevelt to name the day for a meeting with Platt. In the course of the letter Quigg said that in his report to Platt upon their conference he had said 'that you would take the office, if at all, intending in good faith to act the part of his friend personally and politically; to acknowledge and respect his

[1] See *New York Tribune*, April 23, 1915.

position as the head of the Republican organization and the Republican Senator from the State of New York;... that you would consult with the Senator freely and fully on all important matters, that you would adopt no line of policy and agree to no important matter of nomination without previous consultation, and that you wanted him to agree to the same thing on his part.' Before closing Quigg felt bound to warn Roosevelt against Mugwump influences: 'The thing I fear is that these plausible and poisonous Mugwumps will at some time or other involve you in some of their "good government" entanglements, intended, as they always are, to help the Democratic party and to create dishonest prejudice against decent Republicans, and that the first thing we know there will be a hitch.'

Roosevelt in reply to Quigg accepted the general tenor of the letter: 'Your representation of what I said was substantially correct: that is, it gave just the spirit,' but he went on to make certain obviously proper reservations: 'I know that you did not in any way wish to represent me as willing to consent to act otherwise than in accordance with my conscience.' Quigg's suggestion that Roosevelt should call at once on Senator Platt resulted in a meeting that took place on September 17. Roosevelt's attempt to obliterate the bad effect which this call was bound to have on the public mind is amusingly set forth in 'The Autobiography of Lincoln Steffens.' Its immediate effect upon the Independents was devastating, for the talk with Platt was promptly followed by Roosevelt's withdrawal of his name from the first place on the Citizens' Union ticket. In a letter of September 19 to Chapman — still 'dear Jack,' even as Roosevelt remained 'dear Teddy' — he wrote, 'I do not see how I can accept the Independent nomination and keep good faith with the other men on my ticket.'

It is impossible that while the Independents were scouring the state for the many signatures required for the nomination of a ticket by petition, instead of in a convention, Roosevelt could have imagined that his name would appear alone upon it. He had approved a statement naming a whole ticket. Platt did not fail to see that the Independents were hitting at his control not only through the governorship but through the other elected officials of the state. As Chapman rationalized the situation when he wrote his 'Practical Agitation' two years later: 'The rumpus among the Republican heelers — following so slight a cause as the action of five or six citizens who took the field with a ticket of their own — resembled the action of a geyser when a cake of soap is thrown into it — rumbling — followed by terrific vomiting.' Quigg, the professional politician, knew his business better than Chapman and his amateur colleagues when he caused Roosevelt to commit himself in writing to the recognition of Platt as the leader of his party. When Chapman was asked afterwards why he and his fellows had not secured Roosevelt's written agreement to stand by them, he replied, 'We didn't know it was necessary.'

The awkward position in which Roosevelt had placed not only the agitators for the Independent nomination but also his fellow-nominees is revealed in the following words from an unpublished statement of George E. Waring, Jr., preserved among Chapman's papers:

> Early in September I was assured by the Independent Committee that Roosevelt would stand on its nomination, and I consented to the use of my name on the ticket. I wrote Roosevelt that even if he ran only on the Independent ticket he would be elected, so great was his popularity. He took this to be advice in favor of such action, which was not my intention, and said he could not run against a candidate of his party.
>
> I have no copy of my reply. I said substantially, that Platt would not nominate him if he could help himself: that if he ran only on Platt's ticket his name might be used to help fill the legislature with 'Yellow Dogs' who, at Platt's bidding, might elect even Quigg to the U.S. Senate — that if he ran also on the Independent ticket, Platt would be bound to put up good men for every place; that he need not accept the Independent nomination, but that he should not decline it; and that it would suffice if he would say, in accepting the Republican nomination, that he was glad to become the candidate of his own party and of all others who might choose to vote for him. I received in reply a letter which began thus: 'With what you say in this letter, I can cordially agree.' ...

It is hard to explain Roosevelt's failure to pursue the course proposed by Colonel Waring on any theory except that of Senator Platt's insistence to the contrary. Of course the Independent Committee did not accept the decision without a struggle, and in the week following the meeting with Platt on September 17 many written and spoken words flew back and forth between Roosevelt and his rejected supporters. One of the letters from Chapman contained the following paragraphs:

DEAR TEDDY,

... You will remember that you told Klein and myself that you would, if nominated by the Republicans, be glad of our nomination, as it would strengthen your hands; and Tucker tells me you said the same thing to him, and that simultaneous nominations would be satisfactory.

You will remember that the first time I visited you, we were unwilling to press you to a decision; that is to say, to get you to let us go ahead with our canvass before you had an opportunity to see your friends and talk over the situation, which was manifestly a complex one.

I know that you are the least astute of men, and this led me into an almost brutal frankness in explaining the situation, and in giving you a week to think it over. As a practical matter, our petitions are now being signed in every county in the State, and the returns are coming in by each mail. We expect to conclude the work about the middle of next week, and if by that time you are convinced of your duty to decline our nomination, it will be an easy matter for you to file the certificate of your declination. Our committee for filling vacancies will on October 1st be in a position to place another man at the head of our ticket and proceed with the canvass.

I am satisfied, however, that you misapprehend the situation and that you never will decline. Of course my own sense of honor would force me to stop the signing of the petitions by telegram the moment you positively reject our nomination, no matter at what cost.

Yours sincerely
JOHN JAY CHAPMAN

On September 22 Roosevelt wrote to Chapman, setting forth with more elaboration than in his letter of the 19th, his reasons for the course he was taking. This letter was published in the *Tribune*, of September 25. 'I write this with great reluctance,' he said, 'for I wish the support of every Independent.... I fully appreciate the importance of the Independent vote.'

When Chapman, after his visit to Oyster Bay, had finally to give up his faith in Roosevelt, the surrender was complete. He entered with enthusiasm into the substitution of the name of Theodore Bacon, of Rochester, for that of Roosevelt as the Independent candidate for Governor, and labored valiantly in what was known to be a hopeless campaign. A sample speech in an upstate stumping tour is preserved, and contains these sample sentences: 'It is hard to believe that ambition has addled the brains and rotted the moral sense of Theodore Roosevelt — but the thing has happened. It is a tragedy. I have no desire to denounce him. I pity him. But I do want you to look calmly at his words and his acts and see whether there is any other explanation of them.'

Another trace of Chapman's intensity in the campaign is found in a letter to his wife from Ithaca (Oct. 27, 1898): 'I gave the professors a nasty jolt by saying, "I don't mind Roosevelt's being a damned fool, but I do object to his taking me for a damned fool. His buglers and tomfool campaign, his thinking himself the American flag, his saying that a vote against him puts courage into every Spaniard, is all right because he is sincere — he really believes he is the American flag; but when he endorses the administration of McKinley in words that are intended to cover, and do cover, Alger, I despise him, for I know him to be dishonest."'

When Roosevelt came to deal in his 'Autobiography' (1913) with his election to the New York governorship he referred to 'a lunatic fringe to every reform movement,' and dismissed the Independents as 'another knot of extremists who had at first ardently insisted that I must be "forced" on Platt, and as soon as Platt supported me themselves opposed me because he supported me.' As if to corroborate this view of the matter, he quoted a letter from John Hay after the election: 'The exhibition made by the professional independents in voting against you for no reason except that somebody else was voting for you, is a lesson that is worth its cost.' In the 'Selections from the Correspondence between Theodore Roosevelt and Henry Cabot Lodge,' Senator Lodge gave a letter from Roosevelt (September 26, 1898) saying, 'The Citizens' Union or Independent Movement has been worse than silly, and some day I will tell you of their exceedingly tricky conduct to me.' In an immediate answer, written (September 28) before Roosevelt could possibly have told his story, Senator Lodge wrote: 'The conduct of the Independents toward you is the most emphatic exhibition of their dishonesty I have ever seen.'

Thus it appears that if Roosevelt felt misgivings about the episode, his most trusted advisers were encouraging him to dismiss any such thoughts. Indeed it may be doubted whether any misgivings occurred to him. He had dealt with the whole matter in the intensely practical fashion of a rising political figure who wished to become Governor of New York. Chapman dealt with it in the spirit of an idealistic and, if you will, impractical reformer. A conflict was inevitable, and the consequent long estrangement was natural enough.

In amplification of the reference to George E. Waring, Jr., in Chapman's 'Memorandum' on the Roosevelt affair, a letter to Colonel Waring's son, the late Guy Waring, is given here:

To Guy Waring

Dean Hall Plantation
Strawberry, South Carolina
March 30, 1924

Dear Guy

I hate to leave just as you are coming, and especially to miss meeting Mrs. Waring — to whom please give my greetings and great regrets. Do you remember John Moors at Harvard? — good as gold and always working for citizenship and Uplift. Well, he's now old and honorable, an LL.D. and a Fellow of Harvard. I met him last summer at the Tavern Club, and it appeared that he was making historical studies into Roosevelt's relation to the Independents, and had come across the N. Y. Governorship campaign — during which Roosevelt accepted an Independent nomination and then withdrew his name at the behest of Tom Platt, etc. I gave Moors some correspondence of the period as I was one of the Independent gang with

471

whom Roosevelt dealt during the episode. This reminded me of something that passed rapidly and unnoticed at the time. You may remember that your father was then the most popular and respected citizen of New York — for his street sweeping and other accomplishments — and was running on our Independent ticket as candidate for *State Engineer*. At the time of Roosevelt's apostasy I happened to go into the City Club and found your father — on crutches, as I remember — and the most indignant man I had ever encountered. I must tell you that at the outset of the campaign he had written a strong public letter in favor of T. R., who was our young war hero, fresh from Cuba.

Your father pulled out of his pocket a letter he had sent to Roosevelt beginning, 'I had thought you were an honorable man,' and proceeding in such a tone of castigation as was unique in my experience. Roosevelt had returned the letter to him without comment. Boudinot Keith, another of our committee, tells me that your father also showed the letter to him, and told him that T. R. had returned it. Your father almost immediately afterwards went to Havana and died suddenly. Now on the Saturday (or Monday) before election Roosevelt or his Committee republished the *original laudatory letter* which your father had written him at the beginning of the campaign. Roosevelt accepted the praise.

I went to Lawrence Godkin at the time (he was your father's Executor) and told him that among the testator's papers the denunciatory letter would be found, and that our Committee would like to have it, if possible. The family had naturally enough little interest in the controversy, and so the matter rested.

It occurs to me that if, by any chance, your father's papers are in existence his second letter to Roosevelt may be among them. The republication of the first letter can easily be found in the New York papers of the period, and I should like to turn over both of them to John Moors for historic preservation. Write me how all this strikes you. Many things are whirled under in this world and some of them come to light again....

Yours affectionately

JOHN JAY CHAPMAN

Appendix B

COATESVILLE

The larger portion of Chapman's speech at Coatesville, Pennsylvania, on August 18, 1912, not quoted in Chapter VI, follows:

I will tell you why I am here; I will tell you what happened to me. When I read in the newspapers of August 14, a year ago, about the burning alive of a human being, and of how a few desperate, fiend-minded men had been permitted to torture a man chained to an iron bedstead, burning alive, thrust back by pitchforks when he struggled out of it, while around about stood hundreds of well-dressed American citizens, both from the vicinity and from afar, coming on foot and in wagons, assembling on telephone call, as if by magic, silent, whether from terror or indifference, fascinated and impotent, hundreds of persons watching this awful sight and making no attempt to stay the wickedness, and no one man among them all who was inspired to risk his life in an attempt to stop it, no one man to name the name of Christ, of humanity, of government! As I read the newspaper accounts of the scene enacted here in Coatesville a year ago, I seemed to get a glimpse into the unconscious soul of this country. I saw a seldom revealed picture of the American heart and of the American nature. I seemed to be looking into the heart of the criminal — a cold thing, an awful thing.

I said to myself, 'I shall forget this, we shall all forget it; but it will be there. What I have seen is not an illusion. It is the truth. I have seen death in the heart of this people.' For to look at the agony of a fellow-being and remain aloof means death in the heart of the onlooker. Religious fanaticism has sometimes lifted men to the frenzy of such cruelty, political passion has sometimes done it, personal hatred might do it, the excitement of the amphitheater in the degenerate days of Roman luxury could do it. But here an audience chosen by chance in America has stood spellbound through an improvised *auto-da-fé*, irregular, illegal, having no religious significance, not sanctioned by custom, having no immediate provocation, the audience standing by merely in cold dislike.

473

I saw during one moment something beyond all argument in the depth of its significance. You might call it the paralysis of the nerves about the heart in a people habitually and unconsciously given over to selfish aims, an ignorant people who knew not what spectacle they were providing, or what part they were playing in a judgment-play which history was exhibiting on that day.

No theories about the race problem, no statistics, legislation, or mere educational endeavor, can quite meet the lack which that day revealed in the American people. For what we saw was death. The people stood like blighted things, like ghosts about Acheron, waiting for someone or something to determine their destiny for them.

Whatever life itself is, that thing must be replenished in us. The opposite of hate is love, the opposite of cold is heat; what we need is the love of God and reverence for human nature. For one moment I knew that I had seen our true need; and I was afraid that I should forget it and that I should go about framing arguments and agitations and starting schemes of education, when the need was deeper than education. And I became filled with one idea, that I must not forget what I had seen, and that I must do something to remember it. And I am here today chiefly that I may remember that vision. It seems fitting to come to this town where the crime occurred and hold a prayer-meeting, so that our hearts may be turned to God through whom mercy may flow into us.

Let me say one thing more about the whole matter. The subject we are dealing with is not local. The act, to be sure, took place at Coatesville, and everyone looked to Coatesville to follow it up. Some months ago I asked a friend who lives not far from here something about this case, and about the expected prosecutions, and he replied to me: 'It wasn't in my county,' and that made me wonder whose county it was in. And it seemed to be in my county. I live on the Hudson River; but I knew that this great wickedness that happened in Coatesville is not the wickedness of Coatesville nor of today. It is the wickedness of all America and of three hundred years — the wickedness of the slave trade. All of us are tinctured by it. No special place, no special persons, are to blame. A nation cannot practise a course of inhuman crime for three hundred years and then suddenly throw off the effects of it. Less than fifty years ago domestic slavery was abolished among us; and in one way and another the marks of that vice are in our faces. There is no country in Europe where the Coatesville tragedy or anything remotely like it could have been enacted, probably no country in the world.

On the day of the calamity, those people in the automobiles came by the hundred and watched the torture, and passers-by came in a great multitude and watched it — and did nothing. On the next morning the newspapers spread the news and spread the paralysis until the whole country seemed to be helplessly watching this awful murder, as awful as anything ever done on the earth; and the whole of our people seemed to be looking on helplessly, not able to respond, not knowing what to do next. That spectacle has been in my mind.

The trouble has come down to us out of the past. The only reason that slavery is wrong is that it is cruel and makes men cruel and leaves them cruel. Someone may say that you and I cannot repent because we did not do the act. But we are involved in it. We are still looking on. Do you not see that this whole event is merely the last parable, the most vivid, the most terrible illustration that was ever given by man or imagined by a Jewish prophet, of the relation between good and evil in this world, and of the relation of men to one another?

This whole matter has been an historic episode; but it is a part, not only of our national history, but of the personal history of each one of us. With the great disease (slavery) came the climax (the war), and after the climax gradually began the cure, and in the process of cure comes now the knowledge of what the evil was. I say that our need is new life, and that books and resolutions will not save us, but only such disposition in our hearts and souls as will enable the new life, love, force, hope, virtue, which surround us always, to enter into us.

This is the discovery which each man must make for himself — the discovery that what he really stands in need of he cannot get for himself, but must wait till God gives it to him. I have felt the impulse to come here today to testify to this truth.

The occasion is not small; the occasion looks back on three centuries and embraces a hemisphere. Yet the occasion is small compared with the truth it leads us to. For this truth touches all ages and affects every soul in the world.

Bibliography

BOOKS

Emerson and Other Essays. New York: Charles Scribner's Sons.
1898. Pp. 247.

> *Contents:* Emerson
> Walt Whitman
> A Study of Romeo
> Michael Angelo's Sonnets
> The Fourth Canto of the Inferno
> Robert Browning
> Robert Louis Stevenson

(Republished, with added Preface. New York: Moffat, Yard &
Co. 1909. Pp. x, 247.)

Causes and Consequences. New York: Charles Scribner's Sons.
1898. Pp. x, 166.

> *Contents:* Politics
> Society
> Education; Froebel
> Democracy
> Government

Practical Agitation. New York: Charles Scribner's Sons. 1900.
Pp. x, 157.

> *Contents:* Election Time
> Between Elections
> The Masses
> Literature

(Republished, with added Prefatory Note, New York: Moffat,
Yard & Co. 1909. Pp. xii, 157.)

Four Plays for Children. New York: Moffat, Yard & Co. 1908.
Pp. viii, 156.

> *Contents:* The Lost Prince
> King Ithuriel
> The Hermits
> Christmas in Leipsic

The Maid's Forgiveness. A Play. New York: Moffat, Yard & Co.
1908. Pp. 95.

A Sausage from Bologna. A Comedy in Four Acts. New York:
Moffat, Yard & Co. 1909. Pp. 114.

Learning and Other Essays. New York: Moffat, Yard & Co. 1910.
Pp. vi, 242.

Contents: Learning
Professional Ethics
The Drama
Norway
Doctor Howe
Jesters
The Comic
The Unity of Human Nature
The Doctrine of Non-Resistance
Climate
The Influence of Schools
The Aesthetic

The Treason and Death of Benedict Arnold: A Play for a Greek Theatre. New York: Moffat, Yard & Co. 1910. Pp. 76.

William Lloyd Garrison. New York: Moffat, Yard & Co. 1913. (Republished, with added 'Chronology' and 'Preface for Second Edition, 1921,' Boston, The Atlantic Monthly Press. 1921. Pp. xii, 289.)

Homeric Scenes. Hector's Farewell and The Wrath of Achilles. New York: Laurence J. Gomme. 1914. Pp. 76.

Deutschland über Alles, or Germany Speaks. A Collection of the Utterances of Representative Germans — Statesmen, Military Leaders, Scholars, and Poets — in Defense of the War Policies of the Fatherland. Compared and Analyzed. New York and London: G. P. Putnam's Sons. 1914. Pp. vi, 102.

Memories and Milestones. New York: Moffat, Yard & Co. 1915. Pp. x, 270.

Contents: Art and Art Schools
William James
Shaw and the Modern Drama
Dr. Horace Howard Furness
Henry Grafton Chapman
The Function of the Church School
Mr. Brimmer
Mrs. Whitman
Greek as a Pleasure
Charles Eliot Norton
Ethical Culture
President Eliot
Notes on the Teaching of Art
Maria Weston Chapman
Coatesville
Julia Ward Howe
The Negro Question
Alfred Q. Collins

478

Notes on Religion. New York: Laurence J. Gomme. 1915. Pp. 100.

>*Contents:* The Roman Church
>The Effect of Hebraic Thought on Western Europe
>The Indestructibility of Religion
>Memories and Half-Thoughts. (In 25 sections.)

Greek Genius and Other Essays. New York: Moffat, Yard & Co. 1915. Pp. vi, 317.

>*Contents:* Euripides and the Greek Genius
>Shakespeare
>Balzac
>La Vie Parisienne

Neptune's Isle and Other Plays for Children. New York: Moffat, Yard & Co. 1916. Pp. vi, 196.

>*Contents:* Neptune's Isle
>A Family Quarrel, A Play for the Nursery
>Wilfred the Young, A Dragon-Play for Boys
>Christmas Once More, a Sacred Cantata for Children

Cupid and Psyche. New York: Laurence J. Gomme. 1916. Pp. 92.

>*Contents:* Cupid and Psyche
>Lafayette
>Romulus and Remus

Victor Chapman's Letters From France, with Memoir by John Jay Chapman. New York: The Macmillan Co. 1917. Pp. 196.

Songs and Poems. New York: Charles Scribner's Sons. 1919. Pp. viii, 86.

A Glance Toward Shakespeare. Boston: The Atlantic Monthly Press. 1922. Pp. 116.

>*Contents:* Introduction
>The Plays as Poetry
>On the Stage
>Romeo and Juliet
>Richard III
>Hamlet
>The Merry Wives of Windsor
>Othello and Henry V
>King Lear
>Macbeth
>The Comedies
>Shakespeare's Types
>The Sonnets
>Appendix
>Notes on Enunciation
>American Speech

Letters and Religion. Boston: The Atlantic Monthly Press. 1924.
Pp. 132.

> *Contents:* Part I. Words and the Spirit. (Four sections.)
> Part II. Comment and Reflection. (Nineteen sections.)

Dante. Boston and New York: Houghton Mifflin Co. 1927. Pp.
xxiv, 99.

Two Greek Plays. The Philoctetes of Sophocles and the Medea of
Euripides. Done into English. Boston and New York: Houghton
Mifflin Co. 1928. Pp. 119.

The Antigone of Sophocles. Boston and New York: Houghton
Mifflin Co. 1929. Pp. 70.

Lucian, Plato and Greek Morals. Boston and New York: Houghton
Mifflin Co. 1931. Pp. viii, 181.

> *Contents:* Introductory
> Lucian the Man
> Illustrations (Nine sections)
> Lucian attacks Pederasty
> Plato and Lucian Contrasted

New Horizons in American Life. New York: Columbia University
Press. 1932. Pp. v, 51.

PAMPHLETS AND REPRINTS

The Two Philosophers: a Quaint and Sad Comedy. [Anonymous]
Boston: J. G. Cupples Co. 1892. 37 pp.

The Lost Prince. A Children's Play in Three Acts. Sylvania, 1907.
Red Hook, N.Y. [n. d.] Pp. 19.

Exultations and Insultations. Being a Few Strains and Venturesome
Touches upon the Harp in Prose and Verse in Praise of The Class of
'84 [etc., etc.]. Reprinted from Report of Twenty-fifth Anniversary Celebration, Class of 1884, Harvard College. Cambridge:
1909. Pp. 10.

John Jay Chapman on Lynching: Address delivered at a Meeting held
in Coatesville, Pa., on August 18, 1912, to Commemorate the
Anniversary of the Lynching in 1911. Reprinted from the *Southern
Workman* for January, 1913. Pp. 4.

Washington et Lafayette. Spectacle en Deux Tableaux Composé pour
le Comité du Fond Lafayette et Joué au Century Theatre de New
York, le 4 mars 1915. Traduit par Émile Legouis. Paris: 1915.
Pp. 16.

On the Sailing of Our Troops for France. (Dedicated to President

Wilson.) Reprinted from the *North American Review* for November, 1917. Pp. 6.

Memoir of Isaac H. Klein. Read at the Memorial Service at the Madison House on January 11, 1920. Pp. 7.

Alma Mater. Reprinted from the *Boston Evening Transcript* of March 12, 1924. Pp. 13.

Harvard and Business: John Jay Chapman '84; John Forbes Perkins, '99. Reprinted from the *Harvard Graduates' Magazine* for September, 1924. Pp. 18.

Our Universities. Reprinted from *School and Society*, vol. XX, No. 508, September 20, 1924. Pp. 4.

Strike at the Source. [America and Roman Catholicism.] Reprinted from *The Forum*, April, 1925. Pp. 9.

The Honesty of Al Smith. New York: 1927. Pp. 3.

Thomas Mott Osborne *and* Osborne's Place in Historic Criminology. Reprinted from the *Harvard Graduates' Magazine* for March and June, 1927. Pp. 12, 7.

James L. Ford. [Notes printed for private distribution to members of the Coffee House.] New York: 1928. Pp. 11.

The Roman Catholic Mind: Extract from My Secret Journal. New York: 1928. Pp. 7.

Obsessions and Digressions. Read at the Forty-fifth Anniversary Dinner of the Class of 1884, Harvard College, Algonquin Club, Boston, June 19, 1929.

Chapman's contributions in prose and verse to magazines, and his letters to the press, would furnish forth a list of quite unwieldy proportions. In many instances these writings are to be found under the titles above.

Index

Index